DATE

Visionaries and Planners

VISIONARIES AND PLANNERS

*The Garden City Movement and
the Modern Community*

STANLEY BUDER

New York   Oxford
OXFORD UNIVERSITY PRESS
1990

Oxford University Press

Oxford   New York   Toronto
Delhi   Bombay   Calcutta   Madras   Karachi
Petaling Jaya   Singapore   Hong Kong   Tokyo
Nairobi   Dar es Salaam   Cape Town
Melbourne   Auckland

and associated companies in
Berlin   Ibadan

Published by Oxford University Press, Inc.,
200 Madison Avenue, New York, New York 10016

Library of Congress Cataloging-in-Publication Data
Buder, Stanley,
Visionaries and planners: the garden city movement and
the modern community / Stanley Buder.
p.   cm.   Includes bibliographical references.
ISBN 0-19-506174-8
1. Garden cities.   2. Garden cities—United States.   I. Title.
HT161.B84   1990
307.76′8—dc20   89-26507   CIP

1 3 5 7 9 8 6 4 2

Printed in the United States of America
on acid-free paper

For Rachel

Preface

In 1898 an unknown Englishman published a little book advocating experimental communities as the way to draw populations out of huge, teeming cities. Small garden cities girdled by greenbelts were to meet fully and efficiently the needs of their residents and indeed, in time, to serve as the "master key" to a higher, more cooperative stage of civilization. Dismissed by reviewers as the utopian fantasy of a naive enthusiast, Ebenezer Howard's deceptively simple concept has provided a basis for modern city planning's most elusive quest, the environmental design of the ideal community.

Howard soon founded an organization to build garden cities. For nearly a century his movement has represented a remarkable blend of accommodation to and protest against the role of the city in modern life. To its cause have rallied social critics and planners, including Lewis Mumford, Clarence Stein, and Raymond Unwin, and it has profoundly influenced planning theory and practice in dozens of nations. Moreover, Howard's ideas still intrigue and provoke in the ongoing debate about the problems of large cities and our more recent concerns with their suburbs.

As a historian, I examine the Garden City movement's influence; as a student of planning, I explore the strengths and limitations of the planner's ability to design innovative and superior communities. A history of the

Garden City movement properly told sheds light on the complex transition from the nineteenth to the twentieth century in the way we think of community, the good life, and even the very process of change.

My thesis, simply stated, is that Howard's garden city joined together two very different types of late nineteenth-century experimental communities, creating a tension never fully resolved. Small groups, dismissed by most as "utopians," sought the design of a community as the means of achieving an alternative society, the "Cooperative Commonwealth." More limited in intention were efforts at model industrial villages under the stewardship of enlightened employers and philanthropists. One group sought to challenge conventional values; the other, to reinforce them. Each in their own way tried to right a world turned upside down by the premise that environment influenced behavior.

A tension appeared in the early years of the Garden City movement which persisted as the modern profession of city planning emerged to claim the right to design the ideal community. I follow this and related tensions from the nineteenth-century world of visionaries, self-help, and philanthropy into our own with its reliance on the expert, bureaucracy, and governmental policy. The title of this book is not intended to convey an antipathy between visionary and planner but only the exploration of the relationship between the two. While all agree that planning for community must reflect the hopes and aspirations as well as the resources of a society, the issue then becomes whether our sense of possibility or limitation will dominate.

The first six chapters of this book trace the various influences that led to Howard's vision of the garden city. These include two previously unexplored but central experiences: Howard's involvement with the Chicago religious leader Cora Richmond, and his participation in a small London group preparing to launch an English experiment based on the ideas of the American Albert Owen. Their significance is to place Howard in the very rich and largely neglected late nineteenth-century tradition of communitarian dissent. This strongly shaped his vision of a supportive community and also provided him with the critical concept of "social cities," the planned clustering of several garden cities to provide sophisticated urban services.

To gain entry into the mainstream of late Victorian reform, Howard offered his Garden City concept as an environmental alternative to urban problems. As such it appealed to diverse groups. With the start in 1903 of Letchworth, the first garden city, Howard's movement attracted international attention and ready acceptance from the first generation of modern city planners. By then, it represented much more than the original vision. Chapters 7–10 explain the remarkable success of the Garden City movement while examining the changes brought about by the rise of the profession of city planning and the effort of building two garden cities.

The final three chapters consider the fortunes of the Garden City movement in the context of the twentieth-century social-welfare state. Central to the latter's development was confidence in the expert to achieve desired societal goals. City planners were to correct the abuses of market forces involving housing, the community, and the environment.

Much of the garden city's appeal was as a way of curtailing urban growth through planned population dispersal. Above all, the allure of the garden city resided in its promise to redefine and strengthen community in a modern world that challenged and reduced community significance. Although other visions of the future city and the ideal community competed for the attention of planners and governments, the Garden City movement, with the postwar British new towns to its credit, achieved the pinnacle of its international influence in the 1960s.

Developments since then call into question the social-welfare state and the Garden City movement. This book ends with a consideration of the future of Howard's ideas and their relevance to the modern community. The explosion outward of the suburbs after World War II occurred in a diffuse fashion that critics refer to as "spread city." Neither city nor country, it is a near parody of Howard's hopeful synthesis of the best features of both. Efforts at an alternative along the lines of a garden city have proven limited, but some suggest this is because they failed to adapt Howard's principles to modern conditions and the Western World's love affair with the automobile. Others argue that modern conditions and not Howard's principles must be changed.

The Garden City movement was very much a British development. Howard, however, drew many of his ideas from American sources, and indeed expected the United States to take the lead in building garden cities. It is the Anglo-American aspect of the Garden City movement that I emphasize, though also indicating developments elsewhere. Nor is this a traditional biography, as my interest is in Howard's ideas and not in his life—except as it sheds light on their formation and development.

Over its long history, the Garden City vision has encompassed several very different movements and causes. Its past until recently has been written by partisans eager to advance their own views. I intend only a detached account. Here I run the risk of appearing critical of many men and ideas that I admire. This is especially a danger in the earlier chapters where I describe social reformers who drew from a well of religious and spiritual views that now lack the power to inspire action. Indeed a major theme of this book is how this worldview as expressed in the Garden City movement was radically reshaped in our own century.

Modern city planning is a vivid example of Max Weber's concept of the rationalization of Western culture: the drive for control of the inner and outer life. The Garden City movement illumines the vitality and even necessity of visionary thinking with its concern for realizing a Platonic ideal. Early in this century, H. G. Wells observed that a break had occurred between his generation and its predecessor in the way utopia was regarded. What had formerly been a static vision was superseded by a sense of progress toward goals themselves always in transition. This remains our way of thinking. It lends itself to a preoccupation with technical means and discourages interest in an overriding order and harmony.

To guarantee that humanity—not things—is the primary focus, we must plan the future attentive to the imperatives of humanistic values as well as long-run ecological considerations. A vital function of the planner is to provide feasible alternative visions of the socially desirable community. This, indeed, is why Howard designed his garden city in the 1890s. Its history hopefully addresses our quest as we approach the twenty-first century justifiably concerned about the damage we leave in our wake.

New York   S. B.
May 1989

Acknowledgments

This study has been supported by grants from the Graham Foundation and, on three critical occasions, the Research Foundation of the City University of New York. I should like to acknowledge the assistance of the librarians and staffs of the International Federation of Housing and Town Planning, the Town and Country Planning Association, the Garden City Museum, the New York Public Library, and especially Eric Neubacher of the Baruch College library, Ronald Mahoney of the Fresno State University of California library, and Michael Hughes of the Welwyn Garden City Central Library.

Along the way, the following have in one manner or another extended helping hands that I greatly appreciated: Ina Baka, Paul Buckhurst, Leonard Buder, Thomas Busch, Deborah Lindrud, Frits Locher, Gary Sabot, Lawrence Sabot. My brother Terry Buder and his wife Ileana Font on several occasions made available to me their lovely home on Flag Hill in St. Thomas, the U.S. Virgin Islands. The late Sir Frederic Osborn, my next-door neighbor for a year in Welwyn Garden City, provided me with much of the background and material upon which this work rests.

Several friends have read drafts of this study or discussed the project with me at length. I should like to thank Myrna Chase, Thomas Frazier, Kenneth Jackson, Edward Pessen, and Richard Wade. Jon Peterson rigorously critiqued the manuscript. Marlene Wortman especially gave me a great deal of the best kind of advice on style, organization, and content. Sheldon Meyer and Scott Lenz of Oxford University Press epitomize the ideal editors, knowledgeable and concerned about the writing of history.

Finally, I should like to thank my children, Rebecca and Micah, for their support and assistance. Without the help and patience of my wife, Rachel, this book would not have been completed, and I dedicate it to her in gratitude and love.

Contents

Visionaries and Planners

1

An Inward Quest

There is . . . reason for believing that there is a spiritual nature in man which will rise from the mass of material elements, and with outstretched wings cleave the upper air for higher and higher flights.

Ebenezer Howard
(Paper read to the Holborn Literary and
Debating Society, Feb. 14, 1880)

On a late Saturday afternoon in mid-February 1893, a middle-aged man animatedly addressed an audience in London's Nonconformist Memorial Hall on Farringdon Street. In a pleasingly resonant voice, he urged those present to undertake an experimental community based upon the principles of collective land ownership and the joining together of the better features of urban and rural life.

Observers reported a keen sense of expectancy among those present. Many belonged to organizations that had sponsored the occasion. Others had been attracted by notices that had appeared for several weeks in small radical newspapers. A turnout estimated at three hundred far exceeded expectations, and at the last moment the meeting was moved from a small room to the building's main auditorium.

The spirited discussion following the speaker's talk revealed "considerable divergence" on details but a strong consensus that some form of experimental community was highly desirable. A resolution favoring the start of a "home colony" was passed, and a committee was elected to arrange the purchase of a suitable site in the vicinity of London. Satisfied that an important undertaking was now under way, the crowd dispersed onto Farringdon

Street into the chill of a winter's early night. A few, though, lingered to debate the merits of the scheme and the meaning of a socialist society.

The speaker, Ebenezer Howard, was a short, bespectacled man of nondescript appearance. An obscure Londoner of the lower middle class, he was raising four children on the uncertain income of a court stenographer, a profession he much disliked. Acquaintances regarded "Ben" Howard as likeable, gentle, and well-intentioned, although too inclined to hair-brained schemes for his family's good. Few expected this latest project—a community of his own design—to prove any more successful than his earlier enthusiasms. Nor did immediate events offer any reason for a contrary view. Within six months, Howard's comments at the Farringdon Hall meeting were all but forgotten, and for the next several years little was heard of the proposed new community.

Nevertheless Howard persevered. Using his kitchen table as a writing desk, he carefully worked out the details of his ideal community. Entitled "New Jerusalem," Howard believed his scheme capable of peacefully transforming society and solving the grave problems of his age. In time his seemingly far-fetched plan, renamed the Garden City, brought Howard international fame as a founder and pioneer of modern town planning.

The origins and history of the Garden City concept can best be understood in terms of the audience which crowded into the drafty London meeting hall and the values upon which it drew. Both Howard and his audience represented a visionary communitarian tradition (now nearly forgotten but extremely important in Anglo-American radical thought of the 1800s), whose roots are traceable to the republican fervor of the eighteenth century.

Tom Paine in *Common Sense* (1776) proclaimed a bold new confidence in humanity's utopian potential when he wrote: "We have it in our power to begin the world over again." Early nineteenth-century enthusiasm for colonies reflected the ideals of social perfection and experimentation inherited from the "Age of Reason." These ideals were, in turn, combined with the exhilarating sense of de novo beginnings experienced by Europeans as they explored and settled other areas of the world. In the early nineteenth century, the Western tradition of intellectualizing an ideal society ceased being essentially a theoretical exercise. At least a few "free thinkers" throughout the century regarded communitarianism as a protean means of social reconstruction, either at home or in the new world, through applying intelligence to the experimental design of a community's institutions and environment. Repeated failures between 1825 and 1850 brought a lull in colonization efforts. In the last quarter of the century, though, a resurgence of communitarian enthusiasm flared briefly and then subsided, leaving little obvious residue.

The Garden City concept provided a bridge between a radical tradition seeking small voluntary experiments in community and mutual aid and early twentieth-century modes of reform, looking toward government and relying on experts. It is in the last quarter of the nineteenth century that the shift became discernible. The scheme Howard presented in Farringdon Hall already reflected certain of these changes.

The final decades of the nineteenth century in Britain were years of intense dissatisfaction. The uneasy sense of social drift in the air, the economist Alfred Marshall told a Bristol audience in 1883, resulted from a century of change that had caused "the breaking up of village life and of the customary duties of paternal kindness, on the one hand, and of respectful service on the other." Recent economic hard times in England had called into question the benefits of change.[1]

Late nineteenth-century apprehension about the future stood in marked contrast to the confidence in progress that had been the hallmark of the Victorian era at the time Howard grew to maturity. That faith, symbolized by the Great Exhibition (held in London in 1851), where Britain proudly displayed its technological prowess and industrial supremacy, remained an integral part of Howard's personality and thought. His naturally buoyant temperament was reinforced by conversion in the 1870s to the "New Dispensation," a congeries of beliefs articulated by the American religious leader Cora Richmond. Buttressed by his new faith, Howard viewed himself a member of a small avant-garde circle gifted with a special message of hope for a suffering humanity. Until he encountered Cora Richmond, there was little unusual about Howard or his background.

Born in London on January 29, 1850, Howard was second in a family of nine children, four of whom died in infancy. His parents belonged to the shop-owning class and were chapel-attending Congregationalists. The father, whom he strongly resembled in appearance and temperament, was a baker and confectioner originally from Harwich. His mother was a farmer's daughter from Lincolnshire. The family enjoyed modest comfort and security. Both parents were industrious and affectionate, but an indulgent father required the mother to act as the children's disciplinarian.[2]

The family resided above their confectionary shop at 62 Fore Street, a street in the midst of the central business district and almost completely given over to commercial activity. At the time of Howard's birth, London still remained the "vast and shapeless city which Dickens knew—fog-bound and fever haunted, brooding over its dark mysterious river." Then during the prosperous 1850s and 1860s, London was transformed into the imperial capital of Whitehall, the Thames Embankment, and South Kensington.

Educated away from London in country boarding schools, Howard early showed some of the character traits that would lift a man in his fifties from obscurity to international renown. His formal education began at age four at a dame school in Suffolk. At age nine, he transferred to a school at Cheshunt in Hertfordshire. Then from ages twelve to fifteen, he attended Stoke Hall at Ipswich in Suffolk. He was considered a slow learner but demonstrated a plodding tenacity and desire to do well and to please. A serious and religiously observant boy, Howard was also noted for being preoccupied and absentminded. The subjects that interested him most were drawing and geography, and his hobbies were stamp collecting and the new art of photography. His personal reading was limited to the *Boy's Own Magazine,* whose stories of adventure emphasized the importance of character, service, and the excitement of exploring unknown regions. What emerges from his early years is a picture of a persevering Victorian youth, more visual and mechanical than intellectual, in search of something larger than the ordinary career and circumstances common to his class and background.

On leaving school at the age of fifteen, Howard took a position as clerk with a firm of stockbrokers. His duties required copying letters into a ledger with a quill pen until closing time, when a small glass of wine was offered to the clerks. He then worked several years for a merchant, Mr. C. Elliot.

A lifelong interest in efficiency and rationality first emerged in 1869 when Howard decided to teach himself phonetic shorthand, a system which had not yet gained wide acceptance. To learn this technique, a student bought the books of Sir Isaac Pitman and enrolled in a correspondence course, which provided tracts written by this ardent Swedenborian on behalf of his many interests. Pitman hoped to simplify reasoning as well as communication through new systems of spelling and numeration. (Forty years later, Howard took up one of Pitman's causes—the development of a universal language to further the brotherhood of man.) Almost at once, though, he set to work to improve the Pitman system.[3]

In 1870 or early 1871, Howard, relying on his new stenographic skill, served briefly as the private secretary to Dr. Joseph Parker, a friend of Pitman and a supporter of his efforts at orthographic reform. Parker, then early in his celebrated and controversial career as a leading Congregational minister who encouraged new currents in religious and social thought, was the pastor of the Poultry Chapel where the Howard family attended Sunday services. His highly popular sermons combined a liberal content for the thoughtful with an emotional delivery that satisfied those desiring a touch of pentecostal flame.[4]

Parker encouraged Howard to consider the ministry, but the young man decided on a more adventurous course, and in 1871 he joined two friends in migrating to the United States to try homestead farming. On a farm of 160 acres in Howard County, Nebraska, he built a shanty and sought to raise a crop with a notable lack of success. After several months of the hardships of pioneer life in a bleak climate, a discouraged Howard and one of his companions decided to leave.

They traveled eastward to the Midwest metropolis of Chicago. The Windy City was already an American marvel. Its population had jumped from thirty thousand in 1850 to ten times that two decades later. Lumber yards, factories, grain elevators, stockyards, warehouses, docks, and depots lined its streets and riverbanks. Great fortunes were quickly made and lost. Everywhere, real-estate developers and speculators transferred parcels. Wooden-frame structures sprawled in all directions to shelter a working population drawn mainly from Europe. Shoddy streets in desirable locations had been widened and paved to provide for handsome commercial establishments and the homes of the city's merchant princes and industrialists.

Howard arrived in Chicago less than six months after the spectacular fire of October 1871 had cut a swath of destruction four miles in length through the city's center. Thousands were left homeless, and property damage alone approached a quarter of a billion dollars. Undaunted, Chicagoans bragged that theirs had been the "greatest fire in history" and rapidly rebuilt the city. A British visitor in 1872 noted with astonishment: "There was built and completed in the burnt district of Chicago a brick, stone, or iron warehouse every hour of every working day." Chicago epitomized an American get-up-and-go attitude that strongly impressed the young Howard who only recently had perched on a high stool in an old-fashioned London counting house, quill pen in hand.

Rushed for time, the Chicago builders introduced labor-saving methods that revolutionized their industry. Howard was a man who learned from observation and experience, and his years in Chicago demonstrated the advantages of trying new ways. The popular emphasis on "striking it rich" possibly contributed to his later interest in making a fortune through an invention to improve the efficiency of the newly invented typewriter, then beginning to be mass-produced by a Chicago concern.

But Chicago also contained an underside. A Boston temperance reformer who came to investigate Chicago's crime and vice warned that the city was "a modern Sodom that must perish if it does not change its ways." To its critics, Chicago was a city of uprooted, lonely people pursuing wealth in a setting of drinking, corruption, and open sin. With its rawness and energy, Chicago offered much to fascinate and trouble the inexperienced and sheltered young Howard. Despite the prevailing materialism that shocked other Americans, Chicagoans engaged in ambitious municipal undertakings. A belt of parks around the city was cited by civic boosters as evidence that theirs was the "Garden City."[5]

In Chicago, Howard found employment as a court stenographer in the legal partnership of Ely, Burnham and Bartlett of 206 La Salle Street, one of the city's most prestigious firms. He lodged nearby at a once grand home now turned into a boarding house on 374 Michigan Avenue. While back in London on vacation in 1874, Howard was filled with enthusiasm for urban life and wrote: "A strange ecstatic feeling . . . possessed me. Then flowed through every nerve of my body as if it were strains of electricity, giving intense and long continued pleasure. The crowded streets—the signs of wealth and prosperity—the very confusion and disorder appealed to me." He was, he recalled, oblivious to the signs of poverty with which London abounded.[6]

Soon after returning to Chicago, Howard experienced a religious crisis brought on by reading Darwin's recently published *Descent of Man* and W. H. Draper's *Intellectual History of Europe.* Crises of the kind Howard experienced were common at this time. Henry Demarest Lloyd's popular column in the *Chicago Tribune* was often devoted to efforts to reconcile science and Christianity. With the weakening of his Christian beliefs, Howard became overwhelmed by a sense of loss and emptiness. But he soon discovered a substitute faith in the teachings of Cora Lavinia Scott Hatch Daniels Tappan Richmond, a much married "trance medium" of substantial talents who espoused a doctrine called the "New Dispensation."[7]

Cora Richmond arrived in Chicago in November 1875 for a month's public engagement. She had been a celebrated trance medium for over twenty years, and the *Chicago Times,* whose editor was one of her admirers, gave her full coverage. He hired Ebenezer Howard to provide stenographic transcripts and sent Alonzo M. Griffin, a young Quaker interested in religious subjects, to write up the story. They reported that a "fashionable and intelligent" audience of fifteen hundred gathered on November 14, 1875, to hear Richmond at the old Congregational Church (on the corner of Green and West Washington), which had been recently acquired by the First Spiritual Society of Chicago.

As Richmond lectured on Spiritualism as a religious movement free of creeds and priests, her face "lit up with a glow of inspiration." Then on finishing, she went into a trance and was visited by several spirit guides who spoke through her to urge the need for moral regeneration of the individual as the necessary first step to universal brotherhood. Finally, still in a trance, she answered questions offered by the audience.

Cora Richmond had first encountered the spirits as a child in 1852 at Hopedale Community in Massachusetts, one of two hundred recorded American communitarian experiments between 1840 and 1860. To American communitarians, starting new colonies represented the opportunity to begin society again along more fraternal and rational lines of organization. The Hopedale of Cora Richmond's childhood reflected the lofty ethical expectations of its founder, Adin Ballou, a leading Universalist minister. Among the conditions for membership were a commitment never to take an oath or hold public office and never to participate in war or even to hate anyone. All property was to be held in common, although, unlike some communities, each family resided in its own individual dwelling. Hopedale, a famous way station for New England's reformers on their way to or from their many conventions and meetings, was also a hotbed of various enthusiasms, such as spiritualism, food reform, and water cures. In 1856, however, two brothers gained control of the community's property, ending the experiment.[8]

By then Cora Richmond (then known as Cora Scott) no longer lived at Hopedale and had begun her career as a trance medium carrying Ballou's message. In 1853, Ballou had sent Cora Richmond's father to Wisconsin to start a colony. Failing in this, he began arranging performances for his attractive blonde daughter in theaters. Widespread interest in spiritualism had begun in 1848 when two young sisters reported mysterious "rappings" in the cellar of their home. By 1874, it was estimated that two million Americans accepted one form or another of "Modern Spiritualism." In that year the American Spiritualist Society, which viewed itself as a new scientifically based and superstition-free religion, claimed a membership of two hundred thousand.[9]

The distinctive characteristic of "Modern Spiritualism" lay in its effort to combine the occult with a commitment to social reform and rational inquiry. Frank Podmore, the foremost contemporary student of psychic phenomena and a founder of the English Fabian Society, was one of many observers who commented on the strong "affinity between Socialism of a certain type and Spiritualism." The type of socialism he referred to was communitarianism.[10]

Podmore judged Cora Richmond the most impressive of the many trance speakers he had observed. Henry James, the novelist, attended several of her séances and is said to have used Richmond and her father as models for the characters of Salah and Varena Tarrant in his depiction of genteel New England "humanity Bohemia" in *The Bostonians*. James, however, was intrigued by her charismatic personality, not by the contents of her trance messages, which he characterized as "a string of . . . arrant platitudes."[11]

In 1872, Cora Richmond carried her message to Britain. She arrived with a letter of introduction from the American reformer, Robert Dale Owen, who like his famous father, the English industrialist and utopian socialist Robert Owen, had become a convert to "Modern Spiritualism." There she met prominent British supporters such as Alfred Russel Wallace, the co-discoverer with Darwin of the theory of natural selection. (Wallace, who had been converted in 1867, used his considerable reputation to gain open-minded scrutiny of psychic phenomena as well as support for such reform movements as land nationalization.) Performing at London's St. George Hall, Richmond drew large crowds and established a small circle of followers. Her serene face adorned the cover of the English spiritualist weekly, *Medium and Daybreak,* on 2 January 1874 with the greatest part of the issue devoted to a discussion of her mediumship.[12]

When Richmond returned to the United States after her three-year stay in England, she assumed the mantle of seer and prophet. Now in her mid-thirties, she soon made Chicago her permanent home and became minister of the First Spiritual Church. She also married for the fourth and last time.

What Howard saw and heard on encountering Richmond in November 1875 was a compelling personality with a message that appealed not only to the despondent but also to the many who at this time were throwing off Calvinist doctrines of guilt and sin and embracing an optimistic view of human potential. The reporter for the *Chicago Herald* thought the meetings he witnessed extraordinary but unconvincing to the nonbeliever. Howard, transcribing for the *Chicago Times,* to the contrary, felt overwhelmed and became a lifelong disciple. Indeed, he underwent the profound and lasting "conversion experience" described by the philosopher William James in his study of mysticism.[13]

Howard joined a study group that met in Cora Richmond's home on Chicago's northwest side. There he was introduced to Tom Paine's *Age of Reason* and soon declared himself a free thinker. He was also taught that all past religions had strayed into error. Now, however, through the guidance of friendly spirits, the correct path was known. When a sufficient number of supporters were organized into groups prepared to act, the millennium would be reached.[14]

Much of Cora Richmond's teachings were a mixture of arcane principles of cosmic unity borrowed from various repositories of the occult and such temporal reforms themes as equality of the sexes, universal education, and the brotherhood of man. Communitarianism was prominent among her nexus of sympathies. One of her principal spirit guides was Adin Ballou's son. His message, as expressed by Richmond in her trances, was a call for moral regeneration. Small efforts at cooperative experiments were to be undertaken as preparation for an eventual attempt at a communal utopia along the lines of her father's earlier failed scheme.[15]

Underlying the occult and novel in Richmond's message was a widely held version of New England radical transcendental thought. The Republic had been conceived on a new continent with a divine mission. Americans in the nineteenth century had strayed by embracing materialism and recklessly exploiting the continent as well as each other. The result was an unhealthy and corrupt civilization centered in crowded cities where people ignored their neighbors. She called, on one hand, for a return to the presumed virtues of the early Republic and, on the other, for the building of a higher civilization based on true brotherhood and scientific advances. People must learn to live cooperatively with each other and in harmony with nature.

Cora Richmond provided Howard, who was strongly conscious of inner questionings, the reassurance of life's higher purpose and of the working of cosmic forces that were pushing humanity in the direction of altruism. Spiritualism contributed to Howard's enduring views that a unifying force or purpose existed and that humanity must arrange circumstances accordingly. Richmond's view of life encouraged involvement in the world and the rejection of evil and aggression. The "New Dispensation" inspired in Howard not only a sense of purpose but, more important, the assurance of being in the forefront of significant developments. He came to view his calling as being to advance the cause of "Modern Spiritualism," with his specific role the "harmonizing of Science and Religion."[16]

In this frame of mind, Howard returned permanently to London in December 1876 and soon thereafter found employment with Messrs. Gurney and Sons, official reporters to the House of Parliament. In 1879, he formed a firm of stenographic reporters with William Treadwell and became a junior partner. Howard now felt secure enough to marry Elizabeth Ann Bills, whose parents managed a hotel in Nuneaton. The Howards set up house in rented quarters in Dulwich, a suburb south of the Thames. Within seven years, three daughters and a son were born, while a fifth child died in infancy.

Despite considerable financial strain, the marriage by all accounts was satisfactory. Elizabeth Howard showed remarkable tolerance for her husband's enthusiasms, although sometimes chiding him for being impractical. In her last letter to him before her death in 1905, she observed: "The Good Lord who made you a reformer should have also provided the means." Initially troubled by her husband's unorthodox religious views, she was won over when she met Cora Richmond during the summer of 1881. In the recollections of Howard's eldest daughter, her father appears as affectionate, gentle, and outgoing, but absentminded and usually preoccupied with one scheme or another; and her mother is depicted as "the family mainspring, keeping things going. . . ."[17]

In the capacity of stenographer, Howard accompanied a parliamentary committee to Ireland in 1879 to investigate unrest among tenant farmers. Greatly upset by the widespread poverty, Howard imagined himself an efficient landlord improving the well-being of all. "To be in the pay of a Conservative Government seems to destroy any enthusiasm," Howard, a Liberal-Radical by party affiliation, wrote his bride. "The cottages of the country are most wretched. I quite wish that I could be a great landowner and for once without a tinge of selfishness. I do think that with your help we might make ours the most comfortable estate as far as the poor tenants . . . in Ireland." These and other letters reveal a personality apprehensive about self-serving motives.[18]

Between 1880 and 1883, Howard's major outside interest was trying to improve the space bar on the typewriter. He hoped accomplishing this would bring his ever-growing family financial security and material comforts. He also participated in the meetings of the newly organized Zetetical Society. This group of young men, interested in enlightening themselves on "all matters affecting the human race," included George Bernard Shaw and Sidney Webb. Members were required to prepare and read a paper to the group. In his paper, Howard claimed that "science would provide demonstration that the soul was capable of existence apart from the material form . . ."—an idea he advanced again in a paper presented in 1880 to the Holborn Literary and Debating Society and later published in *Medium and Daybreak*, a journal edited by James Burns.[19]

Spiritualism had by then become the vogue in certain London circles. A group of young Cambridge dons, with the support of eight fellows of the Royal Society, founded the Society for Psychical Research to inquire into various spiritualist phenomena. Spiritualism, however, never acquired anywhere near the popularity that it did in the United States. British spiritualists tended to more conservative and conventional views. Most considered it complementary to Christianity rather than a new religion.[20]

The spiritualist group most closely aligned to the ideas of the "New Dispensation" gathered about the office of the *Medium and Daybreak* at 15 Southampton Row in Bloomsbury. There James Burns, a friend of Cora Richmond and Alfred Russel Wallace, presided over the Spiritual Institution, trying to make spiritualism a new religion of liberation and science, as well as a force for social reform.[21]

The "New Dispensation" enabled Howard to break with the dominant materialist and individualist ethos of the era in which he came to maturity. Its presumption that life needed to conform to a profound transcendental reality anchored his reform enthusiasms. These would be nurtured by the radical ferment of the 1880s and take concrete form at the beginning of the following decade. By then the missing pieces he needed to assemble his Garden City concept had arisen from ideas generated by several years of radical agitation.

Howard's predilection, however, for communitarian schemes began in 1875 when he first heard Cora Richmond utter her trance message. Her rejection of authority, her insistence on mutual aid, and her notion of natural affinity among people of like conscience would all in time be incorporated into Howard's Garden City concept. He heard that message repeated in 1881, 1884, 1885, and 1896, when she visited London to lead the English circle that had formed around her teachings. A biography of Cora Richmond published in 1895 refers to Ben Howard as a "gifted student, inventor and letterataur [*sic*]" and contains letters of appreciation from Howard and his wife.[22]

Howard's personal struggle fits a common mid-Victorian pattern. As Beatrice Webb has observed: "There was a current belief in the scientific method, in that intellectual synthesis of observation and experiments, hypothesis and verification by means of which alone all mundane problems were to be solved." "Modern Spiritualism" differed in its focus on human perfectibility through the assistance of guides from the other world offering instruction on divine design.[23]

In professing spiritualism, Howard identified with a phenomenon suspected by many conventionally minded as being "crank." His preoccupation with psychic research and inventing kept him more or less aloof at this time from the scores of radical groups springing to life in London. This gave him the time to observe, think through, and decide where to locate himself on the spectrum of social reform.

In the 1880s, Howard entered his middle years. With family responsibilities and a profession, his life had acquired a definite shape. But underlying this apparent stability was a restlessness, a keen sense of dissatisfaction with circumstances, and a continuing effort to redirect, one way or another, the course of his life. It is clear that Howard early on viewed himself as having a calling to do more than labor as a court stenographer. Now in his thirties, he regarded himself as an inventor blessed with strong powers of observation and analytical ability. His interests, though, were not in attempts at originality but in perfecting and making more serviceable ideas and devices already well known. Throughout his life he would strive to reduce "complicated things to method and orderly connection." In "Modern Spiritualism" Howard believed he had acquired knowledge of the God-given harmonious order of the universe and, from this, the road that humanity must travel to reach the higher civilization promised by grand design.[24]

2

Land Reform in an Urban Age

All writers on economics are compelled to make a
distinction between land and other things.

Alfred Marshall
(*Principles of Economics*, 1890)

The decade of the 1880s was a watershed in British history and thought as
Victorian ideas of progress pushed against the sharp edge of hard times. It
was a decade to reflect on the "much good and much harm" produced by
an industrial system. Henry George's *Progress and Poverty* expressed the
mood of many that progress was an illusion in any nation which tolerated a
great disparity of conditions among the classes. Indeed, George's London
lectures in the fall of 1882 elicited a remarkable popular response and
helped spawn the birth of a fiery new radical mood.

At first this excitement was expressed in a revival of older forms of
activity derived from Owenite utopianism and nonconformist humanitari-
anism: among these being the launching of colonies to serve as exemplars
of radical reform. After a break of nearly three decades, a period of intense
interest in communitarianism began that lasted until the century's end.
This second phase of communitarianism understandably differed from the
earlier one in placing greater emphasis on intentional communities as a
response to excessive urbanization and the stresses of a consumer economy
on the family. Alfred Marshall in an 1884 article in *Contemporary Review*
described London as astir with numerous "socialist groups" talking about
launching communities in England to combine "the advantages of the town

and the country." Such efforts at colonies for the purpose of domestic reform were designated as "home colonies," in contrast to those sent abroad to remote areas of the world.[1]

But the communitarian enthusiasm of the late nineteenth century encountered opposition from the radical mainstream, which now moved toward the acceptance of state socialism. Both Fabians and Marxists dismissed colonization efforts as an outgrown primitive stage of early socialist development that only weakened the cause.

For Howard, however, it was the communitarian thinking of the 1880s about the "Land Question" that provided the wellspring from which he would eventually draw for his Garden City scheme. As American spiritualism in the form of the "New Dispensation" awakened his interest in the 1870s in cooperation and radical reform, the next decade provided the ideas and insights which in time led to the garden city. Once again an American, Henry George, profoundly influenced Howard's thinking.

In the revival of "socialist" agitation in the 1880s, the issue of "Land Nationalisation" joined old passions to new causes. Long the battle cry of "individualistic" British radicals, "Land Reform" in the scholarly analysis of David Ricardo and John Stuart Mill was largely reduced to an issue that pitted the middle class of capital against the landed aristocracy—the arena for this contrast being parliamentary debates over primogeniture and entail. Then in the evangelical writings and speeches of Henry George, "Land Reform" reacquired mass support by offering the promise of a thorough transformation of society with near miraculous excision of most social flaws. The journalist and politician John Morley likened George's impact on London radical circles as comparable to the effect on pedestrians of a dinosaur making its way down Pall Mall. William Morris thought that *Progress and Poverty* "had been received in this country . . . as a new Gospel."[2]

The question of why the unknown George elicited this reaction in Britain intrigued his contemporaries. Scholars found *Progress and Poverty* neither original nor profound. According to one early student of socialism, the Austrian scholar Max Beer, "his leading ideas are natural rights, Ricardo and Mill's theory of rent and the schemes of Spence and Dove." Beer believed it was only George's style, an impassioned and moralistic eloquence, which galvanized many to confront a world they perceived had run awry. In short, the American provided his followers with a righteous cause and simple theory around which to rally. Later historians have emphasized also the propitious timing and circumstances—the "dramatic opportuneness"—of George's arrival in Britain. Interest in the "Land Question" had been aroused by the recent "Irish Trouble," in which upwards of ten thousand evictions had caused tenant farmers to strike back in desperate fury.[3]

In 1882, Henry George traveled to Ireland to report on conditions. On two occasions—a day apart—he was arrested and briefly detained in Galway, events well publicized in the press. Alfred Russel Wallace, by now in correspondence with George, quickly arranged for him to speak in London's Farringdon Hall on September 12, 1882. George Bernard Shaw attended and later recalled, "I was thus thrust into the great socialist revival of 1883. I found that five-sixths of those who were swept in with me had been converted by Henry George." A cheap sixpence edition of *Progress and Poverty* sold over one hundred thousand copies in England during the next two years. George returned to the United States a famous man. His ideas now received a broader hearing in his native country, with the prestigious *North American Review* eagerly soliciting his articles.

The distinguished economist and journalist, J. A. Hobson, believed the real importance of Henry George derived from the fact that he was able to drive an abstract notion, that of economic rent, into the minds of practical men. George succeeded because he made landlordism a personal issue for town dwellers. In both Britain and the United States, George appealed to the skilled workers and lower middle class of the cities. Where George broke new ground was in his treatment of urban land values.[4]

Ricardo's theory of rent, the basis of George's philosophy, assumed an agrarian context and the Malthusian premise that the pressure of population growth forced into use increasingly inferior agricultural land. This, Ricardo argued from the tenets of classic economics, pushed rents upwards. Such increases, in turn, necessarily came at the expense of capital and labor. Simply put, land was a natural monopoly whose owners held unfair advantage over laborers and businessmen.

George's experience in a relatively sparsely populated America offered a different perspective. While observing the California land boom of the 1860s, George concluded that rising land values were largely due to speculation based on anticipated use. To George, any theory of ground rent needed to include the "values of locality," meaning that desirability was based on accessibility, either real or potential. Since the "values of locality" were socially created, they and all other forms of unearned income from land should be rightfully returned to society at large in the form of a confiscatory land value tax (the celebrated term "single tax" did not become important to George until 1887).[5]

George, the "prophet of San Francisco," elaborated a common American belief (the same theme satirically employed by Mark Twain and Charles Dudley Warner in their novel, *The Gilded Age*) that the easiest way to make a fortune was to buy land where a railroad or city would eventually be built and to sit tight until land values exploded. While no doubt Americans viewed such behavior as smart business practice, George denounced land speculation for its disastrous social consequences. It reduced living standards, exacerbated inequality of wealth, and created overcrowded cities and underutilized countryside. Not the least of George's complaints was that it caused moral erosion by creating examples of great fortunes amassed through idleness and gambling.

According to J. C. Gavin, Joseph Chamberlain's biographer, Chamberlain and John Morley on reading *Progress and Poverty* concluded that the "Land Question" in its urban aspects of housing, overcrowding, and ground rents must be brought forward as "the great business" of the day. Even George's critics turned their attention to the implications of his ideas for urban life. In drawing attention to the influence of ground rent on the cost of housing, food, and wages, George transformed the "Land Question" into a meaningful issue for urban dwellers.[6]

The responses to George of the historian Arnold Toynbee and the economist Alfred Marshall influenced the views of Howard and his circle. Toynbee, a Balliol tutor and reformer who had chosen to live among the poor of Whitechapel, found the enthusiastic reception accorded George's ideas among London workers disconcerting. Just before he died in 1883, he rose from a sickbed to deliver two lectures rebutting George.

Asserting that the period 1840 to 1880 had registered a considerable improvement in the standard of living, Toynbee argued that the protesters of the early 1880s wanted to improve the quality of their lives. Their dissatisfaction arose principally from expectations having increased faster than wages. *Progress and Poverty* appealed to those earning good wages who "cannot obtain a whole house as a home, nor the decent enjoyments of life," such as leisure or a garden.[7]

Although he thought George wrong in arguing that rent always came at the expense of wages, Toynbee conceded that London provided an instance where it did. Workers in almost any given trade earned higher wages than their counterparts elsewhere, but the differential did not adequately compensate for the capital's inflated costs. Its rents, Toynbee explained, were especially high, because the city suffered from a "keen struggle for space by competing land uses at its center. . . . that a site would go for more if used as a warehouse than as a residence was obvious." Higher rents paid by the Londoner brought him less housing than other Englishmen. While a skilled worker in Bolton and in Lancashire could afford a whole house, the same man living in London and earning more would live with his family in two rooms or perhaps take in lodgers in order to afford to rent a house in "the great suburbs springing up around London . . . mere blocks of brick and mortar . . . without a single space in which you can breathe." This explained why London audiences rose in standing ovations when George denounced "landlordism."

Early in 1883, Alfred Marshall also delivered a series of lectures on

Progress and Poverty. A professor at the University College of Bristol, he would soon become the preeminent economist of his day and hold the chair of political economy at Cambridge. Characterizing *Progress and Poverty* as a work flawed badly by error and obsolete economic theory, whose author was "by nature a poet, not a scientific thinker," Marshall regarded George's views as greatly exaggerated.

In 1884, the *Contemporary Review* commissioned Marshall to write on London's "Housing Question." Public interest in lower-class shelter had been recently aroused by Andrew Mearn's *The Bitter City of Outcast London* (1883) and by a government report on housing which estimated that two hundred thousand families—a fourth of London's population—resided in substandard dwellings. Marshall viewed the core of London's problem as the concentration of great masses in a compact area and the effect of this on ground rents. The "housing question," in other words, was inherent to the growth of "great cities."[8]

Henry George had argued in *Progress and Poverty* that the rise of cities in the nineteenth century was due largely to speculative forces and hence artificially induced. Without going into great detail, he suggested that a confiscatory tax on the unearned increment would automatically disperse population and industry until a nation arose of small towns possessing advanced industry, while retaining a green setting and bucolic surroundings.

Marshall, in contrast, related the rise of nineteenth-century cities to the imperatives of a new industrial technology. Once the railroads in the 1830s freed industry from the need to locate near water power or coal fields, it was inevitable that factories would gravitate toward large centers of population. In turn, the relocation of factories drew a rural population seeking employment into the cities. "So the tide set strongly toward the town." Now in the 1880s, however, the advantages of industrial production needed to be weighed against its negative effects: the depopulation of the countryside and the unhealthy concentration of people in already crowded cities.[9]

According to Marshall, the economic consequences of concentration inflated living costs while holding down wages for the unskilled. High ground rents obviously led to excessive housing costs for the workers and others. Moreover, they were also an important cost factor for a firm or factory doing business in a large city. All of this he viewed as bad, but there were still other negative considerations.

In London, ground rents stood so much higher than elsewhere that its businesses dared not pass along their cost of rent for fear of risking their competitive position against rivals elsewhere. London firms compensated for high rents by paying low wages to their unskilled labor who had little ability to resist. Despite this, the capital continued to lure farm laborers and immigrants to swell crowded and disorderly neighborhoods by the prospect of employment. Thus, if jobs existed elsewhere, they would leave London or, better yet, not go there in the first place. Marshall thought it both possible and desirable to relocate certain types of employment away from London proper to the surrounding countryside.

He believed that recent technological innovations promised to reverse the trend toward concentrating businesses in compact cities. The advent of the telephone, mail service, general newspapers, and business associations now allowed manufacturers to locate at a distance from the city without serious disadvantage. In Manchester and Leeds, he reported, cotton and woolen mills requiring large sites had already relocated to the outskirts in search of lower ground rents. Indeed, Marshall predicted that the general departure of large-scale manufacturing from the central areas of cities would be only a matter of time.

London's economy, however, was not based on large-scale manufacturers but on small specialized workshops devoted to high-priced luxury items. Requiring little space, they could not be easily forced out of central-city locations. Yet their presence in London drew a rural and immigrant population whose health and morale were impaired by residence in slum neighborhoods.

Marshall proposed a most novel way to speed the departure of small shops. He urged the formation of a committee to plant a "colony in some place well beyond the range of London's smoke." It would erect suitable and sanitary cottages before approaching employers with the argument that their employees in such a salutary setting would prove more reliable and efficient. Marshall reiterated this analysis of urban rent in his famous *Principles of Economics,* published in 1890, the most influential textbook on the subject at the turn of the century.

Interest in shrinking the size of cities through deliberate relocation of industry and people grew considerably by the 1880s. Radicals had long regarded the rise of the "great city" as both undesirable and unnecessary. Marxists, for example, perceived urbanization as a phase in the development of a capitalist system to be reversed by the advent of socialism. Marx and Engels asserted this view as early as 1848 in the *Communist Manifesto,* although also suggesting somewhat contradictorily that the rise of cities had saved millions from the stagnation of "rural idiocy." Certainly many radicals in England and America regarded the nineteenth-century growth of cities in numbers and size as symptoms of a generally diseased and malfunctioning system. The new stress on the critical economic role of ground rent in an industrial age altered conceptualization by making the rise of cities appear more a cause rather than merely a consequence of the general problem.[10]

The movement of urban problems to center stage can be traced clearly through changes in the ideas and writings of Alfred Russel Wallace. Wallace's interest in the "Land Question" had been prompted by reading in 1862 Herbert Spencer's *Social Statics*. When John Stuart Mill organized his Land Tenure Reform Association in 1870, Wallace enrolled as a charter member. Concerned about the plight of the Irish tenants and the high-lander clearances in Scotland, Wallace in 1880 wrote an article in *Contemporary Review* calling for land nationalization and in the following year published *Land Nationalisation and Its Aim*. While completing its final chapters, he encountered *Progress and Poverty*, which he promptly hailed as "undoubtedly the most remarkable and important book of the present century."

George's influence on Wallace's book is obvious in the final chapter, "Low Wages and Pauperism; the Direct Consequence of Unrestricted Private Property in Land." The fact that independently of each other the two had arrived at very similar positions through "totally distinct lines of deductive reasoning" was thought by Wallace to prove their validity. An important difference between the thinking of the two was that Wallace called for government acquisition and nationalization of all land with compensation to owners. Nationalized land would then be rented to tenants in parcels of up to five acres for farming.[11]

In the second edition, after reading George, Wallace added an appendix "On the Nationalisation of House Property." He was now convinced that "the crucial test of the practicability of land nationalisation [would have] to be its applicability to towns." Wallace reasoned that the availability of farm-land at low rates would draw large numbers from the city and revive the countryside. Villages would thrive, developing farming and industry in a complementary balance. Over time the price of land and housing in cities would be lowered sufficiently to make it feasible for government to acquire them at the depressed price and to become the nation's sole landlord. In 1881 the Land Nationalisation Society was founded in London to further Wallace's program. Securing offices in the City, it soon employed a full-time secretary who, provided with a bright yellow horse-drawn wagon, carried the message far and wide.

Wallace and Henry George essentially accepted the tenets of a market-regulated economy. Land was to be withdrawn from competition only because its limited supply represented a national monopoly. Both men were also prepared to argue that certain utilities—railroads, telephones, gas—for the same reason should also be removed from the arena of private profit. But once these impediments to competition were removed, they believed, the market system would reverse the economic and demographic concentrations they deplored.

Until the second half of the 1880s, to advocate land nationalization or a confiscatory land-value tax generally identified one as a socialist. socialism was still a catchword for various ideas, efforts, and sentiments to alter a competitive economy through cooperative activity. Attempts, however, were well along to restrict the term to advocates of state ownership, in part or in whole, of the means of production. Often the phrases "Continental socialism," "state socialism," or "scientific socialism" were employed to convey this.

George did not call himself a socialist, but neither did he object when others did. In early 1887, he organized the United Labor party as the vehicle for "the American producing classes" to fight at the polls for the "Single Tax" and "Free Trade." By the summer, a break occurred between George and "Marxists," many of them German immigrants. George read them out of his party, claiming, "The truth is that state socialism with its childish notions of making all capital the property of the state is an exotic born of European conditions that cannot take root or flourish on American soil." Subsequently, until his death a decade later, George would be pushed further away from the main drift of socialism to a position which revealed his philosophy for what it always was—a radical individualism which opposed the centralization of power in the state as much as in any other vested interest.

Reacting to the economic depression of the mid-1880s, Alfred Russel Wallace urged the creation of labor colonies for the unemployed in a book called *Hard Times* (1885). A few years later this idea would be promoted enthusiastically by William Booth, the founder of the Salvation Army. Disturbed greatly by the violent disorders of the late 1880s, Wallace declared himself a socialist. In an article written in 1889, he called for the creation of "home colonies" and the organization of the economy on "collectivist principles." In calling for governmental ownership of land, Wallace was closer to the mainstream of developing socialist thought than George. Yet in urging home colonies as the means for national reconstruction, Wallace harkened to an older socialist tradition under attack from the proponents of state socialism as "utopian."[12]

This latter word—formerly applied in the main to literary exercises depicting an ideal commonwealth, the classical utopias of Plato, More, and their imitators—was now employed widely to derogate experimental colonies. Among the very first to use the word in this negative sense were Marx and Engels. *The Communist Manifesto* of 1848 honored Robert Owen, St. Simon, and Fourier as pioneers of socialism who discerned capitalism's evils but could offer in its place only far-fetched "duodecimo editions of the New Jerusalem." Marx and Engels termed their predecessors "utopian socialists" to contrast a misguided interest in fanciful colonies with the correct approach of "Scientific Socialism."[13]

Communitarians generally were uneasy with concepts advocating class

conflict or revolution and were suspicious of the state. Colonies, as the
model for the Cooperative Commonwealth, represented a peaceful way of
introducing social regeneration through voluntary associations and social
experimentation. Many communitarian schemes, however, lacked a carefully thought-through design of an alternative society or environment and
represented little more than the inclination to start a community based on
one or more cooperative principles combined with an intuitive sense of a
common vision.

Not only those who viewed themselves as socialists or radicals were intrigued by schemes for home colonies. Certain reformers also evinced
interest in the 1880s. The importance of healthy and contented workers as
a factor in production was becoming increasingly evident. The growing
opinion that lower-class malaise and restlessness were intensified by urban
conditions supported the belief that the alternative environmental setting
of a model industrial village might create a contented industrious working
class.

The theme of model industrial villages stems in British history from
Robert Owen's efforts at New Lanark. Disraeli propounded the idea in his
novels. The model industrial community of Saltaire near Bradford
(started in the 1860s) and the spectacular instance of a town of ten thousand people erected almost overnight in 1880 by the American businessman George Pullman were much commented on as examples of how an
enlightened employer could provide his workers with superior and uplifting surroundings.

The line separating model industrial villages from communitarian
schemes sometimes blurred. Robert Owen, after all, created a model industrial village, proposed a home colony for the unemployed, and finally
launched on the American frontier the communitarian experiment of
New Harmony. His conviction that the principal factors in the formation
of character were environmental led him to assert "that any general character, from the best to the worst, may be given to any community, by the
application of proper means."[14]

The best-known examples of model industrial villages, however, only
intended to demonstrate a commonality of interest among employers and
employees without altering the critical distinctions between the two. Then
Alfred Marshall proposed in 1883 a scheme for a home colony as a model
village for the purpose of persuading London manufacturers to relocate
their work force. As a social invention, the idea of home colonies could be
applied in various ways. The common denominator was that the home
colony represented an organized effort at a community, usually new, with
some specific social goal in mind.

Awareness of working-class alienation combined with increased concern for environmental factors in social behavior to foster interest in model factory towns during the last third of the nineteenth century. Though it was not necessarily recognized as such, the model factory town represented an effort of sorts at an industrial utopia which sought to strengthen conventional values and place them in a context which emphasized the harmony of interests of capital and labor. This ideal held promise of appealing to influential circles and certainly seemed less fanciful than colonies—such as Hopedale—intended to challenge prevailing values and relationships.[15]

It was in an apparently propitious climate, then, that the Society for Promoting Industrial Villages was founded with a membership of leading social reformers and industrialists in 1883. The society's intention was exclusively propagandist: to encourage the building by others of model industrial villages. In 1884 its chairman, the Reverend Henry Solly, suggested in his *Industrial Villages: A Remedy for Crowded Towns and Deserted Fields,* that cottages should be well built and sanitary with legal restrictions against subletting or overcrowding. The village, he thought, should contain schools, a library, an art museum, and a social club or coffeehouse in place of the usual public house. Hopefully, the area surrounding the village might be retained as open space and reserved for playing fields and allotment gardens. Solly's model villages were not only to redress urban congestion but also, as his title attests, to staunch the flow from country to city: "for the one evil must redress the other."[16]

By 1887, Solly, grown tired of waiting for benevolent and public-spirited manufacturers to act, founded a limited-dividend company to erect a model village. But he soon conceded lack of interest, and his Society for Promoting Industrial Villages closed its doors in 1889. The building of Port Sunlight by W. H. Lever and Bournville by George Cadbury kept alive the hopes of those espousing model industrial villages as a partial solution to housing and industrial problems.[17]

For the problems of the city, land reform offered more promise. In the 1890s, land reform largely lost its millenarian fervor for a more moderate and promising future. In the guise of separate valuation of land for rating purposes, with improvements assessed separately and taxed less stringently, land reform entered into the mainstream of turn-of-the-century politics. After Gladstone's retirement in 1895, an increasingly radicalized Liberal party pushed separate valuation to the top of its agenda. From the impractical panaceas advocated by Alfred Wallace and Henry George, land reform emerged as one of several prominent socially oriented reform political issues by the decade's end.[18]

As adherents of land reform abandoned their extreme assumptions, they successfully related the issue of separate valuations to the particular problems of urban overcrowding and unemployment, agricultural depression, and business cycles. By 1906 a land valuation tax was an overwhelming parliamentary concern. Its backers claimed broad support, though mainly from urban quarters—such as municipal rating councils, trade unions, and cooperative congresses.[19]

While ethical condemnations of landlordism remained present in the period from 1889 to 1906, land reformers also developed more sophisticated and pragmatic arguments. They claimed that separate valuation by eliminating speculation would end the common practice of retaining unimproved and lightly rated land near growing cities to await a future windfall. This greater availability of land would contribute significantly to lowering rents by encouraging housing construction. Furthermore, a land-valuation tax would swell the public coffers to reduce other taxes (especially on buildings and improvements) while funding improved public services. By 1906, the Land Nationalisation Society, then at the height of its influence, claimed eighty members of Parliament as members and another fifty openly sympathetic to its program. This, however, was considerably more modest and urban oriented than the one offered by Alfred Russel Wallace twenty-five years earlier. In the interim, land reform had been successfully transformed into a relevant political issue for an urban society.[20]

Municipal governments during the 1890s were increasingly obliged to acquire privately held land at inflated prices in order to undertake improvement schemes. Bills appearing before Parliament in 1904, 1905, and 1906 sought to remedy this problem in a most ingenious manner. Owners were to declare the value of land for rating purposes, with the stipulation that at public acquisition their figure would also serve as the basis for compensation. As early as 1892–1893, London Liberals sought the enactment of a "betterment levy," whereby property holders profiting from large improvement schemes might be taxed accordingly. With officials in London and Glasgow taking the lead, municipal governments joined in demanding land-valuation taxes as a critical need of modern urban reform. Land reform thus contributed greatly to the remarkable radical revival of the 1880s, being transformed in the process into the new vernacular of social-issue-oriented politics.

Howard was an interested onlooker in the intellectual debate of the 1880s. His circle of friends and acquaintances in spiritual groups, the Zetetical Society, and elsewhere were people of active social conscience. Themes pushed forward in the decade—colonization efforts, the proposed model industrial villages of Marshall and Solly, and the "Land Question"— were considered with a sense of urgency. All found their place in his formulation of the garden city.

The discourse of the decade dramatically brought forward the problems of the "Great Cities" and their poor. Howard's youthful excitement at urban growth and change fell by the wayside to be replaced by concern for the consequences of crowding people into cities. The communitarian theme of seeking to combine the advantages of city and country into a harmonious whole was familiar to him from the "New Dispensation." It was now being suggested that advances in technology made such an ideal feasible. Henry George and Alfred Russel Wallace urged land reform as a way of reversing the movement from countryside to city. Howard had much to ponder.

At a time when many who viewed the existing social system as inequitable or inefficient moved in the direction of social-issue-oriented politics, Howard clung to an older radical tradition that emphasized self-help and volunteerism. Perhaps he shared George's foreboding that an involved government would be paternalistic at best and tyrannical at worst. From his perspective, a higher civilization would only come about as the result of enlightened individuals leading humanity by their example to the acceptance of a grand design inherent in the order of the universe.

3

Ebenezer Howard and Hard Times

> It may . . . be safely affirmed that industry can only be
> found where artificial wants have crept in, and have
> acquired the character of necessities.
>
> John Pendleton Kennedy
> (*Miscellaneous Papers*, 1849)

For much of the 1880s, Howard remained dissatisfied and restless. Many of his concerns were particular to his own situation and personality, while others were of a more general nature in this decade of depression and social friction. And at least some of these reflected an unhappiness felt by many with the circumstances of daily life in a city becoming a modern sprawling commercial metropolis of great complexity with the resultant human strain. A frequent moving about from one residence to another reflected an inability to find a home within his means that met his expectations. Howard's disappointments with life in London were doubtlessly shared by others who crowded into Farringdon Hall in February 1893, intent on a social experiment that promised to better their lot.

With little formal education, scholarly inclination, or indeed time, Howard drew upon London and his experiences in it during the 1880s for many of his ideas. A radical mood permeated the city in this decade, and Howard was responsive to complaints of social inequity. Still, his actions and thoughts were shaped by his own frustrations and experiences.

In the 1880s, Howard sought vainly to escape from mediocrity and what he described as an "exhausting profession." During the depression years of extensive unemployment and stark want, his sense of personal deprivation derived from the unrealized expectations of the dreamer who envisioned a special destiny for himself in which he benefited while also contributing to society's welfare. In a more general sense, his frustrations resulted from wanting what others above him on the economic scale enjoyed.

British historiography in its consideration of the early impact of industrialization on society has long been preoccupied with the "standard of living question"—whether it was raised or lowered for the working classes. My interests, however, are the process by which Howard's class—the lower middle class of some education and means—arrived at a sense of what constituted a decent standard of living, and the significance of that process for social thought and action. Howard, advancing to his middle years, realized the elusiveness of his goals. The great advances in material largess, ease, and leisure promised by an era of technological innovations were not being realized rapidly enough to satisfy him and numerous others of his background.

During the early 1880s, Ebenezer Howard pursued two lines of activity apart from his vocation: thought transference and spiritualism, and mechanical inventing or tinkering to improve the typewriter. These activities took time which his partner, Treadwell, believed should be devoted to the business. The firm had never made much money and in 1882 experienced financial difficulties. The two men, decidedly uncomfortable in their relationship, gave thought to ending it.

Howard hoped to solve his professional and financial problems through the sale of an improvement on the typewriter he had recently patented; therefore, in early August 1884, he sailed from Southampton for the United States. Howard visited New York and Chicago, meeting with Cora Richmond during his sojourn in the Midwest, before returning home on October 25, 1884. To his disappointment, he had failed to interest the Remington Rand Company or several smaller firms in his invention.

New York and Chicago had grown greatly since he had last seen them. Once again he was awed and delighted by their feverish moods of excitement and expectation. At age thirty-four, Howard had not yet reached the point in his life where he viewed "great cities" as undesirable. (Within a few years he thought differently. By the late 1880s, he had concluded that much of a city's growth and change was purposeless and wasteful, demanding an incessant activity which was altogether exhausting and alienating.)

Howard's letters home contain no mention of two planned communities on Chicago's outskirts—the commuter suburb of Riverside and the model industrial town of Pullman. Pullman, constructed in 1880 on a grand scale and according to plans provided by an architect, landscape architect, and engineer, was attracting worldwide attention and acclaim at this time. It appeared to personify the advantage of applying social intelligence to the design of a community in the interests of efficiency and social cooperation. Pullman's provision of superior housing for factory workers amidst rural surroundings was eagerly cited as an important example of enlightened capitalism. In 1885, a young economist, Richard Ely, published an article in *Harper's Monthly* exposing the paternalistic ethos that underlay the model town's imposing façade and challenging its value as a social experiment. Ely reported that the residents viewed themselves as living in a "gilded cage" where their personal liberties had been curbed by an employer determined to use the town as a "showcase."

George M. Pullman's experiment intended to demonstrate that a superior community for workers could be built and managed on business principles. He had subordinated every aspect of the town, including the wishes of the residents, to this end. A copy of Ely's article with indecipherable marginal notes in shorthand was found among Howard's papers after his death. When he acquired and read the article is unknown. The international fame of the town, Howard's long-standing interest in social experiments, the publicity it had received, and the fact that he knew its area from fishing there when he had lived in Chicago suggest strongly that Howard joined the many curious visiting Pullman in 1884.[1]

Ely's forebodings were realized when in 1894 the town of Pullman became the site of the most important strike of nineteenth-century America; overnight its fame was reduced to notoriety. Despite its shortcomings, Howard long continued to be fascinated by the example of a town planned from the start in a comprehensive manner and referred to it several times in his writing.

The rustic town of Riverside, Illinois, represented a far different type of model community. It attracted relatively little notice from the press, and it is not known whether Howard ever went there or even knew of its existence. Riverside, a railroad suburb due west of Chicago, offered a pastoral setting for an affluent middle class seeking to live at a distance from the disorder of the metropolis.

Laid out in 1868 by Frederick Law Olmsted (the noted American park designer and landscape architect), Riverside featured an open plan of winding, tree-lined, curved streets—emphasizing the privacy of each home—as well as public walks with attractive views. Olmstead was one of the first to celebrate suburban flight. He regarded the city as properly a place of business. Those able to leave should, as "the more attractive, refined, and most soundly wholesome forms of domestic life are found in residential suburbs." His considerable talent provided in Riverside just such a pastoral and safe environment for the affluent able to afford the beauty and high commuting costs. Rustic suburbs comparable to Riverside could be found near London in the 1880s but only at a cost that generally excluded the Howards and their class.[2]

On his return to London, Howard found Treadwell irate at his long absence, and the two decided to dissolve their partnership. For legal and other practical reasons, though, the firm continued for another four years. After September 1888, Howard set himself up as a free-lance stenographer. From 1884 to 1890, he remained financially hard-pressed. At earlier times of need, Howard had received help from his father, but he also was now suffering financial setbacks, including the loss of his shop. In early 1885, Howard told his wife that they could pay as much as 40 pounds per annum for rent, suggesting an annual income in the range of 150 to 170 pounds. (£300 was often regarded as the dividing line between the lower-middle and middle-middle classes.) This income could not provide the home he wanted.[3]

After their marriage in 1879, the Howards lived south of the Thames in Dulwich, an area of attractive dwellings still at the time largely surrounded by open fields. With the birth of their third child, Howard suggested moving to larger quarters, but his wife, noting they were short of money, refused. By 1885 the Howards had four children. They looked at various estates being erected in the better suburbs—such as Hampstead—only to find them financially out of reach. While away on a business trip in March 1885, Howard wrote his wife to propose a novel solution to their problem.[4]

He assumed their inability to find "a nice house with a garden within our means" in a satisfactory neighborhood and then suggested that they and his brother Harry and his family jointly rent a large house for eighty pounds a year with all costs shared. This, Howard thought, offered many advantages which he carefully enumerated: (1) "a nicer neighborhood which would mean that the children would associate with children of a better class"; (2) "a really nice garden with perhaps a lawn tennis ground"; (3) a "savings in railway tickets for they always grant [a rebate] to all in a family"; (4) "in our long summer holidays we need have no difficulty about leaving the house for burglars to make free with as they not infrequently do."

Howard dwelt on the various advantages of a common kitchen in reducing costs, lessening labor, and even allowing for a greater variety of food. But he then assured his wife that within the house each family would retain its own privacy and have separate sitting rooms. He ended by imploring her not "to be too strongly prejudiced in favor of separate houses, but try and perceive the advantages there would be" in a joint household. Though nothing resulted from the scheme, Howard retained interest in what was known as "cooperative" or "associated" housing.

Communitarians in this period endlessly debated the merits of associated housing. Some saw it as a way of breaking down the isolation of the family from society at large. Others, such as Howard, favored it for reasons of economy and expedience as well as increased sociability, but only as long as family privacy was left inviolate. At Letchworth, the first garden city, Howard put his ideas of 1885 to use in the form of an associated housing scheme for the middle class called Homesgarth and also sought vainly to secure financing for a project along similar lines for the working class.

The Howards finally did move in 1885 or 1886 to Islington, once a stronghold of respectable chapel-attending clerks, small businessmen, and petty professionals. This was the area and social type which Mathew Arnold savaged when he wrote: "Your middle-class man thinks it the highest pitch of development and civilization when his letters are carried twelve times a day from Islington to Camberwell . . . and if railway trains run to and from them every quarter of an hour. He thinks it is nothing that the trains carry him from an illiberal, dismal life at Islington to an illiberal, dismal life at Camberwell." A considerably gentler picture of its residents appears in G. W. Goldsmith's turn-of-the-century minor classic, *The Diary of a Nobody,* with its inimitable Mr. Pooter.

At the time of Howard's arrival, Islington was rapidly losing its middle-class character. Perhaps because of this, the Howards soon moved to nearby Stoke Newington, a new district being built up to resemble what Islington had been only a short while before. Here they remained for three years in cramped circumstances. By this time Howard's enthusiasm for "great cities" had definitely waned.

At the beginning of the nineteenth century, the population of London and its immediate environs stood at one million. By 1881, this figure had risen to four and a half million with nearly one of every four Britains residing in or very near the capital. Railway commuter lines in the 1860s and the 1870s and the introduction of "cheap workmen's trains" after 1880 provided the means for London to thrust outward. The development of new residential neighborhoods relieved somewhat the congestion of older inner-city districts. Housing in the central area of London, where Howard had been born, was razed for offices or warehouses, railroad construction, and public works (such as street widening). As a consequence, much of the population relocated often, provoking further social change and dislocation.[5]

Manifestly present by the 1880s was the separation of the social classes into segregated residential neighborhoods. Many observers believed this pattern contributed to social estrangement and indifference on the part of those living in the affluent outer suburbs toward the conditions among the poor of Whitechapel and other inner-city districts. Reformers in the 1880s devoted much energy to bringing the plight of the poor to the attention of the better classes, who rarely came into contact with them in their slum neighborhoods—or for that matter with little else in London except for the shopping, businesses, restaurants, and theatre of the West End or the City.[6]

London emerged in the 1880s as a modern metropolis, a paradigm of the Anglo-American city. In place of a former compactness and clearly defined and limited reach, it now spread beyond the horizon with suburbs linked to suburbs "like onions on a string." When in 1888 Parliament passed an act to create the County of London, this entity included 120 square miles, which was still only a fraction of the metropolitan expanse. London by now was more a region than a city. The continued outward movement of population in the next decades, encouraged by the introduction of electric traction, called these developments to public consciousness as a matter for attention.

Charles Booth in his pioneer social survey, *London Life and Labour,* begun in 1888 and completed ten years later, carefully documented many of London's physical and social changes. Booth considered Stoke Newington representative of London's lower-middle-class neighborhoods—neither better nor worse. He described it as a place totally lacking in "symmetry or convenience or natural order of any kind. . . . All seems haphazard." Though not a neighborhood to attract the notice of settlement-house workers, Stoke Newington offered its residents little in the way of pride or amenity. Here was an instance of a new neighborhood thrown by the actions of numerous speculative builders, each constructing several houses to fall within the limited means of lower-middle-class purchasers and renters.[7]

Between 1890 and 1894, the Howards resided as 1 Norcott Road on a straight and treeless street. The small terrace house of yellow brick, indistinguishable from its neighbors, contained six rooms. Their size may be judged by Howard's bitter comment in a letter to his wife that he had espied an enormous quarried flagstone set in the sidewalk before a mansion which was "considerably bigger than our drawing and dining room put together." On another occasion, he observed that furniture stores in Stoke Newington and similar neighborhoods regularly carried specially scaled-down furniture, "little more than children's things," since ordinary sofas, chairs, tables, and beds often proved too bulky for the houses. The contrast between 1 Norcott Road and its neighborhood with Howard's depiction in 1885 of what he wanted leaves little doubt of his disappointment with the homes that London offered its lower middle class.

Victorian attitudes toward the home differed sharply from those prevailing a century earlier. In *London Life in the Eighteenth Century,* Dorothy George noted that size, arrangement, amenities, and location of the home were relatively unimportant to much of the population. "All classes lived so much at coffeehouses, alehouses or clubs that house rooms were a secondary consideration."[8]

To the Victorian middle class, in contrast, the home represented "the

temple of family life." Regarded as crucial to the formation of good character in children, the home was the center of adult social life. Its comforts
were hailed as life's true pleasures. To the wife fell the "sacred and noble"
role of converting a house into a true home: "a place of Peace, the shelter,
not only from all injury, but from all terror, doubt, and division"; to the
husband, the role of provider of the wherewithal. This vision of home and
gender roles, designated by historians "the cult of domesticity," anchored
the middle class's pervasive sense of "respectability."[9]

In a general sense, the Victorian emphasis on home life and its inviolate-
ness appears related to the rise of an urban and industrial society. These
developments made the external world more disordered and threatening
and older urban neighborhoods less stable and desirable. Families of means
drew away from the city's center to the less-developed periphery in order to
separate home life from urban problems and to gain greater control over
their lives.

Victorian attitudes toward the home also reflected important changes
occurring within the family and the increasing dependence on a market
economy. The "cult of domesticity" in its emphasis on the importance of the
home promoted the consumption of goods and services such as wallpaper,
pianos, potted plants, and sundry "objects d'art."[10]

Managing the expenditures of a Victorian household proved especially
onerous to lower-middle-class wives, such as Howard's, who, to cling to
their status, had to employ a maid. In general, they disposed of resources
above the subsistence level while lacking the means to escape into a leisured
or even anxiety-free existence. The changes taking place in both the economy and culture required longer schooling and made children a growing
economic burden. Family size declined from a norm of five and six children
early in the century to around two and three children by century's end, a
shift particularly evident in London's suburbs. The savings from smaller
families might be devoted to the new luxuries of life, like holidays at the
seaside and bicycles. Omnipresent billboards, shop windows, and newspaper advertisements temptingly proffered an ever increasing variety of
"crinkum-crankum" to drain the family budget.[11]

In the course of the nineteenth century, housing and neighborhood became the key factors in the family's style of life and its related aspirations
for status. Perhaps a third of the family budget was spent in providing and
furnishing the house. By a process sociologists have termed "stratified diffusion," each level of society tended to identify its hopes and aspirations with
that group perceived as immediately above them on the social ladder. Nowhere would the desire to emulate one's betters receive more social sanc-
tion than in the areas of housing and home furnishings. Money spent here,

it was thought, elevated the family's sense of respectability and well-being. The importance of these was obvious in a society where the family was increasingly venerated as a vehicle for moral uplift and security in a world being turned upside down.[12]

Howard was not alone in thinking that only through collective action could he and many others of limited means participate to their satisfaction in the waxing consumer economy. By the 1880s nearly a million individuals had joined cooperative societies to enhance their purchasing power by eliminating the middleman's role in the distribution of goods.

Consumerism originally had been only one of the goals of the cooperative movement. The original pioneers also started cooperative stores in the 1840s to raise capital to begin colonies. Within three decades of its origins, however, the cooperative movement achieved considerable success and respectability, but it had largely lost its reform impulse and was beset by dissension of an ideological nature. Many of the societies in the south of England became notorious for paying their employees low wages and refusing them any share of the profit. Rejecting Robert Owen's philosophy that cooperation represented a "concert of many for encompassing advantages . . . in order that the gain may be fairly shared by all concerned in its attainment," these societies viewed their only obligation as maximizing the rebates returned to their membership. This businesslike approach incurred the ire of many northern societies still attached to Owenite principles.[13]

The cooperative movement's success in the area of distribution was not matched by gains in extending cooperation to production. In 1884 the Labour Association for Promoting Cooperative Production Based on the Co-partnership of the Worker was organized to remedy this shortcoming. Its objective was "to bring about an organization of industry . . . in which all those engaged shall share in the profits, capital, control, and responsibility." In other words, distinctions between employer and employee, while not necessarily ended, were to be lessened by establishing a common interest. In addition to encouraging the creation of outright cooperative workshops, the association tried to persuade private firms to adopt schemes of profit sharing and stock distribution. These later arrangements proved more successful and soon became the association's major activity. Enthusiasm for profit sharing and stock distribution was strengthened by the strong current of Comtean thought which flowed in certain British circles in the 1880s and called for a new cadre of selfless, enlightened businessmen to direct social change by reconciling social inequities.[14]

Howard's direct involvement with radical groups at this time was slight. In the spring of 1884, he heard Henry George speak in London. Soon thereafter he read *Progress and Poverty* and Alfred Russel Wallace's writings on the land question. Howard agreed with Wallace's view that property owners should be compensated, while Harry, his younger and more radical brother, supported George's position that they should not.

In August 1885, Ebenezer Howard visited the fair held annually at London's Crystal Palace by the Cooperative Union, a loose federation of some one thousand local cooperative societies. The fair displayed cooperative exhibits and products as well as featuring lectures and discussions on the movement's progress and future. Here Howard acquired a tract published by the Labour Co-partnership association entitled "Ethics of Cooperative Manufacturing." Howard and a friend by the name of Jordan, one of the two young men who had accompanied him to the United States in 1870, had been thinking about opening a jobbing press. They now decided that this venture should operate along co-partnership lines, but the severe economic downturn of the years 1886 and 1887 made a new business undertaking out of the question.

The events of 1886 to 1889—rising unemployment and keen want on one hand, disorders and strikes on the other—exposed society's fractious nature: "the scramble for profits and wages, the war of clashing interests." If in the main the national mood was glum and anxious, there were those who in their anger at the established order welcomed any sign of its coming apart. In his autobiography, Edward Carpenter, the Whitmanesque poet, recalled the late 1880s as a "fascinating and enthusiastic period preparatory to great change. The Socialist and Anarchist propaganda, the huge Trade Union growth, the Theosophical movement, the new currents in the Theatrical and Artistic world, the torrent even of change in the Religious world promised much." This sense of impending transformation was particularly exciting to those who viewed themselves as radicals. British socialism at this time can best be described as heterodox and highly moralistic.[15]

Amidst the swirl of radical ideas, Edward Bellamy's utopian romance, *Looking Backward*, made its debut in Britain, appearing from January to July 1889 in J. Bruce Wallace's *Brotherhood*. Before the serialization had completed its run, however, *Looking Backward* was published by William Reeves, who specialized in radical literature. Within two years one hundred thousand copies of *Looking Backward* were sold in Britain. Ebenezer Howard later claimed a role in Bellamy's British success.[16]

According to Howard, an American friend in early 1889 gave him a copy of Bellamy's novel. He read the book in a night and was overwhelmed by its vision of a "new civilization based on service to the community and not on self-interest." The following morning on traveling to his office in the City, he looked about with a fresh sense of the possibility of imposing order and harmony on London's pervasive chaos. He approached William Reeves and personally guaranteed to sell at least a hundred copies if the publisher would print a British edition.[17]

What excited Howard and countless others was Bellamy's depiction of a new social system he had named "Nationalism" (since he thought the term "socialism" was acquiring a Germanic ring in American ears). This called for the organization of both economy and society along the lines of an army under the direction of a highly centralized state. All citizens were guaranteed security from cradle to grave, including employment, considerable leisure, early retirement, and indeed the full satisfaction of all reasonable needs and wants. Bellamy's vision was of an egalitarian society of highly moral and responsible citizens living a serene, contented, healthy life while developing their aesthetic and intellectual faculties to the fullest. His means to this end were novel, but the goals were an echo of a long-established radical tradition—the truly fulfilled individual and the Co-operative Commonwealth.

Bellamy's utopia was addressed to a middle-class readership aspiring to a fuller social life, one free of insecurity over bills or concern with status and downward mobility. They desired genteel amenities, attractive surroundings, and more leisure, but not a life of idleness or luxury. *Looking Backward* is consumer oriented and devotes little attention to either the details of the factory system of 1887 or the new industrial technology of the year 2000. It, however, describes in great detail the process of distribution—use of credit cards, the ordering of goods from large warehouses and their delivery by means of pneumatic tubes.

Bellamy also envisioned an environmental setting suitable for his new social order. His Boston of the year 2000 is a small city of parklike appearance. Neat, unostentatious homes filled with conveniences face broad tree-lined boulevards. Conveniently located public laundries and central dining halls relieve the drudgery of housework and end the isolation of domestic life. Dominating the city are handsome and commodious public buildings of classical architecture and gleaming whiteness which provide the center of community life. Needless to say, slums, saloons, and the excitement of crowds or the enticement of loitering before shop windows have been eliminated. An efficient, ordered life is what Bellamy's future promised. The author ingeniously combined state control in matters of production and distribution with private initiative in the arts to project what he regarded as a truly satisfying and liberal society.

Throughout the United States, Nationalist Clubs sprang into existence to promote Bellamy's visionary future. On July 3, 1890, twenty people met in London to form the British counterpart, the Nationalisation of Labour Society (N.L.S.). A year later several provincial and London branches claimed a membership of over twelve hundred, including "Socialists, Trade Unionists, Cooperationists, Anti-Cooperationists, Theosophists, gentlemen holding important positions under Government."[18]

Ebenezer Howard recalled joining with a group of friends to discuss the principles outlined in *Looking Backward*. Circumstantial evidence suggests that he became a member of the Nationalisation of Labour Society. An E. Howard is listed on the organization's executive board in 1893. By then Howard was involved in an effort sponsored by the N.L.S. to design and begin an experimental colony in the vicinity of London. He was also, however, experiencing second thoughts about Bellamy's utopia.

Some radicals found Bellamy's future world distasteful. William Morris, reviewing *Looking Backward* for the journal *Commonweal,* thought Bellamy's vision smug and philistine. It revealed an essential satisfaction with modern civilization "if only the injustices, misery, and waste of class society could be got rid of." Morris, the leading spokesman of the emerging Arts and Crafts movement, sought to resurrect an ideal of craftsmanship as an antidote to modern ills. The Middle Ages with its guilds and "organic communities" represented a time when collective values imbued daily life and work with dignity, meaning, and beauty.

In *News from Nowhere,* Morris in 1890 offered a "romantic" alternative to Bellamy's ideal world. He depicted a future London reduced to a network of villages separated by woodlands and streams, whose inhabitants would be organized into agricultural and manufacturing guilds. Life would be sweet and simple and based on brotherhood and craftsmanship. His view expressed a coherent integration of the individual, society, and culture. The Arts and Crafts movement attracted a variety of types who sought to transcend an ugly present by both looking backward to a past "golden age" and then forward to new forms of "organic" community. For his part, however, Howard never challenged or even doubted Bellamy's celebration of the efficiency and wonders of modern technology or the machine's superiority to the Arts and Crafts' handloom and potter's wheel.

In either 1886 or 1887, Howard and his family joined the Rectory Road Congregational Church. The sermons of its new minister, C. Flemming Williams, at least in their references to this world, complemented the teachings of Cora Richmond's "New Dispensation." Williams, a year older than Howard, was an ardent Christian socialist and a leader in the largely successful effort to lead Congregationalism away from Calvinist theology and toward social responsibility. In 1890, Williams remarked that socialism was growing at a rapid rate, and "God alone knew what the next year would see. Christ was king and Christian Socialism was His cause." The congregation that listened to his impassioned sermons, however, was solidly middle class, with many of the men still coming to church in frock coats and top hats.[19]

Williams was more than Howard's pastor; he was also his friend, and their families socialized frequently. In 1889, Williams was elected an alderman in the "Progressive" sweep of the newly created London County Council (L.C.C.). From 1890 to 1906, he served on the Public Health and Housing Committee. From 1893 to 1895, he was chairman of this important group which had responsibility for slum clearance and for the provision of new housing under the Housing of the Working Class Act of 1890. During the 1890s, Howard acted as a stenographer for the L.C.C. and various of its committees. He had stationary printed: "E. Howard, Shorthand Writer to the London County Council, New Court, Carey Street." His knowledge of London and its problems would thus be broadened and deepened, and his conversations with Williams no doubt underscored in his mind the difficulties involved in municipal efforts at improving conditions.

Though Howard certainly cannot be said to have been active in the radical upsurge of the 1880s, neither was he unaffected or unresponsive. During these years, he heard Henry George lecture and read both *Progress and Poverty* and *Looking Backward*. He became interested in the cooperative movement and labor co-partnership in particular. His life experiences during this decade provided an increasingly critical perspective on existing conditions and the circumstances of the ordinary citizen of London, capital of a vast empire and the world's largest city. During the 1880s, public attention was drawn to the sufferings of the poor. The pressures of lower-middle-class life in London went largely unnoticed.

H. G. Wells wrote to this very point in 1906 when he broke with the Fabian Society and presented a penetrating critique of its shortcomings. In essence, he believed the organization elitist, overly concerned with reaching those of influence, and, because of this, indifferent to an element very susceptible to its ideas. "In London," he wrote, "particularly, under the peculiar conditions of London, the hope of socialism resides in the middle class, in that indeterminate class of which the poor doctor and the Board School teacher may be taken as the best types. . . . It is in London particularly that you find educated people living under such conditions as to make them socialist."[20]

London, whatever its shortcomings, also provided particular advantages to radicals. Here was the center of networks keeping abreast with and discussing developments and ideas not only current in Britain but also on the Continent and in the United States. In the very early 1890s, Howard would involve himself in just such a network, and from this connection would emerge his scheme of a garden city.

4

The American Cooperative Commonwealth

We may hope to learn something from every experiment.

John Humphrey Noyes
(*History of American Socialism,* 1870)

American radicals, like Americans in general, at the end of the nineteenth century thought their nation on the cutting edge of modern change. The influential *Our Country* (1885) by the Reverend Josiah Strong boldly assumed as "America goes, so goes the world." In reforming their own nation, American radicals often anticipated fulfilling its destiny as "a wonder-working providence," a nursery for social experiments.

They associated Marxism with immigrant groups of low status. As such, it held little appeal for native-born Americans, who came to radicalism with an ethical vision of Christian brotherhood and were appalled by strident rhetoric of class conflict. Cooperative and communitarian schemes long had provided the matrix for what they thought of as socialism. The end of the century was in America as in England a time of intellectual ferment and the subtle transformation of old dogmas to bring forth a new emphasis. For many, including a notable list of prominent radicals, a tug of war occurred between their hearts, which remained attached to communitarianism, and their heads, which rejected it as ineffectual. Themes would be ripped out of the older tradition to be joined with newer ideas. Reformers moving away from communitarianism continued to envision beautiful and rationally planned communities combining city and country as centers of self-fulfillment and happiness. The search for the Cooperative Commonwealth was a vague yearning for a just and supportive world, embodied in the form of a nurturing and uplifting community where life was no longer hostage to market forces, and human beings related to each other as caring family. By about 1900, communitarianism, as such, ceased to be a significant part of this search, but it left a legacy of ideas and values to be picked up by other kinds of reformers who looked to the community as the spearhead of social progress.[1]

American radical circles, at least those composed of middle-class reformers of native background, regarded England and the United States as partners in the forging of a new humane civilization and culture based on reform. Temperance, anti-slavery, penal reforms, and Christian missions were all Anglo-American campaigns. In part, this affinity rested on a mutual delight in such writers as Emerson, Thoreau, Ruskin, and Whitman as spokesmen for a shared culture with a common language. Many believed that the new century would see the United States replace Britain as the world's most important nation.[2]

A network of informal connections based on common hopes and culture linked British and American middle-class reformers, and this was particularly true of those who in the 1880s viewed themselves as adherents of the Social Gospel or Christian socialism. Reciprocal institutional influences mirrored the movement of ideas back and forth across the Atlantic. Two ministers, J. Bruce Wallace (1853–1939) and W. D. P. Bliss (1856–1926), editors of journals devoted to radical reform within a Christian context, played important roles in this cross-fertilization. For the nineteenth-century moral reformer, America, even late in the century, remained a laboratory for social experiment.

J. Bruce Wallace in *Brotherhood* introduced British readers not only to *Looking Backward* but also to the writings of Lawrence Gronlund, whose book, *The Cooperative Commonwealth* (1884), popularized this term to distinguish a socialist-type economy and moral order from the existing society. In *The Cooperative Commonwealth*, Gronlund predicted that "populations will leave the city and will bring the pleasures and comforts of city life, the blessings of our civilization, into the country to begin a new and better civilization." Wallace also reported enthusiastically on American communitarian experiments.[3]

One colony in particular attracted his fervent support. This was Albert Kinsey Owen's grandiose project for an American colony and planned city in Topolobampo, Mexico. Intrigued by Topolobampo, Wallace in 1892 organized a small weekly study group of Londoners to employ Owen's ideas, known as "integral cooperation," as the basis for an English "home colony" in the vicinity of the capital.

Ebenezer Howard was a member of this group. Here in the company of followers of Bellamy, cooperators, socialists, and land reformers, he involved himself in discussions on the literature of radicalism and colonization. Serious problems in the operations of the colony at Topolobampo also became known and were considered. In time, Howard formulated his Garden City scheme as an alternative to the original intention of a colony based on Owen's "integral cooperation." Howard offered this alternative in February 1893 to the audience in Farringdon Hall.

J. Bruce Wallace's counterpart in the United States was the Reverend William Dwight Porter Bliss. The American's interest in socialism began in the 1880s through a reading of Henry George. Bliss was editor of the *Dawn*, the publication of the Society of Christian Socialists, which he helped found in 1889. In its pages, Bliss promoted such British contributions to reform as the social settlement and the social survey. In the 1890s, he became president of the American Fabian Society and espoused a "gas and water socialism" based on municipal ownership of utilities. A little later, in 1906, Bliss founded the Garden City Association of America to further Ebenezer Howard's ideas in the United States.

In their numerous enthusiasms and optimism and as peripatetic organizers and publicists, Bliss and Wallace were remarkably similar. But in one way they differed. Bliss did not share J. Bruce Wallace's fervent advocacy of colonization schemes. He argued along with Henry George and Edward Bellamy that as isolated attempts they ran counter to historical tendencies. Society's ever-increasing economic and technological interdependency inevitably doomed the small-scale, communal-size unit of production. For this reason Bliss identified himself with efforts at institutional reform on a national scale.

Still, communitarian enthusiasm was very evident in American radical circles until the new century, and there were those in England, including Ebenezer Howard and J. Bruce Wallace, prepared to follow. Communitarianism represented more a means than an end. Schemes for colonies throughout the century differed dramatically from each other in critical ways. Some permitted private property and individual economic activity; others did not. The motives of the colonists varied widely from those seeking a heavenly kingdom to those concerned with only realizing a better life. Almost all, however, shared the conviction that society could not be altered significantly by political means. In the 1880s a colonist noted that "cooperators" usually thought in terms of an eventual network of colonies to exchange products among themselves and "transform society without disturbing politics."[4]

For colonists, efforts to create a new society represented only a logical extension of their search for the right way to live, creating an environment conducive to the flourishing of the spirit or soul. An intentional colony was intended to be a social laboratory and an example for all humanity. In Arthur Bestor's apt phrase, communitarians strove for a "patent-office model" of social perfection.[5]

By century's end, communitarians were conspicuously out of step with the direction American social thought was taking. Even in the first phase of communitarianism (1825–1855), many regarded them as "peculiar people." However, in this earlier period, when most Americans were engaged in farming and many were moving westward to the frontier as a matter of course, to separate from settled society for the purpose of starting a colony was not as extreme as forty years later. By the 1880s, the contrast between life in a settled civilization and life in a pioneer colony was more readily apparent and, accordingly, the psychological hardships involved in beginning a colony all the greater. Unlike many earlier Americans who assumed the need to be more or less self-sufficient, most at the century's end readily relied upon civilization's amenities and well-stocked store shelves. The idea of colonies, therefore, appeared more unrealistic and extreme in the last years of the century.[6]

Still, undeterred by the general view that they quixotically moved against the times, little cliques of men and women sought to create a counterculture through colonies. To critics who warned them that communitarianism was utopian, unscientific, and destined to fail, they replied—not necessarily correctly—that it represented an American approach to socialism unlike imported ideologies urging class divisions and street barricades. To others who sneered at their rejection of civilization, they responded that their proposed colonies promised greater comforts than an individualistic society. Often they argued that advances in technology made their success possible though earlier efforts had failed.[7]

No one sang this siren song more persuasively than Albert Owen. Over twelve hundred Americans were lured by him from cities and farms across the high Sierra Madre mountains to a remote bay in Mexico to build his dream of a gleaming city in which all would live like millionaires. Owen's was a singularly American utopia in that it was based on the model of a business corporation intertwined with a scheme for land and railroad promotion. Owen expected the latter to earn him a fortune, while the first would insure his fame as a benefactor of humanity. Get-rich schemes proliferated among Americans of the time, and even communitarians were not immune. Because Topolobampo proved so important to J. Bruce Wallace and Ebenezer Howard, at least as a point of departure for their own thinking, both the colony and Albert Owen deserve notice.

Albert Kinsey Owen was born in 1848 into a prominent Quaker family of Chester, Pennsylvania, and studied civil engineering at a local college. After working briefly as a surveyor for his native city, Owen (at age twenty-three) found employment with the Clear Canyon Railroad of Colorado Springs, whose head, General William J. Palmer, had developed the resort town of Colorado Springs—often cited as one of the most successful examples of town development by an American railroad.[8]

In 1872, Owen traveled to Mexico on railroad business. Along the western coast of Sinaloa on the Gulf of California, he came upon the partially hidden and sparsely populated Topolobampo Bay. For the next decade, Owen promoted the building of a transcontinental railroad from Galveston, Texas, over the high Sierras and down to Topolobampo Bay. Here a city and harbor were to be constructed. Such a line, he argued, would be the shortest route between the southern states and the Pacific Ocean and ultimately to the Far East where a vast market existed for cotton.

Promising to bring settlers, Owen received valuable land concessions from the Mexican government. But his efforts for over a decade to interest American investors met only with rebuffs, despite President Grant's son being identified for a time with the scheme. Finally in 1884, Owen proposed a cooperative venture by colonists who would incorporate themselves as a development company, the Credit Foncier, for the purpose of creating a city, towns, and farms. A second company, the American and Mexican Pacific Railroad (with Owen as chief engineer and principal stockholder), was to build and operate the railroad.

Owen legitimately claimed a long-standing interest in reform. In the late 1860s, he advocated women's suffrage. A few years later he joined the Greenback party and subsequently became a supporter of script money based on social credit. He was also involved in turn with the Sovereigns of Industry, the Brotherhood of the Union, and then the Knights of Labor— all efforts at joining together the producing element of the population in a national federation.

Owen viewed himself as an inventor and engineer and what the next generation called an efficiency export. He believed that social progress required eliminating the blatant corruption and waste of a competitive economy. In its place, he urged that a cooperative economy should be organized along the lines of a business corporation. But Owen arrived at "integral cooperation" only in 1884 after other efforts to attract settlers and to build his railroad had failed. Owen was not a disinterested social reformer, nor indeed did he claim to be one.

Integral cooperation was a much discussed idea in radical circles. A Johns Hopkins University study of the American cooperative movement in 1888 described its advocates as the most radical faction among cooperators. As expounded by Owen, integral cooperation denoted a "system of interdependent interests" modeled on the multi-divisional organization of a big business. Railroads and other great enterprises, he argued, demonstrated the advantages of large-scale operations.[9]

From this, Owen drew the conclusion that the means of both production and distribution should be collectively owned to allow for economies of scale. But he scorned those communitarians who rejected all private property. In his way of thinking, this ignored man's need for personal incentives and status symbols. "Equity, not Equality" was flown as Owen's banderole. The radical thrust of his thinking lay in his insistence upon the collective ownership of farms, factories, stores, and banks. His colony would be owned and operated by a chartered company. Self-employment would be permitted only in certain artisan trades, while all others would work for the company and be paid according to skill and productivity. Initiative and industry, claimed Owen, must be rewarded for social advance to occur.

In striking contrast to his collective organization of the economy, Owen's scheme for his colony featured private ownership of homes and residential lots. These were to be acquired by the purchase of company stock. Resale would be permitted only to the company which would allow for appreciation in values. Rental housing would be provided only for singles and the elderly and those temporarily lacking sufficient capital to build a home. To attract pioneer settlers, Owen priced his lots so that their purchase cost increased greatly for latecomers. Thus, those who delayed paid a surcharge for settling in a developed community.

Indeed the entire scheme, as a practical matter, hinged upon land sales. Owen anticipated $200,000,000 in sales revenue. This huge sum would enable the company to build a town with the most advanced public utilities, develop an industrial and agricultural base, eliminate taxes, and finance such social services as free medical care and pensions for early retirement at age fifty-five.

In 1885, Owen incorporated the Credit Foncier to buy land, to build a town, and to operate the town's utilities and businesses. All settlers were required to own at least one share in the company. Stockholders casting one vote for each share held would elect the board of directors who in turn appointed a chairman. The chairman would then select from among the directors the heads of the ten departments which handled the company's different activities. Such an organization, Owen argued, avoided the pitfalls of American government where "political ringsters seize control and the boodle becomes the aim."

Utopia, to Owen, included the totally and meticulously planned Pacific City at Topolobampo. To be based on modern technology, it would offer a superior, safe environment, including "wide streets, single homes, artesian water, river or bay for public use, sewerage recycled, pipes underground." Several six-lane avenues would facilitate movement in either direction by foot, bicycle, or electric traction. All heating and lighting would utilize electricity. Sewers would convey human waste to be treated and then spread as fertilizer on giant farms surrounding the city and providing it with fresh produce year-round. Owen described his future city to a reporter as "the first city which will be town and country combined. There will be little or no smoke. The factories are placed on the main avenues. Movement at all times will be fast, safe, and clean."[10]

His design for Pacific City called for a parklike setting. Twenty-nine square miles would be laid out on a grid of broad, tree-lined streets overlaid with a crisscross pattern of similarly spacious and diagonal roads (as in L'Enfant's plan of Washington, D.C., although much more mechanical). Parks located at regular intervals would form ordered rows through which the diagonal streets would run. Eventually the city would house a population of about five hundred thousand. This allowed for an overall density of twenty-six people to an acre in an open, uncluttered, green environment with all housing restricted to a Moorish design as most compatible with the climate. Owen promoted Pacific City as modern developers now advertise resort communities in Arizona or Florida.

Those attracted wanted not only to advance a social experiment but also to improve their circumstances. Unlike earlier nineteenth-century utopians, Owen sought, as did many communitarians at century's end, to salvage rather than recast traditional ethical and domestic values by providing a supportive environment. The home as "palladium of civilized life" was proclaimed the key to Owen's design of Pacific City.

Albert Kinsey Owen's scheme for Topolobampo was innovative in basing cooperation on the organization of the modern business corporation. In "integral cooperation" Owen claimed a new "system" that provided the mechanism for joining together both production and distribution. Capital to put it into practice would be obtained through sales of shares in the Credit Foncier in return for homesites.

Indefatigable as a propagandist and a promoter, Owen generated a steady stream of tracts, letters, and articles expounding his ideas. Despite the highly confused and contentious argumentation of his discourse, he still attracted a following. In particular, Owen won the support of a small New York bohemian circle which included the Harvard educated dilettante Edward Howland and his wife Marie, the author of a popular feminist romance. This novel, *Papa's Own Girl* (1874), had for its principal theme the starting of a model industrial village. Both Howlands were proponents of a cooperative factory and "associated homes" experiment, "Familistère," begun in the 1860s by the French industrialist Jean Godin at Guise. Another member of the circle was the well-known publisher John Lovell, who published Owen's miscellaneous writings and correspondence in 1885 under the title *Integral Cooperation: Its Practical Application* as part of an inexpensive series on radical and occult subjects.[11]

In the spring of 1886, Owen's New York supporters received unexpected attention from Edward Aveling and Eleanor Marx, guests in the United States of the Socialist Labor party. Aveling, a nonpracticing medical doctor, had recently aided William Morris in founding England's Socialist League. His companion and common-law wife was an aspiring actress, the favorite daughter of Karl Marx who had died in 1883. Their hosts, the German immigrants who mainly comprised the American Socialist Labor party, were soon startled to find the Avelings submitting extravagant bills for traveling expenses while preferring the company of Owen's circle to their own.[12]

Aveling arranged for John Lovell to publish a book on his American visit. In it, he reported that "scientific socialism" had made little headway among American-born radicals, and he commented on the considerable talk in labor and radical circles about colonization schemes, especially Owen's proposed Mexican venture. Of Topolobampo, he wrote that "the whole scheme . . . is on broader and larger basis than any that has as yet been started."[13]

By now Albert Owen was in contact with other British radicals. Through the Howlands, he entered into a correspondence with Evacustes Phipson (a mean of independent means from a prominent Birmingham Quaker family), interested in developing a socialist aesthetics. On Phipson's promise to introduce Owen to wealthy Englishmen prepared to financially support the Topolobampo scheme, Owen traveled to Britain in 1889. His effort proved disappointing.[14]

Owen made at least one convert in the course of his British sojourn, J. Bruce Wallace. An aquaintance has described Wallace as a "man of intensely devoted and spiritual nature, who was convinced that it was possible to establish some kind of cooperative system in place of the present capitalist system." Wallace, born in India in 1853 to missionary parents, gave up his position as a Congregational minister in 1885 to devote himself to Christian socialism. At that time he located himself in a small village outside of Belfast, Limavady, in County Berry, hoping thus to set an example for others to return to the countryside. In 1886 he became a member of Alfred Russel Wallace's Land Nationalisation Society, and a year later he started *Brotherhood*, which appeared intermittently on a weekly or monthly basis for nearly twenty years.[15]

Aspiring to a holistic approach to reform, *Brotherhood* railed against efforts to transform radical reform into sectarian and exclusive causes. Wallace espoused diet and clothing reform, temperance, the eight-hour day, and also led anti-vaccination and anti-vivisectionist campaigns. Above all,

he desired the "Cooperative Commonwealth," and *Brotherhood* reported
with enthusiasm on efforts at colonization and cooperative living.

On August 30, 1890, Wallace sailed to New York to visit several American
colonies, including Topolobampo. In New York he met with Henry George,
and then he traveled to Boston to speak with William Dwight Porter Bliss.
Bliss also came from a missionary background. After attending Amherst
College and Hartford Theological Seminary, he became minister of several
Congregational churches; in 1886, however, he entered the Episcopal
Church, which he believed offered more opportunity for the ecumenical
Christianity he sought. At this time he also became active in the Knights of
Labor and soon organized the highly unconventional labor-oriented Church
of the Carpenter in Boston.[16]

Bliss was one of the founders of the first Nationalist Club in 1889. At the
same time he helped organize the Society of Christian Socialists and edited
its journal, *Dawn*. Given Bliss's interests, Wallace was surprised to find Bliss
skeptical about colonization efforts when he met the American in September 1890. Edward Bellamy at this time struggled to curb interest among his
followers in starting a colony, and Bliss supported him in this. Bliss did,
however, think small residential communities worthwhile in terms of providing fellowship and comforts for their members, and he toyed in the 1890s
with several such schemes. It was the idea of a community as a self-
sufficient colony or pilot project for general social and economic experimentation and regeneration which he and Bellamy rejected.[17]

From Boston, J. Bruce Wallace journeyed to British Columbia, where the
provincial government included many followers of Henry George who ostensibly were prepared to support the creation of a colony as a "Cooperative Commonwealth." He then traveled south to visit the Kaweah colony,
begun in 1885 by radical workers from San Francisco. Kaweah, high up in
the mountains of east central California in Tulare County, was intended to
realize in miniature Lawrence Gronlund's "Cooperative Commonwealth."[18]

Even a sympathetic observer depicted the Kaweah colonists as a "motley
lot . . . ranging from word purists to uncooked food faddists to spiritualists . . . and with some who are all three and more." In any case, when
Wallace arrived the community was already doomed. Congress had just
enacted a bill reserving most of the land claimed by the colony for the
Yosemite National Park. Leaving California, Wallace sailed down the coast
to Topolobampo in December 1890.

Albert Owen's colony was now four years old and numbered about two
hundred settlers. Most of the original advance party had returned to the
United States. Wallace found the colonists living in a collection of shacks
and ragged tents. One large ranch structure held the colony's newspaper

and library, both presided over by the irrepressible and by now controversial Marie Howland. Howland's wearing trousers and her insistence on riding horses astraddle rather than a ladylike sidesaddle disconcerted the local Mexicans. Moreover, her consorting with various male settlers after the death of her husband disturbed some colonists.

Wallace accepted the harsh conditions as necessary to pioneering. In his reports to England, he preferred to dwell on the colonists' indestructible spirit and Owen's claims that work on the railroad would soon begin. Wallace returned home in January 1891 determined to assist Owen's venture, which he described as "the greatest cooperative scheme in the world." For this reason, he decided to move to London.

Despite Wallace's optimism, Topolobampo's affairs did not improve. In 1892, although there were now a reported five hundred settlers, disgruntlement over Owen's dictatorial leadership and the primitive conditions festered. Since few shares of the Credit Foncier's stock had been sold, capital was very short and "integral cooperation" remained untried. The settlers desperately struggled to eke out a subsistence through farming and tin mining, while digging a seven-mile-long irrigation canal.

A last glimmer of hope for the colony was offered by a wealthy German industrialist, Michael Flürscheim. Flürscheim, a leader in the German Land Nationalization Society, promised to invest a large sum of money in Topolobampo. In March 1893 he arrived in New York and accompanied Owen to Topolobampo. After reviewing the situation, Flürscheim suggested that Owen change his goal and lease his two hundred thousand acres to enlightened employers, such as himself, who would start factories on the principles of labor co-partnership as well as erect model towns. Owen angrily refused. Over the next two years, all but a handful of colonists straggled home. As a colony and dream, Topolobampo did not so much die as fade away.[19]

Topolobampo's failure and the ugly rumors afloat about Albert Owen's actions did not immediately end American communitarian enthusiasm. Several other colonies were started between 1894 and 1897. These included Fairhope, Alabama, where followers of Henry George sought to combine "cooperative individualism" with common ownership of land; the Ruskin Cooperative Colony of Tennessee, started by J. A. Wayland, a self-made businessman and editor of *The Coming Nation,* to be operated along "Nationalist" lines; and Equality in the state of Washington, sponsored by the Brotherhood of the Cooperative Commonwealth. All proved short-lived, at least in their original experimental form. Fairhope became a successful suburban real-estate development. By 1903, Wayland of the Ruskin colony was telling his readers not to put "confidence in anything but the organization of our class into a political party for the purpose of capturing the powers of government." Interest in communitarian colonization experiments was by then largely exhausted.

Organized in Maine in 1895, the Brotherhood of the Cooperative Commonwealth tried to join communitarianism with more au courrant radical themes. Its stated purpose was the novel fusion of communitarian and political activity. This was to be done through the systematic settlement of colonies in one state, Washington, "until said state is socialized." The colonists would then elect the state's congressional delegation as a radical spearhead in the very heart of national government.[20]

In a short time the Brotherhood claimed among its supporters such radical luminaries as Eugene Debs, Henry Demarest Lloyd, and William D. P. Bliss. Eugene Debs, however, was the only one who worked actively with the Brotherhood, though for his own reasons. Interested in building a new labor party, Debs sought to join together the Brotherhood with the remnants of his American Railway Union in a new political party, the Social Democracy of America. Debs's union had never recovered from the defeat suffered in the Pullman or Chicago strike of 1894, and he himself had spent six months in jail for violating a federal injunction. Even at the time the strike was collapsing, there had been talk among the die-hard Pullman workers about starting a cooperative factory and model town in Hiawatha, Kansas. But this represented the idle fantasizing of beaten men. By 1897, Debs was interested in colonies for the unemployed and in providing for his own officers as the paid organizers of the colonization effort in the event of his union's collapse. A three-man committee sent out to find possible sites displayed poor judgment and a weak sense of geography, ending up with a salted gold mine in Arizona.[21]

At a convention of the Social Democracy of America held in June 1898, a majority of the delegates (fifty-three to thirty-seven) supported colonization as the best means of achieving socialism. The minority, led by Victor Berger, denounced colonization as naive and quit the convention to form their own political party. In July 1901, Berger's Social Democratic party joined with dissidents from the Socialist Labor party to create the Socialist Party of America which nominated Debs as its presidential candidate. In 1908, William Alfred Hinds, a conscientious student of communitarian experiments for over thirty years, observed that the leaders of the Socialist party "have for years been lively in discouraging cooperative experiments in colony life, and have unquestionably been successful in diverting much attention from the colony movement"—so successful indeed that communitarian colonization schemes by now had virtually ceased being regarded as a legitimate activity of socialists.[22]

Long after communitarianism had lost much of its intellectual appeal, it still retained an emotional hold on many reformers of moralistic impulse. They acknowledged that the modern way of thinking required replacing the older view that socialism was an ideal or static state with a new conceptualization of socialism as a "mode or process which must gradually develop." Emotionally, however, reformers clung to the dream of the kingdom of heaven on earth as embodied in a small community designed for the highest degree of social harmony and rationality. Often their writings bear witness to an effort to graft communitarian themes onto what they regarded as a more scientific perspective of social change.

This effort to salvage something from the wreckage of communitarianism represented not so much a conscious attempt to join together different ideas as a conflict between the soul and the mind. Such a struggle certainly occurred in Henry Demarest Lloyd (1847–1903). Lloyd, like Bellamy, was the son of a minister and had chosen to be a writer. As a newspaper editor in Chicago, Lloyd criticized the prevailing business ethic of greed and domination. A series of articles for the *Atlantic Monthly* in 1881 on the Standard Oil Company, the first modern trust or holding company, was later expanded into *Wealth Against Commonwealth* (1894). This documented the corporation's manipulation of government and brought him national attention.

Lloyd infused his writings on social issues with a strong sense of evolutionary progress and positivism. But they also reveal his continuing sentimental attachment to communitarianism as a process for social change without conflict between parties, classes, or even individuals. On one occasion, when the press gleefully reported yet another collapse of a colony, Lloyd sorrowfully entered into his journal: "Always failures? They are little oases of people in our desert of business."

Lloyd, however, reluctantly concluded that the repeated failures demonstrated that the coming of socialism needed to be "solved in the womb of society by all," and not through the isolated example of colonies. "The Parable of the No Mean City," written in November 1893 on the closing of the Chicago Columbian Exposition, reveals Lloyd's attachment to very different radical approaches and his attempt at a synthesis. To many Americans, the famed "White City" of the Chicago exposition, an exhibit of temporary plaster-of-paris buildings collaborated on by America's best-known architects, suggested the importance of coordinated action in building the city of the future. Lloyd sought to capitalize on this sentiment in proposing a scenario for a way America could be peacefully transformed into a higher civilization.[23]

In "The Parable of the No Mean City," he projects how the abandonment of the "White City" of the Chicago Columbian Exposition of 1893 causes a spontaneous civic movement to revive it and make it permanent. In time, the civic enthusiasm extends outward to embrace Chicago as a whole, with the city becoming a laboratory for social and scientific experimentation. Highly trained municipal experts are sent throughout the world to learn the latest improvements. Municipal government takes over the ownership and management of the utilities. Horses are banned and all transportation electrified. In time, members of the middle class leave the city for model suburban communities and commute to work by trains moving at a speed of 125 miles an hour. Lloyd's account of the rise of a transformed Chicago depicts developments not out of line with the thinking of Sidney Webb and the Fabians with their emphasis on municipal socialism.

Lloyd's essay then veers abruptly off in the direction of evolutionary communitarianism. Colonies created for the unemployed eventually become the residence of choice for all. Technological advances and increased production, in Lloyd's scenario, led to considerable unemployment. His solution for this problem was to enroll the unemployed in colonies distant from the city and built from the first along rational lines. These colonies possessed advantages which could not be matched by Chicago. Their success lured the remaining population from the city center while also attracting farmers from their isolated landholdings to engage in mechanized agriculture. "It had always been idle," wrote Lloyd, "to ask the ambitious, the social among the younger people of the farm districts, not to take themselves to the city. It had been equally useless to ask the enervated or the unequipped of the city to brave the solitude of the farm. But here was a solution to both these difficulties. Here in the same place was country for the city people and city for the country people."

Eventually the colonies expand to absorb Chicago. On the centennial anniversary of the Great Fire of 1871 the old city is razed to make a vast people's park. It is of passing interest to note Lloyd's observation that when Chicago's famed skyscrapers were dismantled their steel was found crystallized "owing to the incessant oscillation of the molecules by the swaying of the wind and . . . were in danger of going to pieces."

"No Mean City," Chicago's successor, was free of the congestion, disorder, dirt, tenements, and mansions of the large cities. It is also of apparently unlimited horizontal expanse. Indeed, "No Mean City" does not resemble a recognizable urban form. Lloyd tells us specifically what "No Mean City" will not have. The future city will not contain urban blocks, nor does it permit tall buildings. At its center is a "people's park" wherein will be universities, libraries, museums, and civic buildings. Lloyd's future city will also be a mixture of agriculture and industry with homes placed in planned residential areas. Everything else is vague. Lloyd could not fully conceptualize and describe his preferred alternative. For him the present was unacceptable, the future promising but uncertain.

The redirection in socialist thought about colonies and their role comes out sharply when comparing the 1898 edition of William D. Bliss's *Encyclopedia of Social Reform* with the 1907 revised edition. In his article on socialism in 1898, Bliss reported that most socialists looked to the state as the vehicle for change but that some sought socialism through the success of colonization schemes. Ten years later, he stated that all socialists, whatever else their disagreements, accepted the necessity of enlarging the state. In 1907, Bliss reported that communitarian interest was principally exhibited by religious cults. There are in the 1907 edition, however, favorable articles on colonies for the unemployed, on associative housing, on model industrial villages, and on various types of model housing experiments, including the Garden City movement. Colonization schemes originally perceived by communitarians as a way to launch the Cooperative Commonwealth had for the most part become a reform tool for improving the conditions of urban life. Perhaps for this reason, the connection between nineteenth-century colonization efforts and twentieth-century reform themes has remained obscure.

In the year he died, 1899, Edward Bellamy published *Equality* as the sequel to *Looking Backward*. This second work offered a more comprehensive and satisfactory account of social change than the first. It went, however, largely unsold and unread. A shift in social thinking was under way: a movement toward a consideration of change as a slow, incremental, and evolutionary process and away from the near miraculous transformations offered by the panaceas of Henry George and Bellamy or the advocates of colonies. Reform was becoming piecemeal, pragmatic, and technical. An alternative vision of society was something reformers sought to work toward in the future rather than achieve all at once in the here and now. The reform-minded no longer prophesied that the kingdom of heaven was about to descend, and few now subscribed to the view that voluntary efforts at cooperation in the form of colonies or otherwise could bring about social transformation.

In this more cautious and tentative mood, communitarianism, with its dependence on "naive enthusiasm" and unlimited optimism, could no longer retain a place as a legitimate form of radical activity. More and more in the twentieth century, it would be shunted to the sidelines—divorced from the mainstream of historical development and widely considered to be a sideshow for social deviants. Yet in the late nineteenth century, all radical thinkers still for a time needed to come to grips with communitarian colonization schemes, if only to reject them. Looking down his pince-nez, Sidney Webb in 1889 bemoaned the fact that "modern socialists are still reproached with the domestic details of an imaginary Phalanstery" by their enemies. By the end of the first decade of the new century, no such problem existed. Socialism had acquired its modern meaning of state ownership of the economy in one form or another.

Late nineteenth-century visionaries of a Cooperative Commonwealth reacted to rapid urbanization. Still, they also indicated concern with the loneliness and hardship of rural life; the mindless, endless domestic chores of the housewife; and the sense of the family as isolated and vulnerable. The alternative sought was a new type of community—a synthesis of town and country—providing public baths, playgrounds, promenades, common kitchens, libraries, museums, theaters, and public rooms, as well as homes with gardens to enrich individual life, ease domestic chores, and bring the family out into the community. Frequently the department store was employed as the metaphor of a society stripped of inefficiency and waste, capable of providing a general life of abundance amidst a multiplicity of easily available conveniences, services, and goods.

Freedom was redefined by radicals such as Bellamy to mean not only the absence of repression but also new opportunities for individuals to develop themselves to their highest potential through the support of community. The socialism of the Cooperative Commonwealth as expressed by enthusiasts rested not on political theory or economic analysis but on the presumed innate goodness, rationality, and altruism of human beings once they were provided a nurturing setting. What was sought and promised was a community capable of creating a more progressive and ethical humanity. Society was considered as a social organism with laws and needs of its own rather than only the sum of individual actions. Social duty in the Cooperative Commonwealth was to be a joyfully and freely offered fact of life.

All in all, the Cooperative Commonwealth proffered a genteel and ethical vision of the future rooted in a deep longing for community as an expression of true brotherhood. The community as a collective force was to be at the heart of change. Obviously attractive to some, this vision was also open to the charge that it failed to square theory with reality. In response to the criticism of their utopianism, social visionaries faced the necessity of demonstrating that their ideas were feasible. Not all aspirations to the Cooperative Commonwealth rested on colonization schemes, but this tendency was strongly present and especially vulnerable to ridicule. Communitarian enthusiasts, however, developed an inventory of ideas concerning the good community for others to draw on.

As Ralph Waldo Emerson early on discerned, the real value of colonies "is not what they have done but the revolution which they indicate as on the way." Writing in 1913, Gustave Stickley indicated the debt of a certain type of reformer in the Progressive era to the communitarian vision. "We do not need to be reminded that the dream of the world for ages has been the ideal city of the future—a community which will unite with the fullest civic life and opportunity, the freedom and healthfulness of the country, and in which the citizens, merely because of their citizenship will be entitled to

share in all the benefits of the commonwealth. In this ideal community . . .
the very failings of human nature . . . will be transmuted by the new conditions of life into recognition of the wider good which includes the whole
community; all alike will have the opportunity to live, work and enjoy." In
the twentieth century, reformers relying on politics and the positive state
often echoed an older communitarian set of values.[24]

5

Toward a New Urban Vision: Howard in the 1890s

> The essential idea is that a city can be founded, planned and governed de novo even in an ancient land like England.
>
> Ebenezer Howard
> (*Daily Mail*, October 27, 1899)

In the 1890s, a professor at the University of Edinburgh commented: "The kind of Socialism most in repute at present is one which cannot be carried into practice by the voluntary action of individuals, or illustrated by experiments on a small scale. It is the Socialism which can only be realized through the State and which must have the whole nation as a subject on which to operate." The emergence of the Independent Labour party and the growing prominence of the Fabians gave a collectivist and political thrust to British socialism. From the embers of communitarian interest, though, a spark was thrown off in the form of the Garden City movement.[1]

J. Bruce Wallace's decision to start an English colony based on "integral cooperation" set in motion the events leading to Howard's appearance at Farringdon Hall. In October 1891, Wallace, busily lecturing on Topolobampo and vigorously publicizing the colony in his journal, *Brotherhood*, rented office space in London, inviting Owen to make it "the British or European centre for your colony and railroad." He also acquired an old derelict Congregational chapel on Southgate in Islington. Renaming it the Brotherhood Church, he built up a congregation of about two hundred and opened a cooperative store.[2]

In place of theology and ritual, the Brotherhood Church offered fellow-

54

ship, an intellectual forum, and more—a sense of participation in helping the dawn of a brighter new age. Wallace and his congregation were not concerned with sin, believing only that human frailties like ignorance and selfishness posed the obstacles to the building of the New Jerusalem. They aspired to individuals achieving their full potential and the correction of social flaws.

A brief Sunday service was followed by an improvised vegetarian meal and a general discussion lasting late into the afternoon. In 1907, when Wallace's Brotherhood Church was rented by the Sixth Congress of the Russian Social Democratic party meeting in exile, Maxim Gorky described it as a small, faded red-brick building with a tin roof whose intentionally austere auditorium contained "no trace of anything ecclesiastic and even the pulpit placed low."

In February 1892, Wallace wrote to Owen that a small party of Englishmen had left for Topolobampo. This group consisted of two single men and Mr. J. A. Kinghorn-Jones, a London printer, with his wife and nine children. Wallace had by now concluded that many not prepared to travel six thousand miles to Topolobampo would join an experiment closer to home. He asked Owen to send literature on the Mexican colony and other experiments. His Sunday discussion group would use this material to think through the design of a British "home colony."[3]

Members of the Nationalisation of Labour Society earlier had tried to stir up interest in the idea of a British home colony and had adopted a "declaration of principles" (which it claimed Bellamy had approved) calling for such a scheme. In February 1892, notices appeared in both *Brotherhood* and the *Nationalisation News* asking those interested in participating in an English home colony to contact J. Bruce Wallace. Two months later only a handful had volunteered—most of them middle-class and few with the requisite manual skills needed to construct a colony. Nonetheless, J. Bruce Wallace and John Orme, president of the Nationalisation of Labour Society, decided to proceed.[4]

They called a meeting for Sunday, April 2, 1892, at the Brotherhood Church to discuss the start of a colony. This group declared its intention to organize their proposed community according to the principles of Albert Kinsey Owen. By September 1892, one hundred twenty individuals had expressed interest. Among them was Ebenezer Howard, soon to lead an effort to steer the proposed colony away from the idea of "integral cooperation."[5]

J. Bruce Wallace's fascination with Owen had both an emotional and intellectual basis. Wallace had developed a theory he called "circle cooperation." This envisioned a gigantic network of interlinked producer and consumer cooperatives which, when combined with land nationalization, would lead to a Cooperative Commonwealth, a fully socialist society. But Wallace was pain-fully aware of the criticism that cooperative schemes represented at best no more than a form of "combined individualism." Owen's "integral coopera-tion," with all elements and interests of the community represented by a single company, seemed the solution. In addition, Wallace shared Owen's view that it was necessary to pay individuals according to the value of their work. Both looked to an "individualistic form of socialism" rather than a communist society, which still meant to them the older communitarian mean-ing of total sharing.[6]

Wallace had long been fascinated by the idea of starting a colony. For Wallace and others like him, communitarianism provided a means of with-drawing from a turbulent society and searching inwardly while justifying this action in terms of universal applicability and significance. It is clear that even without Owen's example, Wallace was ready to involve himself at this time in some effort at a British home colony.

"Integral cooperation" was not the only idea considered by Wallace's group. Marie Howland, the librarian of the Topolobampo colony, prepared a thirty-five-page bibliography of nineteenth-century communitarian litera-ture and forwarded this to London. Moreover, in March 1892, an English translation of Theodore Herzka's *Freeland,* a utopian novel, appeared and immediately attracted the group's attention. Herzka, a highly regarded Viennese economist and journalist, had moved during the 1880s from the laissez-faire of the Manchester School to radicalism. In *Freeland,* the Aus-trian proposed combining the freedom of "individualism" with the social justice of "socialism." In his novel, a group of Europeans establish an experi-mental colony in Kenya for this purpose.[7]

Herzka assumed his colony's evolution into a Cooperative Common-wealth, but that decision was left to the colonists—hence the name Freeland. All he required was that the colony collectively own the site and all of its banks. Settlers were free to lease land and borrow capital while awaiting the rise of a "higher form of collective organization." Herzka's scheme appealed to land reformers and to those radicals suspicious of strong central control (views that frequently coincided). Led by a German artillery officer, a party of Herzka's followers soon set off for Kenya. But Masai tribesmen, indifferent to their message of an altruistic higher civiliza-tion, forced a retreat home under a hail of spears.

Wallace's London group made efforts in 1892 to bring Herzka and Al-bert Owen together. They proposed to the Austrian that he consider a colony in Topolobampo rather than Kenya. Herzka's response ruled out a joint venture until the American allowed private economic enterprise. This Owen refused to do. Members of the circle meeting in Wallace's "chapel of the tin roof" had much to discuss in the differences between the two.[8]

There were other reasons for second thoughts about Owen's "integral cooperation." Rumors of trouble in his colony mounted. Flürscheim, the German industrialist, wrote Wallace in a critical vein regarding the Mexican experiment. One of the party that had gone to Topolobampo, Kinghorn-Jones, also wrote to denounce Owen's authoritarianism and then left for San Francisco where he told the press that Owen had stolen his life's savings invested in the colony's stock. His voice was added to those of others who charged that the entire scheme was a hoax to enrich Owen and his friends.

In May, Wallace told Owen of the need for a response to the ugly stories circulating concerning his colony. Another member of Wallace's group, Evacustes Phipson, informed Owen that many in England interested in a scheme by which "increasing land values were turned to community profit . . . were concerned that Topolobampo did not adequately allow for this." Now in the spring of 1892, the London group pressed Owen to provide details about the arrangements for ownership of the vast tract of land the Mexican government had awarded him. In July 1892, Owen wrote to Wallace, defending himself from charges of profiteering while acknowledging that some land was kept apart from the colony as his own.[9]

By the time Owen's letter was received, if not before, a faction within the London group announced opposition to a home colony based on integral cooperation. Its leaders came from the Land Nationalisation Society. In September 1892, a provisional committee to resolve differences between Herzka's and Owen's schemes for a colony started biweekly meetings at the Land Nationalisation Society offices. Three months later, in December, a public meeting to launch a home colony was called for February 11, 1893, to be held in Farringdon Hall. The scheme presented would represent a compromise between two very different plans for a colony.

Howard emerged briefly at this time as a central figure in English communitarian circles. Called upon to work out the terms of compromise, Howard presented the Garden City idea for which he later became famous. At the time, however, his proposal reflected an attempt to devise a workable communitarian experiment upon which divergent radical groups could reach agreement. This experience permanently altered the trajectory of Howard's life. He now determined that his personal mission was to realize a new form of community.[10]

In 1892, Howard stood at a crossroads. For much of the previous year he had experienced a deep depression precipitated in March 1891 by the unexpected death of a relative and by his inability to raise sufficient capital to start his job printing firm. Howard writes that one night his depression inexplicably lifted, and he was filled with desire to help resolve the social dilemmas of his age. He recalled many years later experiencing on this occasion an energizing surge of hope: "I was brought back to the supreme value of Christ's teaching that the individual is given free will to choose the good." Then sometime early in 1892, Howard recorded a sense of expectation "in some great approaching change."

At the time, Howard was a court reporter with the Royal Commission on Labour which met irregularly from 1891 to 1894. For once his profession dovetailed with his interests in a way which profoundly influenced his thinking. The commission, which included among its members the Cambridge economist Alfred Marshall and the rising young working-class politican John Burns, investigated the causes and extent of unemployment and the problems of poorly paid unskilled labor. Of particular concern was the continuing flight of a surplus rural population into urban slums, adding to the ranks of the unemployed. Several of those called to testify, including General William Booth of the Salvation Army and author of *Darkest England* (1890), proposed philanthropic efforts at labor colonies as a way of helping the poor and easing urban unrest and misery. To Howard, the circumstance of his being present while recognized authorities grappled with problems that he himself was interested in resolving proved a fortunate concurrence of events to match and promote his "good assembly of thought."[11]

In 1892, Howard put down on paper his first tentative ideas concerning social reform. This unfinished manuscript, entitled "Commonsense Socialism," is filled with anger at the poverty and squalor surrounding him in London and at the tales told to the commission of exploitation by rackrenters and jerry-builders. In his later writings, he would attribute the housing problem not to the landlord's greed but to the system. His change of heart may have been influenced by George Bernard Shaw's first play, produced in the fall of 1892, *Widower's House*, which offered this very perspective.[12]

In "Commonsense Socialism" Howard assumed humanity's natural right for "ample space to live healthy and useful lives." He blamed the landlord for the huddling of people in cities while the countryside was being deserted. "The landlord is in everyday life what the priest is in religion. He says in effect, if you want to go to God's earth you must go through me." Howard proposed a colony based on collective land ownership to eliminate the landlord. The rents which formerly provided the exploiter with "carriages and houses, and servile attendants" would now finance roads, hospitals, open space, and assist the sick and the helpless.

Howard offered very few details of the actual community, although significantly his minimum widths for roads and dimensions for homesites are very nearly those suggested by Owen for Pacific City. One highly prescient thought is present in the essay. Howard observed that the inventor is in a sense more practical than the practical man because he sees what is possible and desirable long before the other, yet "it is generally the practical man who possesses the faculty of execution." Ten years later, Howard gladly stepped aside to allow those more experienced and influential than he construct his garden city.

Drawing on Bellamy's "nationalism," Howard had initially thought of a home colony in terms of a centrally managed and collectively owned economy. Circumstantial evidence suggests that he entered Wallace's discussion group as a member of the Bellamite Nationalisation of Labour Society (N.L.S.). In any event, Howard quickly came to the view that a collectivist economy, such as Owen and Bellamy sought, posed great problems and could not be effectively imposed. If it were to come at all, it needed to evolve slowly and cautiously through trial and error. For this reason, he quickly moved to the position favored by the Land Nationalisation Society (L.N.S.) that the colony at its outset should only own the land.[13]

The provisional committee, meeting in the fall 1892, unsuccessfully attempted to reconcile differences. Its membership consisted of three men from the N.L.S., three from the L.N.S., and Ebenezer Howard. A consensus was arrived at only on preliminary details, not on the colony's purpose. Differences were not resolved but circumvented.[14]

The provisional committee agreed to lay out the colony on the pattern of a spider's web, rejecting Albert Owen's radial-grid design. The principal avenues were to radiate from a central place around which would be grouped the chief public buildings, "while the subsidiary streets are arranged in concentric circles." They also decided that the site of the colony should be within a thirty- to forty-mile radius of London, preferably near or on a railroad line. The reason given for this was that such a distance would allow them to acquire land at agricultural (rather than speculative building) rates while still being near enough to London to benefit from proximity. Colonists could commute to London to work until the colony offered them an adequate livelihood. If the colony failed, the site could be sold profitably to suburban developers or even leased to industrialists interested in labor–co-partnership experiments and model housing. This idea of leasing to enlightened industrialists was the scheme Flürscheim was proposing to Albert Owen.[15]

The decision to locate near London represented an important change in perspective. Until the 1880s communitarians favored locating colonies at a distance from civilization, preferably in a virgin or foreign region. Such placement was desired to strengthen a colony's self-sufficiency while lessening the seditious influences of the external world. A reaction to these views had set in by the 1890s, fueled by the hardships endured in such colonization efforts as Topolobampo and the growing recognition that no colony oriented to progress could divorce itself completely from a national market economy—the futility of such an effort being a major argument against colonies by their critics.

The celebrated Russian anarchist Prince Peter Kropotkin, then living in Britain and widely regarded as an authority on the subject of colonies, attempted to revise older communitarian values to make them more relevant and attractive. In a letter to an English admirer published in *Brotherhood,* he called for "home colonies" in preference to foreign adventures and pleaded for colonies sited in the "neighborhood of large cities." Furthermore, he rejected the emphasis in many schemes on "barrack housing" and argued for separate family dwellings. Communitarians, he asserted, needed to discard any similarities between their approach to colonies and the "monastary or factory" in order to think in terms of "the life of independent families, united together by the desire of obtaining material and moral well-being through combined efforts." Colonies, according to Kropotkin, needed to offer comfort, convenience, and civilization, as well as a more harmonious and moral manner of life.[16]

Finally, the committee agreed that under no circumstances would the colony divest itself of the land, thus insuring that all increase in land value would revert to the community. An ingeniously devised stratagem sidestepped differences over economic organization. Both parties would join together to support a colony based solely on collective land ownership. Once in existence this colony would rent space to the N.L.S. interested in a more radical and far-reaching experiment based on "integral cooperation." Ebenezer Howard was designated the principal speaker for the Farringdon Hall meeting. After Howard presented a scheme of his own design, however, John Orme would then describe briefly the plans for a second colony to be carried out once the first was under way and within the other's borders.[17]

At 3:00 p.m., Saturday, February 11, 1893, the meeting was opened, and Howard spoke for an hour. His proposal, while modest in scale when compared with the schemes offered by American communitarians, was highly ambitious by the standards of their English counterparts. It called for a site of approximately nine thousand acres near London to contain a population of some thirty thousand.

Howard's premise was simple. The colony was to be based only on common ownership of the site. A chartered company with trustees would develop the colony and retire the mortgage. All ground rent would be used to pay off this debt and to provide for public improvements. The colony's principal purpose was to demonstrate the social value of eliminating private landlordism. In the role of landlord, the colony was prepared to accept groups interested in other forms of social experimentation, but would maintain "vigilance against intrusion by cranks and scoundrels."

The questions that followed Howard's talk tended to be critical. Many in the audience argued that it did not go far enough in the direction of socialism. The initial resolution in favor of Howard's proposal was voted down until speakers from the Nationalisation of Labour Society spoke in its favor. They viewed Howard's scheme as a useful first step upon which to build their own collective scheme at a future time. Finally, a committee was elected to raise twenty thousand pounds, to find a site, and to purchase it.

In *To-morrow*, Howard acknowledged several men whose ideas foreshadowed his Garden City concept but then quickly observed that he alone had assembled all the pieces and carried them to a logical conclusion. He referred by name to only one experimental colony of the hundreds launched by communitarians in the course of the nineteenth century—Topolobampo. Owen's colony and "integral cooperation" were cited as negative models, an instance of what could go wrong when a colony was exclusionary, overly repressive, and highly centralized. These comments help explain the most attractive feature of the garden city—Howard's emphasis on the need for freedom and experimentation.[18]

Owen prescribed a static, predetermined, and closed plan which demanded obedience and acceptance. In contrast, Howard proposed diversity, gradualism, and practicality. He refused to dictate any fixed future for his community. Only time and the democratically expressed choices of its residents, he believed, could determine this. Howard had a view of a dynamic society in constant change and development but moving forward as individuals realized their potential and "spiritual forces assumed a materialistic form." This approach was directly in line with twentieth-century liberal thought.

In April 1893, a suitable site of nine hundred acres was located near Hockley in Essex, and negotiations were entered into. By June 1893, it was apparent that the committee could not raise even the five hundred pounds necessary as a guarantee of good faith. Perhaps through oversight, a list of committee members appearing in *Brotherhood* at this time omitted Howard's name. Certainly in July, when the committee had abandoned its efforts, Howard was unaware of its failure. In that month he went on business to Manchester, which he described as a "horrid place . . . a very pandemonium. It is more squalid even than London." On his way home, Howard wrote his wife that he planned a visit to the estate in Essex, "the site of the New Jerusalem."[19]

After the failure of the Farringdon Hall scheme, J. Bruce Wallace called a meeting for mid-December 1893 at the Brotherhood Church to consider other proposals for colonies. The following year, he organized the Brotherhood Trust to promote a complex network for carrying on both trade and industry that he hoped would lead to the building of a cooperative colony.[20]

Associated with Wallace in this new grandiose undertaking was the Reverend J. C. Kenworthy, the minister of the Brotherhood Church in Croyden. Kenworthy visited the great Russian novelist Leo Tolstoy at Yasna Polyana in 1895 and 1896 and returned to England with the rights to Tolstoy's British royalties. With a few friends, he established a short-lived community in Purleigh, one of nine small English efforts at founding communities between 1895 and 1899 based on Tolstoy's vision of a primitive Christianity which fitted nicely with certain themes of the Arts and Crafts movement. These fin de siècle colonies illustrate marked communitarian decline. They were attempts by a few middle-class discontents to find refuge from a bleak reality and "live according to the light within" rather than to erect a beacon high on a hill.[21]

Howard chose to follow the other side of the communitarian coin—the ideal of a colony as a means to universal reform by inspirational influence as a model. He spent the next few years working out in book form the details of the Garden City scheme he had presented at Farringdon Hall. Longhand pages written in the evenings or on Sunday on a kitchen table were typed by a niece he could not afford to pay. With compass, ruler, and watercolor paint, he painstakingly prepared seven illustrations to accompany the text. Howard first considered calling his proposed community "Rurisville" to emphasize its synthesis of the desirable aspects of city and country. A year later, in 1895, he thought of calling the colony "Unionville," but in the end he decided on "Garden City," a choice he later regretted. In 1896, he sent an article on his scheme to *Contemporary Review,* whose editor rejected it, claiming lack of space.

Howard sent his manuscript to several publishers and found none of them interested. Then in the spring of 1898, an American friend, George Dyckman, the director of the Kodak Company's British branch and "a great admirer of Mrs. Cora Richmond," offered fifty pounds toward the publication of *To-morrow: A Peaceful Path to Real Reform.* Howard now arranged with the firm of Swann and Sonnenschein for the publication of the book on a commission basis. The author was to provide Swann and Sonnenschein with printed sheets that they were to bind and arrange to distribute, charging him for the service. On the sale of books, his account received a credit. No royalties were to be paid, and neither Howard nor the publisher bothered to seek a copyright.

The details of the colony proposed by Ebenezer Howard on February 11, 1893, were essentially identical to the famous garden city advanced five years later in his book *To-morrow: A Peaceful Path to Real Reform* (known since 1902 by the title *Garden Cities of To-morrow*). Howard's involvement with J. Bruce Wallace's group and the connection through them with Albert Kinsey Owen's project at Topolobampo and Theodore Herzka's novel *Freeland* escaped notice by historians for the simple reason that Wallace's

Brotherhood in its accounts of his group's effort to begin a colony never referred to Ebenezer Howard by name. Aside from being reported in *Brotherhood*, the meeting of February 11, 1893, received coverage only from small obscure newspapers whose accounts focused on the events of the day and did not detail any of the preliminary activity. In his later recollections of the origins of his scheme, Ebenezer Howard never referred to Farringdon Hall or his membership on the provisional committee. This was at least in part because Howard feared such references might bring into question the originality which he eagerly asserted for his scheme.[22]

Howard's perseverance reflected his conviction that he had a gift for seeing things differently and more clearly than others. Cora Richmond, on a visit to London in 1881, had told him "you have a message to give the world." Howard thereafter thought his purpose in life was "to put forward . . . practical proposals to uplift society." Howard's desire for reform rested on a solid belief in a God-given purpose of harmony and unity in the universe. In the world vision offered by "Modern Spiritualism," humanity needed to align itself with this divine order. This, he now believed, required the garden city.

Howard was very much the stereotypical Victorian in combining an enthusiasm for science and material progress. To this, he added an essentially altruistic ethic and faith in evolutionary progress derived from Cora Richmond's "New Dispensation." Society erred, he believed, in its overemphasis on material possessions, in its exclusive reliance on individual self-interest, and in its skepticism toward radical novel ideas. Howard knew full well that he was going against the grain. He needed to convince a skeptical world that a remarkably simple solution to the problems of great cities and rural depopulation was at hand and only awaited implementation.

6

The Search for Environment

Environment—or the sum total of the external conditions of life.

George John Romanes
(*Fortnightly Review,* December 1881,
as cited in the *Oxford English Dictionary*)

Howard's eventual success is directly related to his decision to direct *To-morrow*'s message to a general audience rather than to one inclined toward communitarian experiments. To persuade the skeptical reader, Howard knew he needed to avoid any suggestion of faddism, sectarianism, and, most important, utopianism. In 1893, Howard had presented his scheme essentially as an experiment in collective land ownership and only secondarily as a planned community designed with the problems of the great city in mind. In *To-morrow,* this approach was reversed, and priority was given to the garden city as a novel environmental order.

The shift in emphasis allowed Howard's scheme and the movement it started to acquire in time a place of prominence in a rising reform movement directed toward the dramatic improvement of urban conditions. His search for a new environmental ideal provided the passageway for ideas and individuals to cross over from the small fervid world of late-nineteenth-century communitarianism to the twentieth-century profession of town planning. *To-morrow* reflected both society's concern with the rise of an urban civilization and the concomitant hope that the social cataclysm this seemed to portend could be avoided.

The book opens with the premise that it is the general view of all parties and ideologies, "not only in England, but all over Europe and America and our colonies, that it is deeply to be deplored that the people should continue to stream into the already overcrowded cities." Howard's intended appeal, then, was to all disturbed by the overcrowding of cities in the modern world. He offered them the Garden City concept as a universal and encompassing solution. The name "Garden City" appears to have been selected as pictorially evocative while politically neutral.[1]

To-morrow employs a style of reasoning common in communitarian writing of the period. A problem is posed in terms of antithetical developments. Then a colony is offered as the comprehensive solution. In *To-morrow*, the dialectic appears in the form of Howard's famous metaphor of the "Three Magnets." Under a diagram of two magnets—"The Town" and "The Country"—he delineated in terse phrases the advantages and disadvantages of each as he perceived them. Urban living provided economic and social advantages negated by social alienation and inadequate and expensive housing. The country offered fresh air and natural beauty but lacked social and economic opportunities. Under the final or third magnet, "Town-Country," only advantages are noted since the negatives of the other two are balanced out. As the synthesis of city and country, Howard claimed for the garden city: "all the advantages of the most energetic and active town life, with all the beauty and delight of the country. . . ."

Howard, however, distanced the Garden City concept from the usual communitarian effort by presenting it as an environmental ideal rather than as an alternative social order. Communitarian thinking from Robert Owen onward attached great importance to environmental design because a new social order and the reshaping of human behavior required an appropriate and purposeful setting. In Howard's work, though, the design of the environment is presented as the "raison d'être" for a colony. His community is offered as an alternative to the great city, not to challenge prevailing values.

Collective land ownership, the most radical proposal presented, is treated as a necessary condition of orderly community growth and development rather than as a social ideal. The elimination of speculation meant, in addition, that the appreciation of land values resulting from community development would be exclusively channeled into collective goals such as schools, libraries, and theaters. Other types of reform are regarded as secondary and tentative. Economic and municipal experimentation were to be permitted and encouraged but not, as was usually the case in communitarian colonies, predetermined. Howard personally hoped that such experiments as municipal socialism and a cooperative economy would evolve through the initiative of the residents.

Howard called his approach to community organization "social individualism." This he explained as individuals "grouping themselves in a social manner with nothing cut and dried. People will go as far as they desire in the direction of a collective effort." He told a trade-union meeting that the workers must despoil the rich not through laws "but by cooperative action which will set an example and gain the support of the rich until extremes of wealth are voluntarily abolished." Addressing the Fabian Society in 1901, he described himself as a "socialist in spirit," although unable to accept the "doctrine that all land and industrial developments should be communal." Indeed, Howard did not join the Labour party until 1917, when in a speech Ramsay MacDonald stressed that the Labour party would work with all progressive forces and not represent a class ideology.[2]

Howard believed that the garden city, by its very nature, must lead to important social changes and impel civilization's higher evolution. This assumption relieved him of the need to put forward a new social order, the very aspect of communitarian thinking dismissed by its critics as the essence of utopianism. *To-morrow* promised a superior community and in time a new humanity, but these did not entail a far-reaching redesign of social values or institutions.

The garden city provided the preconditions, in Howard's mind, "for a peaceful path to real reform." His ultimate goal—a network of garden cities to replace the existing arrangement—allowed for a democratic society committed to free choice, individual and family well-being, and evolutionary progress. Few could object to Howard's social goals as such.

Howard's assumption that social and economic changes would evolve from the popular will enabled him to avoid addressing the usual perennial communitarian concerns, such as socialism versus individualism. An increasingly healthy, educated, contented, and altruistic citizenry could be relied on to decide for itself. This, in fact, had been Howard's position in 1893, but only while writing *To-morrow* did he think through the implications of his novel environmental order and push it firmly forward as the primary civilizing agent. His shift in emphasis reflected the dominant social thinking of the 1890s, which sought environmental explanations for social problems.

Howard considered many details of the physical plan of the garden city tentative and hypothetical. All his illustrations were carefully marked "Diagram Only—Plan Cannot Be Drawn Until Site Selected" in the second edition of his book. The garden city as presented in *To-morrow* does, however, contain an irreducible element. A de novo community must be carefully planned in advance in terms of basic services, street and road patterns, as well as in the location of public buildings, open areas, residences, industry, and shops. All of these must be considered in terms of the others and correlated for efficiency and convenience with considerable segregation of land-use functions to minimize incompatibility. Furthermore, the population and area of the town were limited by the permanent presence of a surrounding rural area to permit immediate access to nature and a balance of industry and agriculture.

The principal characteristics of Howard's community are that it is a town and not a suburb, that it is planned in advance of construction, and that its layout is characterized by an ordered pattern with adequate land devoted to homesites and open areas. Above all, a balance was to be struck between town and surrounding country through restrictions on development and population. Such measures would create a small city of sufficient size to offer the sophisticated opportunities of town life without congestion, crowds, or inconvenience. These constitute the sine qua non of Howard's garden city.

Howard sensed that presenting the garden city solely in terms of its theory would not generate mass appeal. For this reason, Howard depicted it visually. The most vivid and easily remembered sections of *To-morrow* are the illustrative details devoted to the town's layout and organization. Howard asks the reader to imagine a kite-shaped estate of six thousand acres, of which one thousand near the center is the site of a garden city with a population of thirty thousand. The estate is laid out in a circular plan, about three-quarters of a mile from center to circumference. Radiating out from the center, as spokes in a wheel, are six boulevards, 130 feet wide, which divide the town into six equal, self-contained wards.

In the exact center of the town site is a small circular garden. Around this are grouped the larger public buildings—museum, library, theater, concert hall, and hospital. They are separated from the remainder of the city by a central park of fifteen acres, which is surrounded by the "Crystal Palace," an arcaded series of structures (divided by radial boulevards) which contain the shops. Beyond this is the residential area containing 5,500 house lots averaging twenty-five by one hundred feet in size, allowing for a density of about seventeen houses to an acre and providing each house with a small garden.

Circular avenues give further definition to the plan, and one of these, Grand Avenue, contains sites for schools and churches in a parklike setting. The outer ring of the town is a circular railroad. Adjacent to it are factories, warehouses, and a coal yard. Outside the town is a permanent agricultural greenbelt of five thousand acres devoted to small farms, orphan asylums, and convalescent homes. Allotment gardens are also provided for town residents to allow them to grow fresh produce to reduce food bills.[3]

Howard's presentation of the design of the garden city is an elaboration of the "spider's web pattern" discussed in the committee meetings in the fall of 1892. This may indeed explain why in later years Howard expressed great concern in private that others claimed credit for the garden city's design. In any event, Howard's town design in *To-morrow* was never directly employed in a garden city.[4]

Success of the first garden city was expected to initiate a familiar communitarian cycle. Others would be begun and organized into cluster patterns. While each garden city was to remain a basic unit of settlement for residence and work, a number of them arranged in proximity to each other and linked by canals and rapid electric transportation would facilitate interchange and cooperation. In this way Howard envisaged an arrangement of towns with a total population of approximately 250,000, so that "each inhabitant of the whole group, though in one sense living in a town of small size, would be in reality living in all the advantages of a great and beautiful city."

In time, London and other large cities would be drained of their excess populations. A new age would dawn. Town planners have seen in this suggestion a seminal form of regional planning. It should be noted, though, that the idea of a cooperative network of towns was clearly a variation on the common communitarian theme of federated communities espoused by J. Bruce Wallace, Peter Kropotkin, and many others. It was also a more articulate expression of Henry Demarest Lloyd's concept in "The Parable of the No Mean City" of how the proliferation of planned communities transformed the urban fabric.[5]

To argue, as many have, that Howard exemplified an anti-urban bias—much in evidence in the late Victorian period—is to miss the significance of his ideas. Howard agreed with Alfred Marshall that cities were the cutting edge of civilization and progress. They served a necessary and vital role in expediting technological and industrial improvements. Unfortunately, gigantic cities also generated social ills. But new forms of transportation, particularly electric traction, permitted dispersal of people away from "great cities" to his new garden cities without loss of urban advantages to the individual or to civilization.[6]

A highly concentrated population was no longer required by an advanced industrial economy. "The crowded cities have done their work. . . . they are in the nature of things entirely unadapted for a society in which the social side of our nature is demanding a larger share of recognition." To Howard, the garden city promised not a return to a more idyllic past age envisioned in the literature of the Arts and Crafts movement but the basis for the evolution of an advanced and altruistic civilization.

Howard did not consider his criticisms of the Victorian city in any way original. He assumed his readers held the same views. In 1898, over 70 percent of the population of England and Wales lived in cities. The transformation of a rural into an urban society had occurred in the span of two or three generations. The American statistician Adna Ferrin Weber expressed in 1899 a widespread view in the Western world that "the dramatic increase in the numbers and size of Great Cities was the most remarkable social phenomenon of the present century." Among Western cities in 1801, only London had a population approaching one million (864,845). In 1901, twelve cities exceeded a million people and London numbered nearly five million. The United States alone contained three cities with over a million, and New York, the largest, counted three and a half million. The press, politicians, scholars, and reformers of many nations expressed a general concern about the consequences of the mounting urban population.[7]

Howard's analysis of the Victorian city relied on the example of London. He regarded the city as an arena of commerce which greatly exaggerated certain modern social attitudes—materialism and competitive individualism—harmful only when unrestrained. The physical expression of these social excesses posed a striking urban kaleidoscope of contrasting conditions—the "cheek by jowl" presence of mansion and slum, gin palace and museum, church and brothel. The city also offered great social, economic, and cultural opportunities, but these benefits were offset by the inconvenience and high cost of urban life, an unattractive setting, and the "loneliness of the crowd."

The view of the large city as an unwholesome environment required little elaboration for a Victorian audience. In *To-morrow*, there is only a brief general presentation of urban problems. Indeed, various attempts over the course of the nineteenth century to improve conditions accomplished much. But continuing rapid urban growth only aggravated problems and deepened the anxieties that had given rise to reform movements. Appalling urban conditions had spurred the birth and development of the British public-health movement and, in turn, a vast expansion of municipally supplied vital services such as drainage, sewerage, and street cleaning. Starting with the Public Health Act of 1875, building and street bylaws were adopted to ensure adequate open space on a building lot and straight wide streets in new subdivisions.[8]

Remarkably high urban mortality rates in the earlier "cholera decades" declined sharply after 1868, but not social tensions. Gareth Stedman Jones's provocative study *Outcast London* (1971) captures middle-class fears in the 1880s that casual laborers might drag the respectable working class down to their level. As employment revived in the next decade, the sense of urgency waned, but urban problems continued as an overriding national concern. Reformers discussed relocating the lower classes to the suburban periphery and even beyond to labor colonies in the country or abroad.

What is striking about the seemingly endless discussions on the nature of city life is the pronounced environmentalist cast. Carlyle coined the word environmentalism in the 1830s to denote the view that human behavior is significantly influenced by the external setting, including housing and neighborhood. Dismissed then by the essayist William Hazlitt as the view of a "hair-brained few," environmentalism by century's end had superseded the "time worn doctrines of original sin, grace, election and reprobation" as an explanation for behavior and character. This development in social thought can only be described as protean. It greatly expedited shifting responsibility away from the individual to a broad social canvas.[9]

The modern roots of environmentalism are to be found in John Locke and the "empirical psychologists" of the eighteenth century who argued for outside stimuli as the basis of all ideas. Geographic and climatological determinism, forms of environmentalism, were employed by Montesquieu and the Encyclopedists to explain national or racial characteristics. Both Beccaria and Bentham dabbled at the end of the century with ideas of a controlled physical environment as a means of penal reform. Robert Owen in 1813 argued emphatically against any suggestion that personality was present before birth, asserting instead that the infant emerged "plastic." He went on to contend that a man's character was "made for him and not by him" and that "circumstances" explained almost all. This conviction underlay Owen's interest in model industrial villages and communitarian experiments.[10]

An environmentalist strain is very evident in the thinking of temperance reformers of the 1830s who urged providing parks and reading rooms to act as "counterattractions" to the public house and believed attractive and sound dwellings an inducement to self-respect and sobriety for the working classes. In 1849, James Silk Buckingham designed the model home colony of Victoria as a proposed temperance experiment relying on a controlled and ordered environment.[11]

The public-health movement provided a powerful impetus to the spread of environmentalist thinking. Medical doctors early in the nineteenth century asserted that such factors as miasmic air, high overall density levels, overcrowding within the house, dirt, dampness, and the absence of adequate sanitary facilities led to a physical debilitation. Lowered energy levels, in turn, created a craving for artificial stimulants, such as strong drink, which further reduced the individual's ability to control impulse or even to anticipate. Cities with their varied activity and excessive stimulation only aggravated the "morbidity, irritability, and impairment of moral judgment" of the befuddled urban masses.[12]

Sanitary reformers advanced far beyond urban amelioration in their thinking to define what constituted a positive environment. In a paper read before a London congress of social scientists in 1875, Dr. Benjamin Ward Richardson described an ideal community, "Hygiea, A City of Health," where each family occupied a house of stipulated minimum size with a garden in order to limit density. In addition, wide and tree-lined streets encouraged the free circulation of air. Spatial, sanitary, and design features of the houses were specified in considerable detail. Richardson noted that his recommendations "had been worked out by the pioneers of sanitary science."[13]

The decision made by countless middle-class families to leave crowded urban neighborhoods for the new low-density residential suburbs with house and gardens fed into and reflected the emerging vision of a positive environment. Although directed to curbing the effects of an unhealthy environment, the public-health movement was rich in suggestions for wide-ranging environmental reform. It contributed greatly to the development of a concept of a desirable or positive environment that stressed the importance of providing superior housing and surroundings to the lower classes.[14]

Model-dwelling societies arose in the 1840s and 1850s to demonstrate that acceptable low-rent housing could be provided at a 5 percent return on capital through careful attention to the details of design, construction, and management. For the Great Exposition of 1851, no less a luminary than Prince Albert designed a model workman's dwelling for four families, which he proudly exhibited in Joseph Paxton's Crystal Palace. As with the public-health movement, the British model-dwelling societies were quickly imitated in the United States and on the Continent.

By 1901, nearly sixty thousand London families lived in model dwellings provided by the societies, almost all being barrack-style housing in the center districts of the city. From the first, the model-housing movement had been oriented to housing large numbers of people in limited space created by street clearances for public improvements. The obvious dislike of London's lower classes for this type of housing challenged the tactics and assumptions of the model-dwelling societies. Moreover, their critics by 1900 argued that since high density was the root cause of urban problems, barrack tenements at the city center, model or not, only exacerbated matters.[5]

The increasing importance of Social Darwinism at century's end extended the focus of reform from the home to its general surroundings and then to entire urban districts. It also added, according to Gareth Stedman-Jones, an ingenious and reactionary strand which he has termed "hereditary urban degeneration" to environmental thinking. "Hereditary urban degeneration" expresses a bleak argument that each generation raised in urban crowding was successively more physically and mentally stunted. Since these traits were progressively passed on, the urban environment threatened, unless altered, racial degeneration and even racial extinction. The eminent statistician G. A. Lonstaff in a frequently quoted article in 1893 asserted that an urban population required the replenishment and revitalization of a constant influx of healthy country stock. With only about 10 percent of Englishmen still engaged in agriculture, a dwindling rural type could no longer fulfill this vital function. "Social Imperialists" argued that unless such demographic trends were reversed, the English race would lack the stamina and vitality to beat back the rising American and German threat to British industrial and world hegemony.[16]

This gloomy prognosis was reinforced by Booth's and Rowntree's empirical studies of London and York and by the well-publicized poor health of potential military recruits from urban distracts during the Boer War. Many conservatives concluded with reformers that the nation's welfare required the imposition of minimum standards of life in order, at the very least, to guarantee a supply of industrious workers and vigorous soldiers. Issues such as housing, population density, land development, and the salubriousness of country life received much attention. In the 1890s, reform began to move in the direction of a series of connected social goals that were to be achieved incrementally through government action. Good housing and a positive environment emerged as necessary social goals, not simply desirable amenities, and, as such, a matter of political concern. Reformers, while rejecting the utopianism of communitarianism, believed (as did communitarians) that a positive society was one where applied social intelligence established an efficient society and offered all citizens a rewarding life, however that was to be defined. New social values reflecting collectivist concepts, often conveniently described as the "New Liberalism," came to the fore.[17]

Not only in Britain but also throughout the Western World environmental views emerged around the turn of the century as the foundation of modern social philosophy. Writers on social issues stressed the functional and social interdependency of all elements of a modern industrial society. This perspective challenged older values of self-reliance and promoted a philosophy of reform which strove to address not personal failings but social causes. It looked not to the individual and charity but to society and national legislation as the truly relevant arena of action.

Land-reform schemes served as a transitional theme in the evolution of the "New Liberalism." Originally an economic and moral issue involving rent, land reform by the end of the century had been extended into an attack on a system of private land development, primarily concerned with profit making rather than with the healthful and efficient use of the nation's most precious natural resource. It was now argued that land must not be viewed as previously almost solely in economic terms but must be utilized to ensure a proper social environment. Questioning of the market's ability to render decisions in the best interests of the community in this latter regard had become widespread.[18]

By the turn of the century, reformers were moving beyond concern with the slums to define the city as a whole as the correct field of interest. They sensed the need to replace, or at least rein in, haphazard market forces with social intelligence and to fashion a unified approach to urban and even national environmental problems. What formerly constituted diverse urban causes were brought together in the next century, very largely in the guise of the new profession of town planning.

Reformers warned that the unchecked individualism of the nineteenth century had destroyed the historic environmental equilibrium between town and country by stressing manufacturing over agriculture. The disastrous consequences were a dangerous and unhealthy overcrowding of cities and the depopulation of rural districts. Together, these two developments largely explained the physical deterioration of the race. The sense of a balanced environment and integrated social order, always critical to nineteenth-century communitarian thinking, had entered the lexicon of "statist"-oriented reformers.

Although decentralization schemes had been long discussed, only in the 1890s did urban reformers believe it feasible to anticipate a major redistribution of population. Electric traction and reduced fares for working men on commuter trains allowed many London families a new freedom to move away from the older inner-city neighborhoods. A building boom under way during the decade encouraged large-scale relocation. This development coincided with the acceleration of the earlier trend for industries dependent on large sites to move away from the urban center. Even from London, which Alfred Marshall had noted as a special case, a few industries (notably printing, bookbinding, and furniture making) were leaving.[19]

The model industrial villages of Port Sunlight, begun in 1888 by William Lever, and Bournville, started in 1894 by George Cadbury near Birmingham, attracted attention. They were hailed as demonstrating by example how to help solve the problem of urban congestion—their low-density housing in close proximity to the workplace worthy of the attention of municipal councils empowered under the Housing Act of 1890 to erect working-class housing on vacant land at the periphery of their cities.

The Scottish biologist-sociologist Patrick Geddes expressed the emerging reform perspective. Geddes's interest in ecology had led him to the study of the human habitat. Geddes concluded that the middle class's discovery of the "bijou suburb" as an alternative environment to the crowded town represented the single most important development of the Victorian era. The coming century's challenge was to provide a comparable low-density pattern for those of low income still dwelling in cities. Geddes's opinion of the middle-class suburb was not without reservation. He disliked an ostentatious architecture reflecting rampant individualism and materialism that sacrificed community to family privacy. Geddes preferred an architecture of suburban housing supportive of social cooperation.[20]

Environmental issues, then, were very much in the fore of public thinking at the time Howard wrote *To-morrow* and in the following years when he
founded a movement. The rising reform mood, the "New Liberalism," with
its concern for applying social intelligence and collective methods to raise
national standards, colored discussion of the future of the city. Moving
away from a singular concern with the negative environment of the poor,
housing reformers now urged a more ambitious and inclusive program.
Housing, as such, remained at the core of concern, but less exclusively so.
Urban reformers broadened their purview to the total community and its
environs and argued that low-density development must replace unacceptable urban congestion.

In the course of the nineteenth century, the public-health and model-
dwelling movements had developed a technical understanding of what constituted unsanitary and poor housing. Building codes from mid-century
onward sought to eliminate the most egregious of these features. On the
other hand, the question of what represented good housing and desirable
environment was not definitivly answered. After assuming the absence of
negative qualities, criteria for the positive entered the realm of the subjec-
tive. Positive features could be pushed only so far before becoming impossi-
bly expensive and thus utopian, but where the line was, no one knew for
sure.

By definition, desirable housing and the positive environment would
promote the health, comfort, and happiness of the inhabitants. Good housing would clearly offer sufficient space, privacy, and facilities for the effective functioning of family life. The environment must be free of pollution
or disorder. The community needed to provide not only essential services
but also those services that allowed and even encouraged individuals to
elevate themselves. As many of these ideals had meaning only in terms of
expectations, styles of life, and practical considerations, they would of
course alter greatly in detail over time.

When reformers were preoccupied with the housing of the poor, priority
was placed on avoidance of a negative environment, not on issues of amenity. As the housing issue slowly evolved from the area of private philanthropy to become a matter of national policy, this emphasis shifted. More
interest was now manifested in providing a positive environment, of which
housing as such constituted only a part. Rather than the bare-bone concerns of providing sanitary structures, reformers came to think in terms of
a desirable and even ideal community.

By focusing on environmental issues in *To-morrow*, Howard moved his
Garden City concept toward the mainstream of social reform. It is important to remember that reform was on the move, too. The relatively new
concern with community and environment brought social reform into areas

of traditional communitarian interest. Whatever their other differences, radical communitarians had been long preoccupied with the vision of a balanced environment and the need to heal the widening breech between town and country brought on by the excesses of modern civilization. They always sought, as Dolores Hayden (among many others) has noted, an architecture and spatial organization indicative of and complementary to the functional and supportive nature of a designed social community. Such interests now came to the fore among social reformers interested in urban conditions.[21]

The theme of the feasibility of large-scale population relocation by means of patterns of settlement based on low density figured prominently in *Tomorrow*. It clearly reflected Howard's awareness of new currents of social thought as well as the opportunities created by transportation improvements in his era. What is distinctive to his ideas is the effort to disperse the population into a new form of environmental order offering the best aspects of both country and city; this explains his opposition to decentralization schemes based on residential suburbanization.

What sets Howard apart from other environmentally oriented social reformers of the twentieth century is the communitarian core of his vision. The idea of balancing city and country, agriculture and industry, was a commonplace of communitarian thinking. Howard's originality is found in the attention to the details of how this was to be done, and at least some of this detail rests on ideas and technology only present in the last decade or so of the nineteenth century. Howard's central concern was not housing or even low density as such but the development of a cohesive community in a balanced environment.

The communitarian ideal represented, above all, an effort at banding together for the purpose of expressing a shared social life. The small community, regarded by earlier communitarians as the sine qua non of an unalienated and simple life, was redefined by Howard on a grander scale. It would be large enough to offer sufficient variety and to allow support for a wide range of shops, factories, and civic institutions necessary for full human development. Although Howard supported fully the growing sense of a national society imbued with a collective moral purpose and social program, he remained loyal to an older radical tradition. This identified progress with relatively self-contained communities and decentralized government and distrusted direct political action as inviting the contamination of vested interests.

In an age of individualism, communitarianism rejected an existing social order to seek the Cooperative Commonwealth. With the rise of "New Liberalism," the lines of division between radical and respectable reform blurred. The view that man was inherently good and tied in an organic relationship to society by the early twentieth century imbued a broad-ranging reform mood. The search for a positive environment in the form of experimental communities would in time interest professional planners and government officials. Howard's own Garden City movement would encourage this development.

At the turn of the century, reform drew on diverse themes: sincere interest in issues of social justice combined with concern over national efficiency and anxiety over class conflict. Many were eager to shape a more socially responsible form of capitalism while not abandoning individualism altogether. Environmentalism and housing reform, lending themselves to such an approach, proved especially attractive to those who envisioned a working class more like the middle class in values, behavior, and circumstances of external life. Moreover, they represented concerns over which a social consensus might emerge and promised to redirect the lower classes away from more intractable issues. Since the 1870s, municipal authority for the urban environment had been tacitly accepted and pursued ever more vigorously. By 1900, with nearly four Britons out of five dwelling in towns, an ambitious and comprehensive approach to the urban environment was an often noted need. The nineteenth-century lines of development of public-health and housing policies did not present such potential. Focused on urban pathology, they offered little of the positive thinking the new mood of expectancy demanded.

In *To-morrow*, Howard offered a community free of the sectarian and open to all. In this way, he invited acceptance of the garden city as an instance of comprehensive environmental reform rather than a naively utopian effort at instantaneous social reconstruction. Howard launched his scheme into a society eager for change and prepared in part to redress the environmental imbalances of the nineteenth century. Still, he needed to convince others or his ideas would lack the opportunity of the experiment he sought. Publication of *To-morrow*, he realized, was only the first step in this direction.

7

The Building of
a Garden City, 1899–1920

It is not so many years that an able and enthusiastic
book by Mr. Ebenezer Howard ... divided its readers
between those who said its ideas were those of a
"crank" and admirers. Today we all know that the
crank was splendidly right.

Daily News (London, October 26, 1907)

Not surprisingly, *To-morrow* was dismissed cavalierly by reviewers. They
found it a moderately interesting and well-done instance of a type of utopian thinking spurred by the commercial success of Edward Bellamy's *Looking Backward*. The reviewer for the *Times* described Howard's garden city as
"ingenious" and snidely noted: "The only problem is to create it; but that is
a small matter to utopians." Edward Pease in the *Fabian News* reflected:
"proposals for building new [cities] are about as useful as arrangements for
protection against visits from Mr. Wells' Martians." According to Pease, the
problem was to learn to make the best of existing cities. Behind his opinion
was a strong and important ideological stance.[1]

Pease was one of those who had left the communitarian-inclined Fellowship of the New Life in early 1884 to found the Fabian Society. In 1890, he
became its paid secretary and editor of the *Fabian News*. McBriar, in his
study of the Fabians, described him as "shrewd, hard-headed, skeptical,
determinedly unimaginative ... the perfect secretary." To Pease, the rejection of colonization schemes and utopian thinking had been the first important step in working out Fabian doctrine. Writing for the socialist newspaper the *Clarion* in 1893 he unequivocally asserted: "Home colonisation and

77

all cognate experiments . . . are distinctly foreign to the Fabian method. This Society first arose out of an association for the purpose of communal life, which came near to such an experiment, but which after a careful examination deliberately abandoned that purpose . . . and expressly excludes it from its methods of action as more likely to retard than to advance the attainment of socialist aims." Sidney Webb spoke and wrote often against colonization schemes as futile attempts to introduce socialism horizontally rather than vertically. Another Fabian, George Bernard Shaw, on receiving his review copy of *To-morrow,* "glanced at the maps and put the book down with the thought, 'The same old vision!' "[2]

Despite disappointment with the reviews, Howard was determined that his scheme should gain a wide hearing. In December 1898 he lectured on the garden city before his congregation at the Rectory Road Church. He then appeared before meetings of religious groups, cooperative societies, and Arts and Crafts guilds. Here he found a sympathy for his ideas denied him by the reviewers and soon approached friends to start an association for the purpose of promoting a garden city.

In the midst of a record-breaking heatwave on June 10, 1899, twelve men met to form the Garden City Association (G.C.A.). Several present, including Howard and J. Bruce Wallace, had been present at Farringdon Hall in 1893. The association's purpose was to promote "in its main features . . . the project suggested by Mr. Ebenezer Howard in *To-morrow.*" Soon a score of committees scurried about on various projects. In the *Fabian News,* an amused Edward Pease dismissed the goings-on as the usual short-lived busywork of enthusiasts.

Though intended by Howard as a broad, nonpartisan group, the Garden City Association mainly attracted lower-middle-class and middle-aged Londoners with prior involvements in "crank enthusiastic causes." Many came from the Land Nationalisation Society or J. Bruce Wallace's Brotherhood Trust. And both these groups offered the new association support within their meager means. The L.N.S. volunteered its office; the *Brotherhood,* Wallace's journal, carried news of G.C.A. activities. The *Morning Light,* the publication of the small Swedenborgian Society, also provided free publicity. Despite its efforts, the new organization had not broken out of the marginal world of well-intentioned reformers whom the world regarded as "cranks" and "faddists."

By 1900, the G.C.A. claimed 325 members who had enrolled at a shilling per subscription. Howard proudly spoke of its membership as including "Manufacturers, Cooperators, Architects, Medical Men, Financial Experts, Lawyers, Merchants, Ministers of Religion, Members of the London County Council." Efforts were soon under way to organize local branches in Manchester and Scotland. Demonstrating an initial staying power, the association received occasional brief attention by the press. Even so, by the beginning of 1900 there were good reasons for discouragement.

Attempts to reach out encountered little response. J. Bruce Wallace failed in an effort to organize a cooperative congress to ally the two groups. Trade unionists told Howard that labor's resources were husbanded for strike funds and not to build a garden city. Overtures to leading industrialists also led to no practical results. The association's weakness became apparent when in the summer of 1900 it raised less than one hundred pounds toward the acquisition of a town site. By early 1901 the odds against founding a garden city remained overwhelming. Howard's vision was alive and circulating, but it had not overcome one of the more intractable of communitarian problems, the financing of a colony.

The first question invariably asked Howard was: "How will the money be raised?" Given the absence of a profit incentive, venture capital needed to be attracted in ingenious ways. Fifty years earlier, Marx and Engels noted that the discrepency between limited means and grandiose visions often required "an appeal to the feelings and purses of the capitalist class." Indeed, Fourier punctually waited in his study every afternoon for twenty years for a benefactor who never arrived.[3]

In *To-morrow,* Howard cleverly skirted the issue of money by imagining his garden city well under way and self-sustaining. He did assume, though, that his book would evoke "sustained collective voluntary effort" and in time support, sufficient to start the venture, would come from individuals, cooperative associations, congregations, trade unions, and enlightened industrialists. This support he proposed to channel into the purchase of debenture bonds issued by a trust chartered for the purpose. As the garden city materialized and started to generate revenue in the form of rents, the trustees were to set aside money for the payment of interest and to build a sinking fund to retire the bonds. The balance would be returned to the community for use by a board of management elected by the town's residents. Once the bonds were liquidated the trust was to be dissolved. All appreciation of the value of the community's land and buildings accordingly provided for the general good.[4]

Unfortunately, Howard's scenario did not materialize as anticipated. Then, in Howard's words, "a change came over the Association [and] its affairs took a practical turn." This sudden turnabout resulted from Howard's recruitment to his cause of Ralph Neville, a prominent barrister. Some ten years earlier, Howard had remarked that the inventor usually required a practical man to make his project a success. Ralph Neville met Howard's need. Lending the G.C.A. his considerable personal prestige, he quickly placed Howard's venture on a strictly businesslike course and in effect replaced Howard as the leader of the Garden City movement.[5]

Neville solved the practical problem of raising the money but by means different from Howard's proposal. By 1904, the first garden city at Letchworth was under way. A decade later, Howard's movement and its model town were considered by press and public as successful and even highly influential. By then the once obscure Howard was well known to housing and environmental reformers throughout the world.

This remarkable success concealed a largely unexamined history of tension and conflict within his movement. Between 1899 and 1914, the scope of social reform, widening dramatically, transformed the political agenda. As part of this redefinition, visionaries gave way to pragmatists and enthusiasts yielded to professionals. So it was within Howard's young movement. In consequence, Howard was largely reduced to a mere figurehead, with his ideas misinterpreted by others who purported only to advance them. In 1905, when his scheme's success was being hailed, Howard had reason to reflect that "the entrance of the ideal into the practical is a descent; it is surely attended with pain and difficulty."[6]

Howard knew of Neville by reputation when an essay by the lawyer, published by the Labour Co-partnership Association in March 1901, brought him to mind. In his essay Neville wrote of Britain's need to promote population and industrial dispersal and singled out Howard's Garden City concept for praise. An overjoyed Howard called on Neville to ask him to take charge of the G.C.A.[7]

With startling speed Neville assembled the pieces necessary for the founding of the first garden city. He rented an office for the G.C.A. and hired a full-time secretary—a thirty-year-old Scotsman, Thomas Adams. Adams, in turn, quickly demonstrated unusual ability and drive which, aided by Neville's strong connections to the reform wing of the Liberal party, thrust the Garden City Association into public prominence among those seeking environmental reform. Under their leadership the Garden City Association shed overnight its identification with crank enthusiasms and gained respectability.

Educated at Tonbridge and Cambridge, Ralph Neville (1858–1918) was admitted to the bar in 1872 at Lincoln's Inn and named a Queen's Counsel in 1888. As a Liberal member from Liverpool, he sat in the House of Commons from 1887 to 1895. Highly successful in his profession, with a specialty in the railroad industry, Neville would soon be appointed to the Chancery Bench and knighted. Though of the same generation, Neville by education and position contrasted greatly with Howard. These differences in background became readily apparent in the affairs of the Garden City Association. Liking and respecting Howard, Neville knew Howard's limitations.

For Thomas Adams (1871–1940) appointment as secretary of the G.C.A. started a brilliant career as an internationally acclaimed city planner. Raised in Scotland, Adams briefly attended college in Edinburgh. During the

1890s, while working a farm, he became involved in the land-reform movement, finding the time to contribute articles on the agricultural crisis and the need for tax reforms to Scottish newspapers. This activity brought him into the Liberal party, where he acted as an agent for a parliamentary candidate. Seeking a career as a journalist writing on social issues, Adams moved with his family to London in January 1901 and shortly thereafter was employed by Neville.[8]

As secretary of the G.C.A., Adams quickly became knowledgeable in matters related to his new career. He studied surveying and advanced himself as a professional estate planner and manager. Self-confident and ambitious, Adams soon was at odds with Howard and his band of enthusiasts. A down-to-earth man, Adams thought "it a waste of time to set up idealistic utopias of what we would like to do but cannot."[9]

Adams in his first important action as secretary called for a national conference at Bournville in September 1901 on the theme of industrial decentralization. A marked success, the Bournville conference drew over three hundred delegates from urban district councils and reform groups. In July 1902, a second conference at Lever's model village of Port Sunlight was attended by nearly a thousand representatives of various public bodies and societies. Both conferences received extensive coverage in the press, which was now prepared to treat the Garden City Association as a serious and even important reform organization.[10]

Sponsorship of the conferences propelled the G.C.A. into the forefront of the environmental reform movement. The Garden City concept assumed the eminently respectable guise of an experimental type of a model industrial village along the lines of Bournville and Port Sunlight. As such, it was regarded as a legitimate and worthy effort at bettering the health, housing, and values of the working classes. By August 1903, membership in the G.C.A. stood at 2,500, a sevenfold gain since Neville and Adams had arrived. The association's strategy was to identify itself closely with the two model communities which had hosted the conferences. In this manner the association won the support of their influential founders and others who admired these experiments, while also gaining the argument that Bournville and Port Sunlight proved a garden city practicable.

Both conferences had as their themes the desirability of lowering urban density by the relocation of population into model low-density housing of one kind or another. The extensive press coverage reflected the importance accorded this subject. To Howard, urban dispersal, while generally beneficial, was of real consequence only if directed into the creation of garden cities. By and large, the conferences ignored the distinction. The praise lavished on Bournville and Port Sunlight only blurred the differences between them and Howard's scheme. The Garden City concept was being

promoted as low-density model housing for the industrial worker, rather
than as an experimental community seeking a novel environmental order.
A process had begun by which Howard's vision was being diluted in an
effort to join the Garden City movement to much more general interests in
urban dispersal and low-density cottage-type housing.

The change of heart experienced by George Bernard Shaw and the
Fabian Society is illuminating. We know that Shaw on receiving *To-morrow*
put it down without a reading. Earlier, in 1896, he had denounced schemes
for home colonies as implausible efforts at "the establishment of socialism
by private enterprise." When Howard addressed the Fabians in January
1901, Shaw and Pease both expressed their skepticism. The Irishman asked
Howard what assurance was there that if the scheme worked, the private
company owning the garden city would voluntarily dissolve and transfer its
valuable property to the community. After the Bournville conference, Shaw
wrote to Neville. He critiqued the idea of a garden city at length and
expressed his guarded approval, although reiterating the question he had
asked Howard earlier. He now suggested that Howard's real contribution
was in offering a community which appealed to enlightened industrialists.
In this regard, Shaw believed, Howard had set his scheme apart from those
of so many other dreamers.[11]

In the following years, the Fabian Society regularly devoted meetings to
discussion of the Garden City movement (in which many of its members
were involved). Others on the left also ceased rejecting the Garden City
concept as utopian foolishness, but not necessarily to extend their approval.
An anonymous writer in the periodical *The Race Builder* observed that many
radicals warily "regard it as a ditch for the hard-pressed forces of capitalism." In the labor movement, some derided Howard's scheme as a "happy
hunting for capitalists on the lookout for cheaper labour." The Garden City
movement had become part of environmental reform. It was also more, but
what exactly became less clear with time.[12]

Enlightened employers, such as the Levers and the Cadburys, wanted
businesslike forms of cooperation between capital and labor to eliminate
wasteful and dangerous social divisiveness. Their message, bluntly put, was
that the poor need not rise up against the rich to obtain their fair share.
The weakness of such an otherwise commendable approach was that since
the parties involved were unequal, it tended to paternalism.

This was the direction the Garden City movement took in advocating a
new type of model industrial village. Overjoyed by the enthusiasm prompted
by the conferences, Howard saw no need to draw lines firmly. It was enough
that the association sat firmly astraddle issues of considerable interest and
significance. As for Thomas Adams, he intended from the first to broaden

the Garden City message to encompass a variety of environmental reform interests.

Encouraged by events, the council of the association decided in December 1901 to move forward on the start of a garden city. With Neville providing direction and enlisting the support of his influential friends, developments proceeded quickly. The Pioneer Garden City, Ltd., was registered with an authorized capital of twenty thousand pounds on July 16, 1902, to acquire a site. At Neville's insistence, all promotional literature explicitly warned of the risks involved. Despite this caveat, the offering was subscribed fully by a small group of wealthy men that included the press lord Alfred Harmsworth and the industrialists J. P. Thomasson, George Cadbury, and Lever. Howard, appointed its director at a salary of three hundred pounds per annum, was also placed on the board of directors. Neville soon found it necessary to caution Howard on his casualness in advising potential investors of the risks.[13]

At the Bournville conference, Howard predicted that the "Garden City will not come into being except as the result of a great outburst of moral enthusiasm. . . . It will not come as the result of cold calculations." Neville, however, intended to be businesslike. Furthermore, he saw the experiment's significance in a different light than Howard.

To Neville, a garden city was important primarily as leading the way toward urban dispersal into "hygiene, beauty, and comfort in an industrial town made by foresight and scientific development." Although sympathetic to Howard's ideas of community land tenure, he viewed this as a lesser concern and was not "prepared to risk the success of the undertaking by any unyielding determination to carry it through."[14]

Despite progress toward a garden city, not all of Howard's original followers were pleased with Neville and Adams. One, Evacustes Phipson, believed they had tied the association to the "paternalistic wing of the Liberal Party" whose intent was a community "drawn along high Tory lines." Furthermore, according to Phipson, old members of the movement were being pushed aside, while newcomers were brought in as experts.[15]

It should be noted that Phipson in 1892 had strongly supported the idea of a colony based on "integral cooperation." As late as 1903, he corresponded with Albert Kinsey Owen and even urged the American to offer his services in the building of Letchworth. His comments only indicate that at least some of Howard's enthusiasts were dissatisfied with developments. The earliest settlers of Letchworth did, however, come from Howard's first followers. One, a Mr. R. Morrell, wrote Thomas Adams to object to a remark the Scotsman allegedly made that he would not "coddle cranks" associated with the movement.[16]

Neville's leadership, despite whatever else may be said, brought results. In July 1903, a site of some 3,800 acres near Hitchin in Hertfordshire was purchased at a price of three hundred thousand pounds. The building of Letchworth Garden City had started and in a context no longer easily dismissed as utopian. Having achieved its purpose, the Pioneer Garden City, Ltd., was dissolved and its subscribers received an exchange of stock in a newly formed company, the First Garden City, Ltd. The latter's charter, drawn up personally by Neville, limited dividends to 5 percent. From the first, Neville made it clear that the company's ultimate responsibility was to its stockholders, not to the four hundred tenants acquired with the site nor to Letchworth's future residents. Such a policy was required by law, and its neglect would only discourage similiar ventures.[17]

By now the scheme differed significantly from Howard's ideas. He had assumed the community would be built under the control of elected representatives of the community. Instead, the experiment was to be handled by a private company. This critical change explains much of the later tension at Letchworth. Yet without Neville's changes, an experiment in building a garden city almost certainly would not have occurred.

The First Garden City, Ltd., rapidly raised funds sufficient to survey and grade the site. In January 1904, the company invited several architectural firms to enter a limited competition to draw up plans for the town. Three designs were submitted. The one prepared by the partnership of Parker and Unwin was selected, with the partners also named the company's consulting architects. As had Neville and Adams, the two partners also found it necessary to modify Howard's original scheme. Again the consequences proved far-reaching. At Letchworth, Parker and Unwin identified, perhaps even overwhelmed, the Garden City movement with the aesthetics of the British Arts and Crafts movement and their own approach to low-density housing.[18]

As an effort at comprehensive planning of a small city, Letchworth was a pioneer venture. To this challenge, the partners responded with considerable skill. In their approach to the town design, they relied on a set of aesthetic principles derived from the "domestic revival"—the architectural expression of the late-nineteenth-century British Arts and Crafts movement that sought a functional and yet vernacular approach. As compared with Howard's crude compass and ruler attempts at layout in *To-morrow*, the Unwin-Parker plan of Letchworth skillfully demonstrated the technical expertise involved in the art of town planning. The professionalism displayed at Letchworth became closely identified with Howard's movement, and their work soon epitomized "garden-city-type planning." Unwin, indeed, ranks only behind Howard in importance to the history of the Garden City movement.

The two architects, Parker and Unwin, were brothers-in-law and partners from 1896 to 1914. Barry Parker's career was considerably less influential than that of the extroverted Raymond Unwin (1863–1940), who was a gifted speaker and writer. As a practitioner, teacher, theoretician, and public official, Unwin evolved into a leading spokesman for the new profession of town planning. His views on the subject remained seminal for at least two generations of planners and influenced the government's housing policy between the two world wars. For this reason, it is useful to compare Unwin with Thomas Adams, who also played a major role in shaping both the early years of the British town-planning profession and the history of the Garden City movement. Both men contributed profoundly to changing Howard's movement, but for different reasons and from a different perspective.[19]

Adams, throughout his career as a town planner, sought to separate this emerging profession from too close an attachment to Howard's ideals, which he viewed as limited and narrow. From his perspective, this divorce was imperative if town planners were to acquire an important function in modern society. In contrast, Unwin was strongly sympathetic to Howard's Garden City concept as an ideal. His work represented an effort to transform Howard's ideas into a workable set of planning principles.

In this, Unwin inevitably altered Howard's scheme. Of the greatest consequence was the fact that Unwin's planning and design principles could as easily be applied to housing estates and suburban subdivisions as to garden cities. His ideas and Howard's could and did work at cross-purposes. All sorts of model housing laid out at low density in some semblance of Unwin's principles were hailed as "garden-city-type planning," ignoring the critical ways they fell short of Howard's vision.

Unlike Adams, however, Unwin always accorded homage to Howard. He made no effort to distinguish between his own increasingly technical and professionally oriented approach to town planning and Howard's visionary effort at designing an experimental community. Unwin's loyalty to Howard and the Garden City movement can be interpreted as a continued attachment to his own youthful ideas which his professional work adapted to a twentieth-century reality. In a certain sense, Unwin, within his own career and without conscious effort, made a transition from enthusiast to a professional planner and then to a governmental bureaucrat.

In *Social Radicalism in the Arts,* Donald Drew Egbert has asserted that late Victorian England, with the Arts and Crafts movement, emerged as "the major radiating center of aesthetic doctrines having radical social connotations." Unwin as a young man had been much taken by the message of Ruskin, Morris, and Carpenter of the artist's need to rebel against the commercial and puritanical aspects of society and to end the artificial distinction between applied and fine art. They singled out the architect's role as particularly important. Architecture had to reconcile individual tastes and needs with the collective ethos of a culture, as had the anonymous designers of the great medieval cathedrals.[20]

These views influenced Unwin's choice of career and the nature of his work. It was through Unwin that a late-nineteenth-century aesthetic-romanticism rooted in Christian socialism entered the Garden City movement to flesh out Howard's straight-forward and simple notions. Indeed much of the early appeal of the Garden City movement throughout the world rested on its association with the influential Arts and Crafts movement.

From a prominent Derbyshire family, Unwin originally trained as an engineer. While working for a coal and iron company, he decided to become an architect. This career change reflected Unwin's increasing interest in the ideas of Morris and Carpenter, both of whom he knew personally. By the middle of the 1890s, Unwin and Parker (whose sister Unwin married in 1893) were busily involved in designing inexpensive working-class cottage housing.

In his architectural work and later in his planning activity, Unwin evinced an engineer's strong concern with details of cost and function. To this he joined the aesthetics of the Arts and Crafts movement. Given their political orientation, it is not surprising that Unwin and Parker regarded middle-class villa housing as ostentatious and impractical. Selecting the simple country cottage as their working ideal, they brought to it an open floor plan in order to encourage family intimacy and lessen domestic labor. In addition, the partners grouped their housing to achieve economies and more attractive, varied settings, having first considered topographical and natural features. The resultant savings in land, they believed, permitted setting open space aside for common use. Most important, this and other savings in construction allowed for economical working-class housing at relatively low density.

Efforts to innovate in the design of building sites and street layouts brought Unwin and Parker to an interest in town planning. This activity, in turn, made them leaders in the struggle against the bylaws which required the layout of new streets according to rigid specifications and on straight lines. Here they marshaled arguments based on practical and aesthetic considerations. Not the least of these would be the contrast between their own work as architects and bylaw housing. Unwin by 1901 had prepared a Fabian pamphlet, *Cottage Plans and Common Sense*, and several other articles on housing design.

In the fall of 1901, Unwin had addressed the Bournville conference "On the Building of Houses in the Garden City." He used this occasion to attack the practice of "covering large areas with houses of exactly the same size and type" as leading to "a dreary monotony of effect." Instead, Unwin called for siting buildings according to a town plan designed with "complete acceptance of natural conditions" and local traditions as well as with an eye to function.[21]

In his talk, Unwin lauded the medieval English village as expressing a close interrelationship of nature, built form, and social organization. This harmony of form and function—or organicism—needed to be provided in the town plan of the garden city. Already Unwin was seeking to bring together Howard's ideas and those of the Arts and Crafts movement as unifying forces for a society in which individuals enjoyed a sense of place and purpose and where life's various activities complemented each other.

The architect ended his paper by expressing enthusiasm for the idea of a garden city. Until resources for a garden city were available, however, small experiments in estate planning and housing would be useful preparation for the larger undertaking. Along these lines, Unwin urged on the conference a crusade to encourage cities to purchase land on their outskirts for experimental low-density development. A certain pragmatism always characterized Unwin's outlook toward the Garden City concept. While committed to Howard's ideal, he also accepted other low-density approaches. Soon after the Bournville conference, Parker and Unwin were engaged by the cocoa manufacturer Joseph Rowntree to design industrial housing at New Earswick, a few miles from York.

By reason of both interests and experience, the partners represented an obvious choice for the Letchworth competition. They came with definite ideas in mind, the foremost being to let the site's natural features determine the town plan. They discovered instead that the presence of a railroad and existing roads required primary consideration. For this reason, the town site was treated as an off-angled quadrant surrounded by a greenbelt. Within the town Parker and Unwin planned distinct residential, industrial, and public areas—the most important of which was a civic center in the bottom-left sector, organized along a mile-long axis leading to the railroad station (see illustration 6). As C. B. Purdom characterized the plan, it provided for "a group of connected villages around a civic center with a factory district on the outskirts."

The critical weakness was an overall lack of coherence and central focus. There were other problems as well. Treatment of the civic center was mishandled and inadequate provision made for movement between the several areas of the town. Nevertheless, the plan received lavish praise. Most visitors who came to Letchworth to examine an experiment did so intending to find a success; the need for an exemplar of planned development inclined them to praise.

Considerable attention was devoted to Letchworth's most attractive

feature:—the middle-class residential streets. Numerous published photos
of landscaped cottages ostensibly provided vivid visual evidence that planning worked. In a short time, charming "street pictures" became the Garden City movement's logo or signature. Soon speculative suburban builders
advertised their wares as "garden-city housing."

Parker and Unwin utilized a highly irregular street pattern in Letchworth's residential areas that created odd-shaped blocks, including a few
cul-de-sacs. Curvilinear streets with picturesque houses, some built by Parker and Unwin, and amply endowed with trees and shrubbery, provided the
"street pictures" so favorably received. Not all of Letchworth's residential
areas, however, were picturesque.

Parker and Unwin encouraged the company to impose aesthetic controls
on the various builders and architects employed either by private parties or
housing societies. Among other requirements, the company stipulated that
all roofing be of red tile and that prior approval be given for the layout of
building lots. Eager to hurry the building of Letchworth, however, the
company permitted numerous exceptions, disappointing the partners with
its lack of commitment to aesthetic unity.

Parker and Unwin relied in their design of the civic center on an elegant
Baroque formality. Unlike for the residential areas, nothing in the partners'
background prepared them for this assignment. No doubt their formal
treatment aspired to an appropriate grandeur for the principal public area
of the world's first garden city. In this they erred. Out of scale with the
remainder of the town plan and endowed with broad straight vistas, the
civic area offered only a hollowness at Letchworth's center instead of the
sense of urban enclosure required. Furthermore, their civic-center concept
proved too grandiose for the First Garden City, Ltd., to realize. In 1913 the
partners redesigned Letchworth's center along more modest lines.

Letchworth's plan failed as a powerful depiction of a new form of urban
community. Except for the flawed concept of the civic center, it really was
more a village than a city. The principal achievement of Letchworth was in
the layout and architecture of middle-class residential areas. Here Parker
and Unwin worked in an area familiar to them and in which a generation of
British architects led by Philip Webb and W. R. Lethaby were pioneering
the new domestic Arts and Crafts aesthetic. Until World War I, the low-
density and open residential layout of Letchworth symbolized by tree-lined
curved streets and picturesque cottages possessed much appeal in Britain
and elsewhere. This, though, was far from an urban metaphor. Certainly
such residential streets could be planned in a suburb or village and did not
require a garden city for their setting. As Letchworth's street scenes replaced Howard's concepts as the banderole of Howard's movement, it conveyed an ambiguous message.

Howard, however, always remained satisfied with Parker and Unwin's plan of Letchworth. Other aspects of the first garden city, however, disappointed him. As it slowly took shape in the years between 1904 and 1914, Letchworth represented only a pale embodiment of his vivid dream. Refraining from open criticism, Howard only said "that it has shrunk into somewhat smaller and humbler dimensions than I pictured it." Howard fully realized the problems confronted by the First Garden City, Ltd., in constructing a de novo modern community with modest funds. Still, as he noted, the transformation of his ideas into the reality of Letchworth represented a painful descent.[22]

Howard's role in the building of Letchworth was limited largely to the symbolic; he had little influence on the company or its policies. Howard's brief performance as manager of the Pioneer Garden City, Ltd., convinced Neville that he lacked the practicality for an important assignment at Letchworth, and after 1903 he was paid a small stipend by the company to travel about Britain lecturing on Letchworth. In 1906, Howard, shortly after the unexpected death of his wife, moved to Letchworth. There he concerned himself with starting an experiment in "associative housing" as he had called for in *To-morrow*. Barry Parker, who respected Howard greatly, later recalled how officers of the company, especially Thomas Adams, condescended to Howard as an amusing figure not to be taken seriously.[23]

From 1904 to 1906, Ralph Neville, as chairman of the board of the First Garden City, Ltd., and Thomas Adams, who was appointed estate manager, were in charge at Letchworth. Their principal problem was a lack of capital. Slow progress in building Letchworth placed great strain on resources while limiting revenue from rental. Much of the initial difficulty resulted from the company's inability to sell shares. Three years after its formation, less than half the authorized amount had been marketed.

While raising less capital than expected, the company also found its initial expenses greater than anticipated. Preparing the site, providing roads, electricity, sewerage, and drinking water involved considerable costs since they required anticipating future needs at a time when the community had few residents to draw on for revenue. Faced with this conundrum, the company made two important decisions. It would reserve its limited resources for the provision of public services and refrain from any residential construction. It also decided to give first priority to attracting people and industry quickly.

This decision led to the abandonment of Howard's position in *To-morrow* on leasing and rents. There he had called for short-term leases permitting periodic rent revisions to allow the community to gain from the appreciation in land values. Instead the company instituted a policy of long-term leases at low fixed rates. Neville thought this necessary to attract businesses as well as individuals interested in building homes. He also decided to separate rates from rents rather than to employ Howard's idea of combining them.[24]

The "unearned increment" was not returned to the community during its history as a garden city. Letchworth's lesson was that the cost of infrastructure in a de novo community was staggering. The price of land had been anticipated as the major financial burden, but the cost of roads, streets, and utilities proved its approximate equal. Howard's idea in *Tomorrow* of building the community in stages with the rent from a completed section financing the development of the next was never attempted and, in any case, could not have solved the financial problems confronting the company.

When the site at Letchworth was purchased, approximately four hundred residents lived there. Sixty families of Garden City enthusiasts soon joined them. For the most part they commuted to work in London, thirty-five miles to the south (or an hour by train to Kings Cross Station). Journalists soon depicted these "pioneers" as simple souls of modest incomes and few material wants. Accounts of them dwelt on individuals strolling the newly paved streets, wearing sandals and smocks, and forming committees to conduct cultural and reform activities. Early on, Letchworth acquired the reputation as a community of "cranks."[25]

A founder of the Land Nationalisation Society, Anthony Swinton, bequeathed three thousand pounds to found the Alpha Union, named after the title of an 1851 novel on the starting of a new civilization by E. M. Denny. J. Bruce Wallace, as trustee of the union, started a Letchworth adult summer camp providing courses oriented to promoting a moral uplift. Topics offered in the summer of 1906 included "health and food," "thought transference and world peace," and "spirituality and science." Possibly influenced by the Alpha Union, Howard in that year became a vegetarian. A few years later the Alpha Union led him to an interest in Esperanto, another enthusiasm of J. Bruce Wallace.

A community of "cranks" was not what the First Garden City, Ltd., wanted. Eager to attract industry into the town, it feared that outlandishness would frighten off potential employers. The company's promotional literature described a healthy, stable, and inexpensive model industrial community well suited to business. Moreover, the company vigorously protested Letchworth's identification in the press with bohemian types.

C. B. Purdom in his autobiography recalled that "every member of the staff treated the middle-class utopists [*sic*] with contempt." A clerk of the company and sympathetic to the "pioneers," Purdom also remembered that the company "set out to demonstrate that the town was intended to be all that could be expected in any town not called a garden city. . . . The nonsense of the idealists was to be squashed."[26]

In time, two other elements were added to the original residents and the pioneers. One was the working class employed in the industries, at first drawn from surrounding communities but then augmented by Londoners relocating as factories moved to Letchworth from the metropolis. The other was shopkeepers and professionals attracted by the commercial opportunities offered by a new community.

Most of these came to lead a conventional life. A very few, however, arrived eager to participate in a social experiment. Peter Myles, a former chemist who once resided in the Whitelaw Colony, established a hand-loom weavery. George Adams, who trained with Edward Carpenter to craft "Indian-type" sandals, opened a small shop. Other "simple lifers" started a "health food store," a "food reform restaurant," and a "good-health and simple-life hotel."

Tension developed between the groups as well as between the groups and the company. According to Purdom, there was "no cohesion in the new community." The commercial types and the "simple lifers" avoided unnecessary interaction, but the workers and their families he found an "incongruous element" with no ties to the community. When a Garden City enthusiast asked three recently transplanted London workers about their view of Letchworth, one said, "Well, you see guv'nor there aint no life in this ere place." They missed the nightly meetings with friends at the Blue Dragon at the corner of Bermondsey Street and the lights and shops of their old East End dockside neighborhood.[27]

A major issue dividing the community was whether a licensed public house should be allowed. The company, though it had the authority to make the decision, wisely decided to submit the question to a referendum. When the middle-class opponents of the public house prevailed, members of the company's board of directors provided funds for a coffeehouse with a reading room where the workers could relax in the evening.

In 1907, a community center was erected through private contributions. Since it was hoped that working-class families would use this facility, Thomas Adams in a public meeting urged that representatives of the workers be included in the management of the center to insure that their class would feel welcome. Raymond Unwin argued against Adams's position, and the architect's views won the support of the audience. In late 1907, a reporter for the *Daily Mail* observed that Letchworth offered a profusion of lectures on "vegetarianism, social Christianity, the raising of the moral tone of dustmen" but no forms of amusement wanted by "the mass of men who are childlike in their tastes," such as a music hall.[28]

This same reporter claimed that many transplanted Londoners pined for the excitement of their old neighborhoods and streets. When he asked the Garden City enthusiasts about this, they told him that the working class would realize in time the advantages of Letchworth and adjust. As late as the 1920s, however, there were those who believed that the worker residents of Letchworth felt uncomfortable in a community dominated by a middle class who looked down on them.[29]

For their part, the middle class complained of working-class vandalism and rowdyism. In July 1910, the officers of the Letchworth Guild of Help wrote the company "that a considerable number of undesirable tenants have become residents in the town." The company was urged to put pressure on those renting cottages to screen out applicants of intemperate and improvident habits.[30]

Some "pioneers" placed pressure on the company for a very different reason. They believed it encouraged businesses to leave London for Letchworth to escape trade unions and told them that workers could be paid less than London wages since living costs were cheaper. By 1912, a campaign was under way to persuade the First Garden City, Ltd., to require a minimum wage for all companies doing business in the town.[31]

A leader in this effort was the editor of the *Letchworth Citizen*, who also served as chairman of the local Independent Labour party. When he was suddenly dismissed by the paper, meetings were held to protest what was believed the company's role in his firing. By now some of the original enthusiasts, including J. Bruce Wallace, departed the community which they considered hostile to unions and labor. They preferred soldiering at dissent to accommodation. In 1920, another sizeable group of pioneers relocated to the second garden city of Welwyn, which they hoped would provide a more supportive context for the social experimentation still sought. By then, one disaffected resident dismissed the first garden city as a "practical ideal of bourgeois villadom, a rest haven."

The company had more pressing concerns than the community's contentment. Above all, it needed to promote the town's rapid development in order to earn revenue. Thomas Adams's work as town manager was criticized by some board members. It was charged that he was not adequately cost conscious, nor sufficiently successful in attracting businesses. After Neville resigned as chairman in 1906, Adams found his situation untenable and soon resigned under pressure.[32]

The problem was that the community required essential services before businesses would locate there. By late 1906, however, shortly before his resignation, Adams reported significant achievements. Two large printing firms, W. H. Smith and Son and J. M. Dent Ltd., and an embroidery firm had signed leases. The trail having been broken, other large companies followed. By 1914 Letchworth's factories employed over a thousand work-ers. Ironically, the largest plant was an engineering shop which during the war produced ammunition, resulting in the bombing of Letchworth by a German zeppelin in the summer of 1915. To Howard, long involved in the peace movement, the presence of an arms factory in his garden city posed a painful reminder of how far reality fell short of his vision.

A major reason for the difficulty in attracting industry to Letchworth was a serious shortage of working-class housing. To acquire housing quickly, the company allowed Letchworth to be the site in the summer of 1905 for the Cheap Cottage Exhibit sponsored by J. ST. Loe Strachey's *Country Life*. The company was also eager for the publicity provided by the exhibit—which drew some sixty thousand visitors to Letchworth. More important, after the exhibit closed, it acquired gratis a hundred or so houses erected for the occasion.

Many of these were highly experimental in the use of building materials and style and cost the town in adverse criticism. Several score of buildings, some markedly bizarre, occupied a prominent site very near the railroad station. The resulting eyesore distressed Parker and Unwin. It also puzzled visitors who arrived at Letchworth expecting architectural unity and har-mony only to confront structures of bewildering variety and appearance.[33]

At the end of 1906, only four hundred new homes had been built in the garden city. Roughly a fourth were the legacy of the Cheap Cottage Exhibit, and another third were built by private contractors. The remainder had been erected by the Garden City Tenants Association. This was a tenant co-partnership association with no formal connection to the First Garden City, Ltd. It had been assumed that the Garden City Tenants Association would provide housing for workers who were required to purchase shares in the association to establish a sense of equity in the housing. In practice, though, its tenants were mainly middle-class—a development justified on the grounds that the housing erected was of a superior standard requiring higher rentals than workers could afford. When pressure was placed on the Garden City Tenants Association to erect less costly homes, it refused. For this reason, the First Garden City, Ltd., reluctantly created in 1907 the Letchworth Cottages and Building Ltd., with an authorized capital of thirty thousand pounds in shares which were to pay a guaranteed return of 4 percent. The intention was to erect three-bedroom cottages at a cost of under two hundred pounds. This would allow rental at five shillings and twopence per week, well within the range of working-class families.

It was intended to employ Parker and Unwin's open floor plan in these inexpensive cottages. Working-class tenants, however, preferred a separate living room and kitchen as "more proper," no matter how tiny each of these rooms were. After the first efforts, the housing erected was of a conventional nature. Within six years, over 180 homes had been constructed, easing, though not ending, the shortage of working-class housing in Letchworth.[34]

By the summer of 1914, Letchworth Garden City contained a population of 8,500. The *Pall Mall Gazette* referred to the community as "undoubtedly the greatest experiment that has ever been tried in the housing of all classes of the people since modern conditions have been obtained in England." The directors of the First Garden City, Ltd., had reason for satisfaction. For the first time they were in a position to pay dividends to their shareholders. Both in practical and planning terms, the community was widely hailed as a success.

Even so, some reservations were expressed. Thomas Adams stated his concern that the company's role in the town was paternalistic, if benevolent. He also noted that the agricultural areas of the estate had been largely ignored. Visiting in late 1910, the American planner F. L. Olmstead, Jr., thought the community much less attractive than Bournville or Port Sunlight. The architect A. T. Edwards went further in his criticism. He thought the town plan suitable for a suburb but not adequate for an urban community. In their design of the garden city, Parker and Unwin, according to Edwards, had sacrificed the latter in favor of the former.[35]

A more poignant comment came from an anonymous H. A. G. He had been present at Farringdon Hall in 1893. A member of the Land Nationalisation Society, he joined the G.C.A. in 1900. Visiting Letchworth for the first time in 1908, his reaction was one of keen disappointment. The most he could say for it was a "local palliation of the housing problem; but . . . it is [not] the social revolution we hoped for."[36]

In one regard, Letchworth represented an unqualified success. Letchworth served as a standing example of the modern art or science of town planning. Its lesson, or so supporters contended, was that model communities were greatly superior to those erected by speculative builders. Letchworth's very existence provided a rallying point and a showcase for the emerging profession of town planning. As Henry Vivian wrote in 1914, "few movements in this country have taken such a hold on public opinion in so short a time as that in favor of better housing and town planning. It is not many years ago that we had a few voices crying in the wilderness, and they were regarded by the so called practical men as utopians and dreamers." Letchworth contributed significantly to this changed view by providing an instance of town planning conducted along businesslike lines rather than the fiasco skeptics anticipated.

Letchworth was both more and less than the garden city promised in *Tomorrow*. Falling far short of the idealized cooperative community envisioned by Howard, it identified his movement with a set of design principles he had not anticipated. Parker and Unwin's winding streets with white gabled cottages and red roofs were now the garden-city signature, a visual shorthand for a low-density and open form of housing development.

The significance of Letchworth is best assessed in the context of the emergence of modern British town planning and the latter's influence on the development of planning in other nations. The early history of Letchworth provides a background for such a discussion. In this sense, its most important lesson was that visionaries and enthusiasts had made way for practical and pragmatic men inclined to work within a system of conventional ideals and values. Letchworth legitimized a Garden City movement no longer dismissed as utopian. The movement had moved away from its roots and now appealed to a new membership. Letchworth and Howard's Garden City Association had acquired lives of their own apart from their inventor.

8

The Garden City and Town Planning, 1903–1918

> The Twentieth Century marks the dawning of an epoch in Western Civilization. . . . never before has society been able to better its condition so easily through the agency of government.
>
> Frederick C. Howe
> (*The City*, 1905)

Howard and his type of reformer yearned for alternative cultures based on grand design rather than incremental reforms. By 1900 a more complex vision of the good society was largely in place. Darwin impelled thinking individuals to try for an understanding of progress through themes of evolutionary development and endless change. These views challenged the teleologic reasoning favored by communitarians. In *A Modern Utopia* (1905) H. G. Wells contrasted the old and new ways of thinking about progress: "The Modern Utopia must be not static but kinetic, must shape not as a permanent state but as a hopeful stage, leading to a long ascent of stages." The mark of modern thinkers was their assumption that government, when staffed by highly trained experts, provided the means for the rational management of an ongoing process of social change.

The rise of cities, with their profound problems and tensions, contributed greatly to shattering residual faith that actions based on individual self-interest when added together would equal the common good. A modern urban order required purposeful action to control land use and improve housing which the private sector's "invisible hand" failed to provide. Modern town planning emerged early in the twentieth century as a call for expertise to complement market factors in determining urban developments.

From its inception, modern planning was closely associated with a new approach to reform. This emphasized an organizational framework, a scientific approach, and an increasing reliance on professional experts to impose purposive controls in the interest of society as a whole. The extent and nature of state intervention was open to debate, but the need for the redefinition and expansion of government's role was not. The state was now expected to be dynamic not static. Increasingly it came to be regarded as the instrument by which society secured for the individual the necessary conditions to live a good life. The "Age of Organization" had dawned.

The Garden City Association, an organization started with the purpose of launching a single experimental community, soon joined the ranks of reform organizations advocating institutional change. Some of its members perceived opportunities for careers as town planners. Expanded governmental activities created new bureaucracies that required new types of professionals—experts with technical skills. Often both skills and expert personnel needed to be created.

Neville's success in promoting Letchworth in 1903 presented unexpected problems for an association whose purpose was to encourage an experiment along the lines proposed in *To-morrow.* Since this was now being done by a private company acting independently, the association had to decide how large a role strictly garden-city activities should play in its future.

The Garden City Association responded by placing itself in the forefront of a reform movement which sought urban dispersal into low-density model cottage housing. These efforts soon fused with a call for parliamentary legislation requiring land-use control in the design of new suburbs along what would be called "garden-city lines." In 1909, a Town Planning and Housing Act was passed by Parliament, and modern town planning, both as concept and profession, emerged.

In Britain, town planning initially focused on the suburb or town extension. By enlisting in the cause of town planning, the Garden City Association assured itself of an important role in a national movement concerned with housing and environmental reform. But in accepting the desirability of planned suburbs, it diluted and confused its original message. The association involved itself in various small-scale model housing efforts entitled "garden suburbs" and "garden villages."

Howard's Garden City movement attracted international attention but delivered a double message: claiming the garden city as the only valid alternative to metropolitan growth, though welcoming suburban planning or even model suburban housing estates as acceptable correctives of urban congestion. Obscuring the Garden City theme even further was the identification of the association with cooperative and industrial housing ventures, as long as these were low-density model cottage housing. The movement absorbed an older tradition of model housing at the same time it extended itself into the new area of town planning and professed loyalty to Howard's ideal. As a result, the public, professionals, and even the association's membership became hopelessly confused about the nature and purpose of the Garden City Association.

The seemingly inevitable movement of the Garden City Association away from Howard's vision can be traced in the activities of Thomas Adams. In January 1904, Thomas Adams submitted a confidential memorandum to the association's executive board. A few months earlier, his policies as secretary had been criticized at a public meeting as straying from the association's purpose. Now Adams explained his position and offered to resign.[1]

Adams's memorandum urged the association to rethink its role. In his view, to advocate garden cities alone was not sufficient justification for its continuation. He believed it necessary for the association to encompass a variety of environmental approaches to urban reform and to recognize that promoting garden cities would not be necessarily the most important of these. Adams's statement was the opening salvo in a battle over the question of remaining loyal to Howard's ideas—a battle that flared intermittently over the next fifteen years.

Adams began his report by observing that the association had endorsed *To-morrow* only as providing an experimental guideline and not as detailing fixed principles. He then proceeded to demonstrate that Neville's actions in setting up the First Garden City, Ltd., had already departed significantly from Howard's concept. The association, having relinquished all authority at Letchworth to the company, had no significant role in building the first garden city. Moreover the association could not realistically encourage or promote a second venture until Letchworth proved itself, which would take at least ten years.

In the meantime, the association needed to find a worthwhile cause. He suggested, "the function of the Garden City is surely the higher one of teaching sound principles in regard to a particular aspect of social reform. . . . There is room for a strong, active, educational institution to take up a definite *line of action* [*sic*], and press its objects forward not only on the public generally but on all public bodies throughout the country."

Adams, for political reasons, was not specific about the association's "line of action." But earlier, in September 1903, he suggested its mission should be "to give general encouragement to manufacturers to move out of crowded cities, stimulate interest in and promote the scientific development of towns, and encourage the erection of sanitary and beautiful dwellings with adequate space for gardens and recreation."[2]

Adams groped not only for a broader mission for the Garden City Association but also at an elusive concept which within a few years would be called "town planning." In Britain, this concept was to be closely identified with ideas of urban dispersal and low-density development. In particular, Adams was interested in model estate layout, which offered the potential for professional fees. His involvement in two small efforts along these lines had, however, provoked the anger of Herbert Warren, the association's lawyer and one of his principal critics at the September 1903 public meeting.[3]

Adams prided himself on a practical turn of mind. The suggestions he offered in his memorandum doubtlessly appeared to him as the common-sense acceptance of reality and a logical extension of the association's original purpose. Lacking an ironclad allegiance to Howard's vision, he clearly perceived its limitations. Distant from the communitarian frame of thinking of the older man, but not necessarily less idealistic, Adams's social philosophy was more flexible and less visionary. He, too, stressed voluntary cooperation to engage in schemes which served the interests of all parties, but he eschewed the programmatic and relied on the practical. As Adams well knew, such leading figures in the association as Neville and Cadbury were essentially interested in encouraging manufacturers to relocate away from cities. They might prefer garden cities for this end, but they supported other types of activities as well.

The Scotsman's memorandum was probably intended to persuade the wealthy Liberal industrialists that Neville had involved in the movement. Their support could bring the association around to his position. To preserve harmony, the Executive in early 1904 decided instead that Adams should resign as the association's secretary. George Norcroft, a journalist recently returned from ten years abroad, replaced him, but he soon proved ineffectual.

Norcroft did, however, initiate the quarterly journal *The Garden City* in the fall of 1904. A statement of the association's goals was drafted to provide a masthead for the new journal. The general objective of the association was "to promote relief of overcrowded areas and to secure a wider distribution of population." Garden cities were designated the preferred but not the exclusive means of achieving this end. This formula, while professing loyalty to the Garden City cause, allowed the association considerable latitude to support other approaches to housing and environmental reform.[4]

This statement no doubt honestly reflected the views of the association's leadership. As the Garden City Association's president until 1914, Sir Ralph Neville consistently argued the superiority of the Garden City concept over any other housing or planning strategy. Still, he allowed the association to move off in other directions and opposed as impractical Howard's urgings to begin a second garden city.

The reform wing of the Liberal party, to which Neville belonged, valued

highly individual home-ownership as enhancing social stability. To achieve
the verisimilitude of this, Neville identified the association after 1905 with
Tenant Co-partnership and its low-density housing estates, regardless of
their setting. In tenant–co-partnership schemes, a building society was incorporated to erect housing whose residents purchased shares. The spokesman and leader of the tenant–co-partnership movement was the M.P.
Henry Vivian. Its connection with the Garden City movement brought
favorable attention and even imitation in other countries. By 1908, the
Daily News wrote of Tenant Co-partnership: "It is impossible to exaggerate
the importance of this movement, which is an application of the Garden
City principle to the existing cities, and is capable of infinite expansion."[5]

In the 1900s, the environmental reform movement assumed the stature
of a national crusade whose ultimate goal was the transformation of the
urban fabric. Though gravely dissatisfied with the bylaw suburbs which had
proliferated in the 1890s, most reformers still regarded the suburbs as the
best hope for housing reform and urban decentralization. The issue now
evolved into how a superior suburban environment might be achieved.
Reform interest in the Garden City movement, apart from those who believed as Howard did in garden cities, largely rested on the fact that at
Letchworth an effort was under way to comprehensively design a low-
density community which could serve as a pilot model for superior types of
development, including working-class dwellings.

In 1904, Thomas Coglan Horsfall, a Manchester industrialist long involved in housing-reform efforts, published his highly influential *The Improvement of the Dwellings and Surroundings of the People: The Example of
Germany*. Horsfall called for English local government, staffed by trained
professionals, to assume control over town-extension development by employing the model of Frankfort. In this German city, extensive laws had
been passed to provide for municipal laying out of suburban streets, the
acquisition of land for working-class housing, and, in general, strict regulation of private development.[6]

Horsfall's proposals gained enthusiastic support among environmental
reformers. Among his recruits was a member of the Birmingham City
Council, John S. Nettlefold. By 1906, Nettlefold had persuaded his colleagues to request parlimentary legislation along the lines proposed by
Horsfall. It was in the context of this mounting campaign for municipal
control over suburban development that the term "town planning" acquired general usage.

Along with other organizations, notably the National Housing Reform
Council, the Garden City Association helped orchestrate a campaign which
led to the passage of the Town Planning and Housing Act of 1909. Ebenezer Howard viewed these years as a period in which large numbers of men

professionally interested in the prospects of town planning entered the association and diverted it from the Garden City path. They had, he believed, redirected its energies into the struggle for passage of planning laws.[7]

The environmental movement of the 1900s involved a two-fold effort. The first was the rejection of the bylaw street. The second and more ambitious rested on the premise that society and its experts could promote improved communities which would fully meet all human needs. This latter aspect reflected an interest in transforming the older housing and sanitary movements into the broader activity soon regarded in England as town planning.

In this struggle, the Garden City movement's most important contribution was inspirational in nature. "Garden-city-type planning," the low-density cottage-housing layout advocated by Unwin, provided the banderole under which environmental reformers assembled. It allowed them not only to promise a brighter future of superior housing and attractive communities but also to be specific concerning their details. Thanks notably to Unwin's contribution to the Garden City movement, British planning emerged with a theory and practice derived in large part from the blending of Howard's vision with the Arts and Crafts movement. Although nominally focused on the development of the new community, British planning's preoccupation would in practice be with suburban development or town extension, not Howard's garden cities.[8]

For over a generation, suburban development had been viewed as a solution to urban problems. The extensive housing activity during the building boom of the period 1896–1905 had results that called this expectation into serious question. By 1904, a writer in the *Times* railed at London's new suburbs as "appalling monotony, ugliness, and dullness." The architect H. V. Lanchester went much further to describe the emerging suburbs as "that no-man's land where the country is wrecked and broken up only to give place to . . . the slums of the future." Such criticisms were, of course, not directed at suburban growth as such but only at bylaw development.[9]

Even critics conceded, however, that the bylaw imposed standards of light and air for housing while restraining overbuilding. Their complaint, though, was that the bylaw provided an inflexible mechanistic approach to street layout, not allowing for attractiveness, economy, or functional adaptation. Raymond Unwin observed in this regard: "the remarkable fact remains that there are growing up around our big towns vast districts under these bylaws which for dreariness and sheer ugliness it is difficult to match."

The Edwardian environmental crusade attempted to go beyond late Victorian urban sanitary ameliorism. Circumstances dictated that much of this effort to redirect the pattern of suburban development was along "garden-city lines." Interest in town planning brought Ebenezer Howard and his movement increasingly to public attention and at the same time obscured his message. His Garden City concept soon became associated in the public mind with town-extension planning and Unwin's iconography of cottage housing.[10]

The Garden City Association, no longer under Howard's leadership, encouraged this confusion. In November 1905, Thomas Adams returned as secretary. This time he remained only nine months, until the summer of 1906, and then launched a new career as a "land agent and consulting surveyor." The contacts acquired through his connection with the Garden City Association allowed Adams to become Britain's first planning consultant. His position as secretary of the association was assumed by Ewart Culpin. Culpin, a young journalist living at Letchworth, took steps soon after his appointment to qualify himself as an architect and town planner.

Culpin was Adams's friend, and the Scotsman suggested him as his successor. Like Adams, Culpin used his position to obtain lucrative outside employment. He served as the association's secretary for twelve years. During this time he continued Adams's policy of identifying the Garden City movement with a design approach to low-density model housing, even when these were built in or adjacent to existing towns. By 1912, Culpin claimed some forty limited-dividend ventures designed along garden-city lines. To Culpin, the true importance of the Garden City Association was its influence on town extension and estate planning.[11]

In July 1906, the Garden City Association sought to harmonize the activities of proliferating and often rival housing associations by inviting several to appoint representatives to its Executive. Among these were the Workmen's National Housing Council founded in 1898, with strong support from labor unions, to propagandize for municipal housing. Its general secretary, Fred Knee, had accused Thomas Adams and the Garden City Association of opposing municipal housing as "socialistic" and likely to be located in congested areas. Knee also denounced Adams and the association as partisans of paternalistic housing schemes that ignored the interests and participation of the workers.[12]

Earlier that year the Joseph Rowntree Trust, started two years before by the Quaker philanthropist and builder of New Earswick, promised both organizations an annual stipend on the condition that they devote themselves to different tasks. The Workmen's National Housing Council was to promote council housing, while the Garden City Association was to advocate model tenant–co-partnership housing schemes.[13]

In 1907, the Garden City Association hosted conferences calling for a town-planning act "in order that existing towns should be brought as near as possible to the Garden City ideal." John Nettlefold described town planning as the anticipating of needs in advance of development and providing abundant parks and small open spaces while designating the future sites of public buildings. He also called for the retention, when possible, of an agricultural belt around new suburbs.[14]

In 1909, the name of the Garden City Association was changed to the Garden Cities and Town Planning Association (G.C.T.P.), and the journal was retitled *Garden Cities and Town Planning* to reflect the new "Aims of the Association." The G.C.T.P.'s program was enlarged to encompass the promotion of town planning, the improvement of local bylaws, the influencing of legislation on housing reform, and finally "to advise on, draw-up schemes for, and establish Garden Cities, Garden Suburbs, and Garden Villages."[15]

The movement of his association to the center stage of the environmental reform crusade presented Ebenezer Howard with a dilemma. He had never been enamoured of the enthusiasm for suburban dispersal. Indeed, his position on this subject was always that it could only further complicate modern life by exacerbating the time and expense involved in commuting. At best, he regarded the suburb as a palliative to urban problems with only the garden city a valid alternative.[16]

As the association became committed to the cause of a town planning bill, Howard sought to rally the organization behind an effort at a second garden city. By then Ralph Neville and Aneurin Williams, his successor as chairman of the First Garden City, Ltd., had concluded that considerable governmental assistance was required before future garden cities could be built, and that the "national machinery for instituting new towns is still some years off."[17]

Under the circumstances, even Howard could not withstand the suburban tide. In an effort to clarify a confused situation, Howard in 1907 prepared definitions for three critical terms: "garden city," "garden suburb," and "garden village." Garden villages were miniature "garden cities" in the sense of combining workplace and residence, but without the requisite scale or greenbelt and usually dependent on one major industry as well as a neighboring city for services. "Garden suburbs" were defined only as urban extensions along "healthy lines." Culpin, on publishing Howard's definitions in the journal, thought it useful to append a statement that the association approved of garden suburbs, was actively involved in planning several, and "hopes to continue that work, being engaged week in and week out in preaching the advantages of the principle."[18]

No man contributed more to the development of the "principle" of the "garden suburb" than Raymond Unwin. His work at Hampstead Garden Suburb and elsewhere provided vivid street pictures of the "possibilities offered by town planning." True to his youthful conviction, the highly esteemed Unwin continued to strive to improve the housing of the working class by applying the art of site and street design to low-income, low-density home construction. Not content with design as an aesthetic exercise, he also sought through it to lower the costs of construction and maintenance of housing and its public services in order to bring the ideal of cottage and garden within the reach of the urban masses.

Unwin provided the theoretical framework for "garden-city-type planning" in a 1912 pamphlet entitled *Nothing Gained by Overcrowding! How the Garden City Type of Development May Benefit Both Owner and Occupier.* Focusing on the economics of housing and street and site layout, Unwin suggested that his principles of low-density estate development, with a maximum of twelve houses to an acre, cost less than intensively built terrace bylaw streets. By the means of diagrams of a ten-acre site developed in several ways, Unwin argued his point (see illustrations 10 and 11). These illustrated considerable savings in land and utility costs resulting from reducing areas devoted to public roads through the use of irregular shaped blocks and cul-de-sacs.[19]

Nothing Gained by Overcrowding represented Unwin's most important statement of his ideas. Summing up his twenty years of work in the field of housing, it marked the culmination of the creative and innovative phase of his career—a career perhaps best described as the social visionary engaged in the role of professional town planner. As a visionary, Unwin aspired to create community through architecture and layout; as a planner, he sought to prove that the ideal was also practicable.

Although professing loyalty to Howard's goals, Unwin's little book explicitly presented "Garden City principles" as relevant to suburban expansion. In this regard, Unwin revised rather than, as he thought, extended Howard's vision to render it compatible with contemporary trends. He did this by endorsing the view that the Garden City ideal could be identified with the dispersed form of estate layout which he had done so much to pioneer. He even proposed its employment by speculative builders wherever a site of several acres was available. Unwin realized, of course, that estate design schemes, as such, could not approximate Howard's vision of a transformed urban world. Accordingly, he developed another line of thought. Unwin tried to demonstrate in *Nothing Gained by Overcrowding* how planned town extensions could in time result in something resembling Howard's concept of clustered garden cities, or "social cities."

This was to be done by organizing planned suburbs, each encircled by a greenbelt, as a ring around London or any great city. Unwin tried to prove that the resulting low-density conurbation would not lead to sprawl by employing the theorem that the area of a circle increases proportionately to the square of its radius. Thus his ring of contained suburbs, he argued, required less conversion of countryside to development than the usual suburban ribbon pattern of spread. These ideas received further development in an essay Unwin contributed in 1921 to the volume *The Future of London*. Here he promoted them as the Garden City movement's approach to the postwar interest in regional planning. By this time Unwin, through his practice and writing, was the principal interpreter of Howard's vision to professional town planners.[20]

The true importance of the Town Planning and Housing Act was to extend official recognition to town planning as a local government activity. By offering legitimacy to town planners and creating opportunities for their employment, the 1909 act spurred greatly the emergence of the new profession. Indeed, its development occurred considerably more quickly than did the actual application of the planning ordinances.

The act as passed was more tentative than its supporters expected. Few in Parliament opposed planning in principle, but the implications of planning powers for private property led to their being sharply weakened before the bill's passage. Thomas Adams, for example, wanted the mandatory requirement of town-extension planning as well as provision for means by which local government could acquire land at its agricultural value.

Instead, the exercise of town-extension planning was left to the discretion of local government. Furthermore, its application required a protracted process, involving extensive consultations with all concerned parties and parliamentary approval of the general provisions of any town-extension planning scheme. Under these circumstances, few local governments engaged in planning. Over the next two decades, suburban development was little influenced by the presence on the law books of the new planning powers.[21]

The act, however, did have important consequences for the profession of town planning. Thomas Adams's disappointment with the provisions of the act was mollified by his appointment in December 1909 as town-planning advisor to the Local Government Board. Others were soon employed as planning consultants by local governments, and local government officials quickly indicated interest in learning the art or science of town planning to advance their careers. If planning were to be a function of government, then government had need to employ planners and planners, in turn, had to establish credentials.

In 1909, as the campaign for the planning act reached its conclusion, W. H. Lever endowed a department and a chair of civic design at the University of Liverpool. He also provided funds for a journal, the *Town Planning Review*. Lever's actions encouraged the training of specialists to be available "for Towns and Cities . . . to deal on broad lines with their suburban areas." Departments of planning were introduced at the Universities of Birmingham and London. Soon architects, surveyors, or municipal engineers could no longer rely on these backgrounds to consider themselves town planners. Additional training and credentials would be expected. Individuals already engaged as planners led the way in imposing professional requirements.[22]

As early as 1910, Thomas Adams suggested the need for a professional organization for the new field. On the founding in 1913 of the Town Planning Institute, Adams was elected its first president. Perhaps because of their involvement with this fledgling professional institute, both Thomas Adams and Raymond Unwin resigned from the council of the Garden Cities and Town Planning Association, although still retaining their membership and interest in the organization.[23]

When Adams left England for Canada in October 1914, Unwin succeeded him as both president of the Town Planning Institute and as town-planning advisor to the Local Government Board. The two men obviously sensed that the Garden Cities and Town Planning Association as a propagandist body could not meet the professional needs of the new specialist, the town planner. A separation of sorts between the planner as a professional and as a reformer had to occur, but the line between the two remained unclear. The roots of British town planning were too deeply embedded in the soil of reform for easy extrication.

As Ebenezer Howard observed, the association entered a new phase with the campaign for a planning act. Among those attracted to it were many involved in planning activities. During the years 1906 to 1911, several men joined the Garden Cities and Town Planning Association who remained important figures in British planning until well after World War II. Among them were W. R. Davidge and George L. Peppler, articled surveyors, and the architects S. D. Adshead and C. R. Ashbee. Writing in February 1911, Ewart Culpin commented on the recent changes: "Town planning is passing to the realm of the practical, and the engineer, the architect, and the surveyor are succeeding to the work of the propagandist. The state has adopted an important part of our principle, and the municipalities have taken in hand the putting of them into practice."[24]

The association received much credit for the 1909 act. Influential and respected, it easily called upon important personages for its meetings and conferences. Tours of Letchworth, the garden suburbs, and the garden villages for foreign visitors or Englishmen interested in town planning were incessantly organized by the association. Despite this apparent success, the G.C.T.P. experienced a decline in membership from 1910 until after World War I. Readership of its journal also fell dramatically.

Between 1909 and 1912, membership in the association plummeted from 4,200 to 1,600. During the war years, membership fell below 500. This decline appears closely related to the professionalization of town planning.

1. This photo, the frontispiece of the 1902 edition of *Garden Cities of To-morrow*, shows Howard at age 52. He was only newly emerging from obscurity and acquiring recognition as the leader of a respectable reform movement.

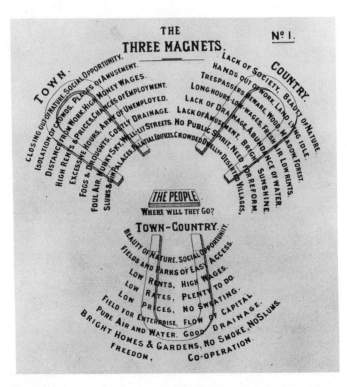

2. Howard's diagram of "The Three Magnets" from *Garden Cities of To-morrow* (1902). Dialectical reasoning to arrive at an ideal synthesis was common in communitarian thinking and writing.

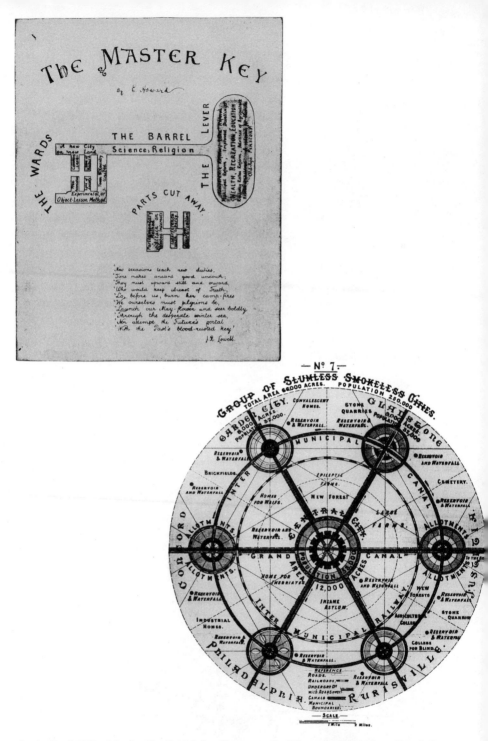

3., 4. Both "The Master Key" and the diagram of a "Group of Slumless, Smokeless Cities" appear in *To-morrow: A Peaceful Path to Real Reform* (1898) but not in the 1902 edition (renamed *Garden Cities of To-morrow*). They were probably omitted as too radical in one case and too visionary in the other. It is from the 1898 text that Howard envisioned "social cities" as the next stage after the first garden-city demonstration: "The idea of a carefully planned town lends itself readily to the idea of a carefully planned cluster of towns."

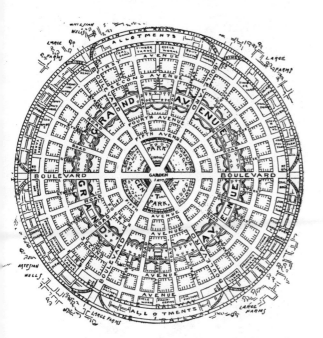

5. This illustration of the garden city accompanied the earliest interview (July 1899) with Howard published in an English newspaper. It offers greater detail than the "Ward and Centre" section of a garden city used in the book. Not until the 1902 editon were the illustrations marked "diagram only, plan must depend upon site selection."

LETCHWORTH: TOWN-PLAN

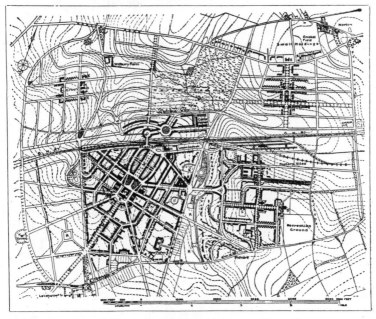

PARKER & UNWIN'S ORIGINAL PLAN OF LETCHWORTH GARDEN CITY
AS FIRST PUBLISHED (APRIL 1904)

Key to Plan

A. Main avenue
B. Goods yard and sidings
C. Central square
D. Sites for public hall, museum, etc.

E. Sites for schools
F. Sites for places of worship
H. Sites for hotels

K. Open spaces, greens, or parks
L. Site for post office
M. Site for municipal buildings

6. A major weakness of this plan is its lack of overall coherence. A resident characterized it "as a group of connected villages around a civic center with a factory district on the outside." Parker and Unwin's formal treatment of the civic center was an awkward effort at creating an "urban order."

7. Self-parody by a "pioneer" of Letchworth's reputation as a community of cranks. The development company believed this view discouraged businesses from locating. The bottom figure at a drawing board is a caricature of Raymond Unwin.

CARTOON No. 3.—WHAT SOME PEOPLE THINK OF US.

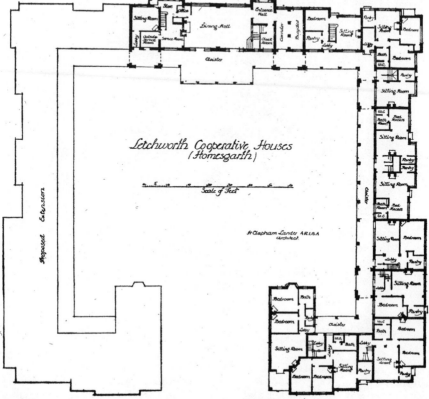

The Ground Plan of the Co-operative Houses.

8., 9. Associative or cooperative housing, where individuals or families lived independently while sharing common services and amenities, was popularized in the years before World War I by the writing of the American feminist Charlotte Perkins Gilman. Homesgarth at Letchworth was intended for the lower middle class. H. Clapham Lander, its architect, combined the quadrangle arrangement of a Cambridge college with the architecture of the "domestic school."

Diagram I.

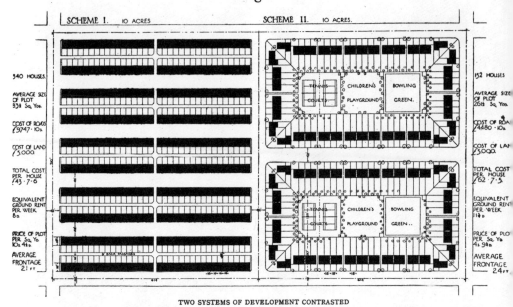

TWO SYSTEMS OF DEVELOPMENT CONTRASTED

10., 11. The residential design and architecture of Parker and Unwin derived from the arts and crafts movement and originally represented an attack on bylaw speculative housing as these illustrations demonstrate. Grafted onto the Garden City movement, they blurred the clarity of Howard's concept of the garden city. Lending themselves to various types of estate housing, Parker and Unwin's work furthered the Garden City Association's identification with Edwardian reform enthusiasm for the "suburb salubrious."

Example of the ordinary working class street made under by-laws—a type of street which can be found in every city in Great Britain.

Example of Garden City method of road construction metalled part of the width, with trees and grass margins, and houses set back from street frontage.

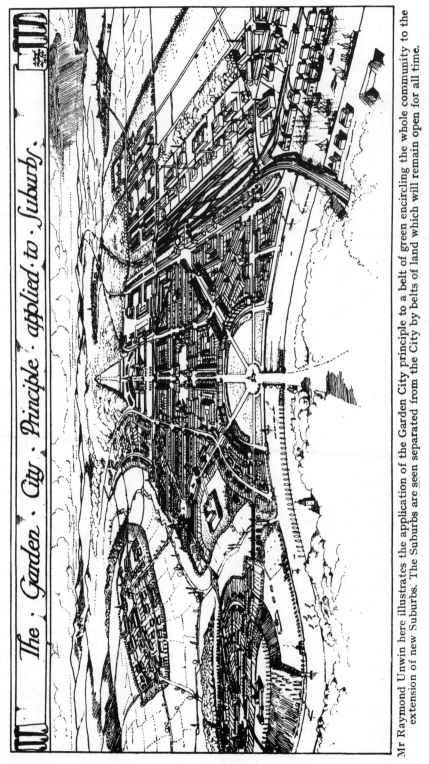

The · Garden · City · Principle · applied · to · Suburbs ·

Mr Raymond Unwin here illustrates the application of the Garden City principle to a belt of green encircling the whole community to the extension of new Suburbs. The Suburbs are seen separated from the City by belts of land which will remain open for all time.

12. This illustration from *The Garden City Movement Up-to-Date* (1912) is an early effort by Unwin to interpret Howard's ideas in terms of metropolitan or regional planning.

13. Walter Burley Griffen's prize-winning entry for the City Club of Chicago's 1913 competition for the design of a suburb along "Garden City lines." Griffen, the planner of the new Australian capital of Canberra, suggests here a more appropriate civic center than the Parker and Unwin effort at Letchworth. (*Courtesy Chicago Historical Society*)

14. Early plan, about 1921, of Welwyn Garden City by Louis de Soissons. The site was divided into four parcels by the main line and two east-west spur lines of the Great Northern Railroad. Soissons placed the civic and commercial centers in the southwest parcel with the two sections east of the main line reserved for an industrial district with adjacent working-class housing—creating, in effect, a "wrong side of the tracks."

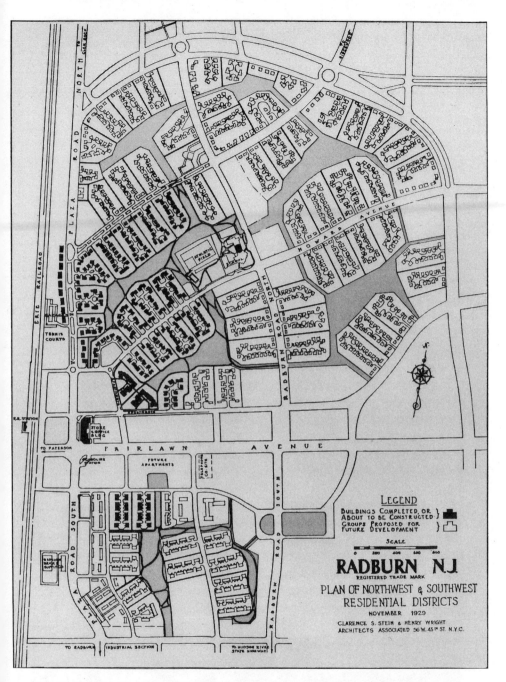

15. Planned at the end of the 1920s, Radburn employed the cul-de-sac found at Welwyn Garden City to arrive at the concept of the "superblock." Homes were turned around to face an "interior park." Pedestrian walkways led to underpasses and overpasses between the superblocks. Radburn was advertised as "the town for the motor age." Note the street named for Ebenezer Howard and the central placement of the school.

16. As early as 1882, the Spaniard Soria Y Mata suggested linear cities built along their main arteries of transportation and capable of indefinite extension. Linear planning was popular among anti-garden-city planners in the 1930s. This 1942 plan for redevelopment of London by the MARS Group offered a "herring bone" variation. The "spinal column" is surrounded by commercial and office space. The "bones" are residential areas with local industry at their ends. The remainder is open area for parks, schools, etc. An encircling interurban railroad also runs through the central axis and residential zones. Still, movement between the various parts of the city appears difficult.

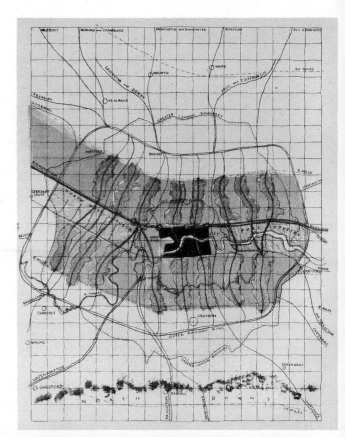

17. An aerial view of Cumbernauld near Glasgow. This Mark II new town sought through high density and architectural diversity to escape the "suburban monotony" of earlier communities. In the center of the photo, running along the crest of hill is a multilevel enclosed town center. Cumbernauld won praise from architects, but the plan lacked the flexibility to accommodate easily to change.

18. The Milton Keynes plan broke with the earlier new-town reliance on the neighborhood unit, centralized road system, and defining and enclosing borders. A grid road system emphasized flexibility in planning and easy movement by auto. The small black rectangles along the road system are "activity centers" which were placed to discourage neighborhood communities. Residents refer, though not necessarily in criticism, to Milton Keynes as the "eastern-most suburb of Los Angeles."

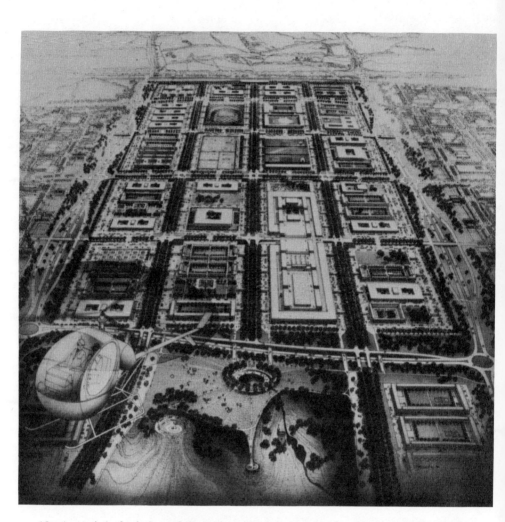

19. An artist's depiction of the Milton Keynes Center's future development. The plan called for a rigid grid and large structures to achieve an urban sense of concentration, diversity, and excitement. Critics, however, have likened it to a supermall, but this, of it self, does not mean it will not work—only time will tell.

Other organizations and journals now competed with the G.C.T.P. for the attention of the professional town planner, while the increasingly technical activities of the association as it tried to keep up with the field only discouraged lay interest. Falling membership probably also reflected an inability to sustain high enthusiasm for environmental reform after the passage of the Town Planning and Housing Act of 1909.

The fact that the Garden Cities and Town Planning Association was devoted to propaganda work for planning along "garden-city lines" made it unsuitable for advancing town planning in a strictly professional sense. For this, an organization had to limit membership to those with professional credentials and espouse an open-minded and technical view of planning. Still the relationship between town planner and reformer remained strong. Town planners assumed that their profession was a progressive force related to the rise of modern science and technology. They viewed their role as overcoming the inefficient wasteful operations of land speculators, developers, builders, and even local government in order to impose rationality over the environment and attend to the public good.

Planning ideas and projects from around the world were reported on at length and with regularity in the *Town Planning Review* after 1910. These accounts made it clear that planners outside of England concerned themselves primarily with the central city. In the summer of 1910, over 1,300 delegates assembled in London to attend an International Town Planning Congress sponsored by the Royal Institute of British Architects. Germans read papers on the "Städtebau." The Americans reported on their treatment of park systems, boulevards, civic centers, and their efforts to integrate all of these into a comprehensive city plan. In turn, the English spoke of garden-city planning as their particular contribution to the new profession. Several speakers noting the variety of interests and techniques brought forth at the conference remarked that town planners needed to include them all in their professional purview. The consensus of the conference was that town planners had to be concerned with health, beauty, convenience, order, and economy in every aspect of the urban environment.[25]

Interest in efforts to improve the center of existing cities was, of course, never entirely absent in Britain. Especially in the north of England, local societies had long been involved in promoting schemes of civic improvement and beautification. Reconstruction of the slums had remained a strong interest of the housing movement. Still, for the first decade of the new century, enthusiasm for low-density suburban development distracted from interest in the older urban areas. Now concern with the city center revived as the ideas and work of foreign planners came to British attention.

Raymond Unwin in his *Town Planning in Practice* (1909) lauded the Viennese architect Camillo Sitte's (1843–1903) ideas on the functions and proportions of town squares and the siting of monuments and churches. In 1911, both Unwin and Thomas Adams attended a planning conference in Philadelphia. On their return, they reported fully and sympathetically on American planning in the *Garden Cities and Town Planning* journal. American city planners had virtually ignored the suburb, stressing instead park and circulation systems along with civic centers. Their approach focused on the preparation of comprehensive city plans intended as an agenda for municipal action with the goal being a "City Beautiful."[26]

In 1911, George Peppler published a series of articles proposing a "transit ringway around London." For this scheme, Peppler drew extensively on the work of the Chicago architect Daniel Burnham, the pioneer and leader of the American "City Beautiful" approach. Thomas Manson's *Civic Art* (1911) presented wide-ranging central-city improvement schemes for the attention of town planners. In his *Town Planning in Relation to Old and Congested Areas* (1911), Arthur Crow developed still another scheme for London's traffic circulation. By 1913, Ebenezer Howard complained that town planners, out of misplaced civic loyalty, were more interested in promoting great cities than acting to contain them.[27]

The movement away from preoccupation with the "suburb salubrious," the theme closely identified with the Garden City movement, continued unabated. C. R. Ashbee in *Where the City Stands* (1917) described town planning as an exercise in "intelligent coordination, the imposition of functional unity," and he made clear his view that the large city should be the planner's principal concern. By then, town planning was regarded as a discipline rather than as essentially a cause. Its practitioners were required to be knowledgeable on all aspects of the built environment and on a variety of techniques and approaches. As a consequence of these professional developments, the Garden Cities and Town Planning Association no longer occupied the center stage of British town planning. Town planning increasingly encompassed the existing city, its efficiency, and civic aesthetics.

In 1913, Trystan Edwards, a young Australian-born architect, attacked garden-city-type planning as anti-urban. According to Edwards, it created semi-rural communities lacking the necessary population density and architectural mass for city living, while also devoid of the simplicity and beauty of the old English village. Edwards's analysis meant that the desirability of low-density site planning had to be recognized as relying on a set of social and aesthetic values open to challange and debate, not a self-evident truth. Garden-city-type planning continued to have its champions, but no one argued any longer that it be accepted as a town-planning dictum.[28]

Howard and the Garden City movement were often credited by contemporaries with having founded modern British town planning. Indeed, this claim provided much of the movement's cachet both in England and abroad. Such a view, however, distorts its two-fold contribution to the origins of town planning. First, it provided a setting for the coming together of reformers interested in model communities. Here Letchworth acted as a "city on a hill," validating and generating enthusiasm for the idea of de novo planning of communities based on an environmental vision. Second, the movement's propaganda on behalf of a new positive environmental approach to housing helped reorient reformers to expect higher standards and to consider housing in terms of a broad community and environmental context.

It is necessary to reiterate that the Garden City movement was only one of several factors which explain the rise of British town planning in the Edwardian age—and far from the most important of these. The passage of the Town Planning and Housing Act is only explicable in terms of the long-term reshaping of British social thought and public policy. The act, above all, reflected the enhanced emphasis on the role of the state and its expert officials in all aspects of social welfare. This mood was described somewhat awkwardly by H. G. Wells in his 1910 novel *The New Machiavelli* as an enthusiasm for ways "to develop a new better living generation with a collectivist habit, to link raw chaotic activities in every human affair . . . and bring it back to the general good." In this sense, town planning served as a metaphor for the application of collective and scientific intelligence to achieve the good community. Advocates of a society oriented to purposeful social action regarded the town planner as providing the technical expertise necessary for collective control of environmental change.

Shortly before the passage of the 1909 act, Ewart Culpin wrote: "everyone is for town planning, and possibly that is the danger." Town planning was advanced as a progressive reform that benefited everyone and harmed no one. Society was expected to gain greatly from better health, good housing, and attractive communities. Furthermore, it was suggested, the costs would be offset through greater efficiency and a stable social order. The apparent plausibility of this reasoning won a ready acceptance for planning as a state function—in theory. It was translating theory into practice that presented problems and allowed for the play of vested interests.[29]

For Howard, the garden city always remained an idée fixe, while any other environmental reform was grudgingly viewed as a palliative at best. *To-morrow* served not only as the first but also as the final statement of Howard's thoughts. As the years passed, developments in the field of town planning progressed beyond his scope and interest.

Events during the war years, however, again made Howard a significant force in the Garden City movement. Important in these developments was

C. B. Purdom. In 1904, at the age of twenty, Purdom had found work with the First Garden City, Ltd., as a junior clerk. By 1912, he was its accountant as well as the author of a book on the Letchworth experiment.[30]

Purdom was an attractive man of compelling personality and with broad-ranging intellectual interests. He came to know Howard well while researching his book on Letchworth, and the older man asked Purdom to be his biographer. In the course of their relationship, Purdom concluded that the G.C.T.P. had seriously erred in departing from Howard's program of new towns. By 1914, Purdom had enlisted two other men living at Letchworth in support of his views—W. G. Taylor, an editor at the publishing house of Dent, and Frederic J. Osborn. Born in 1885, Osborn was a Londoner and an ardent Fabian who had recently moved to Letchworth for employment as an estate agent.[31]

In 1914, the G.C.T.P. experienced great difficulty. Membership had declined for several years, and funds were short. Howard and his early supporters were less and less active in the association and town planners by now had their own strictly professional organization to absorb their interests. For reasons not fully evident, a rift had developed between the London association and Letchworth's First Garden City, Ltd. The latter refused to contribute funds to advertise in the journal or to send representatives to the association's council. Perhaps disheartened by the bickering, Sir Ralph Neville declined in the spring of 1914 to be reelected as president.[32]

His place was taken by Lord Salisbury. Though he had allowed Adams and then Culpin to closely identify the association with town planning, Neville insisted that the organization continue to acknowledge publicly that the creation of garden cities remained its primary purpose. Salisbury, who had only lately become involved with the G.C.T.P., was a busy man who permitted the association to go its own way.

Purdom and his circle identified Ewart Culpin, the association's secretary, as their major opponent. Culpin in 1913 had visited the United States for a period of four months and while advancing his own contacts had done little in the way of advocating Howard's ideas. To Culpin, as he made clear in a pamphlet written in 1912, *Garden City Movement Up-to-Date,* the association's real function was in "encouraging the growth of the suburbs" along garden-city lines by advising large landowners and local authorities on estate layout, as well as recommending trained personnel to them.

In 1914, Purdom fired the first shot in a struggle over the control of the association—a struggle which continued until late 1918. An article by Purdom openly critical of the association's policies appeared in its journal. Here Purdom demanded the exclusive advocacy of garden cities and the renunciation of support for "garden suburbs or town planning on Garden City lines." Purdom admitted little support among the membership for his proposal but predicted that this must change as the problems inherent in suburban extension became apparent. The article ended with Purdom's comment: "I always regretted the day the Garden City Association weakened its good wine with the water of town planning."[33]

Since 1907, Howard had vainly sought to enlist the association in starting a second garden city. Stymied by the opposition of Culpin and the directors of the First Garden City, Ltd., Howard now joined Purdom's attack. He informed the association in 1914 that he was resigning from both the Executive and the council to protest the organization's policies but then allowed his mind to be changed before the news became public.[34]

At the war's start, Purdom volunteered for military service. Discharged in early 1917, he immediately resumed his struggle with the G.C.T.P. By then it was evident that the government was preparing an ambitious program of financing postwar housing. In May 1917, Seebohm Roundtree authored a report for a committee considering postwar reconstruction in which he described a dire housing shortage which the private market could not possibly meet. Housing as a political issue was now moving to the fore. In July 1917, the president of the Local Government Board appointed an eight-man "experts committee," chaired by the Liberal M.P. Sir John Walter, to propose ways for constructing working-class housing. The most knowledgeable and influential of the committeemen was Raymond Unwin.

In a small pamphlet, "The Garden City After the War," Purdom urged that local government be provided the power and funds to purchase land for the purpose of building Howard's garden cities. In November 1917, Howard informed the Garden Cities and Town Planning Association that he would shortly advertise a lecture series on "One Hundred Garden Cities After the War," the beginning round of a campaign for a national program. Later that same month Purdom with a new ally, Captain Richard A. L. Reiss, informed the Executive of the formation of an ad hoc National Garden Cities Committee "to propagate Garden City principles as distinct from garden suburb or village proposals."[35]

Despite the hostility of the Executive, Purdom's group, now known as the New Townsmen, continued their campaign. At Purdom's request, Frederic J. Osborn prepared a tract calling for the state's financing of garden cities to provide homes and jobs for returning veterans. When summoned for military duty at the end of 1916, Osborn refused to serve and fled to London. For most of 1917, he avoided detection while frequenting the Reading Room of the British Museum to study the literature of experimental communities. Unable to work, Osborn received financial aid from Ebenezer Howard, and the relationship between the two became close.

Osborn published *New Towns: After the War: An Argument for Garden Cities* under the pseudonym "The New Townsmen" in January 1918. Here Osborn attempted a "scientific" rationale for a state-financed program of garden cities built either by local authorities or specifically created development companies. A similar work, authored by Purdom and Reiss, was issued by the National Garden Cities Committee. As the war entered its final stage, concern with flagging morale prompted Lloyd George to step up his promises for the postwar provision of superior housing under the catchy banner, "homes fit for heroes."[36]

The prospect of a major postwar housing drive intensified the struggle for control of the association. In May 1918, the Executive issued an ultimatum: the National Garden City Committee must dissolve or its membership resign from the G.C.T.P. This demand was ignored by the New Townsmen, whose position was strengthened considerably when the well-connected Reiss secured an offer of financial support for the G.C.T.P. from the Joseph Roundtree Trust. In the fall of 1918, the New Townsmen demanded Culpin's resignation, arguing that his work as a private consultant on estate schemes conflicted with his position as secretary.[37]

Culpin's resignation in October signaled the victory of the New Townsmen. The National Garden Cities Committee was absorbed into the G.C.T.P. Purdom replaced Culpin as secretary, while Reiss became chairman of the Executive. In the struggle, Howard contributed his prestige to the New Townsmen, while the actual maneuvering was left to Purdom and Reiss.

The victorious New Townsmen created a committee headed by Howard to list possible sites for garden cities. For this service, he was to be paid an annual stipend of three hundred pounds. The assumption was that any further action would await the parliamentary passage of a national garden-cities program. In this expectation, the New Townsmen were disappointed. They now controlled the association, but Howard acting alone determined developments.

The end of hostilities in November 1918 brought heightened social unrest. Even Conservative members of the wartime coalition government accepted the need for an extraordinary effort by government to insure domestic peace. In March 1919, a draft of a housing bill came to the Cabinet and a month later went before Parliament. Based largely on the recommendations of the Local Government Board committee, submitted four months earlier as the Tudor Walter Report, the proposed housing bill called for a bold new course in the area of providing working-class housing.[38]

Before World War I, state involvement in housing had been accepted as a necessity, but little had been done. For the most part, public housing was related to rehousing those displaced by slum-clearance schemes. Due, in part, to the Garden City movement and a growing interest in housing by the working class, a shift in approach occurred even before 1914. Local authorities then began to look to cheap suburban sites in order to construct a low-density layout of cottage housing of relatively high quality.

According to Mark Swenarton in *Homes Fit for Heroes,* the motivation behind state action in housing in 1919 was to "provide visible proof of the irrelevance of revolution." Whether from fear, as Swenarton claims, or as an expression of a nation's gratitude, the Housing Act of 1919 pledged support for building five hundred thousand homes of superior standards within three years. In most important regards, it followed the recommendations of the Tudor Walter Report, which was largely the work of Raymond Unwin.[39]

Appearing in the same week as the Armistice, the Tudor Walter Report emphatically urged state support for low-density cottage housing containing such middle-class amenities as three bedrooms and a bathroom. Unwin's report argued that the housing shortage provided opportunity to elevate housing standards and lower density by building small houses with gardens. Much of the report was devoted to Unwin's comprehensive analysis of cost factors involved in superior cottage housing and how they might be kept low. However, the report offered little concerning the location of new housing or the planning of new towns. It did recommend, though, that future housing should be regulated by town-planning schemes instead of rigid bylaws. In short, the report by implication proposed massive new housing in "garden suburbs." This of course was not what Howard and the New Townsmen intended.

As secretary of the G.C.T.P., Purdom campaigned for the need to restrict metropolitan growth, thus seeking to redirect policy away from emphasis on suburban estate development. To do this, he pressed for the creation of a National Town Planning Commission to consider the decentralization of population and industry into planned new centers organized as garden cities. For a time, Purdom considered abandoning the term "Garden City" as hopelessly muddled in the public mind and substituting "satellite town" for new towns built in proximity to large cities. Instead, he decided on yet another effort to clarify the concept "Garden City."

Purdom provided the association's new official definition, one retained for the next half century. "A garden city," he proposed, "is a town designed for healthy living and industry; of a size that makes a full measure of social life, but not larger; surrounded by a rural belt; the whole of the land being in public ownership or held in trust for the community." The term "satellite town" was also retained to refer to a garden city proximate to a large town and consequently dependent upon the latter for certain services.

Purdom's campaign was barely under way when Howard derailed it. Acting on his own, Ebenezer Howard in May 1919 contracted for the site of

a second garden-city experiment. Osborn, busily engaged in seeking support from the Labour party for new towns, had by now replaced Purdom as
Howard's favorite, and he tried desperately to dissuade the latter. He wrote
the older man, ". . . any scheme in which you have a hand will be regarded
as the main line of garden city propaganda. Now if you try to repeat the
Letchworth experiment, it is bound to suggest that in your opinion voluntary effort is sufficient to get the movement going. But garden cities can
never be the normal mode of urban development until state facilities are
granted suitable to the task."[40]

Osborn was certainly right, but Howard nevertheless pushed on. For the
first time since 1902, he had reasserted his leadership of the movement.
Suspicious as ever of government and politics, he preferred the older methods of voluntary organization and self-help; a successful second garden city
would inevitably lead to a third, then a fourth, and so on.[41]

With the start of Welwyn Garden City, the New Townsmen reluctantly
abandoned their national campaign to assist in building the town. In terms
of Howard's vision, Welwyn Garden City proved of mixed value. As a
demonstration project for British new towns, it provided an example of
town layout and appearance much superior to Letchworth. Yet it drained
from the G.C.T.P. the considerable talents of the New Townsmen, and this
contributed greatly to the organization's relative inactivity for much of the
1920s.

In retrospect, both Purdom and Osborn recognized that their campaign, if continued, would not have influenced government policy. Housing was wanted quickly and a new-town approach required too much time.
Even in the immediate postwar context of unprecedented state involvement in housing, new towns were regarded as too radical and expensive
for ready acceptance.

Indeed, even the Housing Act of 1919 soon proved too ambitious. The
collapse of a postwar economic boom in the autumn of 1920 brought forth
demands for governmental retrenchment. The housing program was singled out for strong criticism as excessively costly. No longer confronting a
social crisis, the government called a halt in 1921 to the program with only
170,000 dwellings erected. Still there were desirable results even from this
truncated effort. A new standard of housing for council and even privately
provided housing was quickly set. During the 1920s, as William Ashworth
has observed, "low-density housing with gardens before and behind and
often with tree-lined streets became normal for new suburban estates."[42]

The experience of building a second garden city confirmed what the
New Townsmen anticipated—only direct and extensive assistance from gov-
ernment could bring about garden cities as more than an occasional oddity.
Governmental powers were needed to acquire sites with suitable location

and size, while governmental money was needed to build expeditiously. To a very large degree, Welwyn Garden City repeated Letchworth's experience. Once again, it was demonstrated how difficult it was to construct a modern town, given the need for considerable capital well in advance of any significant return of revenue. Howard's second experiment would be seriously underfunded, and its development slow and painful.

The collapse of the New Townsmen's campaign ended the systematic effort by the G.C.T.P. to clarify its principles. The extensive construction of low-density housing in the 1920s and rapid suburban development were in any case closely associated in the public mind with the Garden City movement. Before 1914, identification with the "suburb salubrious" worked to the movement's advantage in winning support. After the mid-1920s the reverse would be true in certain architectural circles experiencing second thoughts about the desirability of suburban development and eager for innovations in urban design.

9

Howard and Welwyn Garden City, 1910–1940

Not this town, nor yet the next is Jerusalem. Jerusalem is far off, and it needs more time and strength, and much endurance to reach it.

Mathew Arnold
(pamphlet entitled *A French Eton*, 1864)

Howard's wife died unexpectedly in 1904. A year later the grieving Howard moved to Letchworth, where he soon became a familiar figure with sparse silver hair and a walrus mustache. By his mid-fifties, Howard had acquired a grandfatherly appearance which conformed well with his image as a gentle, eccentric dreamer—the honored founder of the Garden City movement. Invariably, he wore ill-fitted and baggy clothing—a business suit for London and mismatched jacket and pants at Letchworth—and a battered felt hat. In 1907, Howard remarried a Miss Annie Hayward of Letchworth, a considerably younger woman. The marriage proved difficult.[1]

With the Garden City movement's success, recognition came quickly to Howard. The Royal Institute of British Architects in 1910 selected him (a legal stenographer among a line of bishops, dukes, and earls) as an honorary vice president for its international conference. Two years later on March 12, 1912, a public dinner, attended by four hundred, was given in his honor at a West End restaurant. Here Sir Ralph Neville toasted him as a man whose Garden City concept had revolutionized thinking about cities throughout the world. A telegram sent by the Liverpool University School of Town Planning hailed Howard as the "originator of the modern system of town planning." No longer obscure, Howard for the remainder of his life corresponded with and was visited by admirers from throughout the world.

At Letchworth, Howard participated fully in community life and enjoyed his role as an eminent. He acted in local theatrical productions and lectured for J. Bruce Wallace's Alpha Union. In 1912, he was elected a justice of the peace. Fame, however, did not bring fortune. A stipend, paid him by the Garden City Association and the First Garden City, Ltd., did permit him to cut back on his professional work. As late as 1912, however, when writing to Cecil Harmsworth requesting the publisher's assistance in obtaining appointment as shorthand reporter for a Royal Commission, he complained, "I do not know why it is that though I have frequently applied . . . I have never been lucky enough to succeed, but have often acted as a devil to those who have."

A year later he was named to the Civil List for a pension of seventy-five pounds per annum. Even with this, it remained necessary for him to travel to London two or three days a week for stenographic work. Not until 1924, when in his mid-seventies, did he retire completely. Howard earned his Garden City Association (later Garden Cities and Town Planning Association) stipend through speaking engagements. Though pleased to do these, his schedule was cut back sharply after 1912, ostensibly for reasons of health but probably because Culpin and others did not believe he effectively represented the association.[2]

At Letchworth, Howard's major concern became the promotion of a scheme for "associated housing." This interest went back to at least 1885. As noted earlier, associated housing was a central theme of communitarian thinking since Robert Owens had observed that traditional housing encouraged the family's isolation from the community. From the mid-nineteenth century on, occasional articles on associated housing appeared in periodicals. William Morris in 1884 proposed communal kitchens, laundries, and dining rooms for housing which would clearly differentiate between public and family space. This idea appeared in Bellamy's *Looking Backward* a few years later and was also present in Albert Owen's scheme for Topolobampo.

Declining interest in communitarian experiments at the turn of the century, if anything, encouraged enthusiasm for efforts at associative housing. Individuals who otherwise might have been involved in starting colonies turned their energies instead to the considerably more modest concept of cooperation among families in household management. Howard, although requiring little prodding, was encouraged in this direction by many of his earliest supporters and even one critic.

In the spring of 1905, H. G. Wells began a series on utopianism and the future city in Northcliffe's *Daily Mail*. His first article was a thinly veiled

attack on Howard's Garden City concept. Wells believed that modern transportation now permitted people to live at a great distance from work.
Accordingly, he thought the Garden City scheme with its reliance on compact radial development reflected traditional urban form, disregarding the
potentials for new arrangements made possible by modern technology.
Here Wells anticipated an argument not seriously advanced by others until
after World War I. In the second article of the series, Wells attacked the
"myth of the house in the garden" as socially backward and economically
inefficient, proposing in its place the ideal of associated housing.[3]

Howard responded in a long letter to the *Daily Mail*. Workers, he argued,
should live near their employment to allow them to go home for lunch, to
grow gardens, and to use the money saved on transportation for holidays.
Wells's later articles, however, focused only on associated housing and how
it might relieve the burdens of child rearing and domestic care, observing
that "the future of the world . . . rests upon the quality of its children, and
the profession of mother, therefore, is the most important of all." In a brief
personal note to Howard, Wells urged an effort at associated housing at
Letchworth, a thought Howard had already proposed in *To-morrow*.[4]

As Wells noted in his articles, enthusiasm for experiments in "associated
housing" had gained impetus from the work of the American feminist
writer, Charlotte Perkins Gilmore. In *Women and Economics* (1898) and *The
Home: Its Work and Influence* (1903), Gilmore savaged the traditional view of
the woman's role as properly being housekeeper. To free the wife and
mother from the deadening routine of domestic chores, she advocated the
"kitchenless home" based on cooperative features. The liberated housewife
could then achieve economic independence and self-fulfillment through
outside employment.

Gilmore and Howard shared the premise that major social problems
might easily be corrected through cooperation, physical design, and planning. As with Howard, it was Gilmore's reading of *Looking Backward* that
catalyzed her interest in reform. Gilmore urged associated housing to meet
the wife's needs for economic independence. Howard, for the most part,
only thought to improve the material comfort and life-style of the whole
family. According to the historian Carl Degler, Gilmore's work had great
appeal because "it addressed itself to change already in full swing." Ideas
once associated with radical or "crank" circles had entered the mainstream
of social thought.[5]

"Efficiency experts" redesigned and rationalized aspects of corporate
business and its profits. Reformers sought to do the same for politics and
social problems, and town planners grappled with the needs of city and
community. A conscious search for change through collective and systematic planning was very much in the air. For a while at least, efficiency

seemed a goal all could agree on, whatever their other differences. The architect H. Clapham Lander at the Bournville conference asserted in support of a proposal for associative housing: "what is economically best is invariably morally right. Any system involving material waste stands self-condemned. . . . There are not two laws, one for the spiritual and another for the natural world."[6]

In early 1906, Howard announced plans for Homesgarth, an associated housing scheme at Letchworth for middle-class families. He explained that cooperation was the underlying force of modern life, and he wished to demonstrate its relevance to the home. Homesgarth would show how "the numerous folk of the middle class with meager incomes and a hard struggle for existence" could be inexpensively provided with attractive and comfortable circumstances. Associated housing allowed for amenities of space and privacy, a well-stocked library, domestic help and inexpensive nutritious meals served in a common dining hall.[7]

Raising the capital necessary for Homesgarth required four years. Started in 1910, it formally opened in August 1911. Homesgarth was impressive in appearance. Howard had employed the architect H. Clapham Lander, then living at Letchworth. Lander, a Fabian, had long been devoted to the cause of associated housing and his thinking was influenced by Parker and Unwin's "The Art of Building a Home" (1901). There the brothers-in-law had proposed tenements grouped around quadrangles or gardens as an attractive arrangement. Lander's model for Homesgarth was a Cambridge quad, while he sensibly kept its architecture simple and appropriately domestic.[8]

The experiment consisted of twenty-four small apartments and central facilities arranged around three sides of a quadrangle and part of a fourth. Each apartment provided a small kitchen, dining area, and sitting room. Residents were expected to normally take meals in the large common dining hall, using their own small kitchen only for light cooking. This assumption proved the plan's undoing.

Over time, those dissatisfied with the price of eating in the dining room or the quality of food served prepared meals in their own quarters. As a consequence, the costs for the remainder increased and the expected savings were not realized. In 1916, Homesgarth was converted to conventional rental units. Howard remained in Homesgarth until 1920 when he left Letchworth.

When Homesgarth still promised much, Howard in the spring of 1913 proposed a second and more modest experiment for working-class families, one closer to Gilmore's way of thinking. A common dining hall was not included, although a staff in a central kitchen fully equipped with labor-saving devices would prepare meals for delivery to the separate apartments. A nursery with playground and trained attendants would allow mothers to take employment in nearby shops and factories or, alternatively, to raise vegetables in allotment gardens for sale to the common kitchen.

In a small pamphlet, "Domestic Industry As It Might Be" (1914), Howard suggested that associated housing for the working class would do more to "forward the great women's movement" than even granting women the vote. Although sympathetic to the "suffragettes," Howard was deeply distressed by their then ongoing campaign of civil disobedience, which featured smashing shop windows, chaining themselves to public buildings, and bombing monuments.

The sudden and unexpected outbreak of war in August 1914 halted any further action on associated housing and also ended his planned visit to America later that year. Howard, devastated by the news of hostilities, rushed to George Bernard Shaw's home at nearby Ayot St. Lawrence. The agitated Howard implored a startled Shaw to write a pamphlet calling for an immediate peace and personally promised to drop a German translation from an airplane over Berlin. Later, angered by reported atrocities of the Germans in Belgium, he reluctantly accepted his country's involvement in the war, while urging the war's quick end through negotiation.[9]

Close ties existed between the peace and Garden City movements. Both were of an idealistic and international character, appealed to reformers, and stressed cooperation. The connection between Howard and the peace movement may be traced to Cora Richmond and even Adin Ballou. A sense of heightened crisis in world affairs had, in fact, underpinned a widespread revival of the peace movement in the 1890s. Howard opposed the Boer War (1899–1901) and the growing jingoism displayed by people in Britain and elsewhere. In 1906, when Germany and France edged to the brink of conflict, residents of Letchworth, including Howard, formed an Esperanto Society to aid the cause of international understanding.

Esperanto represented the most successful of several nineteenth-century efforts to construct a universal language. Its inventor, the brilliant Russian Jewish physician Lazarus Zamenhof, believed that national hatreds were heightened by barriers of language. By 1900, his followers claimed some one hundred thousand speakers of Esperanto in twenty-three countries.

A reporter from the *Daily Mail* visiting Letchworth in 1907 encountered sandal-shod residents conversing in what he assumed to be Latin until informed it was Esperanto. In 1907, Howard delivered a short speech in Esperanto to delegates attending the Second International Esperanto Congress meeting at Cambridge. To those delegates who toured nearby Letchworth, Howard spoke in Esperanto of the Garden City movement and Esperanto as allied efforts in the cause of international understanding and peace.

From at least 1907, Howard sought the start of a second garden city, different from and superior to Letchworth. On the death of Edward VII, he called for a national subscription to erect a garden city as a memorial. To Howard, a second experiment would reignite a crusade whose fire had long been banked by the misplaced emphasis on the "suburb salubrious." In wanting to demonstrate his arguments by example, Howard disregarded developments which were tying planning to government. He supported the New Townsmen in so far as they called for a return to the garden city, but he did not share the view that this required a governmental planning strategy.

Howard found the site of Welwyn Garden City in 1919, arranged for its financing, drafted the articles of the Second Garden City Company, and then handpicked its preliminary directors. When none wanted the responsibility of being chairman, he looked outside the ranks of the Garden City movement for the right man. This was Theodore Chambers, a well-known London surveyor, who shortly before had impressed Howard with a published article on land values and the public interest. The pace of activity continued to be hectic throughout the fall. Surveys were made; a preliminary town plan was prepared by the architect, C. M. Crickmer; a staff was engaged; and preparation for a capital offering was begun.[10]

The site consisted of nearly 2,400 acres on high ground twenty-one miles north of London and astraddle the main line of the Great Northern Railroad. Proximity to London was stressed as the key to the success of the second experiment. In 1919, Howard and the New Townsmen stated the purpose of Welwyn Garden City as the "illustration of the right way to provide for the expansion of the industries and population" of London.[11]

Until Chambers arrived on the scene, Howard acted very much on his own. As chairman, Chambers promptly took charge. The Second Garden City Company was reorganized and renamed the Welwyn Garden City Ltd. in 1920. An exhausted Howard, ill-suited for the politics of a complex organization, once again retreated from the center of power. Chambers had much experience running board meetings and making decisions. Purdom (who emerged as Chambers's right-hand man) noted of Chambers: "In a sense he was the company." Other directors complained that he kept them in the dark. To Osborn, Chambers was a "Welwyn Garden City man," indifferent to the larger fortunes of the Garden City movement and concerned only with the success of Welwyn Garden City.[12]

Chambers shared Howard's view that the company in Welwyn needed to play a more active role than had its counterpart at Letchworth. Both Howard and Chambers were interested in a scheme by which all residents of the community must own at least one share in the company, an adaptation of tenant co-partnership, but nothing came of this. Other experiments, however, were tried.

Among the more interesting of these was Howard's idea of three "civic directors" sitting on the company's board to represent the residents. These were to be appointed by the local authority and thus were also to expedite relations between the local authority and the community. Unfortunately, neither goal was realized. The "civic directors" quietly acquiesced in company policy. Nor did the other members view them as bona fide directors. The civic directors were instructed not to discuss company business outside the boardroom, and matters of "intimate concern" were not considered when they were present. In 1934, during a reorganization of the company, this experiment in democracy ended without protest.[13]

The company's capital offering coincided with the onset of the postwar financial downturn. Interest rates were forced upward. Of an initial offering of 250,000 pounds in ordinary shares, only about a third were subscribed by one year later. The directors saved the company by personally subscribing for another one hundred thousand pounds. Even so, they still needed to borrow additional funds from the banks and to issue bonds. This created a burdensome debt load with revenues still far in the future.

The question of how to push ahead with essential urban services created serious policy differences among board members. Efforts to raise capital to speed up lagging development met with limited success. A clause written into the Housing Act of 1921 provided governmental loans at low interest for the building of garden cities. When this was sought, a disappointing sum was offered and only under conditions board members deemed intolerable. Financial strains help explain the forced departure of Purdom in 1928 from the company amidst charges and rumors about his professional and personal life.[14]

A major reorganization of the company occurred in 1931 with temporary relief obtained when the town's sewage structure and waterworks were sold a year later to the district council. Finally in 1934, the bond holders forced a drastic reworking of the company's finances and organization. Though grim times obviously had much to do with the company's problems, the creditors and some board members viewed a major source of the difficulties as the limit on stock dividends. This was now removed to make the company's stock more appealing to speculators counting on a future rise in values at Welwyn Garden City. The directors of Howard's second experiment had broken a basic premise of *To-morrow*—that the unearned increment in land values must benefit the community rather than profit the speculator.[15]

The prospectus of the Second Garden City Company stressed the importance of the company undertaking a broad variety of enterprises incidental to the town's development. Dissatisfied by the experience of Letchworth and its cautious development company, Howard and the New Townsmen with Chambers's later concurrence sought experimentation of the kind anticipated in *To-morrow* under the awkward rubric "pro-municipal work." Economic distress encouraged this development. The dearth of private capital for investment at Welwyn Garden City underlined the necessity of an ambitious role for the company if the town were to be built.

Subsidiaries of the company were quickly formed to construct and manage housing as well as provide gravel, sand, bricks, and horticultural plantings. Others were registered to supply electricity, transportation, public houses, and, most important, a central store. Some of these ventures, in time, proved profitable and others were terminated.

In *To-morrow*, Howard suggested that all retail shops be gathered in one central location, the Crystal Palace, a wide glass arcade encircling the central park which was "to be one of the favorite resort places of the townspeople." He had considered and then rejected the idea of a single store. Instead, he proposed the issuance of exclusive franchises to shopkeepers in various trades on the condition that their prices and services remain satisfactory. The disappointing experience at Letchworth changed his thinking.

At Letchworth few controls had been imposed. Shop space had been leased to any interested parties. The results proved highly unsatisfactory— a relatively large number of unattractive structures housed small shops with meager inventory on their shelves. A 1913 survey of industrial firms at Letchworth indicated considerable concern about the inadequacy of local shopping. Howard acted decisively to guarantee against any repetition of this failure.

In the fall of 1919, he offered a retail monopoly to Selfridges and when this was refused, to the St. Albans Cooperative Society, which also declined. More thought was given to the subject by Purdom and Chambers. In May 1921, the decision was made to create an organization, the Welwyn Stores Ltd., to provide for the town's shopping needs. The parent company (the Welwyn Garden City Ltd.) retained a controlling interest in this subsidiary in return for providing the latter with exclusive rights to all shopping sites in the town for a period of ten years. Apart from attending to the community's needs, this experiment in retailing had another interesting aspect— the effort to retain for the Welwyn Garden City Ltd. future increases in the potentially lucrative rental value of commercial property.[16]

It was thought necessary that residential and industrial sites be leased for the customary 99 to 999 years in order to attract newcomers. On the basis of the Letchworth experience, however, it was believed that the length of the lease with retail property was not critical. Retail businesses, in any case, would not venture too far in advance of population. Furthermore, the value of a retail site, more than other forms of property, depended on location and a flow of traffic. This latter would become apparent only once the town's development acquired a definite form. The Welwyn Stores Ltd. was to provide a permanent shopping center and, through attracting trade, enhance the retail value of the nearby sites.

In operation, the Welwyn Stores combined retail departments and businesses in a single establishment—ranging from provisions to clothes to furniture and appliances—seeking to cater to all classes. Rental space was provided for privately owned service shops such as tailoring and a hairdressing salon, as well as social clubs and public activities. Commercially successful, the Welwyn Stores incurred the vociferous anger of the residents, especially of the middle class, who complained of its monopoly position and high prices while enjoying the well-stocked and eventually handsome structure erected in the late 1930s.

The success of the town, both in a practical and theoretical sense, depended on its ability to lure established industries from London. In this regard, Welwyn Garden City initially was a disappointment. Most of its first firms were newly formed. Several were branches of American businesses, the best known of these being the Shredded Wheat Company, who sought through their dry cereal to revolutionize British breakfast habits. In general, though, the industrial development of the new town fell far short of expectations. Until World War II, the building trades were the largest form of employment, engaging 1,100 workers of a total town work force of 6,900.[17]

While industrialists often gave us a reason for not moving to Welwyn Garden City the shortage of affordable housing for their employees, many of the middle-class residents of the town commuted to work in London. These facts called into question the success of achieving a satellite garden city as an alternative to the rise of suburbia. Even more troubling to the friends of the garden city was its slow growth. The town, intended for 50,000, in 1938 had a population of 13,500. In its defense, they mentioned formidable obstacles overcome and pointed out that the town and the experiment had survived.

The town plan provided for an agricultural belt of some six hundred acres, the maximum considered possible under the circumstances. Among those who followed Howard from Letchworth to Welwyn in 1921 was a group of Quakers interested in various experiments in cooperative activity. They organized the New Town Trust and leased five hundred acres to establish a cooperative farm and dairy for the marketing of "certified" milk (or milk meeting the highest standards and thus exempt from the need to be pasteurized). In addition, chemical fertilizers and commercial methods of food processing were avoided. With prices high and the market for its produce limited, the cooperative farm failed after about ten years. Its land was then rented to tenant farmers of a conventional kind.[18]

The Quakers in Welwyn Garden City also attempted an experiment in associative housing. In 1922, the New Town Trust erected a quadrangle of kitchenless flats designed by H. Clapham Lander, the architect of Homesgarth. Sometime in the 1930s, this experiment ended, and the buildings were converted into a hotel. Enthusiasm for associative housing schemes went into decline in the mid-1920s. Here and there an effort occurred, but the excitement of a movement whose time had apparently come, clearly present in the decade before World War I, dissipated, not to be reborn until the cultural upheaval of the 1960s spawned a brief revival.[19]

To a steady if small stream of visitors from Britain and elsewhere who studied the experiment at first hand, no part of the work at Welwyn Garden City was of greater interest than its appearance. As the young American writer Catherine Bauer suggested in her influential study *Modern Housing* (1934), Welwyn Garden City presented to the world a "three-dimensional model of a planned town."[20]

Sketchbook and box cameras in hand, architects, planners, and housing reformers strolled its streets, scrutinizing everything in sight. They evaluated buildings in terms of setting, style, use, and floor plan; traffic patterns were observed, and vehicles counted. But above all, they endlessly analyzed the town plan. This was the core of the experiment, and it was generally judged a success. Open, informal, and allowing for numerous green areas, the plan proved logical, cohesive, and more attractive than the first garden city.

Louis de Soissons (1890–1962) prepared the town plan in 1921. A Canadian, Soissons trained at the École des Beaux-Arts and had a brilliant academic career until it was interrupted by war service. Appointed architect planner for the Second Garden City Company by Chambers in late 1919, Soissons remained in charge of the town plan until his death. As the company's architect and also as the partner in a private architectural practice, he designed numerous structures of all types within Welwyn Garden City. His influence on the architecture of the town extended, moreover, well beyond his own work.[21]

The company imposed tight control over building quality and architecture. Soissons administered this control and selected as appropriate a neo-Georgian architectural style, then enjoying a renaissance in certain architectural circles as a logical outgrowth of the earlier Arts and Crafts movement. The consequence of Soissons's long and very comprehensive supervision of the physical development of Welwyn Garden City is a high overall standard of harmony, which some critics thought uninspired and even monotonous. To others, and they were well in the majority, Welwyn Garden City stood out as a handsome town whose aesthetic order contrasted greatly with the usual suburban hodgepodge.[22]

Inheriting a preliminary plan prepared by C. M. Crickmer, Soissons retained its roughly circular composition but significantly altered the details. The site's most important feature was its division into four parcels by the main line and two east-west spur lines of the Great Northern. Crickmer handled this problem by recommending two formal civic centers. They were to face each other at a distance on opposite sides of the main line and to be connected by a broad avenue given over to commerce. This would have proven awkward, and Soissons developed a different treatment (see illustration 14).

His plan placed the civic and commercial centers in the southwest parcel and reserved the two sections east of the main line for an industrial district with adjacent working-class housing. He treated the commercial center formally as a grid divided by a broad avenue, Howardsgate, running at right angles from the future site of the railroad station for four hundred yards and terminating at another broad avenue, the Parkway. The tree-planted Parkway divided the commercial from the residential districts. At its northern end, the site of the civic center was organized as a semicircle flanked by parkland.

In contrast to the formal arrangement of the commercial and civic areas, the residential districts featured a highly irregular layout of roads and spaces. The resulting odd-shaped blocks often contained cul-de-sacs and closes. This, of course, represented an effort at applying Unwin's principles given in *Nothing Gained by Overcrowding*. The first houses built avoided the conventional "front gardens" separated by hedges or fences, providing instead open lawns. Residents, however, expressed preference for the "English front garden" and the "American practice" was discontinued. As greenness was the hallmark of garden-city-type planning, the planners paid careful attention to landscaping with "a rural-like effect sought and obtained."

Class segregation by neighborhood occurred as the town developed, despite some effort to counter this. Soissons's scheme had destined the area east of the main line as the wrong side of the tracks and essentially working-class. The privately owned homes of the middle class were almost invariably built in the northwest and southwest parcels. In the sense of creating a community which transcended social distinctions, Welwyn Garden City proved no more successful than Letchworth. It is highly doubtful that even if the town plan had been designed with this as its specific goal, the results would have been very different. All that probably would have happened is that many of the middle class would not have moved there, for most sought only a pleasant place to live within commuting distance of London and a safe investment in their homes.[23]

Less a novelty than Letchworth, the second garden city attracted neither the public attention of its predecessor nor many residents interested in a social experiment. The population of the latter never acquired the reputation for the eccentricity of Letchworth's pioneers. More important, the press did not watch its development. Urban problems and efforts at their solutions had been pushed far from the center of social concern.

Welwyn Garden City was regarded as a quiet community of no particular cachet, where middle-class Londoners of modest means and interested in gardening might move. Until after World War II, the difficulty of building lower-cost housing in the town meant that the working class was a minority of the residents. Keeping to their neighborhoods, they stayed aloof from the general life of the community.

The second garden city had been promoted as an approach to redirecting the pattern of metropolitan expansion into satellite new towns. Such an approach certainly could not be conclusively demonstrated by a single experiment, no matter how impressive. The rapid rise of automobile ownership added impetus to the outward thrust of the metropolis. Soon roads leading out of London were festooned with "ribbon developments" of housing and shops. The building of Welwyn Garden City offered no serious challenge to the appeal of suburbia. Indeed, many who lived there thought of the community as a commuting suburb of London rather than as the intended experiment in metropolitan growth and regional planning. If Letchworth had appeared ahead of its time, Welwyn Garden City had not.

Still, to a small group of planners, especially in the United States, Howard's ideas retained their appeal. Resisting the fascination of many architects and planners with the futuristic possibilities offered by a new technology, they looked to the small planned community as the building block of a humane society. To them, Welwyn Garden City rose as an exemplar of the community of the future, an alternative to the normal pattern of unplanned urban expansion through suburban growth.

Howard died in 1928, before progress on his second experiment had advanced very far. He had continued to be a member of the board of the Welwyn Garden City Ltd. and also of several subsidiary companies, being particularly interested in the Welwyn Stores Ltd. After 1920, however, he had not played an active role. Purdom described him as sitting silently through meetings, busily taking shorthand notes of the transactions. Living in a small home at 5 Guessens Road near the Parkway, his interests had returned to those of his earlier days—mechanical inventions and spiritualism which had experienced a revival among grieving relatives of wartime fatalities.

Awarded an Order of the British Empire in 1924 and a knighthood in 1926, he was not happy. By the early 1920s, he was attending séances to communicate with his first wife. In 1923, Cora Richmond died. Whether the two had contact in the preceding years is not known. In his last years, however, he often referred to her teachings and their importance to him in conversation with friends.

In late March 1925, Howard traveled to the Continent. After ten days, he sailed from Hamburg to New York. There on April 15 he was met at the pier by a reporter for the *New York Times* in search of an interview. The circumstances were quite different from his last visit in 1884. Then, he had come unrecognized and had failed to interest American manufacturers in a typewriter which was to make his fortune. Now forty years later, he headed a group of thirty prominent Englishmen attending an International City and Regional Planning Conference.

A small group of young Americans who had organized in 1923 as an informal discussion group (called the Regional Planning Association of America) eagerly awaited him. Several of the members already knew Howard from their visits to England. They now talked to him of their plans to build an American garden city for a population of twenty-five thousand on a square-mile site near New York City.[24]

From the window of his room in the newly opened Commodore Hotel on East 42nd Street, Howard watched cranes lifting into place the steel frames of sixty- to eighty-story office skyscrapers. Manhattan's midtown business district, which had mushroomed overnight after 1914, was the nonpareil instance of the metropolis whose growth he sought first to halt, then to reverse, and finally to eliminate. In the midst of a record building boom, the America of the 1920s must have recalled to Howard the optimism and big plans he heard a half century earlier. Unfortunately, he kept no account of this visit.[25]

Howard returned to a Britain lacking the prosperity he had encountered in the United States. In 1925, Winston Churchill, as chancellor of the Exchequer, returned sterling to the gold standard, which overpriced British goods on the world market. Manufacturers and exporters tried to restore their competitive position by reducing wages, and this led to industrial unrest. When the wages of coal miners were threatened in early 1926, they walked out. The recently formed Trade Union Council called for a general strike. For nine memorable days, the nation teetered on the brink of open class conflict.

A much disturbed Ebenezer Howard, while sympathetic to the workers, wrote letters to the editors of several papers and gave public speeches on the negative consequences of a general strike to the nation and the workers. The developments of 1926 must have reminded Howard and his generation of the sense of crisis caused by the serious strikes of the late 1880s. But the times were very different.

John Maynard Keynes prepared a "Yellow Book" for the Liberal party entitled *Britain's Industrial Future*. He called for far-reaching economic planning by the state through a program of public works to be financed by deficit spending. Another able economist, J. A. Hobson, produced an outline of governmental expansion for the Labour party called *Socialism in Our Time*. The welfare state no longer appeared a will-o'-the-wisp urged by hothouse intellectuals but an ineluctable evolution. Under Stanley Baldwin, the Conservative party, with the slogan of "safety first," tried more to slow and cushion than resist the welfare state's growth.

To a friend in June 1927, Howard complained of a "severe pain in my right leg which makes walking difficult and also sometimes prevents my concentrating my efforts." Sensing his end, Howard spoke to his old friends about his belief in humanity's goodness and his faith in progress. To one, an agnostic, he said, "Whatever you may say . . . we shall meet again hereafter." On May 1, 1928, Howard, to use the phrase he preferred, "passed over." His life had begun a year before Prince Albert's Great Exhibition of 1851 and had lasted into the decade of the radio and the talking movie.

Howard's death had little impact on his movement, for it long had had a life of its own. His final legacy was the need to concentrate on building Welwyn Garden City, but this was not enough. To be significant, the movement needed to influence governmental policy, and for this, the example of Welwyn Garden City alone would not suffice. Actions to propagandize the idea of decentralizing population into planned communities were required. An economic crisis provided the context for such a campaign.

The American depression enfeebled the world economy throughout the 1930s. Unemployment in Britain was concentrated in areas of Wales, Scotland, and the north of England, which relied on staple industries of the nineteenth century—coal, textiles, and shipbuilding. London and the south were much less affected. There, companies had sprung up in the 1920s around the newer technologies of electricity, automobiles, radios, chemicals, and prepared foods.

The regional nature of the distress was evidenced by unemployment statistics in the southeast of England, which stood at 14 percent in 1932 and a little over 6 percent in 1937. Comparative figures for Wales were 36.5 percent and 20 percent. This regional disparity encouraged the migration of population toward the Home Counties. London and southeast England along with the west Midlands gained a million and a quarter new inhabitants between 1931 and 1938 at the expense of the older industrial regions.[26]

The existence of areas of grave economic misery, powerfully described in such novels as George Orwell's *Road to Wigan Pier* (1937), provided impetus to consideration of some effort by government to revive employment in "distressed regions." Prime Minister Neville Chamberlain in 1937 appointed a royal commission to be chaired by Sir Montague Barlow. Extensive hearings were held over the next three years.

This commission occasioned the revival of the Garden Cities and Town Planning Association under the leadership of Frederic J. Osborn, the junior member of the New Townsmen. For the next thirty or more years, Osborn orchestrated the association's efforts to influence governmental planning policy.

Osborn determined to rescue Howard's ideas from neglect. While interested in influencing public opinion, he was even more concerned with reaching individuals of power and influence, no matter their party or ideology. An ambitious man, Osborn, unlike others who used the G.C.T.P. primarily as a stepping-stone in their careers, saw the movement as the way to advance himself on the national scene while engaging in a battle for a cause he never doubted. Highly energetic, talented as a writer and a speaker, personable, shrewd, and self-promoting, Osborn deliberately assumed the mantle of Howard's successor.

He, too, presented himself as the exemplar of common sense and the simple desires of the ordinary Englishman. As Howard had battled the landlord and speculator, Osborn projected himself as the opponent of vested interests, bureaucrats, insensitive politicians, and woolly-headed intellectuals. But, while Howard looked to self-help and voluntarism as the means to achieve his ends, Osborn strove for state promotion of decentralization through garden cities.[27]

Osborn and Howard were very different types and would have been so even if they had belonged to the same generation. There was nothing of the dreamer in the younger man who made no claims to any originality of thought. Still, some differences between the two can be attributed to the fact that Osborn was born thirty-five years after Howard.

As Walter Lippmann has observed, most men have central conflicts running through their lives. For Howard, it was reconciling religion and science, his personal ambitions and his need to be the instrument of a higher social purpose. These were very much Victorian preoccupations, and Osborn was free of them. An agnostic since his youth, he did not accept any vision of evolutionary progress or the need for a spiritual faith of any kind. For these, he substituted a modern skepticism, which still left room for hope. Modern man, he believed, had to adapt to the world as it was while rationally planning a better tomorrow. Osborn's view "that a vivid and happy life is its own justification and completion" doubtless would have startled the Victorian Howard and still retains a contemporary ring to the modern ear.[28]

His central conflict was highly personal—to overcome a severe sense of inferiority due to a harelip not cosmetically corrected until his middle years. He also suffered from a sense of disadvantage because of his lower-middle-class origins and lack of formal education and professional credentials. To overcome these disadvantages, Osborn double-timed through life, promoting the movement—and in so doing, his own claim to distinction and a place in history. In the process, Osborn sought to define Howard and his ideas. Above all, he wished to eliminate any trace of fuzzy or utopian thinking from a movement he virtually regarded as an extension of himself. Osborn was to become not a planner but the single-minded advocate of the need for governmental planning along garden-city lines—and by this he did not mean planned suburban estates but garden cities.

From 1920 to 1936, Osborn served as secretary to the Welwyn Garden City Ltd. and also acted as its estate manager. In addition, he was part-time clerk to the local Urban Council from 1921 to 1930 and the treasurer of the Town and Country Planning Summer School, which he began with Thomas Adams in 1933. All of these were responsible positions, but certainly not of the first order or of great influence. His opportunity to emerge from the shadow of others occurred in 1936 at age fifty-one. Then he lost his position with the company and found employment with the highly successful Murphy Radio Corporation of Welwyn Garden City. The owner was a friend, and there was an understanding that Osborn would enjoy considerable free time.

He now became honorary secretary of the G.C.T.P. The organization, in the absence of effective leadership, had long been moribund. Osborn quickly returned it to health. Gilbert McAllistair, a future M.P., was hired as secretary, and Osborn provided a new program in the form of a memorandum. The Executive was won over to Osborn's view that the association's primary goal must be "the municipal or State promotion of satellite towns or garden cities and the control of the size and development of towns by statutory planning machinery. . . . "[29]

Now he sought to persuade others. To do this, Osborn tranformed the association into a modern pressure group or planning lobby. From its London office, Osborn and McAllistair issued a steady flow of pamphlets and reports; letters went out to the press and government officials. Osborn wanted to convey not only the urgency of his message but also the formidable forces at his command. To achieve this, he attempted to fashion a coalition of environmentally minded groups.[30]

Osborn's principal concern initially was to influence the outcome of the Barlow Commisssion. Its report appeared as bombs rained down on London and children jammed railway stations awaiting evacuation during the summer of 1940. The distressing vulnerability of the metropolis to the vicissitudes of modern aerial warfare strengthened the hands of those arguing for population decentralization. The outbreak of war, however, meant that Osborn needed to rethink his strategy, although his goals remained constant.

Though the Barlow Report referred to garden cities and satellite towns as a desirable means of population dispersal, Osborn was dissatisfied. He had wanted the report to recommend the enactment of new-town legislation. Concealing his chagrin, however, Osborn determined on two courses of action. The first was to argue that the report represented a major commitment by government to a postwar planning policy. The second was to hail the report as an impressive victory for his movement and its influence. In effect, Osborn sought to co-opt the report for his own cause, a strategy he used repeatedly with future governmental commissions. In 1940, though, government had more pressing concerns than postwar planning.[31]

10

The International Movement, 1900–1940

In all Civilization the "modern" city assumes a more uniform type. Go where we may there are Berlin, London, and New York.

Oswald Spengler
(*The Decline of the West,* 1918)

1900–1918

Howard believed the Garden City's appeal universal. "To solve the great problem of the city for England," he wrote in 1901, "is to solve it for all of Europe, America, Asia, and Africa." Many outside England heard his message, but its ambiguity left much room for misunderstanding.

The Garden City movement abroad attracted diverse groups and types. Prominent among early supporters were enthusiasts interested in the Garden City concept as a middle path between state socialism and unbridled individualism, as well as Anglophiles entranced by visions of tasteful cottages in picturesque English settings. Urban critics found in it a comprehensive means to lessen congestion, while those desiring a more humane capitalism hoped to reconcile the classes by way of model industrial villages and tenent co-partnership.

The confusion in purpose and focus characteristic of the English movement appeared elsewhere. The Garden City movement spoke to a very generalized apprehension provoked by the proliferation of great cities in Western civilization and the very real problems of health and housing this posed. National cultures and attitudes toward the city, however, differed greatly. In time, these differences profoundly shaped each country's Garden City movement.

Searching for answers to perplexing problems, reformers in the period 1890–1914 traveled far and wide to learn from others. Nor was this phenomenon dependent upon individuals. It was strongly promoted by a network of reform and professional organizations and even governments. Over sixty foreign delegates attended the Bournville and Port Sunlight conferences. At the London Town Planning Congress of 1910, the American Daniel Burnham expressed the prevailing view when he asserted: "The best that any one nation can do for itself cannot be equal to that done by them all working together and interchanging their ideas."[1]

Urban concerns loomed large on the reform agenda of most Western nations. It was assumed that with rapid growth all large cities experienced similar serious problems of housing and congestion, even if details necessarily differed from city to city and country to country. As reform acquired an international context, a shared pattern of concerns stimulated a transnational discourse on urban problems. In the area of model housing, Britain was accepted as a leader among nations—the pioneer in cottage design and low-density residential layout.

Given this favorable context, the Garden City movement immediately attracted considerable attention in Europe and America. Howard's little book, revised in a second edition in 1902 under the title *Garden Cities of Tomorrow,* was published in French in 1903, in German in 1907, and in Russian in 1912. By World War I, Garden City associations existed in eleven countries, and the International Garden Cities Association had been organized.

International discussion of urban affairs flourished in an atmosphere of apparent goodwill. While it was accepted that the Garden City movement of each country would reflect national values and traditions, it was thought that these would result in relatively minor differences and mainly in the area of architectural aesthetics. Rational and well-intentioned individuals confronted with similar situations should arrive at comparable responses.

The cultural consensus that liberal reformers premised did not exist. For a few years, though, it was possible to sustain belief in cooperation, not only between classes in one nation but also between the countries of the world. Eagerly received by communitarian groups on the Continent, the Garden City movement soon moved outward to professional groups. The architecture and design layout of the Garden City movement attracted attention, as did the theme of working-class dispersal to planned suburbs. Class and ideological divisions sundered most European societies, and the Garden City movement's emphasis on social harmony through the cooperation of classes held appeal. On the Left, however, some suspected a paternalism intended to shore up capitalism.[2]

Readily evident by 1914 was the rise in intellectual and artistic circles of a self-conscious avant-garde. Committed to radical social and cultural innovation, this group encountered the hostility of those seeking the return to traditional society. Paradoxically, the Garden City movement, at least initially, appealed to both camps. Germany provided the central arena for the playing out of these conflicts.

Germany experienced urbanization and industrialization late and rapidly. Between 1870 and 1900, the percentage of Germans living in large cities spurted from 35 percent to over 60 percent. German cities soon gained the reputation as among the most crowded in Europe, with Berlin ranking only below New York in congestion among Western cities. The German Garden City Society, started in 1902, claimed over two thousand members ten years later.[3]

Two brothers, Jules and Heinrich Hart, founded the German organization. The brothers, leaders of a Berlin group that began what was known as the New Community movement, intended a communitarian experiment in "real Socialism." Soon, however, architects, municipal officials, and other professionals active in land-reform efforts took control. Many of these new recruits were admirers of Theodor Fritsch, author of an 1896 pamphlet, "The City of the Future," which in some respects resembled Howard's vision of the garden city. A periodical published by Fritsch, *The Hammer,* warned that housing conditions in large cities eroded the vitality of the German people, espoused the Garden City movement, and railed against land speculators.[4]

For understandable reasons, land reform was an important issue in Germany. According to the German Garden City Society, an urban parcel of land cost six to seven times more than a comparative section in England. In consequence, the typical city-dweller's residence within a generation had become an apartment in a barrack tenement (*Mietskaserne*). The four- or five-story tenements, in turn, were crowded on an urban block, massed around small internal courtyards. Held responsible for these conditions were speculators and landlords who allied themselves with banking interests and often influenced municipal governments.[5]

Municipal zoning powers, though greatly admired by visiting reformers, only aggravated the situation by mandating the provision of extremely wide streets in newly laid-out areas. This policy severely restricted the land available for construction, raised costs, and forced barrack tenements as the only economically feasible form of residential building.[6]

Foreigners traveling along a broad avenue and viewing the frequently handsome ornate façades of the buildings might be impressed. For those living within, there was often darkness, squalor, and crowding. The urging of changes in the zoning laws to permit varying road width according to need was a major activity of the German Garden City Society. T. C. Horsfall was told that "a large supply of narrower streets would allow for one-family homes and generally lower land values and in time rents." In addition, a quarrel was under way among planners and officials over the relative merits of curved and straight streets. This involved aesthetic as well as utilitarian concerns. Raymond Unwin's work on street layout spoke to all these issues and figured prominently in German Garden City literature.[7]

Little effort was made in Germany, or indeed elsewhere, to distinguish between the ideas of Unwin and Howard. The Garden City movement thus represented many and sometimes contradictory themes. A semblance of unity was provided by a design signature that emphasized low density as well as the collective layout of housing. A social message was also conveyed that true communities required a firm sense of place, a harmony of interests, and a balance between rural and urban.[8]

Such a message appealed both to those seeking a "Volkish" revival of "the good old days" and to others looking for a new "progressive" form of community to meet modern needs. These sentiments, of course, also existed in other nations. But in Germany they increasingly polarized, while elsewhere they often blurred. One student of the German Garden City movement has viewed its significance as a notable example of a "centrist approach" based on the model of English reform. Germany, however, lacked a politically strong middle class. Moreover the highly regarded German civil servants "identified themselves with the military and aristocracy" rather than with the middle class or the population as a whole.[9]

Despite the Garden City movement's apparent success, Germany did not offer a political or social soil conducive to nurturing the movement's ethos as contrasted to its technical offerings. In this latter regard, German municipalities possessed the authority to control suburban growth. Planning (*Städtebau*) did not have to fight for acceptance in Germany. Municipalities purchased land at the city's periphery for future needs and imposed plans of development. Some erected municipal housing or subsidized limited dividend companies that erected workers' homes. Interest in lessening central-city congestion was widespread. The question remained how this ought to be done, and here the Garden City movement championed single-family and low-density housing.

The German Garden City Society also advocated cooperative housing schemes modeled on the British example of tenant co-partnership. At least a dozen model community schemes became identified with the Garden City movement. The accuracy of this designation for several of these is doubtful. Margaretenhöhe outside of Essen, for example, was started in 1906 by the Krupp Trust. It was a later attempt among several model industrial towns built by the Krupps over a fifth-year period. While Margaretenhöhe significantly differed from the earlier Krupp communities, this may be explained by factors other than the Garden City movement's influence. Indeed its planner, Georg Metzendorf, preferred: "the straight street [as] the natural and best way of layout."[10]

The connection of the best-known German "garden suburb," Hellerau, with the English movement and the Arts and Crafts tradition is indisputable. When four years old, in 1913, it contained a population of eight hundred artists, craft workers, and intellectuals. Very near Dresden, Hellerau attracted attention not only as a planned community but also as the site of a notable experiment in progressive education, Jacques-Delcroze's School for Harmony. In addition, a score of workshops were devoted to high-quality crafts production.

When the American author Upton Sinclair visited experimental European communities in 1913, he found Letchworth disappointingly dull. The residents of Hellerau, however, who included the philosopher Martin Buber, fascinated Sinclair as an intellectual avant-garde. One of several architects involved in Hellerau was Hermann Muthesius. In the years 1900 to 1902, Muthesius served with the German embassy in London as a cultural attaché assigned to report on British housing. On returning home, he published a profusely illustrated three-volume work, *Das Englische Haus* (1904), which was a paean of praise for traditional English cottage housing and the architects seeking its revival. Muthesius's design of English-style cottages at Hellerau earned him in Germany the sobriquet "Garden City architect."[11]

By 1911, the German Garden City Society was torn by a squabble, which contained sharp ideological overtones, over aesthetics. The majority headed by Hans Kampffmeyer, the society's secretary, thought Garden City communities should use a German vernacular architecture and town design which relied on the medieval crooked streets, half-timbered houses, and the steep, gabled roofs traditionally identified with German village life.[12]

Another group derided the antiquarian as romantic and insisted on a starkly rational approach to town planning and architecture. They wanted an architecture and planning that assisted in reforming German society by rejecting and breaking with the past. Design, according to the modernists, must embrace and utilize the newest industrial technology. Retaining the Arts and Crafts ideal of the integrity of Art and Life, they substituted for craft utility an aesthetic vision of mechanization which sought to exploit new materials and means of construction fully.

By 1914, the German Garden City movement had lost its appeal to young architects. One of those responding to a new call was Walter Gropius. A young Gropius had admired Morris and the English Arts and Crafts move-

ment as an aesthetic revolt against industrial capitalism, and had briefly
worked with Hermann Muthesius. Then he moved off in an avant-garde
direction which soon led to the Bauhaus and a perspective antithetical to
the Garden City approach to planning.[13]

Charles Gide was the first and almost only well-known Frenchman to
advocate Howard's cause. An upper-middle-class Protestant and uncle of the
novelist, Gide was a professor of social economics at the University of Paris.
Rejecting the inevitability of class conflict, Gide's social philosophy espoused
forms of "mutualism" or cooperation, including labor co-partnership, earning him the enmity of both the conservative right and the Marxist left.

Gide's scholarship reflected his sympathies. He authored a study of
nineteenth-century cooperative communities and a biography of Fourier. It
was the Garden City movement's promise of reform through moderation,
cooperation, and community which appealed to Gide, not its design principles. To Gide, "class war has no place in the co-operative program for the
obvious reason that the consumer does not represent any class."[14]

Gide's former student, George Benoît-Lévy, organized the French Garden Cities Association in 1903. An unemployed lawyer, Benoît-Lévy busily
promoted the organization. An ambitious man, he wrote highly unreliable
reports on his activity, which he forwarded with frequency to Britain for
publication in the Garden City movement's journal. In 1907, Gide and
Benoît-Lévy fell under the influence of still another English current. A
Captain J. W. Petavel, variously identified at the time as an engineer or
economist, wrote a series of articles urging a plan to decentralize London
by channeling its growth axially along the main intercity highways for a
distance of fifty miles from city center. Petavel based his scheme on ideas
developed twenty-five years earlier by the Spaniard Arturo Soria y Mata
(1844–1920) who created near Madrid a new community developed on a
linear pattern along streetcar lines.[15]

Benoît-Lévy soon merged the planning principles of the Spaniard with
Howard's and renamed his organization the French Garden and Linear
Cities Association, overlooking the clear antithesis of the two concepts.
Indeed, in the 1930s linear-city schemes appealed to many, especially in the
U.S.S.R., who rejected the concentric Garden City concept and sought a
radically different design for a twentieth-century city reconstituted around
modern transportation technology.[16]

In general, however, the French resisted the low density and open planning promoted by the British Garden City movement. Suburban communities on the English model held little appeal to Parisians who prided themselves on urban grandeur and the café life of their boulevards. In 1913,
French architects interested in urban design organized the Société Fran-
çaise des Architectes Urbanistes. This group was influenced strongly by the

young Lyonnais architect, Tony Garnier, who by then had developed the plans of an ideal industrial town starkly "modern" in conception and design and based on high density. For over a half century more, Benoît-Lévy irrelevantly plodded on.[17]

In 1909, a small party of some thirty Russians toured Letchworth and other English "garden-city communities." One of them, Alexander Block, a well-connected member of the Duma or Russian Parliament, translated and published in 1911 a Russian edition of *Garden Cities of To-morrow.* Block then requested a charter to allow the organization of a Russian garden-city society. A reluctant government waited until 1913 before consenting—also allowing the organization of a small Polish organization.[18]

In the years before World War I, Russia remained a backward nation only slowly experiencing modernization. From 1812 to 1907, the percentage of the population living in cities rose from 4.4 percent to 15 percent. Urban growth, moreover, was concentrated in a few large cities. The populations of Moscow and Saint Petersburg almost tripled after 1870. The urbanization that did occur in a still overwhelmingly peasant society exacerbated a growing sense of distortion and frustration among the educated. An inefficient state bureaucracy sought to retain power by directing change and controlling Western influence.

Centered in Saint Petersburg, Howard's Russian organization drew its membership from the capital's professional class. Though its charter required it to stand "outside parties," most of the membership came from the Social Revolutionary party, which, despite its name, was far from radical. The party urged the use of traditional Russian values in reconstructing society. A tract published by the Russian Garden City Society in 1913, *Socialism Without Politics: Garden Cities of the Future and Present,* advocated a nonrevolutionary path to socialism based on municipal land acquisition and housing schemes built by the cooperative movement aided by enlightened capitalists. The organization praised the traditional cottage housing of the Russian village and insisted that wood constituted the preferred building material for housing in Russia.

The influential architectural journal *Goradskol Delo* vigorously promoted efforts at "Garden City ventures." Among these was the Kaiserwald suburb of Riga. Occupied by middle-class Germans, it presented the remarkable sight of an English-appearing community whose residents spoke German while living in Latvia under Russian rule. More important, however, was Prozorvskaia near Moscow.

Erected by the Moscow-Kazan Railroad as a model community for its workers, Prozorvskaia was planned by Vladimir Semionov, a civil engineer who remained a leading Soviet planner until his death in 1960. Semionov had met Howard and Unwin in 1909 during a lengthy stay in England, and at Prozorvskaia he combined Unwin's principles of street planning with traditional wooden cottage housing.[19]

Hailed widely as a success, Prozorvskaia catalyzed interest in garden sub-urbs. In 1914, the Moscow City Council considered several schemes for worker housing on municipal land, while the prestigious Moscow Architec-tural Society sponsored a competition for the design of a garden city (in Howard's sense of the term) to be built near Ostankina.

The Russian Garden City movement's message survived the revolution, though the society disbanded in 1916. A strong Garden City influence was present in planning proposals for several years after the Bolsheviks as-sumed power in November 1918. A new Russian association even started in 1922 under governmental auspices. By then, however, the official position was moving to the view that housing and planning in the new Soviet state must lead to a "socialist way of life." In this regard, the Garden City move-ment was soon found wanting.[20]

In 1924, a leading architect, Moisei Ginzburg, dismissed "the sentimental cottages of the garden city" as contrary to socialist ideals. Moreover, he maintained that cottage housing did not permit an efficient use of modern construction technology. In 1928, the second Russian association was termi-nated as a "bourgeois relic." The entry on garden cities in the *Great Soviet Encyclopedia* of 1932 stated: "All of Howard's reasoning is that of a petit-bourgeois intellectual and has a purely idealistic character."[21]

In the years before World War I, small garden-city societies appeared in Italy, Spain, Holland, and Austria. According to the British association, its London office in 1912 received many inquiries from other nations (includ-ing Ottoman Palestine, the Dutch East Indies, and Japan) for information and assistance. Consideration was now given to an international organiza-tion to be headquartered in London. Howard was eager for this effort as a contribution to international cooperation. Speaking before the Eighth In-ternational Esperanto Congress held at Cracow in Russian Poland in the summer of 1912, he announced the new International Garden Cities Asso-ciation. Hailing this announcement was D. de Clerq, the president of both the Dutch Garden City and the Dutch Vegetarian leagues and a vice presi-dent of the Esperanto Society, who soon after established an Arts and Crafts community near The Hague.[22]

The International Garden Cities Association was formally launched on August 22, 1913. On this occasion, consideration was given to the new organization's purpose, with delegates from seventeen countries debating two very different proposals. One urged the new organization to devote itself exclusively to advancing the Garden City approach to town planning. The other was for a much broader mandate encompassing "the promotion of social and civic science covering the whole scope of municipal organization and activities and general social and economic problems."

Proponents of this latter proposal had circulated a memorandum beforehand, and a heated discussion ensued. Speaking against it, Adolph Otto of Germany stated that the Garden City point of view was distinctive and should not be confused with a general interest in improving housing or cities. He noted that many in Germany advocated planning methods contrary to Garden City principles, "and these differences were growing not narrowing." On a vote, the advocates of the Garden City case won, with Howard elected the new organization's president. In the next year, little was done aside from the holding of a congress in July 1914; the delegates returned home to learn war had been declared.[23]

The discussions of August 1913 underscore the difficulty of assessing the international influence of the Garden City movement in the years 1900 to 1914. Interest in the movement was strengthened greatly by the fact that it was without rival as a leader in the area of community design and town planning. Simply as a progressive and novel development, it attracted many who were indifferent to the specific contents of its message. Employers of housing companies and municipalities often joined the movement because it represented a professional affiliation in a new field.

In general, the Garden City movement outside of Britain benefited greatly from widespread admiration among the educated classes for the English Arts and Crafts movement and British leadership in the field of housing reform. Even before 1914, however, it is evident that some younger Continental architects had a very different view of housing and planning which emphasized the effective utilization of modern technology. On the very eve of war, the Italian Futurist architect Antonia Sant' Elia wrote of the need to "invent and rebuild ex novo the modern city . . . active, mobile and everywhere dynamic." Sigfried Giedion has observed that the experiences of the war only encouraged the view that architects, as an elite group, needed to unshackle their imaginations and project a very different and better world.[24]

On the Continent, even more than in England, the Garden City movement became identified with the cooperative movement. The Dutch society reported in 1907 a membership drawn primarily from "co-operators." In this regard, it is important to note that throughout Europe, with the exception of Belgium, a sharp division existed between the cooperative movement, generally regarded as middle-class in appeal, and workers' organizations and parties. The latter had gravitated toward the Left and Marxism.[25]

The Garden City movement came to be regarded with suspicion by workers as paternalistically oriented. Its encouragement of model industrial

housing and advocacy of reconciliation of capital and labor reinforced this
view. In Germany, many on the Left envisioned creating a workers'
counter-society, including worker communities, in opposition to bourgeois
culture. A hardening attitude of hostility expressed in revolutionary rhetoric left little room for movements of class reconciliation.[26]

1919–1923

In 1919, however, the future still looked bright for the Garden City movement. Even before the war's end, efforts were under way to revive the
International Garden Cities Association. Homes had not been constructed
for four years on the Continent, and broad swaths of northern and eastern
Europe had been devastated in the fighting. All of this created the need for
much activity once peace came. As the only world organization in the increasingly important areas of housing and planning, the International Garden Cities Association anticipated shaping postwar development along Garden City principles.

The postwar housing shortage and rising building costs promoted the
view that housing conditions were matters of general concern requiring
state intervention. The industrialized nations of Europe quickly accepted
this responsibility. Formerly the concern mainly of middle-class reformers,
environmental issues entered the stormy realms of politics and ideology to
a degree unknown before 1914.

Older arguments between "minimalists," concerned with inexpensive
sanitary shelter for the poor, and "maximalists," seeking higher housing
standards for the average family, continued in more varied and complicated guises. Amateur reformers now tended to leave direct involvement in
housing and planning to those who viewed themselves as professionals. On
the other hand, working-class parties and the Marxist Left became increasingly interested. It was apparent that government and its resources represented the critical levers of any significant policies or programs.

In 1919, the new Weimar Republic required all large German cities to
create housing agencies. France, Austria, and Belgium enacted similar laws
the following year. State intervention was exercised in two ways. Public
bodies directly built and managed housing estates or governmental credit
and other concessions were offered to nonprofit building societies. In time,
the latter approach lost favor. Economic circumstances and ideological drift
supported an increasingly active and direct state role in the 1930s.[27]

With the state as principal client and often employer, those working in
the field of housing and planning gained acceptance as professionals or
technicians. Enlisted into their ranks were thousands of civil servants and
employees of housing societies. Although some universities offered degrees

and specialized curricula to impart skills, no real consensus on the nature of training and professional preparation appeared possible because of the diverse and inchoate nature of the two areas. Instead, a new class of bureaucratically oriented technicians emerged, accustomed to contact with political and administrative authorities and attuned to the demands of collaborative or team effort. Outside their ranks remained the occasional architect, a Corbusier or a Frank Lloyd Wright, who insisted on an approach to planning as an exercise in creative genius.[28]

Professionals in housing and planning were trained for the most part as civil engineers, lawyers, architects, and surveyors, or had backgrounds in public administration, accounting or economics. What all shared was the conviction that housing reform and planning represented the forefront of an effort to shape a more rational environment. Also present was the conviction that the correct housing policy required reliance on large-scale building operations utilizing a comprehensive and systematic approach to design, construction, and management. In brief, they sought instead an order, largely of their own making, for the traditional private housing market. Although recognizing that ultimate decision making remained in the hands of political leaders, they hoped that their technical expertise provided the means for a decisive influence.[29]

The postwar International Garden Cities Association straddled a dual role. Intended primarily as a propaganda body for garden-city planning, it also served as the conduit for the exchange of ideas and experiences among housing and planning professionals throughout the world. Perceived as complementary, in time these roles conflicted. By the mid-1920s, the international organization had edged away from propaganda in an effort to widen its membership.

In July 1919, three hundred fifty delegates assembled in London's Olympia Hall for the first postwar congress of the International Garden Cities Association. A small exhibit and most of the papers delivered concerned the reconstruction of war-torn Belgium along garden-city lines. Reelected president, Ebenezer Howard called for an international effort to finance privately a Belgian garden city. Such a gesture, he suggested, would serve as a symbol of international reconciliation and provide a model for Continental planning. Little action resulted from his proposal. The international organization needed to husband its meager resources simply to stay alive.[30]

For financial reasons, the 1920 congress was postponed. Nevertheless, an office was opened in London, and the librarian of the British Garden Cities and Town Planning Association, Henry Chapman, was appointed the international organization's full-time paid secretary. In his thirties and a friend of Purdom, Chapman held few fixed convictions in housing and planning matters. His time was largely spent preparing for the annual congresses, which soon became the organization's principal activity. Within a few years, Chapman was perceived by members from the Continent as an unwelcome instance of British domination of an international organization. They demanded Chapman's resignation and the removal of the organization's office to the Continent. The Germans in particular regarded the English as too casual toward systematic research on construction techniques and housing design.[31]

In the summer of 1922, the organization renamed itself the International Garden Cities and Town Planning Federation—the first of several such changes. This action was prompted by the decision that the organization be comprised of affiliated housing and planning groups, though individuals could still apply directly for membership. At the same time, the purpose of the organization was reconsidered and agreed upon. It was to promote "Garden City principles" as adapted to varying national circumstances.[32]

Raymond Unwin delivered the keynote address at the annual convention in October 1922. Twelve hundred delegates were present from most major Western nations, Japan, and colonial administrations throughout the world. However, Unwin addressed a problem—the automobile and suburban sprawl—which only a handful of countries (notably the United States, Britain, and Canada) were then experiencing.[33]

Here Unwin emphasized the need for metropolitan and regional planning based on "Garden City principles." Once again, as with his design of the garden city, he grafted his own thoughts on the ideas of Howard until the two were inextricably linked. He did this by using Howard's concept of "social cities" as the basis for planned metropolitan growth.

In *To-morrow*, Howard presented his notion of "social cities" as the means by which the first garden city would lead to a complementary network of garden cities allowing for individual specialization and mutual support. As such, Howard's concept of "social cities" represented an extension of communitarian thinking—how to transform an existing society by means of the multiplication of a new form of experimental communities. In his conceptualization of this process, however, Howard had been highly original and provocative. Particularly important was his suggestion that once the population of a garden city reached a desirable minimum, the next would be created "some little distance beyond [the first's] zone of 'country,' so that the new town may have a zone of country of its own." Lewis Mumford believed that the idea of channeling urban growth into confederated communities represented Howard's most important contribution to town planning.[34]

Following his discussion of "social cities," Howard, in the next chapter of *To-morrow*, discussed how the multiplication of garden cities led in time to the scaling down of London's population as migration occurred into the new towns. At least explicitly, Howard did not connect his concept of "social cities" with a strategy for transforming London and its environs through a system or network of surrounding planned communities. In Howard's presentation, then, "social cities" were constructs of entirely new communities.

With the enthusiasm for the suburb and interest in planned urban growth that emerged after 1904, Howard, Unwin, and others sought to make the Garden City movement relevant to these developments. *Nothing Gained by Overcrowding* (1912) noted that Howard's scheme of "social cities" must be regarded as a "constituent part of the Garden City movement because of its applicability to existing towns." Rather than allowing large existing cities to spread further and further from their original center, growth should be channeled into subsidiary centers, firmly linked to the main center. In 1912, Unwin called this approach "federated town development," but in a few years he referred to it as metropolitan or regional planning along garden-city lines.

As early as the spring of 1912, Unwin became involved with the London Society, a small group interested in thinking through a plan for London and its region which focused on the provision of open and recreational areas as related to transportation systems. By now, the English planners were well aware of the American "comprehensive" approach to city planning. Relying heavily on the American example, Unwin's group published in 1921 a thin volume of exploratory essays entitled *London of the Future*.

Unwin's contribution, "Some Thoughts on the Development of London," was concerned with urban decentralization as expressed in spatial organization. He proposed an encircling greenbelt around the capital to limit its expansion with further development to occur through the creation of satellite towns beyond that belt. The planner's principal concern was to establish the correct relationship between the parts and the whole—satellite towns, central city, and metropolitan region. This required a "maintenance of proportion between urban areas as units of design or pattern and open land as frames and background." Among the factors to be considered by the planner were the distance between the parts, time required to commute between them, and population size and character of each area.[35]

In the 1920s, Unwin further developed his ideas on metropolitan decentralization, presenting them to several annual congresses of the International Garden City and Town Planning Federation. Metropolitan and regional planning were of considerable interest, and Unwin's prestige guaranteed a wide hearing. As the most influential planner identified with the Garden City movement, Unwin's efforts to interpret Howard's ideas were once again critically important. After the latter's death in 1928 Unwin replaced him as the president of the international organization until 1931.

Unwin's thinking on metropolitan planning soon advanced beyond his original spatial design concepts. He became particularly interested in the

linkage between central city and satellite towns in the allocation and organization of services. Unwin assumed that the central city must provide highly
specialized services—such as universities, great museums, and research
libraries—and also act as the center for the administration of the various
services to be distributed among the satellite towns. Still, he wanted the
satellite towns on their own to provide a rich range of services and opportunities. The problem was that sophisticated services depended upon a population's size and character. Increasing the population of satellite towns allowed for more specialized services but risked losing intimacy and social
cohesiveness.

The key to planning was the establishment of the right relationship between the part and whole in all aspects of metropolitan organization. Unwin
called this balanced relationship "proportion." The planner had to promote economic efficiency while seeking cooperation among communities to
facilitate convenience, culture, diversity, and individual opportunity. As
much as possible, the satellite town had to be made self-sufficient and the
metropolitan region decentralized in population, services, wealth, and political power. Without planned metropolitan decentralization, Unwin argued, urban growth only exacerbated congestion, confusion, and social
conflict.

Unwin grappled in the 1920s with the problem of a comprehensive Garden City approach to all aspects of modern planning. To Unwin, "Garden
City principles" were now applicable in a variety of ways: for residential
layout; for the planning of new communities of various types; and even for
redesigning existing older areas of the city. Taken together, they provided a
complete set of tools for metropolitan and regional planning. However, he
never pulled these ideas together in a single important synthesis, as he had
done earlier for his design principles. Nor did he really have much to say
about the reconstruction of existing cities except to urge the infusion of
open space and the provision of greenbelts.[36]

Unwin's ideas appealed to planners appalled by the proliferation of suburbs which occurred after World War I. The resulting strains on transportation facilities and utility systems gave many second thoughts about the
desirability of such outward thrusts, which a few decades earlier had been
eagerly anticipated. A special concern was that the extension of the suburbs, especially in the form of ribbon developments, only added to metropolitan sprawl, devastating rural beauty without fundamentally addressing
many grave problems of the city.

Regional planning as a response to metropolitan growth was the theme
of the 1923 congress of the International Garden Cities and Town Planning
Federation. One American planner, Arthur Comey of Massachusetts, challenged Unwin's ideas about funneling metropolitan growth into planned

new communities. In Comey's view, the probability of such communities being built in sufficient numbers to prove significant was small, and in any case, the results would only be "unnatural and contrived." To Comey, regional planning should focus on technical problems, such as how the city of Los Angeles had been able to draw on a vast area to provide sufficient water for the growth of the city and its environs.[37]

The 1923 congress was the last one free of serious dissension. The Dane Kai Erickson cheerfully observed that "we are city builders, town planners and the like and we find no difficulty in talking to each despite differences of nationality and sometimes politics." This was about to change. In short order, the organization became a battleground between pragmatists or realists (drawn mainly from the field of housing) and the planners in control of the federation (who the "housers" thought too theoretical). At stake was whether the international group would remain part of the Garden City movement.

An action of the 1923 meeting helped precipitate the conflict. It was decided to step up efforts at recruiting organizations and individuals whose principal interest was in housing rather than in planning. Unlike in Britain, where the Garden City movement acted to bring housing and planning together, in several countries the two fields had developed separately, maintaining different organizations. Postwar developments, however, had accented the common concerns of housing and planning. It became generally accepted that good housing involved more than the issue of shelter and a single building and required the grouping of houses into a community with planned services and amenities.

1924–1940

An approach to housing as part of a planning strategy formed the basis of what was by the late 1920s known as "Modern Housing." In a general sense, this approach expressed the values that had long prevailed in the Garden City movement: good housing required the design of neighborhoods, while town planning had to begin with attention to good housing. Such a view, though, was easier to profess than practice. While most housing people accepted it as an article of faith, they also knew that the realities of their work did not usually permit its employment. To them, the pressing problem was the need for providing a great deal of housing quickly, and they recognized that compromises on principles would often be necessary. The Garden City movement for over two decades had provided a model of what was now being called "modern housing," but it was not the only path, and doubts had developed over whether it was the best way.

In advance of the 1924 meeting, the international federation sought to attract the broadest possible attendance, "including technical and education bodies, housing societies, state and municipal governments concerned with the related areas of housing and town and country planning." To promote the federation's appeal, it played down its identification as a propaganda body for the Garden City movement.

In 1924, the organization changed its name to the International Federation of Town and Country Planning and Garden Cities. Two years later it was renamed for a final time. The name selected in 1926 was the International Federation of Housing and Town Planning (I.F.H.T.P.). Shorter and more convenient, this last title also reflected changes in the organization's sense of mission.

The purpose of the International Federation of Housing and Town Planning was succinctly given in 1926: "to function as the central organization in the international study of town planning and improved housing." Eliminated were all references to garden-city work. Identification with Howard's movement had been attenuated at the very time that alternative visions of ideal housing were coming to the fore. In late 1925, the federation absorbed the Congrès International des Habitations des Bon Marche, a leading public housing organization headquartered in Brussels. Reflecting this new orientation, almost half the papers at the 1926 congress were devoted to government-managed housing.

Moreover, most of these did not deal with so-called "garden-city-type cottage housing" or even low-density suburban layout. Their principal concern was with inner-city multi-story housing compounds. In part, this was due to the fact that the 1926 meeting occurred in a city, Vienna, where the long discredited model barrack tenements for the working class were being rehabilitated in the context of an experiment in municipal socialism.

After the dismemberment of the Austro-Hungarian Empire in 1919, Vienna had absorbed a massive influx of displaced nationalities. Confronted by an acute housing shortage, the socialist-controlled municipal government erected nearly seventy thousand units between 1920 and 1934. All but a handful of these were in large blocks of flats. This housing arrangement soon acquired an ideological significance.[38]

Each block complex contained playgrounds, wading pools, nurserys, cooperative stores, and "mechanized community laundries." Innovative in design, the "Viennese Experiment" was hailed by many on the Left as the exemplar of a more efficient and cooperative ordering of community. The celebrated Karl Marx-Hof, for example, contained twelve structures ranging in height from four to nine stories that housed one thousand families and had its own theater group, newspaper, and workers' militia. When the socialists were forced from power by Dolfuss in 1934, the residents of Karl Marx-Hof fortified the compound and offered spirited resistance.

The socialist government's decision to erect block tenements originated in political as well as economic factors. While it was argued that barrack buildings represented the most economical form of construction for the working class, they were also praised as reducing the isolation of the family and encouraging community integration. From a Left-wing perspective, it was easy to deride the low-density cottage housing identified with the Garden City movement as ideologically backward and even petty bourgeois. Such a view also received support from the ideas and work of those Continental intellectuals who propounded "modernism" in the arts, including the areas of architecture and town planning.

The connection between the Garden City movement and Arts and Crafts "rusticity" by the mid-1920s appeared anachronistic. The movement's identification with a design signature and architectural iconography reflecting the tastes and values of English progressives in the period 1900 to 1914 held little attraction to those who sought a brave new world. Much of the prewar appeal of the Garden City movement had rested on its promise of a genteel, green, and picturesque alternative to urban congestion and disorder. A decade and a world war later, the Edwardian era and its aesthetics seemed distant and largely irrelevant. The various prewar strands of modern architecture by now had converged into the broadly shared qualities of the "International Style." Along with the "rationalist" approaches to technology and construction went a concern with stark geometrical and spatial character analogous to the strivings of Cubism and abstract art for an integrity through unadorned pure form. From this perspective, Unwin's picturesque was absurdly retrogressive.

The founding of the Bauhaus in 1919 catalyzed and promoted an avant-garde philosophy in all forms of design. Until its doors shut in 1933, the Bauhaus advocated the passionate embrace of the "tenets of an industrial age for the design arts." In exile, former faculty and students continued to advance its cause.[39]

A group of "avant-garde" architects in June 1928 created the Congrès Internationaux d'Architecture Moderne (C.I.A.M.). Initially interested in the design of low-cost or "minimalist" housing, the group soon broadened its purview to include town planning. At its third meeting held in Brussels in 1930, the Belgian Victor Bourgeois presented a scheme for high-density multi-story dwellings to be organized as neighborhood units in urban working-class districts. The unity between housing, architecture, and town and regional planning headed the C.I.A.M.'s agenda throughout the 1930s.[40]

Behind this interest lay the conviction that the design of ideal prototype residential structures would provide the basic building unit for planning outward from neighborhood to city to region to the nation as a whole. Such an approach was as visionary as Howard's Garden City concept. Not concerned with the distinctive fabric of community, however, it assumed a centrally organized nation rationally responsive to the needs of the masses in an industrial age. The concepts of proportion, population dispersal, and economic decentralization—the hallmarks of Garden City planning—were noticeably absent from C.I.A.M. thinking. An emphasis on modern technology and its functional expression in design replaced them. Friends and opponents alike regarded the new architecture as an expression of rapid industrialization, an appropriate symbol of the fast modern metropolis. To this way of thinking, community was only the sum of functional relationships.[41]

With such luminaries as Corbusier, Alvar Aalto, and Walter Gropius, the C.I.A.M. represented an influential elite. Their vision of a metropolis of residential towers in a parklike setting, as presented in Corbu's "Radiant City" or the starkly rectangular four- or five-story apartment complexes of Bauhaus architects, always presumed the continued growth of the city in population and spatial organization. A leading spokesman for the C.I.A.M., the Swiss architectural historian Sigfried Giedion, in his highly important *Space, Time, and Architecture* (1940) and *Mechanization Takes Command* (1948) casually dismissed Howard's Garden City Concept as nostalgia for an idyllic small community that had produced a few small unimportant experiments.[42]

The C.I.A.M. particularly attacked the cottage house as impracticable and even undesirable. Here it found allies within the ranks of municipal officials who for reasons of their own objected to low-density housing. Both the C.I.A.M. and the International Federation of Housing and Town Planning conducted studies in the 1930s on the desirability of different housing types with conclusions that, not surprisingly, differed greatly.[43]

Catherine Bauer reported in *Modern Housing* (1934) that after World War I most professionals involved in housing thought of the small single-family dwelling as the ideal. By the late 1920s, however, controversy erupted over the economic and planning merits of three types of home construction: the high-rise apartment building, the medium apartment building of from three to six stories, and the single-family homes in either row or cluster arrangements. "Modernist" architects, often Left-wing intellectuals, supported the large high rise, as did another group—municipal housing people.[44]

Many in the housing professions were employed by municipal governments. For them a major problem was slum clearance and the construction on site or nearby of low-cost housing for the displaced. With central-city land being in short supply and expensive, construction costs for rebuilding had to be kept low. For these reasons, municipal housing people regarded low-density housing as irrelevant to their professional needs. The economic crisis of the 1930s strengthened this argument.

The marriage of housing and planning in the International Federation of Housing and Town Planning experienced troubles from the start. After 1925, with a growing number of individuals involved in municipal or public housing and less working for cooperative building societies, challenges to garden-city-type planning grew. Furthermore, officers of organizations merged into the I.F.H.T.P. often resented their loss of status.[45]

In particular, the housing people from the Continent regarded planners as theoretical and unrealistic. The Germans prided themselves on their scientific and technical approach, citing the existence in their country of several governmental research centers to experiment with new building materials and construction techniques. Supported by the Dutch and the Scandinavians, they demanded in 1927 that the I.F.H.T.P. take the lead in developing a scientific approach to housing research. Dissatisfied with the response, it was decided in 1928 to form a second organization.[46]

This rival group, the International Housing Association, established offices in Frankfort with Hans Kampffmeyer, a state housing official, as secretary. Frankfort's selection appears deliberate. It possessed a rich tradition of city planning and municipal housing and remained in the forefront in these areas.

Before the war, Frankfort had enacted sweeping condemnation and eviction laws, acquiring large tracts of land for parks and housing developments. This program was revived in 1925 with the appointment of the architect Ernst May as director of municipal construction. Under May, municipal housing in Frankfort became the flagship for "die neue Sachlichkeit," as the "modernist" approach to architecture became known in Germany. May described his philosophy of housing as "an engineering approach to design suitable facilities for all the various human functions."[47]

Both Kampffmeyer and May had been previously active in the Garden City movement. Then in the mid-1920s as the English movement's influence waned, the two moved away. May had worked with Raymond Unwin in Britain. Even after coming to Frankfort in 1925, May continued to admire Unwin's ideas about the desirability of urban growth through planned new communities separated by open space, although questioning the Englishman's views on desirable density, housing type, and layout. May urged new residential communities based on five-story housing built contiguously along a straight building line and organized internally around a large u-shaped courtyard. Within a year of his arrival, May supervised the preparation of a general plan for Frankfort's expansion.

May proposed a series of rings of new communities to be built around the existing city. These rings he separated from each other and from Frankfort by broad stretches of park and cultivated field, yet all were to be joined together by a new rapid-transit system of railroads and streetcars. This conception was never realized, and only one section of the outer ring of the plan was completed before 1933, when the plan was abandoned. About five miles northwest of the city, three large residential developments were erected with nearly four thousand dwelling units. These represented May's belief in a community design that was essentially urban and not suburban, yet showing concern for nature and open space. Their architecture reflected May's enthusiasm for the crisply cubic buildings of German "modernism." In locating in Frankfort, the International Housing Association had selected a center of Continental ideas on community design which strongly challenged the former English hegemony in these matters.

The sharp decline of Garden City influence on the Continent in the late 1920s was evident in the Netherlands. The 1924 meeting of the International Federation of Housing and Planning had been held in Amsterdam. On this occasion, the Amsterdam municipal government established a committee to plan the city expansion along lines recommended by Unwin. Three years later, the committee proposed the construction of satellite towns and the laying out of greenbelts. An independent town planning office was then created to act on these recommendations. In 1929, however, the architect Carnel Van Eesteren, a critic of the plan, became planning director.

Only thirty-two at the time, Van Eesteren was the secretary of the C.I.A.M. and contributed to the *Der Stijl*, the organ of the Dutch avantgarde. Rejecting the earlier plan, Van Eesteren prepared his own, which was officially adopted in 1935. This second plan applied "modernist" principles of town planning. It stressed very compact growth with all new communities firmly tied to and dependent on the concentration of economic activities around the port area.

By the early 1930s, most Dutch planners regarded the Garden City approach to planning as creating a sprawling type of metropolitan growth where low-density suburbs were neither city nor country. Holland's scarcity of land and dependence on the bicycle for transportation required, they believed, an intense form of development utilizing multi-story dwellings. A similar decline in Garden City influence occurred in Belgium. There a number of architects had designed schemes in the 1920s for proposed garden suburbs, but at a planning competition in 1931 all leading entries were based on high-density planning.[48]

Belief in multi-story structures as the shelter for the masses provided a common ground between the "modernist" architects of the C.I.A.M. and municipal housing officials—two groups who otherwise had little in common. The latter acted from practical considerations, while the "modernists" envisioned a new urban order. For different reasons, each criticized the Garden City approach. Taken together, their attacks seriously weakened the influence of Howard's followers. Such an erosion even occurred in Britain.

During the 1920s, government in Britain favored low-density cottage housing. Then in the depressed times of the 1930s, this changed. A number of factors and various groups contributed to the redirection of policy. At the very least, though, it evidenced a collapse of the prewar consensus in housing and planning circles.

The London County Council (L.C.C.) had used the housing acts of 1919, 1923, and 1924 to fund an ambitious building program. The results soon dwarfed the very limited activity of the period before 1919. By 1930, some fifty-five thousand dwellings (with over 80 percent being in cottage-type housing) had been provided for over 250,000 Londoners. Then in response to demands from the London County Council, Parliament passed a housing act in early 1933 which encouraged slum-clearance schemes while providing additional subsidies for the construction of multi-family flat housing.[49]

In July 1933, the L.C.C. announced a program of slum clearance to involve the displacement and rehousing of 250,000 Londoners. By far the greater part of the new housing was to be flats in five-story buildings of brick construction. Among those enthusiastic about this ambitious scheme was the English chapter of the International Housing Association headed by Ewart Culpin, who, on moving from Letchworth to London, had been elected to the London County Council.

The L.C.C argued for the building of flats because of the need to relocate economically families close to their work. Frederic J. Osborn believed that the real reason was the reluctance of politicians to lose voters, taxes, and political power. Pursuing a narrow view of self-interest, they opposed cottage-housing construction since much of this would necessarily occur outside London. Osborn accused the architects of abandoning their previous support for low-density housing out of a desire to appear fashionably progressive.[50]

For a quarter of a century before World War I, architects in the Western World looked to England for guidance in the area of domestic architecture. After the turn of the century, Germany began to be regarded, at least on the Continent, as the center for an experimental new architecture. By the late 1920s, a few younger British architects acknowledged that leadership in their field had passed to Corbusier and the Bauhaus school. In 1934, Wells Coates organized the Modern Architect Research Group or "MARS" as the British affiliate of the C.I.A.M. The group was augmented by the arriving refugees from Hitlerism. Among the exiles were the architects Gropius, Mendelsohn, Breuer, Kaufman, and the architectural critic Nicholas Pevsner. Ten- or eleven-story tower construction was soon advanced as the solution to London's congestion and sprawl.

In 1940, MARS unveiled a "hypothetical" plan for the total reconstruction of London. Directed by the German refugee Arthur Korn, this scheme contained as its "backbone" a rapid-transit system running along the Thames River for a distance of twenty-five miles. Leading into this at roughly right angles were sixteen "districts," separated from each other by open spaces. Each district was intended for a population of six hundred thousand linked with its own rapid-transit system to the central core (see illustration 16). The MARS plan, with its reorganization of London into a series of high-density linear districts, proposed the complete rebuilding of existing cities along "rational" lines.[51]

According to Catherine Bauer, the C.I.A.M. regarded the Garden City movement as "anathema." She also thought that by the end of the 1930s most younger English architects and planners loathed "the very name and idea of the Garden City." They associated it with efforts at picturesque suburbs and lower-middle-class concerns with privacy, propriety, and petty domestic pleasures. In contrast, MARS stood for bold experimentation and avant-garde community building.[52]

Maxwell Fry in his *Autobiographical Sketches* conveyed MARS's contempt for Howard's movement. For ten years, until he left in 1936 to begin a short-lived partnership with Gropius, Fry was associated with Thomas Adams's architectural and planning firm. Fry considered Adams a careerist of little talent, busily trying to find work for his small firm. He found Unwin a comical figure from an earlier era with Swinburnesque flowing hair, glassy eyed, wearing a "Garden City tie," and in a "high-pitched voice always talking Garden Cities." He regarded Letchworth and Welwyn Garden City as dull suburban settings for small-minded people. For Fry and his colleagues in MARS, the Garden City movement represented a nostalgic yearning for suburban diffusion and cottage housing against their timely call for modern architecture and the reconstruction of the center city.[53]

In the late 1930s, Frederic Osborn feared that MARS had influenced the thinking of Left-wing intellectuals in the Labour party. After Unwin's death in 1940, there was no one of his stature to replace him as spokesman for the movement in Britain. Only among the older planners, men in their forties or over, did Osborn find support for a Garden City approach.

In Britain and on the Continent, the Garden City movement had lost its energy and focus by the 1930s. For many people in planning and housing it represented little more than a type of low-density cottage housing, an approach easily and often crudely imitated by the private house-building industry in its search for profits on the suburban fringe of development. The depression of the decade appeared to demonstrate the inadequacy of Garden City planning as an approach to inner-city problems. These very weaknesses removed the Garden City movement as a serious issue in the way of reconciliation between the International Federation of Housing and Town Planning and its younger rival, the International Housing Association.

Both organizations in 1931 held annual meetings at the same time in Berlin, though at different hotels. This scheduling acknowledged their overlapping membership. Efforts now began to bring about a merger. Not until 1937, however, did this occur. The Germans were determined to end English dominance first. In 1938, the I.F.H.T.P. moved its offices to Brussels and appointed a Belgain as its permanent secretary.[54]

Speaking for the English planners, George Pepler commented "we do not forget that we began with the 'Garden City' in the forefront of our title and our propaganda. We are still firmly convinced that men confined in great urban agglomerations cannot lead full, healthy and happy lives. We still believe that isolated improvement of homes, communications, workplaces, or playgrounds are ineffectual unless related to a comprehensive farsighted plan." Many who supported Pepler's views in theory scaled down their expectations in practice when professional circumstances required this.[55]

In the conflict between the Germans and English, there is no recorded reference to ideological differences. Throughout the 1930s, the I.F.H.T.P. viewed itself as a professional organization required to stand apart from politics and ideology. Yet the C.I.A.M., whose members were avowedly socialists (many in flight from their country of origin), vociferously denounced Nazi Germany and Fascist Italy.

In the tension-charged decade of the 1930s, discussions of architecture and layout were often highly ideological. For the most part, though, papers presented to the I.F.H.T.P. on the advantages of various housing types and approaches avoided ideological controversy and were couched in technical terms. In this debate, the advocates of the Garden City movement and urban decentralization were forced to fight a rearguard battle. Its foes stressed the needs of the inner city and that housing for the masses required "industrial methods" impossible in small-home construction. The dramatic decline in the birthrate during the 1930s bolstered the argument against the need for further suburban expansion. Garden-city-type planning was repeatedly criticized as promoting suburban spread. Unwin's effort during the 1920s to extend the garden-city-planning approach to encompass metropolitan development did not maintain its influence among planners in the 1930s. Even Unwin during the 1930s devoted himself largely to studying the problems of central-city commercial districts.[56]

A speaker at the annual meeting of the I.F.H.T.P. in 1938 noted that disagreements among planners led their critics to accuse them of "speaking in a confusion of tongues." Still he found reason for optimism in that all experimentation, no matter intention or design, "formed a continuous sequence . . . and established a sort of permanent collaboration between all planners." As technicians, the speaker said, planners must develop their discipline through the scientific method of controlled experiment and systematic observation. Only in this way would they earn the right to design the future.[57]

Despite their differences, planners did not lose faith in their profession and its mission. The idea of centralized state planning was in the air by the late 1930s. Total mobilization for war in the years 1940 to 1945 strengthened its momentum. During World War II, surprising attention was paid by several governments to shaping the postwar world. Yet if the stature of the planning profession benefited from the adversities of the 1930s, the Garden City movement languished.

In 1919, the Garden City movement on the Continent fell well within the mainstream of environmental reform and toward the center of the political spectrum. As such, it required an era and spirit of peaceful progress in order to flourish. This had not occurred. Within a decade of the Armistice, the prewar consensus among environmental reformers had shattered irrevocably. By the 1930s, there no longer was general agreement on the desirability of low-density housing and the "suburban impulse." Instead, a prolonged debate ensued over the proper approach to housing and planning. Ironically, as housing and planning gained acceptance as tools of government, professionals in these fields became increasingly divided over what should be done.

Even within Howard's international organization, dissension flourished, and an erosion of postwar enthusiasm for Garden City principles occurred. Much had been promised in the way of planned new communities in the 1920s. The following decade of economic crises, however, shifted attention to the central cities with their acute problems of unemployed slum dwellers and creeping urban blight. Moreover, the rise of ideological conflicts and new architectural currents identified with "modernists" altered the manner in which planners defined the ideal community. Finally, the professionalization of the fields of housing and planning contributed to conflict between "realists" and "theoreticians." This often took the form of a struggle between those essentially interested in housing and others mainly concerned with planning issues.

The one country in which the Garden City movement would not decline was the United States. Here a small group of intellectuals, gathered together in the Regional Planning Association of America, sought to bring Howard's movement to their countrymen. In the process, they brought new ideas and a fresh approach to community and regional planning.

11

The Garden City Movement in America, 1900–1941

> There can be no more worlds to be discovered, no fresh continents to offer virgin fields for new ventures.
>
> Edward Bellamy
> (Letter to the People's Party, 1893)

Developments in no other country had interested Howard as much as those in the United States. This reflected his conviction that Americans possessed the resources and inclination for bold undertakings. An American review of Howard's book in 1902 observed: "The new world has long been the nursery for experimental communities such as the one proposed by Howard."[1]

City planning in the United States, unlike in Britain, was not a direct outgrowth of either the American public-health or housing movements. Nor were the first planners professionally involved with schemes for dispersing or rehousing urban populations. American city planning "scarcely concerns itself with housing conditions," remarked Unwin in 1911, "and devotes itself to the creation of the City Beautiful."[2]

The Chicago architect Daniel Burnham advised his colleagues "to make no small plans, for they do not have the power to stir men's blood." In his own pioneer plans for San Francisco (1905) and Chicago (1909), Burnham proposed an approach to development and improvement that purported to encompass the entire city. He, however, avoided any serious concern with urban slums and refrained from recommending controls on private land use. The hallmark of early American city planning was a series of improvement plans prepared for civic organizations that lacked real social content

157

or even means for implementation. Indeed, American planners explicitly promised only greater civic beauty and more efficient municipal services. Though valuable, these hardly constituted a call for radical social reform. Adopting an expedient course, American planners largely ignored the earlier efforts of Frederick Law Olmsted and others to integrate the family into a vision of community and environment. Such concerns were left for the most part to reformers gathered around the settlement-house movement, who welcomed the message of the Garden City movement as an extension of their own interests in environmental and social innovation.[3]

The two decades between 1897 and 1917, the "Progressive era," constituted a period marked by a lively concern with social issues. A mood of reform and civic responsibility engulfed much of the urban middle class, leading to a mosaic of efforts. With the number of people in cities nearing half the national total, with immigration at high tide, and with political machines in control of many city halls, much thought was devoted to the future of urban America. American city planning was at its start conservative and limited in scope, seeking to define areas of consensus such as efficiency and aesthetics while avoiding the controversial, but there would be those who sought to broaden it into an instrument of social welfare. For this very purpose W. D. P. Bliss brought the Garden City movement to America.[4]

In the second edition of his *Encyclopedia of Social Reform* (1907), Bliss asserted that the critical issue for reformers was to "combine individualism and socialism" effectively. Bliss thought to enlist the support of enlightened captialists to bring the Garden City movement to America. He modeled his efforts closely on the British example, but with one important exception. There was no reference to community ownership of the land.

In July 1904, Bliss's close friend and colleague, Josiah Strong, addressed the first International Garden City Congress in London. Strong was then the president of the Institute of Social Services in New York. His well received *The Twentieth Century* (1898) had admonished that immigrant hoards crowded into urban slums threatened the survival of American democracy. Before his London audience, Strong extended his purview to warn that the rise of cities challenged all of Western civilization. The theme of his talk was the importance of dispersing the urban population and lessening the growth of cities. On his return home, Strong helped the English association mount a small exhibit of photos and plans at the St. Louis World's Fair of 1904.[5]

In the fall of 1905, Strong arranged for Bliss to tour Europe as a representative for the newly created Department of Commerce and Labor. His assignment was to report on unemployment-relief practices in Western

Europe. In November 1905, he met with leaders of the British Garden Cities Association and visited Letchworth.

On his return, Bliss set about organizing the American Garden City Association. He recruited civic leaders and prominent businessmen, and in January 1907, the organization was incorporated with Bliss as its secretary. Its purpose did not refer to the start of a garden city, but only to "drawing out of working-class families into villages with urban advantages." Within six months, Bliss announced that his association was involved in a dozen or so schemes to provide housing for thousands of families.[6]

The American Garden City Association did not directly engage in development. It endorsed and sought to promote schemes promising the highest standards of housing and community services. Most of the proposed schemes involved company housing in model factory towns. The theme of enlightened employers relocating their factories away from the center city and offering their workers a model environment, out of favor since the Pullman Strike of 1894, enjoyed a revival of interest in the early twentieth century.

The prestigious National Civic Federation, organized in 1900 to improve relations between management and employees, strongly endorsed the concept of model industrial housing. Among several men active in both the National Civic Federation and Bliss's American Garden City Association was the president of the Long Island Railroad, Ralph Peters. In June 1907, Peters announced his company's support for several model industrial communities to be built along the railroad's right of way.[7]

Critics complained that the American Garden City Association was being used by land promoters and speculators. Many labor leaders among others also believed that model company towns were necessarily paternalistic. Bliss, however, defended his policies. He conceded that his schemes called for outright sale of land and homes rather than community ownership but argued that American workers insisted on home ownership.[8]

Moreover, Bliss believed American skilled workers would not follow their factories out of the city if this meant an indefinite stay in the raw setting of a struggling new community. A virtually completed community needed to be guaranteed within a period of two to three years. According to Bliss, only large corporations had the means to build this rapidly, and that is why the American Garden City Association looked to big business for leadership in model community building. All of this controversy soon proved academic.

The American economy experienced a "financial panic" in late summer 1907, and the American Garden City Association fell victim. As is usual in hard times, business quickly backed away from social involvement as an unnecessary extravagance. Not until the early 1920s was another effort made to form an American Garden City organization. A disillusioned Bliss soon joined Josiah Strong in co-authoring an article calling for socialism and state intervention as the only way to achieve meaningful reform. The idea of "garden-city planning" serving as a model for industrial housing persisted (proving attractive to younger planners such as John Nolen) but was not the only or even more important expression of Howard's ideas in the United States in the period 1910 to 1920. The Garden City concept as an example of social intelligence applied to community along with other European currents in housing and planning were often cited by American social reformers as evidence of the nation's backwardness in clinging to individualism and private enterprise when collective action was required. Interest in the Garden City movement as a way of building superior communities remained strong among reformers and was fed by several sources.

A steady stream of Americans crossed the Atlantic to visit Letchworth. Americans were kept well informed of the Garden City movement in the pages of several periodicals devoted to improving urban life, notably *The American City, Charities and the Commons, The Survey,* and *Municipal Affairs.* One small magazine, Gustave Stickley's *The Craftsman,* early on adopted Howard's movement as its own.

Stickley, a celebrated furniture designer, started *The Craftsman* in 1901 to promote his Americanized version of the Arts and Crafts philosophy of William Morris. In its pages he preached the "simple life" and decried the waste and vulgarity of an industrial consumer society. Stickley advocated a restrained materialism based on possessions of utilitarian good taste in design and manufacture. Readers were urged to form consumer cooperatives, to cultivate vegetable gardens, and to manufacture furniture and clothes in order to lessen marketplace dependency. He himself started an artists' colony in New Jersey and introduced profit sharing in his workshop.[9]

To Stickley, the Garden City movement represented the potential for attractive communities comprehensively designed in terms of health and a full social life as contrasted to the haphazard layout and shoddy housing supplied by the ordinary speculative subdivider and builder. Stickley asked the American cooperative movement to provide the means for garden-city projects in order to demonstrate their superiority over competitive individualism in town building. One man who heeded Stickley's call was Jules Stein, a Chicago lawyer.

Stein was active in the United States League of Building and Loan Societies. In 1911, he visited Britain to meet with Howard. On his return, Stein led an unsuccessful effort to have the U.S. league, whose member-owned banks lent mortgage money to their small depositers, provide funds for an American garden city. The undaunted Stein, however, joined others to persuade the City Club of Chicago to sponsor a competition in 1913 to lay out a theoretical site of 180 acres along "garden-city lines." Frank Lloyd Wright was among some fifty architects who entered the contest, but the prize went to Walter Burley Griffen, who only shortly before had been commissioned to lay out the new Australian capital of Canberra. According to Gwendolyn Wright, the City Club contest was significant in confirming that progressive architects had abandoned the Victorian ideal of the "privatized" suburban home aloof from its neighbors to embrace a view of the family and its residence integrated into a concept of community. Such a shift influenced those housing reformers eager to provide the working class with environmental circumstances they deemed beneficial and helped attract a receptive audience in America for the Garden City message.[10]

A score of American schemes purportedly based on Garden City principles were built between 1910 and 1916. The most important of these was Forest Hills Gardens in New York City built in 1912. Very attractive in appearance, it was sponsored by a nonprofit foundation as an experiment in the community design of a middle-class suburb. Generating considerable publicity, these schemes conveyed to the public that an alternative to helterskelter speculative development was desirable and possible.

The Garden City movement's influence in America served to heighten an already existing interest in planned low-density residential communities at the urban periphery or beyond. Before World War I, however, little serious thought was given to the construction of a garden city in Howard's sense of the term. Among social reformers identified with housing reform, the idea of "garden suburbs" for the working class on the city's green outer rim struck a responsive chord. Though sympathetic, and by now aware of the need to rethink their activities, American city planners proved reluctant to skate the thin ice separating respectable reform from unacceptable radicalism.[11]

In May 1909, delegates to the National Conference on City Planning and Congestion assembled in Washington, D.C. A small group of New York settlement-house workers had initiated this meeting. Their leader, George Marsh, was an ardent "single taxer" who had visited Europe in 1907 to study planning practices. On his return home, Marsh had aggressively crusaded for municipal controls on land use based on German zoning laws. At the 1909 Washington conference, he battled to win the involvement of American city planners in broad-ranging welfare reforms. One delegate arrived in Washington wary of Marsh's radicalism. This was Frederick Law Olmsted, Jr., son of the pioneer landscape architect.[12]

Olmsted taught a planning course at Harvard University and recognized the need to redefine planning activity. Although eager for changes, he intended to steer his profession clear of embarrassing involvement in radical causes. To Olmsted, the importance of city planning was its use as a tool for efficient long-range municipal management rather than for the advocacy of reform nostrums. His views prevailed at the conference, with Marsh's ideas rejected as extreme (as indeed they were for the U.S.).

After a second conference in 1910, housing reformers and city planners went separate professional ways, each creating their own national organization. But their interests inevitably overlapped. American planners now acknowledged a professional concern with housing, although still perceiving their primary role to be the preparation of comprehensive city plans. These, however, they regarded in a dramatically new light. Practical concerns were assigned priority over aesthetic themes and the "City Beautiful" approach ostensibly gave way to the "City Efficient."

Spurred by Marsh's challenge, Olmsted in 1910 urged planners to establish the comprehensive city plan as a municipal undertaking instead of financing it with private-sector money and proceeding without official standing. Moreover, he radically altered its conceptualization. It was not to be approached as a static document analogous to a blueprint but as a periodically revised compendium of vital information, proposals, and projects. The best planning, he reasoned, was not "a spasmodic and dramatic thing to be done in a once-for-all manner, but . . . a continuous process of annually revised forecasting . . . to give intelligent guidance and control." Olmsted wanted to substitute an acceptance of contingency for a quest for certainty. Such a modern perspective need not preclude visionary thinking, as H. G. Wells for one demonstrated, but certainly posed formidable problems for those seeking to reason deductively from the what ought to be to the what is.[13]

Contrasts between European and American approaches to city planning were readily evident. Impressed by their transatlantic counterparts' professionalism, the English found Americans relatively indifferent to social-welfare concerns, worker housing, or population dispersal. Preoccupied with establishing their profession and making careers, American planners scrupulously avoided antagonizing the all-important business community. A planner in *The American City* in April 1914 still advised: "If you want your reform movement to succeed, get the businessmen to back it." In the "City Efficient," planners hopefully demonstrated usefulness by contributing efficiency, stability, and foresight in ways regarded as valuable by a capitalistic ethos.

Olmsted sincerely believed that the distancing of planners from reform enthusiasms was necessary for a professional or scientific detachment. His approach reflected the growth of pragmatic thinking in American academic and intellectual circles. In a *Preface to Politics* (1913), Walter Lippmann, a student of William James at Harvard, advised that the modern age required "a different order of thinking. We cannot expect to meet our problems with a few inherited ideas, uncriticized assumptions, a foggy vocabulary, and a machine philosophy." Modern social thought required a skeptical, tentative, and experimental approach. Though disdainful of visionary thinking as impractical or worse, Olmsted did not consider the possibility that any effort at planning inevitably reflected values and interests, which no methodology, no matter how "scientific," could eliminate.[14]

Differences in philosophy and interests not only separated city planners from housing reformers but also sowed dissension among housing reformers themselves. Older reformers collaborated easily with the planners and shared their conservative stance. Younger reformers dissatisfied with a "minimalist agenda" looked to the Garden City movement and other European practices to fashion a more radical program.

The dean of American housing reform was Henry Veiller, a New Yorker who had single-handedly transformed a diffuse cause of high-minded moralists into a nationally organized campaign for tenement-house codes. Veiller represented an older generation of reformers with roots in the public-health movement, who believed that governmental reform meant only regulatory proscriptions. He aimed to eliminate unsanitary structures, not transform society. The National Housing Association, which he founded in 1910, pushed localities to enact minimal standards of light, ventilation, plumbing, and safety for various housing types. As one of his followers expressed his credo: "We can not ask for those things that make life worth living, only for those that make life less terrible."[15]

There were those ready to ask for much more. The well-known economist Simon Patten urged Americans to replace the classical economist's premise of an economy of scarcity with the optimistic assumption of an economy of abundance. "We no longer live in an age of deficit and pain," he said in 1907, "but rather in an age of surplus when all things are possible if we will but keep our eyes turned toward the future and strip our intelligence for their task." Younger housing reformers in insurgency against Veiller's autocratic leadership, taking Patten's sentiments to heart, called for a "national housing ideal." Their approach went well beyond a reliance on restrictive codes to eliminate environmental evils. Calling for more and better new housing, they embraced a view of the need for large-scale architectural planning to ensure superior homes and communities for the masses.[16]

By 1914, one of Veiller's critics proposed that every American family be entitled to a house and garden at a rent equal to not more than 20 percent of their income. Veiller rebuked the tide of rising expectations as "adopting the goals which belong to the post-graduate period rather than the kindergarten stage of community development." To those who wanted to use the British Garden City movement as their model, Veillers responded that such lofty activity could only benefit "the better-paid members of the community" and not the urban masses. On another occasion he wrote, "city slums cannot by the wave of a necromancer's wand become gardens of delight." Still, when Thomas Adams and Raymond Unwin visited the U.S. in 1911, the latter reported, "the zeal of the American for the *Garden Suburb* [under-lining mine] . . . has converted our journey into something like a triumphal procession."[17]

Veiller prided himself on being a hardheaded realist, the master of the art of the possible. He expressed strong sympathy for Garden City ideals but viewed them as having very limited immediate use. In 1914, he invited Unwin and Adams to speak before the annual convention of the National Housing Association. Sometime after this, he entered into correspondence with Ebenezer Howard. The American indicated his support of the environmental objectives of the English movement but also observed that he strongly opposed the concept of collective land ownership. To Veiller, the building of garden suburbs, which was as far as he was ever prepared to go, required the private ownership of home and land and had to rely on free enterprise for their construction.[18]

As the insurgents fought for more ambitious goals, it was inevitable that they move toward acceptance of governmental involvement in providing the basis for a national housing program. By 1917, the viewpoint was already widely expressed that the United States in "clinging to a frontier tradition of self-reliance" had fallen well behind Germany and Britain in public responsibility for housing and other welfare issues. In this regard, the Garden City movement was often imprecisely employed as a metaphor for Britain's enlightened program of governmental housing and community and was contrasted to America's reliance on market forces. For young reformers in housing, the Garden City movement stood for a progressive, collective approach to a national desideratum.

As Kenneth T. Jackson, the historian of the American suburbs, has indicated in *The Crabgrass Frontier,* American and English attitudes toward city and suburb were strikingly similar. In both nations, the middle class eagerly left the city for the suburb and venerated the single-family house as the most desirable form of residence. The Garden City movement's architectural iconography and design signature encountered universal American praise and conformed to the landscape tradition of Andrew Jackson Downing and Olmsted, Sr., while also embracing the relatively new interest in weaving suburban housing into a tight fabric of community. Only in the association of the Garden City movement with "collectivist ideas" did the movement provoke criticism. On the whole, though, most Americans aware of the movement probably regarded it as did Veiller—as an impractical ideal which to become meaningful in any significant manner had to be adapted to a market economy. Certainly most American city planners viewed it this way. A few, however, did not.[19]

World War I encouraged the temporary entry of the federal government into the field of housing. To provide emergency shelter for war workers and their families, governmental agencies constructed six thousand units of housing. Several young architects, including Robert Kahn, Henry Wright, and Frederick Ackerman, eagerly seized the opportunity for involvement with large-scale site preparation and its accompanying housing. Indeed Ackerman, on assignment for the influential *Journal of the American Institute of Architects,* visited Britain in 1915 and reported enthusiastically on Letchworth and various garden suburbs.

At war's end, a nucleus of American architects allied themselves with the insurgent housing reformers in a crusade for a new approach to housing which emphasized elevating living standards. Housing to them was to be thought of in terms of community design and large-scale construction. Shrugging off criticism that their ideas were socialistic, they defended them as "the modern approach to housing and the community." In the 1920s, this small coalition would utilize the Garden City ideas to shape a small but vital movement, the Regional Planning Association of America.

The Regional Planning Association of America, 1923–1941

Initially conceived of in 1923 as the American organ of the international Garden City movement, the Regional Planning Association of America (R.P.A.A.) almost immediately evolved into something quite different. Howard and Unwin's ideas were joined to those of American social thinkers and conservationists, French geographers, and the Scottish biologist-planner Patrick Geddes to achieve a synthesis distinctive from the British movement's message. In the areas of site planning, community organization, and regional planning, the R.P.A.A. returned a sense of experimentation and vitality to garden-city planning.[20]

The R.P.A.A. origins are traceable to Charles Harris Whittaker, editor of the *Journal of the American Institute of Architects.* An ardent "single taxer," Whittaker was an interested student of European housing experiments and a partisan of the Garden City concept. He introduced many of the individuals who would be the key member of the R.P.A.A. to each other, allowed them to use his journal as a forum for their ideas, and helped gain them useful connections. Until the R.P.A.A. was founded in 1923, the patrician editor nurtured this incipient network only to drift away due to family problems.[21]

The architect Clarence Stein acted as the R.P.A.A.'s central figure. Mumford called him "The most dynamic member of the group" and its "decisive leader." Born in 1882 to well-off parents, Stein trained as an architect at Columbia University and the École des Beaux-Arts in Paris. Very much the urban aesthete, he lived for several years in Europe before returning to New York to an apprenticeship in the prominent New York office of Bertram Goodhue. In 1919, he started his own practice.[22]

During the period from 1919 to 1925, Stein served on several committees investigating housing and other urban problems. His conclusion from this experience was twofold: the first was that the high cost of housing necessitated governmental assistance for much of the population; the other, that new housing must be upgraded and integrated into a planning program based on community development and urban decentralization. These views were not uncommon. The historian Roy Lubove has written: "All progressive housing reformers endorsed the garden city program or its modifications in the early 1920s." This allegiance, however, usually represented little more than an affirmation of the desirability of lessening urban concentration through well-planned large-scale development at low density on the suburban fringe. The British example provided a rallying point. For architect-planners such as Stein and Wright, the design principles espoused by Unwin were of more professional relevance than Howard's vision.[23]

What distinguished the R.P.A.A. was its insistence on regarding housing and planning goals in terms of (to use Mumford's phrase) an "organic ideology" of the human environment. Much of its perspective derived from sources external to the Garden City movement. As a result, the American movement proved more flexible and open to new ideas than the English where Howard's ideas had been reshaped and narrowed by the "suburb salubrious" concerns of Edwardian England and Unwin's approach to design.

In addition to Stein, three men—Henry Wright, Benton MacKaye, and Lewis Mumford—contributed greatly to the R.P.A.A.'s program. Wright, an architect and Stein's partner, was in his forties. Long interested in experimental site planning, Wright was a student of Unwin's work. Like the Englishman, Wright's concern was not only for lowering costs while increasing amenities but also in clustering homes and using design arrangements to promote neighborliness and community.

Born in 1879, Benton MacKaye was Harvard educated. After college he elected for a career in the newly created U.S. Forestry Service and soon through his writings gained a name as a leading advocate of conservation. In the early 1920s, MacKaye promoted his scheme for the creation of the Appalachian Trail. At the core of the proposal was a projected wilderness path for hikers stretching two thousand miles from Maine to Georgia which he intended as the "base for a more extensive systematic development of outdoor community life."[24]

In his twenties, Mumford was the youngest member of the R.P.A.A. By preference a generalist rather than a specialist, he earned his living as a writer on cultural subjects, especially architecture, urban sociology, and literature. His first book published in 1922 was *The Story of Utopia*. His interest in this subject was the preoccupation of utopian writers with imposing a rational and integrated order on social organization and its environmental setting. From the first, his own thinking synthesized widely separated observations drawn from diverse sources in a search for a meaningful pattern.

Belief in a divine order often had inspired utopian efforts. Mumford sought its secular and humanistic counterpart, a natural order, rationally deduced from available knowledge in the fields of biology and sociology. His wide-ranging interests led him well beyond the Garden City movement in developing a philosophy of planning intended as a mode of thinking about the environment and presented as an antidote to the ailments of modern life. Howard's garden city was championed by Mumford because the idea of a cohesive balanced community limited in size accorded with the American's larger picture of a natural order that had to determine the development of civilization.

At the heart of Mumford's beliefs was his conviction that all aspects of the environment, communities and regions alike, were governed by organic rules of growth related to their function. To exceed these limits invited catastrophe. An alert and strong government needed to regulate capitalism and even in part replace it to guarantee that this natural order be heeded. The miracles of modern industrial technology must be subordinated to human needs rather than regarded solely in terms of profit. In his warnings of impending disaster unless civilization radically altered its course, Mumford projected the solemnity and tenacity of an Old Testament prophet. Yet as an admirer of John Dewey, Mumford allowed for uncertainty, a modern Jeremiah who admitted that "reality might in fact be vague, complex, undefinable, perpetually a little obscure and shifty."[25]

These four men constituted a core, with another twenty or so individuals moving in and out of the group's orbit. Started as an informal discussion group in 1923, the R.P.A.A. continued until 1933, almost as an intellectual salon. Initially, Stein intended an organization modeled after the British Garden Cities and Town Planning Association, but the others favored a less-formal arrangement. Mumford has recalled a group content with a membership determined by the number of people who fitted comfortably into Stein's Manhattan living room.[26]

Members came from the fields of economics, law, engineering, housing reform, and architecture. No effort was ever made at attracting a mass membership or at seeking the funding needed for a serious political lobby. The group's influence was expressed essentially by the activity of individual members rather than collectively or systematically. Over time, Mumford proved the group's most prominent spokesman, and his views tended to be accepted by outsiders as representative of the R.P.A.A. They have been regarded as such in this analysis even though it is readily acknowledged that the others did not always agree with him or indeed with each other, and these differences contributed in time to the group's dissolution.[27]

Despite its informality, the R.P.A.A. expected to influence public policy. To test out theory and provide examples of good community housing and planning, Stein interested the wealthy New York realtor Alexander Bing in founding the City Housing Corporation (C.H.C.), a limited dividend company to carry out experimental housing schemes along garden-city lines. Initially the hope was to build a garden suburb for twenty-five thousand on a square-mile site in the borough of Brooklyn. Instead, seventy-six acres in Queens, very near a bridge to Manhattan Island, were purchased. Here, twelve hundred homes erected in the years between 1924 and 1928 created the community of Sunnyside Gardens.

New York's rigid grid street pattern inhibited experimentation in layout at Sunnyside Gardens. Still, Stein and his partner Wright, with the aid of Frederick Ackerman, introduced novelties in construction, operation, and design. An urban façade was provided by rows of attached homes erected lengthwise along the perimeter of each block, leaving the interior of the block as a parklike open space, while garages were erected only at a few well-selected locations.

The C.H.C. soon undertook a far more ambitious scheme—Radburn in New Jersey. A site of thirteen hundred acres some fifteen miles from Manhattan was acquired to erect a true garden city. Difficulty in acquiring additional acreage forced the decision to dispense with a desired agricultural belt. Unfortunately the Depression of 1929 required an even more drastic paring down of the scheme. The idea of a garden city with industry fell, in time, by the wayside. In all, only four hundred homes for about fourteen hundred residents were completed, and Radburn became, in effect, a bedroom suburb of New York. Thus the significance of Radburn is as a brilliant example of subdivision layout by Stein and Wright. In this regard, though, its influence has been profound.[28]

Radburn was boldly promoted as a "town for the motor age." In 1925, the United States possessed over 80 percent of the world's automobiles. From the start, it was assumed that all Radburn families would own a car. A paramount goal of the plan was to minimize the impact of the automobile on the community and especially to reduce the risks to children. To solve this problem, the planners, strong admirers of Unwin's work and ideas, drew on the British experience with garden-city-type layout.[29]

Far from a mere application of English principles, Radburn represented a considerable advance in site planning. Unwin's concerns were with aesthetics and with reducing land costs. The Americans added to these a consideration of the automobile and a more conscious use of design as a sociological tool to enhance social contact. For their purposes, they invented the "superblock." Bounded by traffic streets, a superblock contained thirty to fifty acres. Small clusters of housing lined its perimeter, while much of the interior was utilized for landscaped park. A person could walk through Radburn by way of the interior parks and a system of underpasses without crossing a single street. This design was to become world famous and Radburn's hallmark.[30]

The Depression forced the City Housing Corporation to dissolve. Radburn and to a much lesser degree Sunnyside Gardens represent the R.P.A.A.'s contribution to site planning. Even here it must be noted that Radburn was depicted by its designers as but one example of good site planning. The R.P.A.A. did not intend to be trapped (as had the British movement) into any exclusive design formula. It intended variety in housing types, densities, and arrangements. While the English insisted on a home and garden layout at no more than twelve to an acre, members of the R.P.A.A. viewed this attitude as dogmatic, at times wasteful of land, and tending to require an open plan more suburban than urban.[31]

Large-scale housing schemes, and even garden cities, were viewed by the R.P.A.A.'s members only as means to an end. The ultimate goal was to create a balanced regional order as the basis for a humanistic civilization. Explication of the R.P.A.A.'s philosophy of regionalism rested on MacKaye and Mumford. This was done in a way which set the R.P.A.A. on a course apart from the American planning establishment. The R.P.A.A. presented an appealing and provocative vision which emphasized the relationship of man and his environment on one hand and family-oriented new planned communities on the other. This vision assumed existing communities might be radically reshaped, great cities dramatically shrunk and restructured, smaller communities economically redirected and vitalized. In short, the R.P.A.A. called for a crusade against the emerging metropolis with its commuting suburbs. According to mainstream planners, such a program naively ignored the finality of past development and current trends.[32]

To Mumford, most American planners worshipped at the altar of acquisitive capitalism. For this reason, the typical planner accepted ongoing metropolitan growth and suburban expansion. Indeed, according to Mumford, planners insured their professional survival by serving the needs of important vested economic interests who wanted urban growth, inflated land values, and speculation—regardless of social consequences.

As a profession, Mumford charged, planners embraced palliatives disdaining a meaningful philosophy of regional growth. They relied on zoning ordinances, although knowing this approach as the most elementary and least satisfactory form of land-use control. They called for new highways, whose purpose was to extend central-city hegemony over a region or to temporarily relieve the choking traffic congestion of the commercial downtown. Planners, Mumford exhorted, must identify with and work for positive values, those leading to the good society. This, of course, required a radical redefinition of their professional role. How this might occur never really troubled Mumford. He was too engaged in distinguishing between right and wrong paths to the future to be concerned with such detail.[33]

In contrast to "prevailing superficial standards," the R.P.A.A.'s philosophy of regional planning sought to encompass "the whole environment, including the work, the housing, the recreation, the customs and habits of the people who make up a region." The first step was to limit metropolitan expansion and suburban development which wasted resources on transit systems and expensive utilities without improving environmental standards or the circumstances of family life. Cities must be no larger than the size needed to perform effectively all of their social and economic functions.[34]

To achieve the satisfactory relationship of communities and industries to the natural environment and to cap urban growth, the R.P.A.A. proposed the creation of garden cities. In this regard, the R.P.A.A. harkened directly to Ebenezer Howard's visionary message of social reconstruction in *Tomorrow*. The Americans, however, were prepared in their thinking to venture well beyond the expectations of the British movement. Mumford complained in 1927 that in their preoccupation with Welwyn Garden City, the British were making the garden city into an "isolated objet d'art." Even Unwin's proposals to employ garden cities, satellite towns, and garden suburbs in shaping future metropolitan organization fell short of a truly regional approach and lacked a cohesive philosophy.[35]

Drawing upon a remarkably varied range of sources, MacKaye and Mumford, each in his own way, formulated compatible concepts of decentralized regionalism. The result has been aptly described as "partly romantic-poetic myth and aspiration, partly cultural revolt and partly realistic response to the possibilities and challenges of a new technology in the automobile and electric power." The two men's thinking assumed a natural ecological order as the basis for structuring a new type of urban society.[36]

As a conservationist, MacKaye objected to America's profligate waste of its rich natural resources. By World War I, the American conservationist movement had produced an impressive body of protest literature directed against the operations of mining and timbering companies who had elevated the slash-and-burn tradition of the American pioneer into a profit-driven science. But while some conservationists thought in terms of husbanding expendable resources to achieve long-term efficiency, others wanted a new socio-industrial order conforming to ecological needs. This latter was MacKaye's bent. While a student at Harvard, he had studied the writings of such American geographers and geologists as William Morris Davis and Nathan Southgate Shaler. From them, he concluded that industrialization could be controlled, though not reversed. Thus he rejected any interest in a return to subsistence farming as later expounded by Ralph Borsodi. Instead, his goal was to bring industry and civilized amenities to rural life while carefully attending the natural environment. In 1919, he drafted a proposal for government-sponsored cooperative rural-industrial colonies in sparsely settled areas of the nation. MacKaye always remained especially interested in rural-industrial communities (farming, mining, timbering). These he envisioned as organized in such a way as to provide modern advantages while also conserving resources and minimizing civilization's disruption of the natural ecology. When the Scotsman Patrick Geddes met MacKaye in 1924 and learned of his ideas, he called them "geotechnic." This term conveys MacKaye's quest for a form of middle landscape, neither rural nor urban, characterized by ecological balance.[37]

The polymath Mumford also ventured far afield for his ideas. Mumford read Patrick Geddes, the man he called "my master," at age eighteen. From Geddes, he learned of the French regionalist school of geographers led by Le Play, Duc de Broglie and Prévost-Paradol, who at the end of the nineteenth century protested their country's extreme administrative centralization as harmful to local well-being and cultural distinctiveness. The French geographers stressed the importance of provincial culture for constructively integrating the individual into society. But Patrick Geddes, not the French school, provided Mumford with his biological and sociological rationale for regionalism. Geddes's ideas were integrated into the thinking of the R.P.A.A. in a way that contrasted sharply with his relationship to the British movement.

While Geddes's emphasis on the use of a social survey as a necessary planning tool had gained ready acceptance from British planners, he himself remained distant from the profession. As early as 1904, Howard had corresponded with Geddes to express admiration for his work while inviting him to become a vice president of the Garden Cities Association. Geddes approved of the Garden City movement but proved too idiosyncratic to work within it. After 1914, moreover, Geddes spent much time in

India and then in British Palestine where he planned over fifty cities. His ideas as presented in lectures and writing were highly abstruse, and it is chiefly in Mumford's writings that they have reached a wide audience.[38]

Geddes's most important contribution to Mumford's development was in providing a historical perspective. Geddes organized the past into "ages of man" based on a civilization's technology. To the Scotsman, the nineteenth century with its industrial revolution represented the Paleotechnic Age in which "private dissipation of resources" intensified social and physical disorder: "the perils of slum and conurbation." Geddes's view of history, although not intended as technologically deterministic, certainly inclined in that direction. Writing in the early twentieth century, he celebrated the possibility of a new era, the Neotechnic, where the advent of a superior technology and cleaner sources of power in place of coal and steam allowed for correcting past abuses.

In effect, the Scotsman restated a common belief at the turn of the century that society stood poised on the threshold of a "higher civilization" based on innovative forms of social cooperation. To this, he added an emphasis on the importance of a new technology. Geddes's depiction of the "higher civilization" rested on regional confederations of limited size in a hierarchical order of mutual interdependencies expressing a unity of "place, work and folk." He assumed a critical role for the planner in bringing about a modern regionalism organized around "organic communities."[39]

In Mumford's interpretation of Geddes, the planner's role in achieving this new regionalism was in "building up of old centers, the breaking-up of congested centers, and the founding of entirely new centers to promote social life, industry, culture. . . . " However, Mumford allowed for flexibility and change. He posed no fixed rules or norms for community size or development. These would be determined by function as well as the planner's sensitivity to the desirable optimum. As an essential beginning, though, the speculative market must be deprived of its tendency to warp communities and to distort their relations.[40]

The R.P.A.A. unveiled their effort at a comprehensive approach to community and regional planning in 1925. An entire issue of the journal, *The Survey Graphic*, consisted of articles by Mumford, MacKaye, Stein, and other members of the R.P.A.A. The journal's editor initially rejected the contributions as too theoretical for a publication devoted to social problems. He was persuaded that several articles on the English garden cities were relevant, and therefore the subject of regional planning warranted the whole issue's space. If anything, though, the articles demonstrated the differences between the R.P.A.A.'s approach and that of the increasingly parochial British Garden City movement preoccupied with building the second garden city. These differences soon received expression in an open clash between Lewis Mumford and Thomas Adams. Adams had been admired by the Americans as a pioneer of Howard's ideas and had been employed as a consultant at Radburn. Now Adams's perceived inclination to yield on principles ended his connection with the R.P.A.A.[41]

Between 1914 and 1921, Thomas Adams worked in Canada for the government and as a private consultant. There he promoted a planning approach toward metropolitan expansion and the particularly Canadian need for the opening up of sparsely settled "new primary resource areas." In both Canada and the United States, he spoke often on regional planning or the cooperation of communities "in the solution of their joint engineering and utility problems." His activity in Canada brought him to the attention of the Russell Sage Foundation, which in 1921 decided on a planning study for New York City and its region. Initially hired as a consultant, Adams in 1923 was named the project's director, supervising a team of top professionals in planning, architecture, engineering, sociology, housing, economics, and other specializations. The well-financed and highly publicized plan was intended as definitive.[42]

Taking nearly a decade to complete, the Regional Plan of New York represented the most ambitious American planning effort until the New Deal. For its purposes, the New York region was defined as consisting of a forty-mile radius from Manhattan—an area that encompassed the city's five boroughs and eight counties in three states. According to Lewis Mumford, the monumental study received eager acceptance "as the last word on the subject of city planning and regional development." Indeed, New York's governor Franklin D. Roosevelt lauded the ten-volume report as opening "our eyes to new vistas of the future."

To the R.P.A.A., however, Adams's work fell appallingly short of desirable. In two articles in the *New Republic* in early 1932, Mumford registered his sharp disapproval. Above all, he faulted Adams's failure of vision. The report, Mumford charged, essentially accepted existing economic and social arrangements, thus endorsing the region's continued dependency on New York City as a reservoir of employment for an ever-widening circle of suburban buildup. To Mumford, Adams and his team erred grievously in not proposing a decentralized alternative.[43]

Adams defended his work in the same journal. The Regional Plan of New York, he pointed out, recommended realistic if limited efforts at population dispersal and economic decentralization. Among its suggestions were: (1) planned residential areas near industry, (2) "diffused recentralization of industry" through planned industrial centers throughout the region, and (3) "subcentralization" of shopping into local commercial areas to lessen consumer dependence on New York's "downtown."

Despite these recommendations, Mumford was correct. From his per-

spective, Adams's Regional Plan of New York sought only such amelioration of New York City's congestion as to permit its continued functioning
as the imperial hub of a growing metropolitan empire. For his part, Adams made his own telling point when he dismissed Mumford as an
"aesthete-sociologist" who wanted his own sense of proper order, blissfully
unaware of the complex nature of the planning process in a democratic
society.[44]

With one aspect of the report, Mumford found little fault—Clarence
Arthur Perry's highly important contribution to volume seven, "The Neighborhood Unit." Here Perry conceptualized the design of a neighborhood
oriented to family life. Key to Perry's scheme was a neighborhood planned
around a centrally located elementary school, no more than half a mile
from the furthest dwelling. Access to the school was via a special internal
street system. Through traffic was ideally deflected to thoroughfares,
which bound and clearly set off the neighborhood and around which local
shops would be gathered together at accessible points. Finally, small parks
and playgrounds were to be scattered around the residential area. The
result was to be an architecturally harmonious, safe, residential neighborhood of about twelve hundred people.[45]

Mumford believed that Perry's scheme elaborated on the concept of the
superblock independently developed at Radburn between 1927 and 1929.
Indeed, both Perry and the planners of Radburn drew on similar sources,
such as British garden-city planning. Perry's orginal contribution, however,
was in focusing the community around the elementary school. It was to act
as a neighborhood social center. Most important, the desired enrollment of
the school provided a guide to the neighborhood's size and population. By
this device, Perry offered an intellectual and design coherence to neighborhood design many viewed as previously lacking in residential planning.[46]

In conceiving the elementary school as the neighborhood centerpiece,
Perry relied on his long involvement with the American "community-center
movement," a movement spun off from the social settlement houses at the
turn of the century. Its leaders, most of whom were women, envisioned
family-oriented urban neighborhoods. Perry's "Neighborhood Unit Plan"
quickly gained popularity with planners and housing people throughout
the world. To one admirer, Perry's concept of the neighborhood unit provided "the physical basis to force associations which characterized the old
village community."

In his 1938 work, *The Culture of Cities*, Mumford observed that at various
times in history the church, the palace, the factory, and the marketplace had
each in turn provided the social nucleus for town life. In the future, he
believed, this pivotal function would be assumed by the school endowed with
attendant community facilities. Perry's neighborhood-unit concept often

was regarded as an aspect of garden-city planning, a view the Garden City movement encouraged. Despite this identification, Frederic Osborn thought the concept exaggerated. His own experiences in Welwyn Garden City were that people selected others for friendship based on shared interests and not on neighborhood propinquity. Even Osborn, however, went along with the enthusiasm by British planners for the postwar new towns to "define the urban neighborhood as the basis for an integrated community."[47]

After the election of Franklin Delano Roosevelt to the presidency in November 1932, members of the R.P.A.A. drifted apart, and within a year the group had dissolved. Several members were recruited into various New Deal agencies and projects, although none ever acquired a position of real influence. Despite the considerable prestige of the group in certain housing and planning circles, their program did not profoundly influence New Deal policies, with the possible exception of the greenbelt communities.[48]

Planners enthusiastically welcomed Roosevelt's New Deal. F.D.R.'s favorite uncle, Frederic Delano, was a businessman turned planner who had been instrumental in launching Burnham's Chicago Plan of 1909 and also the Regional Plan of New York. The uncle converted the nephew who even as a young New York State legislator from rural Hyde Park was already a friend of planning. From the point of the R.P.A.A., Roosevelt's election appeared auspicious.

The Tennessee Valley Authority announced in May 1933 promised regional planning along the comprehensive lines envisioned by the R.P.A.A. Moreover, F.D.R. was an outspoken advocate of industrial dispersal and disliked large cities. Above all, the New Deal hopefully represented a novel federal concern for social issues related to the community, environment, and planning. For the R.P.A.A., eager to replace market factors with a system of land-use planning, developments appeared encouraging.[49]

It was, however, the economic imperatives of the 1930s—deflation, high unemployment, and idle factories—as well as Roosevelt's penchant for the role of a political broker—which established the main thrust of the New Deal. The several experiments in community planning were on a relatively small scale and results inconclusive. Roosevelt, while intrigued by the idea of central planning, quickly backed away from themes which either cut across the grain of traditional American values or antagonized important economic and political groups.[50]

An illustration of the New Deal's vacillation was the Resettlement Administration's greenbelt-town program. This program was conceived by Rexford Tugwell, a Columbia University economist who became a New Deal technocrat and then the commissioner of city planning for New York. Tugwell's career was devoted to advancing the administrative state and its involvement in social engineering. In Tugwell, older radical values of a Cooperative Commonwealth received a very different framing from what had been anticipated in the 1880s.[51]

As a student, Tugwell had been profoundly influenced by Simon Patten, the most brilliant of a score of German-trained Americans who revolutionized economics around 1900. Patten firmly believed that a new era of voluntary cooperation leading to the democratic and peaceful acceptance of socialism was dawning. But Patten did not view socialism exclusively in terms of the state believing its role should be to facilitate cooperation and tolerance between groups. Tugwell shared Patten's dream of an emerging collective society but thought this required direct state intervention. He welcomed coercive regulation and involuntary regimentation, even if this engendered class tensions. Planning, for Tugwell, was a means of elevating the expert and strengthening the power of the state as prerequisite for rationally pursuing national goals.[52]

His greenbelt communities were to showcase the efficacy of state planning. He denied that the R.P.A.A. had influenced his ideas which he said reflected a personal conviction that planned suburban expansion was highly desirable. An entry in his diary is remarkable for its brevity in presenting a solution for complex urban problems and its startling resemblance to the ideas of Howard, Bellamy, and Henry Demerest Lloyd. "My idea is to go just outside centers of population, pick up cheap land, build a whole community, and entice people into it. Then go back into the cities and tear down whole slums and make parks of them."[53]

Tugwell originally envisioned fifty experimental greenbelt communities. Only three communities were, however, actually constructed: Greenbelt, Maryland, near Washington, D.C.; Greenhills, north of Cincinnatti; and Greendale, just outside Milwaukee. Stein and Wright acted as consultants for the Resettlement Administration, and the economist Stuart Chase, who also had been a member of the R.P.A.A., served for a time as an advisor to Tugwell.

The greenbelt communities were only bedroom suburbs, and their high rents restricted residency to the middle class. Despite the fact that they provided good housing in pleasant surroundings, the communities provoked savage attacks from the private real-estate industry and often local opposition as well. Hurt by charges of socialism and more valid accusations of management inefficiency, the Resettlement Administration's greenbelt program soon proved a political liability, and construction came to a halt in 1939. After the war, the federal government speedily disentangled itself from the three communities by selling off what it owned. Tugwell had moved on in 1938 to New York City. With the same enthusiasm he earlier had in seeking to dismantle cities, he now aided the ailing metropolis as chairman of its City Planning Commission until 1941.

After a decade of depression, American cities were in serious straits. The decennial census of 1940 indicated many older cities experiencing large population declines. For American communities, this was frightening news. Their sense of well-being depended on economic activity attendant to expansion and development. Accordingly, population loss was regarded as stagnation and pathology. Inner-city areas of older buildings in and around the business districts were attracting attention because of deterioration. Facing an uncertain future, developers avoided investment in and even maintenance of "downtown."[54]

Blighted commercial districts concerned realty interests, banks, department stores, and municipal officials. The National Association of Real Estate Boards (N.A.R.E.B.), aided by municipal officials, mobilized to influence Washington. A well-financed and skillfully managed lobbying effort urged a federally financed program to raze and rebuild central-city areas. It claimed that until business districts revived, billions in property values remained at risk. The N.A.R.E.B. program provided the basis for the important postwar urban redevelopment legislation of 1948. Even then, not until the mid-1950s did business confidence in central-city development return.[55]

Unlike central-city blight, which activated a powerful alliance of leading business interests and city officials, the deepening plight of slum areas in the 1930s attracted the attention mainly of the liberal and philanthropic groups long associated with the "housing question." A major victory for the housing coalition came with the United States Housing Act of 1937 which passed, however, only with the support of a construction industry eager for contracts and jobs. By 1941, nearly one hundred thousand units of federally supported public housing were built, but the program experienced political problems. Among housing reformers, moreover, a sharp disagreement existed about the nature and location of public housing. On one side were those who wanted superior low-density public housing on the urban periphery; and on the other, those interested in razing inner-city slum sites to provide for high-density development.[56]

Throughout the 1930s, many expressed the belief that the era of the "Great City" was over. America's most famous architect, Frank Lloyd Wright, in a book entitled *The Disappearing City* (1932), proposed a new form of community, Broadacre City. Here Americans would live in single-family homes on a minimum site of one acre, while relying on the automobile and advanced technology to enjoy all the benefits of an advanced civilization. No less an authority on urban and business matters than the president's uncle, Frederic Delano, believed that "the day of the larger cities has definitely passed."[57]

Anxiety about the future of the economy and the city encouraged interest in planning. Even during wartime prosperity, many anticipated that peace would bring a return to depression. Especially after the publication of John Maynard Keynes's *General Theory of Employment, Interest, and Money* (1936), a growing number of economists argued that only economic planning and expensive federal programs could sustain the economy. The area of housing was singled out as well suited for federal spending. In *Urban Redevelopment and Housing: A Plan for Post-War America* (1942), the eminent Harvard economist Alvin Hansen called for a postwar federal agency to finance a massive reconstruction of American cities on the grounds that government spending here would stimulate the economy. Among New Deal economists, a consensus developed that a vigorous restructuring of the capitalist system to allow for planning and social investment by government would forestall future depressions as well as serve the public interest.[58]

This emphasis on the state as an influence on future developments assumed an increased importance for the bureaucratic expert. Highly skilled professional planners, no matter their area, would recommend policies or programs based on technically accurate research, rather than relying on their own predilections or philosophies. Membership in the American Society of Planning Officials, an organization composed of planners employed by the government, rose from 450 in 1934 to nearly 1,200 in 1941. Clearly by this later date, planning was viewed as a technical profession. To some, at least, the position of "professional" did not proscribe a statement of values. The American Institute of Planners, smaller and less bureaucratically minded than the American Society of Planning Officials, in the late 1930s urged action to promote urban decentralization and called for "garden-city planning."[59]

The Roosevelt administration never developed a coherent policy in housing or planning. As with much else about the New Deal, actions in these areas were important mainly as a break with past aloofness, signifying a new era of federal involvement. Planning became a portmanteau concept representing a collective rationality in a modern society where human activities were closely interrelated and difficult to treat separately.

Frederic Osborn believed that the R.P.A.A.'s influence was limited because it did not develop into the effective planning lobby needed in an organized world of competing power structures. This is certainly an important insight. It overlooks, however, serious differences within the group, manifest only after it dissolved in 1933. While Stein and Mumford were highly insistent on good design standards, others lowered these to promote building public housing. Edith Elmer Wood, Catherine Bauer, and Robert Kohn threw their weight behind the passage of the United States Housing Act of 1937, even though their friends were distressed that it did not mandate public housing away from the inner city.

By the late 1930s, the ideas of the R.P.A.A. had lost influence among housing people as too theoretical and idealistic. Some regarded its advocacy of the Garden City movement as "cultism" that lauded Welwyn Garden City and overlooked the importance of slum reclamation and other more modest approaches to housing needs. Even as early as 1928, Louis Pink in *The New Day in Housing* described Garden City enthusiasts as "deserving praise for their zeal rather than for their sense." This view now gained ground. Moreover, among architects the "modernist" ideas of the Congrès International d'Architecture Moderne were winning adherents. The proposals of the R.P.A.A. were attractive in the main to design-oriented planners. These were increasingly outnumbered in the fields of housing and planning by individuals who viewed themselves as administrators of programs rather than as the makers of policy. The real significance of the R.P.A.A. was to bring fresh life to the Garden City movement in America by establishing the context of a radically comprehensive planning approach. Its manifest idealism did not, however, accord well with the broker politics of the New Deal. And its intellectual salon elitism did not offer political leverage.

Expressing disapproval of the direction of modern change, the R.P.A.A. offered the ideal of a decentralized society based on the small supportive community. As such, it represented an expression of themes of the New Jerusalem and the "Cooperative Commonwealth" long present in American social criticism, but now expressed by the R.P.A.A. in a strictly modern, secular, and cultural mode. Along with their vision of community went an interest in folk dancing, small theaters, experimental schools along lines espoused by John Dewey, local arts and crafts, and generally a life oriented to self-realization. The R.P.A.A. groped for an alternative culture based on ethical humanism, with planning as a means to this end.

Unlike many earlier social critics, the R.P.A.A. did not view the decentralized society as something to occur spontaneously or through voluntaristic actions alone. It needed to be brought about and nurtured by the planning policies of an administrative state. Change was accepted as inevitable and often beneficial but also requiring controls to guarantee that it enhanced the humane values of civilization.

The R.P.A.A. did not, however, probe deeply the issues involved in planning in a democratic society. The leading members of this intellectual coterie, especially Mumford, were more interested in influencing hearts and minds than legislation. Experiments in planning until then had been too limited to reveal fully the politics of the planning process. Planning was regarded, despite their criticism of the profession, as the means of rising above interest-group politics rather than, as cynics suggested, inevitably one more way it would be expressed.

As heirs of an American tradition of dissent, members of the R.P.A.A. believed planning's rightful function was protecting the people from capitalism's excesses and the depredations of the rich and powerful. Theirs was a *cri de coeur* against interests and forces in modern life contributing to alienation and social friction. Along with Ebenezer Howard, their vision promised the balanced, organic community, ordered to satisfy individual and social needs. Despite considerably greater sophistication, like Howard they overlooked the difficulty of finding agreement on the meaning and implications of their planning philosophy. They expected planners to contribute to lively democratic government because they believed their expertise made possible more meaningful public debate. Citizens would become more interested in the planning process when they realized the benefits it promised.

To Mumford, how men lived in cities provided the foundation of their civilization and the principal expression of their technology and power structure. From his perspective, the modern metropolis brought with it a progressive loss of "feeling, emotion, creative audacity, and finally, consciousness." Only a new form of planned urban order attentive to human needs and scale could prevent castastrophe. A half century later, his convictions have remained unchanged.

The British Garden City movement offered its American disciples a linkage of the concepts of community planning, metropolitan decentralization, and limitations on the size of cities. To this, the Americans had added such refinements in technique as the neighborhood unit, the superblock, and segregated-use road systems, as well as an approach to regional planning based upon ecological and cultural considerations. Above all, however, the Americans insisted on viewing planning as the only way to radically reshape the modern environment to create a humane civilization. In this regard, they sought to return Howard's movement to its original visionary impulse.

12

British New Towns,
1945–1980

On the one hand there is a sense of achievement that
so much has been accomplished; on the other there is
an appreciation that not all the high hopes held in
1947 have been fulfilled.

Hemel Hempstead Development Corporation, 1957

Britain's passage of the New Town Act of 1946 made the building of new
cities for the first time in modern Western history a concern of long-term
national planning. Once again, Britain led the way in a planning experiment which received much attention, especially in the period from 1960 to
1975 when other nations appeared eager to emulate the British example.
Writing in the late 1980s, the future of the New Town program remains in
question, as indeed does the "modern welfare state" with which it is closely
identified. Yet while awaiting history's final verdict, it would be useful to
appraise the enthusiasm for new towns after World War II and what happened to Howard's vision once it became an instrument of government
policy.

In 1941, the Garden Cities and Town Planning Association renamed
itself the Town and Country Planning Association (T.C.P.A.), by which it is
still known. The year before, both Raymond Unwin and Thomas Adams
had died. During the war years, Frederic Osborn was forced to run the
organization out of a small office in Welwyn Garden City assisted only by a
secretary-typist. Despite these circumstances, Osborn worked tirelessly to
influence public policy toward a postwar program of urban dispersal out of
large cities into planned new communities.

After 1946 and the New Town Act, the T.C.P.A. defended the new towns from critics while also assuming a quasi-public function of collecting and distributing data on them that invariably stressed their positive aspects. To the T.C.P.A., a commitment to new towns ideally stood outside the political arena, drawing its justification from a planner's world of universal values and truths. The history of the British new towns reveals a policy buffeted by political winds, troubled by cumbersome administrative problems, and subject to changing architectural and planning styles. For those who look to city planning to impose order and control over the future, the history of the New Town program must be soberly pondered.

This chapter examines changes in conceptualization of the New Town program as expressed in the Reith Report and the New Town Act of 1946. The first postwar new towns, known among planners as Mark I, closely adhered to the older garden-city model. Those designed in the late 1960s, the Mark III, were radically different in design and intention. Critical to understanding this evolution were changes in the way planners, responding to developments in the 1960s, altered their views of planning and community.

The Reith Report and the New Town Act of 1946

Even as bombs rained on British cities in the summer of 1940, Churchill's coalition government undertook consideration of postwar rebuilding. Motivation for this action was concern for civilian morale and to demonstrate confidence in ultimate victory. In October 1940, Sir John Reith was given responsibility for reporting to the Cabinet on postwar schemes. As director of the British Broadcasting Corporation from 1922 to 1939, Reith was a highly regarded national figure. Like Rexford Tugwell, he, too, possessed a faith in governmental planning as the path to modern progress.

With his customary dispatch, Reith established a new central planning authority, the Ministry of Works and Planning. In 1943, this department was divided to create a separate Ministry of Town and Country Planning. Although all schools of planning thought welcomed a national planning authority, they differed on its future policy. Busily setting up the machinery of planning, Reith did not indicate his own preference. In any event, Churchill and Reith did not get on, and he was made a lord to ease him from the Cabinet. With Reith gone, the pace of developments slowed. Then, as victory and a national election appeared imminent, the debate on future housing and planning policies intensified with the political parties preparing position papers.

Osborn navigated the T.C.P.A. into the thick of the fray. Already in 1941, he had proposed a postwar "National Planning Basis." Its main provisions called for restrictions on residential density, urban encirclement by green-belts, the creation of adequate open space in towns, and, most important, a national program of new towns coordinated with the other objectives. Approval in principle for this statement was quickly gained from the Royal Institute of British Architects and various other civic and professional groups. An important victory came when the Greater London Plan of 1944 called for the decentralization of the capital's population and industry.[1]

The Greater London Plan was the work of Patrick Abercrombie, professor of town planning at London University. At age sixty-five, Abercrombie represented a generation of planners greatly influenced by garden-city-type planning and its theme of the need for urban containment. His plan called for a reduction of London's population by over a million to allow redevelopment at lower densities. This would mean adding housing to existing nearby towns and the building of new satellite towns for some four hundred thousand people. Abercrombie even designated ten possible sites for new towns within a twenty- to twenty-five-mile radius of central London, just beyond a proposed greenbelt.

Labour's unexpected landslide victory in 1945 demonstrated an electorate eager for postwar reform. Although all party platforms promised large-scale housing schemes, none had referred specifically to new towns. As in 1919, it was agreed that housing would emerge as the most important single postwar domestic issue. Osborn feared a rush to construction would take the expedient form of a "combination of central flat-building and a great suburban explosion." Nor did Labour's appointment of Lewis Silkin as minister of town and country planning allay his concerns.[2]

As chair of the London County Council's Town Planning Committee (1940 to 1945), Silkin strongly favored postwar high-rise construction in the bomb-devastated inner districts. To Osborn's surprise, Silkin's first important action in office created a committee to recommend guiding principles for new-town development. Headed by Lord Reith and with Osborn as a member, the New Town Committee delivered its report only a week before the passage by Parliament of the New Town Act. Osborn's years of campaigning had suddenly borne fruit.

Silkin's conversion played a pivotal role in Britain's dramatic decision to embark on a postwar new-towns program. His change of heart reflected the post-election mood of the triumphant Labour party. Many in the party's leadership aspired to a "socialist commonwealth," a planned and largely nationalized economy, as an alternative to the inefficiencies and impersonalities of market capitalism. The euphoria of the moment called for bold innovation. A new-towns program appealed to Silkin as promising a human face for socialism: "a living world of men and women content with their homes and community and children happy and safe at play." The program's very boldness met Labour's need to exercise its mandate for sweeping change, striking a resonant chord with a Labour leadership whose formative years had been much influenced by the writings of authors like William Morris, Henry George, and Edward Bellamy.

J. B. Cullingworth's official history of the New Town program credits the T.C.P.A. with placing Silkin under great pressure. But Silkin was not a man moved easily against his wishes. Osborn believed he had exerted influence in subtle fashion. By temperament, Silkin and Reith were inclined to act with speed, decisiveness, and in a grand style. With development moving quickly, Osborn encouraged them to expediently adopt ideas and details already largely worked out for them by the T.C.P.A.[3]

He was eager for the two to use his program, even to take public credit for them, and skillfully massaged their considerable egos. Although not averse to personal publicity and honors (which he justified as strengthening his influence and thus benefiting his cause), Osborn was satisfied with a growing reputation as an éminence grise or power broker. Still, he was keenly disappointed when Silkin failed to appoint him as the head of a new-town development corporation. A reading of the Reith Report of 1946 reveals Osborn's influence.[4]

Nowhere is this more apparent than in the conceptualization of the new communities along garden-city lines. The Reith Report envisioned "towns established and developed as self-contained and balanced communities for working and living." By "balance," it specified that each new town attract a representative variety of social types and classes. "Self-contained" referred to the inclusion of a satisfactory range of social services and amenities as well as sufficiently diversified employment to eliminate any major need for commuting.[5]

The Reith committee set a population of fifty thousand as ideal for a new town, while allowing that "target" populations might range from twenty thousand to sixty thousand. It recommended low-density layout at an average of thirty persons to an acre, the use of the neighborhood unit as an organizing principle of planning, and that each new town be required to have a greenbelt. Essentially, the new towns were envisioned as sophisticated versions of Letchworth and Welwyn Garden City, both in time to be designated as new towns. The postwar New Town program represented the Garden City movement writ large.

The Reith committee, above all, wanted "true communities." It regarded their decline as "one of the most serious of modern urban ills." Undoubtedly, committee members projected the future new towns as miniature societies promoting a sense of individual belonging, social cohesiveness, and educational and cultural uplift.[6]

Osborn quickly discerned that Reith approached new towns from the same paternalistic perspective that had characterized his stewardship of the B.B.C. Reith expected them to strengthen family and traditional values weakened by the instability and social disorder of Britain's cities. Osborn believed the Scotsman yearned for the simple village communities of his youth, only now provided with much more in the way of opportunities. While Osborn was skeptical of "Reithian principles of high and elevating standards," he recognized that they lent themselves to his cause. Based on his own experiences with garden cities, Osborn did not believe new towns altered individuals or social life dramatically. For the most part, Osborn expected residents to sort themselves out by taste and interests along class lines.[7]

Sociologist Meryle Aldridge in a 1977 study subjected the social assumptions of the Reith Report to a rigorous analysis. They included no real consideration of combining the new towns with any radical program of social change. There was an underlying faith that residents, and especially the working class, were to be uplifted, even if incomes remained unchanged. An example of this thinking was Reith's recommendation that each new town provide a concert hall, an art gallery, and two cinemas, one for popular fare and the other for films of high culture and serious content.[8]

In regarding new towns as instruments of social reconstruction, the Reith committee only elaborated on the long tradition of environmental reform. Reformers customarily promised benefits in terms of a double-ledger form of social accounting. Individuals and families were to acquire superior housing and surroundings, and society, in turn, would gain an elevated citizenry. As an ambitious and unprecedented program, Reith expected the new towns to realize a handsome social dividend. He believed "true communities" established strong social bonds among all classes while reinforcing desirable personal values. For Reith, a well-run community buttressed social control and individual self-worth.[9]

As already remarked, Osborn regarded Reith's thinking as vague and overoptimistic. He himself evaluated the benefits of the New Town program in specific, limited terms. For their residents, the new towns would provide good housing, a supportive family environment, the possibility of an active civic and social life, and eliminate the need to commute great distances. For the nation as a whole, the goal was a new pattern of metropolitan development keyed to low density and the preservation of open space. They might also be employed to stimulate regional growth while expanding economic activity. Expectations above and beyond these, to his way of thinking, were visionary. Though not a panacea for Britain's economic and social problems, new towns represented an important and necessary step forward.

Osborn respected Silkin as a forceful politician who, above all, was a realist. Born and bred a Londoner, Silkin did not believe cities a cause of modern ills.

As the minister in charge of town planning, his concern was the program's success. Speaking before the House of Commons, however, even Silkin advanced the possibility that "we may well produce in the new towns a new type of citizen—a healthy, self-respecting, dignified person with a sense of beauty, culture, and civic pride." Enthusiasm and political needs encouraged new-town proponents to dramatize their potential benefits.[10]

As a large-scale effort by government, the New Town program required an elaborate bureaucratic apparatus. Much of the Reith Report considered the machinery of implementation. Here the committee worked without the advantage of precedent and little, except for the two garden cities, in the way of experience. It examined three alternative means of arranging for the provision of new communities.

One possibility was for a central development authority responsible for all details of every new town. A second relied on largely government-financed nonprofit private development companies (modeled on the garden-city example) for each community—the course favored by Osborn. A criticism of the first proposal was that it would lead to overcentralization and discourage diversity, while there was concern that the second would not allow for sufficient governmental control. Both Reith and Silkin favored a third approach which was officially adopted.[11]

Each new town was entrusted to its own development corporation. Appointment of their members fell to the minister of town and country planning who also exercised overall supervision and, most important, the initial designation of a new town and its site selection. As nonelected and presumably nonpolitical agencies, the development corporations dealt directly with various levels of local government and several ministries—such as Transportation and Trades, and the Ministry of Town and Country Planning (renamed in 1970 the Ministry of Environment)—who retained ultimate control. In the main, this represented a sensible arrangement, but the resulting relationship still proved complicated and often awkward. Over the next thirty years, the new-town administrative and governmental machinery represented a constant source of concern and controversy.

Silkin rejected as involving unnecessary expense a recommendation by the Reith committee for the provision of a central advisory commission to offer assistance to the several development corporations. Consequently, the New Town program lacked a national agency engaged in systematic research on new-town problems or even systematically collecting and disseminating information. This glaring weakness was never effectively remedied. To an extent, the T.C.P.A. tried to meet the need, but its nature as a propaganda body limited its usefulness. Individual development corporations did, of course, publish much on their activities, but these did not provide an overview of the program as a whole.

An early effort at research within the Ministry of Town and Country Planning proved counterproductive. In 1948, a research paper examined the relevance of Welwyn Garden City's experience to the New Town program. It concluded that differences in circumstances made the second garden-city example largely irrelevant. Furthermore, the report noted, "Although Welwyn was intended to be a vital social experiment . . . its experience was not systematically observed and recorded, and thus its purpose of providing principles for future planning was not fulfilled." When word of this reached former members of the Welwyn Garden City Ltd., they exploded in indignation.[12]

According to J. B. Cullingworth, the official historian of the New Town program, the resulting furor persuaded the permanent staff of the Ministry of Town and Country Planning that the area of research was fraught with political overtones and was to be avoided. Not until the 1960s would there be serious consideration of a coordinated new-town research program. However, when one was established briefly in the 1970s, its meager resources guaranteed failure.[13]

Mark I New Towns

Fourteen new towns were designated between 1947 and 1951. Eight of these were near London, with the others also located close to large cities. As a planning strategy, the purpose of the new towns in the immediate postwar era was to draw population out of crowded cities and lessen density, while limiting urban sprawl and helping to meet the need for housing. In accommodating urban "overspill," new towns would create the framework for planned decentralized metropolitan development. In general philosophy and specifics the New Town program closely reflected the central themes of the British Garden City movement.[14]

Unfortunately, the New Town program was adversely affected by the economic austerity of the early postwar years. New-town development proceeded much more slowly than anticipated. As priority went to housing, plans for community services and amenities greatly lagged. Moreover, even the provision of new housing, of which the New Town program constituted only a part, was not a notable success for the Labour government.

Some half million dwelling units had been destroyed by bombs during the war. After 1945, rent-control measures provided little incentive for private residential building aside from those intended for personal use. Due to the state of the economy, the number of dwelling units erected during the late 1940s—mostly constructed by local government authorities—annually averaged only half the number built in the late 1930s. In these circumstances, complaints arose. The new towns with their very high development costs

diverted resources from inner-city housing, where building expenses were
much less since municipal infrastructures already existed. Critics thus argued that placing housing in the context of the New Town program had
detracted from total housing construction.

The coming to power of the Conservatives in 1951 for a thirteen-year
tenure brought a temporary hiatus to the designation of additional new
towns. Of three proposed in the 1950s, only one, Cumbernauld near Glasgow, was actually built. Despite the efforts of the T.C.P.A. to remove the
New Town program from the arena of party politics, many Conservatives
regarded it as too socialistic. Instead, the Conservative party supported a
new program to extend existing towns through new large-scale housing
developments (1952 Town Development Act), where impetus and responsibility rested with local government. Despite this policy change, as affluence
returned to Britain in the 1950s the rate of development in the existing new
towns quickened. Indeed, government had little choice but to continue
support for at least existing new towns, if only to safeguard the original
investment and to keep the program from becoming a political liability.

Enthusiasm for new towns waned throughout the 1950s. As the new
towns developed, many who approved of the program in theory objected to
the results. One criticism was that the new towns were not the promised
balanced communities for all classes. Indisputably, they lacked the cachet
and charm of the historic or the architectural avant-garde. Drawing only
upon the middle three-fifths of the population, the new towns inherited the
garden-cities' mantel as places where families on tight budgets embraced a
suburban life-style.[15]

For the most part, the poor did not find affordable housing or employment opportunities in the new towns. The new-town development corporations explained that the problems of housing and employment were connected in a way that worked against the poor. To attract firms to the new
towns, priority in housing had to be offered their employees. Since most of
the businesses locating in the new towns near London required a white-
collar or skilled work force, the initial housing was designed and priced
accordingly. This was true, but as critics noted, the development corporations preferred "cleaner" capital-intensive industries and built the most
expensive and desirable housing their market could bear. Development
corporations did not really want the "problem poor," although provision
for the elderly was made.[16]

New towns also incurred a scathing barrage of ridicule leveled at their
design and architecture. Many complained that the new towns were devoid
of visual excitement and imagination. The important *Architectural Review*
castigated their layout in 1956 as a type of "planning" whose openness contributed to a "depressing provincial or suburban mood." At this time, the

American planner Lloyd Rodwin remonstrated that there were "no sharp divisions between town and country . . . no breath-taking setting off of forms of façades or of central foci. The smells and sounds are monotonous; the shops, the signs, the entertainment and intellectual fare, spartan."[17]

Sociologists soon studied a phenomenon called the "New Town Blues" which reinforced the complaint of "dead communities." Studies reported that many residents experienced a sense of alienation, depression, and a longing for the communities they left behind. Fighting back, Osborn derided the critics as "blue-eyed aesthetes," while diagnosing the "New Town Blues" as a temporary growing pain of new communities whose significance was grossly exaggerated. Attitude surveys done in the 1960s supported his view that most residents were satisfied with the physical environment of the towns and their homes, and "New Town Blues" faded from the attention of academicians and journalists.[18]

Mark II New Towns

Criticism of the new towns strongly echoed earlier attacks of garden-city-type planning before World War II. During the 1950s, the International School achieved ascendancy in architectural circles. Objections to new-town "prairie planning" and insistence on tightly drawn urban composition took hold. Cumbernauld, the only new town started in this decade, broke sharply with garden-city-type planning. Designed in 1958 as a high-density community of seventy thousand grouped around a linear core, Cumbernauld provided a diversity of housing types, including tower blocks of flats. Most of its multi-level town center was reserved for a pedestrian shopping precinct to achieve a "lively urban atmosphere."

Architects enthused at the visually dramatic results. Cumbernauld received considerably more attention in their journals than any other new town. Residents, however, were less pleased. Nor did the town's plan prove flexible. When two additional residential areas were added later, they had to be sited with their own mini-shopping facilities on locations cut off from the center. A heavy reliance on pedestrian paths to reduce use of the automobile proved a failure. In 1974, an extension doubled the original area of Cumbernauld, transforming the nature of the town. Osborn believed Cumbernauld's flaws supported his position that the ordinary Britain wanted cottage-type housing with gardens, which necessarily meant open-type planning.[19]

In November 1957, the Conservative government announced there was no further need for more new towns as the housing shortage had been largely met. To wind down the New Town program the Commission for the New Towns was created in 1959. When satisfied that a new town was sufficiently under way, the planning minister could transfer the property of its development corporation to the new-town commission. It was widely interpreted that the creation of the commission signified a switch from a social to a financial rationale for new-town development and indeed the beginning of the end of their special status.

In 1961, the Conservative government abruptly reversed course. Five additional new towns were designated in the following three years. The New Town program had entered a second phase, surpassing the earlier in innovativeness and even international attention. Exhilarated by prospects for a greatly enlarged program and influenced by changes in thinking within the planning profession, the T.C.P.A. called for additional new towns sited in distressed areas.

Labour, in power between 1964 and 1971, broadened the agenda of town planning to encompass regional redistribution of population and industry. A national plan was announced and regional economic planning councils established. A further seven new towns were designated in these years. In a decade of rising expectations, the central problem of society was no longer regarded as poverty. Instead, creative governmental policies sought to "modernize Britain," which meant, among other things, raising the general standards, lessening class differences, and reducing imbalances in regional development. The T.C.P.A. pushed new towns as a means of meeting these goals.[20]

The major political parties shared an enthusiasm for planning in the 1960s. This development, especially the Conservative reversal on new towns, must be examined. An unanticipated population growth fed by the postwar baby boom required attention, and there was eagerness for a progressive momentum to dispel the post-Suez mood of decline. Elsewhere in the Western World, a similar emphasis on innovative governmental policies occurred. As the T.C.P.A. reminded government and the public, in the field of town planning and new towns Britain still showed the way.

The tumultuous decade of the 1960s was a time of expectancy. Change, however, did not necessarily occur in the way anticipated. Along with a dangerous overestimation of what government could accomplish, a considerable hostility to all forms of authority soon flourished. The suspicion gained ground that experts and professionals, including town planners, did not really act on the disinterested and unbiased principles they purported. The public, or at least a vocal segment, demanded a significant involvement in the planning process, but no one was quite certain what this meant or how it might be effectively implemented.[21]

At seventy-six years of age, F. J. Osborn resigned as chairman of the T.C.P.A.'s Executive in 1961, while remaining as the editor for the association's journal for another four years. Regarded as one of Britain's most influential pressure groups, the T.C.P.A. came under younger leadership, many of them academicians. Remaining resolutely committed to the New Town program, they were also eager for new approaches.

The T.C.P.A. now downplayed older themes of new-town self-containment and maximum population size and showed less interest in the planning of residential layout. It urged instead a highly ambitious program of new-town construction as key to a comprehensive approach to regional planning stressing economic development. Future new towns would be sited in distressed areas of sufficient size and scale to provide "growth points." By attracting dynamic modern industry, the "growth points" could draw population and jobs to where needed and away from more congested areas, especially London and the Southeast.[22]

In the terminology employed at the time, the T.C.P.A. shifted focus from "micro" to "macro" planning. Regional and economic issues were of paramount concern to government; town planners and the T.C.P.A. embraced these new priorities. Indeed, in the 1960s, interest in residential design and layout, so keen a decade earlier, lessened as part of a general dismissal of "physical determinism" as a naive concept with little real impact on the nature of a community. Moreover, even the conceptualization by planners of the meaning of community underwent reconsideration.[23]

Reflecting the new interest in "macro" planning, the T.C.P.A. campaigned in the early 1960s for the creation of an elective regional level of government. This, it was assumed, would provide the mechanism to decentralize services identified with large cities in a "hierarchy of mutually accessible settlements." In 1969, a royal commission report proposed a sweeping change of local government. A dozen large "conurbation" authorities were established to administer wholly urbanized regions, such as Merseyside.

The changes, however, did not achieve the administrative clarity and efficiency intended. Red tape and restrictions annoyed businessmen and developers and seriously undermined the planners' credibility in the 1970s. The New Town program was also marred by much confusion. Contradictory policies by various levels and departments of government characterized the building of the so-called Mark III towns. This has been well described elsewhere. Our concern, then, is how and why they departed from the Garden City tradition of community design employed in the immediate postwar new towns.[24]

Mark III New Towns

The new towns built after 1960 were referred to as Mark III to distinguish them from their predecessors and to emphasize innovations in their policy and design. If the older efforts had been frequently criticized as too conventional and shortsighted, the planners of the Mark III towns determined that they represent the cutting edge of town planning. Most were also eager to give residents a wide range of personal choices. Ebenezer Howard doubtlessly would have approved of all of this in theory, but the results could only have startled him.

Runcorn, designated in 1964 with a target population of one hundred thousand, reflected this new approach. A year earlier, the well-publicized Buchanan report, "Traffic in Town," urged a scientific approach to reduce traffic congestion and pollution in cities. Such concerns were, of course, not new to planners. Still, the Buchanan report went further in regarding transportation as the planner's principal concern. Runcorn's master plan, officially accepted in 1967, reflected this new priority. New-town planning now started with a consideration of the transportation system rather than with residential organization.[25]

The Runcorn plan sought to reduce private auto use through the provision of a reliable mass-transit system. As public transportation is most cost efficient when operating along a densely developed corridor, Runcorn was laid out in a modified linear development to form a crude figure eight. Along this route was placed a segregated roadway for bus use. Major civic buildings, stores, and places of employment were sited around the figure eight near designated bus stops. This break with the compact concentric layout of earlier new towns received little notice. It appeared only logical to redefine town design to lessen traffic congestion and pollution. Moreover, British planners were greatly impressed by American advances in the "science of traffic management," where planners used computers to design mathematical models of traffic patterns and systems.

Another American planning current felt in Britain was "advocacy planning." According to Paul Davidoff, its leading spokesman, planners needed to regard the residents of a planned area as their clients. At Runcorn, procedures were established to provide feedback on resident satisfaction with a plan implemented in stages. Development strategy after any stage could be modified accordingly. This meant, of course, that the master plan should be largely open-ended. The older practice with its once and for all approach to comprehensive land-use planning was soon termed "blueprint" or "end-state" planning. Many planners now dismissed this type of planning as obsolete.[26]

The Mark III towns broke with the postwar pattern of new towns in other ways. Their sites were usually selected to spur regional development rather than to accommodate urban overspill. Some, indeed, were only planned extensions of existing towns. Their size and scale were considerably greater than the earlier efforts. Target populations were in the range of 100,000 to 250,000, and with an average area of twenty thousand acres, they were four times the size of the first new towns. Many planners even believed that it was futile to think in terms of a maximum population which could not really be held to in practice. Flexibility and planning for growth were urged as the real concerns of new-town planners.[27]

These themes were reflected in the layout of the Mark III towns. Instead of the coherent radial pattern and highly specialized land use of the first new towns, the newer ones were characterized by a diffuseness. One planner described them as resembling "an elaborate cellular arrangement" as seen through a microscope. It was soon suggested that the post-1967 new town—such as Milton Keynes, Worthington, and Washington—was not so much a garden city as the equivalent of several of them organized around a unified transportation system. This, in turn, was hailed as representing Ebenezer Howard's concept of "social cities." Peter Self of the T.C.P.A. exalted in 1970: "New towns are now old hat—but long live the social cities."[28]

As Howard's Garden City concept had once yielded to the Edwardian concern for the "suburb salubrious," it was now reshaped to accommodate new planning imperatives. The T.C.P.A. in its enthusiasm for regional economic planning and its eagerness for planning innovations had slipped away from older values to embrace a new set of priorities.

Milton Keynes represented the bold departure of later Mark III planning. Halfway between London and Birmingham, an area of 21,000 acres was designated in 1966 as the site of a projected city of 250,000. The prestigious international planning firm of Llewelyn-Davies and Partners was called in as consultant on the master plan by the development corporation. Reflecting the new emphasis on participatory planning, a series of public seminars and discussions was held over a three-month period to help establish the planners' goals. What emerged was that the participants wanted convenient access to a wide range of choices in jobs, services, recreation, and shopping. Nor did they intend these choices to be limited to Milton Keynes. Clearly the participants regarded rapid mobility as the key to the good community.[29]

Lord Llewelyn-Davies provided an explanation for this. It reflected the fact that residents of Milton Keynes would be more educated, upwardly mobile, and affluent than their parents. Accordingly, not only did they expect more in the way of housing and services, but they preferred to provide this for themselves through a market economy. To Llewelyn-Davies, rising expectations required a fresh way of conceptualizing the new town. He had been much impressed by a 1966 article by Christopher Alexander, "The City Is Not a Tree." Alexander decried the tendency among planners to think in organic terms, employing biological analogies of size, scale, and pattern, and urged instead a strictly functional approach concerned with basic needs and services. He singled out the neighborhood-unit concept as an example of the erroneous belief that a simplistic social pattern could be imposed by a plan. Llewelyn-Davies told his staff to provide a framework for development which was sufficiently flexible to absorb changes while remaining intact and often used the phrase "unfinished planning" to convey what was intended.[30]

In design terms, this meant assigning priority to "quick, free, direct access from any point in the town to any other." Instead of highly defined "catchment areas," such as traditional town centers or industrial areas, the new goal was to create "overlapping areas of service from widely distributed nodal points." As with the free-standing shopping malls springing up in the U.S.A., the planners at Milton Keynes designated a number of scattered but geometrically located points to place various services. While they also sought to retain the traditional planning tool of the neighborhood unit, the low density of housing at Milton Keynes and the "scatter-shot" location of various services necessarily attenuated the neighborhood unit's ideal of cohesiveness.[31]

By deliberate design, Milton Keynes did not attempt to confine and intermesh peoples' lives through a shared spatial universe of work, play, and residence. The "community of place," a commonplace of traditional societies and so vividly embodied in Ebenezer Howard's vision of the garden city, was no longer considered truly viable. Maximizing and maintaining options for both residents and planners were the new goals. For residents, this meant wide-ranging choices; and for planners, flexibility in town development. Even so, critical decisions had to be made which necessarily closed off and limited certain options.

Though relying on the private auto as the principal means of transportation in Milton Keynes, planners also intended to allow for systems of pedestrian paths and comprehensive and adequate public transit. In this regard, they seriously underestimated the inherent conflict in design forms between the various means of circulation.

The optimum design form for the automobile is a low-density, loosely knit and widely dispersed pattern of settlement with peak-hour journeys distributed over a high-capacity grid road system which planners term a "motor box." In contrast, public transportation works best with a high-density, compact form of development which, as already noted, locates transport-generating land use along well-developed corridors.[32]

Completed in 1970, the Milton Keynes plan (see illustration 18) opted for a very low residential density (the lowest of any British new town) and widely dispersed employment centers. Primary roads were organized into a grid to create a "motor box." In turn, the resulting squares were defined as "environmental areas" with a residential population of five thousand each.

Shopping and service areas, called "activity centers," were then located along the grid in such a manner as to be accessible to several different "environment areas."[33]

The highly diffuse plan precluded the effective mass-transportation system originally promised. Encouraging movement by automobile had resulted in inconvenience to those relying on public transport. This included many of the elderly, children too young to drive, those who could not afford cars, and even, on occasion, those families with several family members and only one automobile. In the mid-1970s, the Milton Keynes Development Corporation advised prospective residents "if you have not got a car, getting about can be a bit difficult and expensive. . . . if you haven't got a car you might have to think about buying one." Experiments with innovations in public transportation systems, such as "dial a minibus" did not resolve problems of cost effectiveness, rider convenience, and adequate passenger use.[34]

Milton Keynes has developed as a middle-class community very much along the lines of a comparable American suburban area. In 1987, the *Times* of London (November 16) devoted a special four-page report to Milton Keynes and its rapidly growing population—then at 135,000. Some thirteen hundred businesses had located there, of which a sixth were foreign companies whose "staff can live in affordable high-standard homes often no more than 15 minutes from their homes. People are fresher, healthier, time keeping improves, absenteeism plummets." But it also reported that Milton Keynes did not seem English. "Somehow, 45 minutes out of Easton, one has left England and found oneself whisked abroad, perhaps across the Atlantic, perhaps across the Pacific." Further promoting this resemblance to an American suburb was the heavy reliance of Milton Keynes and other Mark III towns on private developers.

Peterborough, Northampton, and Warrington were designated new towns in the late 1960s, but in reality they incorporated existing sizable communities. In 1971, thirty-five thousand acres of central Lancashire were designated to provide a growth point for the economic revival of the area. Two more traditional new towns were also announced—Llantrisant in Wales and Stonehouse in Scotland.

Writing in 1970, Frank Schaffer, who had served as an officer in the Ministry of Housing and Local Government and then as secretary of the Commission for the New Towns, explained: "The new towns are no longer a political and economic issue. They are now a well-tried instrument of political and economic progress, accepted by all the political parties." Events soon demonstrated this view overly optimistic.[35]

As planners sought "input" from residents, some inferred from this that planning was very largely superfluous. Unfettered free enterprise, they claimed, could provide what was wanted without a planning apparatus and state support. Planners replied that they spurred superior types of development than otherwise occurred, but their detractors remained unimpressed. By promising "to permit individuals to exercise their freedom of choice and allowing these preferences to determine where resources are allocated," planners stripped community planning of its mystique and even weakened the case for government support of new-town planning. Planning, rather than acting to shape or restrict "utilitarian individualistic values" in the public interest, now only appeared to accommodate them.[36]

The Garden City movement had always argued that its communities were special and superior to the ordinary community. They were designed, after all, to be balanced, cohesive, and to promote a sense of community as well as good health and positive values. By accepting freedom of choice as the highest good, planners lowered the barriers to a rush of values from the consumer society. This in turn weakened the Garden City concept of community planning. Residents did not seek, in Howard's words, a society "in which the social side of our nature is demanding a larger share of recognition."

This is not to say that planners enjoyed much choice in accepting the involvement of residents in the planning process. Times had changed, and planning practice needed to reflect postwar developments. Two decades of affluence had escalated expectations. The ubiquity of the family car required a new approach. Moreover, planners were no longer confident that they knew best. They had long disagreed among themselves over the preferred nature and design of community, while agreeing that satisfactory answers to these questions required the planning process. Now planners were no longer even certain of this. Troubled by internal doubts, they were subjected increasingly to external attack.

Their critics marched under the banner "Power to the People." This snappy slogan meant, of course, different things to radical community activists organizing the disadvantaged and free-enterprise advocates of consumer choice. However, they shared the conviction that social engineering was unacceptably paternalistic, and bureaucracy needed to be curtailed. Each in their own fashion chipped away at the cornerstone tenet of the welfare state that modern society must be managed by enlightened experts. Seventy years before, a profession had arisen to impose an order on unregulated market development, and now its practitioners were belittled as the problem, not the solution. Even the most resolute planner winced before Jane Jacobs's slashing attack on the planning trade in her immensely influential *The Death and Life of Great American Cities* (1961).

By the mid-1970s, Britain had lost confidence not only in town planning but also in most forms of governmental planning. Never really a priority of Whitehall, the New Town program had long sailed in the wake of governmental enthusiasm for economic and regional planning. Straining under the problems of the energy crisis, government reconsidered its priorities. The postwar era of building the welfare state yielded to a new period of concern with unemployment, inflation, and disindustrialization.[37]

Economic decline challenged the long-held assumption of an inevitable continuing evolution of a welfare society. For this largely had rested on confidence in an economy of secure abundance. A resurgent Right now advanced the cry of "privatization" as the only effective way of promoting economic growth. A sea change in social thinking was occurring. The hidden hand of the market, not the governmental expert, was to be called upon to build Britain's future.[38]

In this context, a retreat from the New Town program was inevitable. If Thatcherism sealed its fate, the decline actually occurred earlier. Municipal authorities had long regarded the new towns as a threat to their interests. An exception had been London, which, suffering from an acute housing need and land shortage, welcomed the relief offered by nearby new towns. This now changed. In the early 1970s, the Greater London Council joined those seeking the program's curtailment.[39]

Pointing to their "problem populations," the British cities demanded all available governmental assistance. As possibilities for future expenditures shrank, the cities pressed their demands in terms of having immeasurably greater needs than the relatively affluent residents of the new towns. A pull for public funds between those programs specifically directed to the poor and ones of more general spending for the overall quality of life is normally present, but hard times exacerbated this rivalry.

Few denied that urban problems were acute and explosive. The [London] *Times Magazine* in November 1976 reported "Britain's cities are rotting at the core. . . ." The chief constable of Manchester warned a year later that "unless conditions improved, the city centre might need an army of occupation." A disconcerting concentration of chronically unemployed, broken families, and recently arrived immigrants of color with their children lodged in or near the center of major metropolitan areas. Efforts to provide them housing in the 1960s usually took the form of prefabricated high rises which, as Osborn had predicted, proved unsatisfactory and on occasion unsafe. Furthermore, the mishandling of urban renewal schemes had contributed greatly to the planners' precipitous fall from grace. Certainly, the new towns had done little to relieve the cities of their "problem populations."[40]

At the end of the nineteenth century, Howard proposed the garden city as a general answer to urban problems. The New Town Act of 1946 was intended mainly to accommodate urban overspill. By 1970, it was clear that the new towns lacked sufficient scale to handle the postwar urban exodus, most of which went into conventional suburban developments. Critics still insisted, though, that the new towns lured skilled workers and employment from the cities while leaving behind the problems. Nor had the new towns decreased urban land values as Howard had anticipated. With inflation, prices soared amidst rampant speculation and concern that the greenbelts contributed to the scarcity of development sites. From the perspective of municipal authorities, too high a price was paid for the new towns, with much of this coming at their expense.[41]

The Labour government backed away from the New Town program in 1975. Target population and support were cut with the explanation that the end of the baby boom and lowered population projections decreased the need. A designated new town at Stonehouse in Scotland was also abandoned. A year later, it was announced by the appropriate minister that no further new towns were intended.[42]

The Conservative government of Margaret Thatcher, in office since 1979, has reduced the direct role of the government in the economy and has pushed the privatization of public housing and new towns. By 1992, it is expected that all the English new towns will have been handed over to the Commission for the New Towns, whose mandate is to sell them. In 1986 and 1987, almost four hundred million pounds was raised by the government through the sale of bits and pieces. Privatization of the New Town program has proven an unexpected bonanza to the government due to vigorous marketing and a property boom. Some housing land at Stevenage sold in 1986 for 32,000 pounds an acre. A new London motorway doubled the market value of sites in Hempstead and Harlow.[43] Privatized, the new towns will be left to develop much as any British community.

Academic conferences on the decline of the welfare state are frequent in Britain, and town planning must be regarded as among the victims of its fall from favor. The time for ambitious governmental experiments in planning is probably over for the century. Scholars, however, continue to analyze the merits and weaknesses of a program which created twenty-eight planned communities containing nearly two million people. Perhaps sometime in the future, their work will be of more than academic and historical interest.

Seeking to regroup after the collapse of the New Town program, the T.C.P.A. has broadened its interests to include a wide range of environmental and social issues. It long since has discarded its fascination with planning as a process rather than as a means to an end. Familiar themes and interests, such as the desirability of low density as well, of course, as the importance of urban decentralization, figure prominently in its journal. Although not openly breaking with its nonpartisan stance, the anti-planning policies of Margaret Thatcher obviously have forced it into opposition. Less influential and less establishment, the T.C.P.A. is increasingly an organ of those seeking a humanistically oriented program to counter present trends. Of this development, Ebenezer Howard would no doubt approve.

13

The Future of the Garden City

A map of the world that does not contain utopia is not worth looking at. For it is the one place that man is always landing.

Oscar Wilde
("The Soul of Man Under Socialism,"
Fortnightly Review, February 1891)

Many nations planned new communities after World War II. Differing greatly in intention, design, and scale, they ranged from monumental capitals for Brazil and India to modest development towns by Third World nations seeking to modernize—but all fell under the professional rubric of "new-town planning" as the term "garden city" retreated from use. In most urbanized Western nations, however, new-town interest was principally channeled into schemes to decongest the central city and restructure metropolitan land use. Despite great attention given the "British experiment," efforts elsewhere rarely followed its example closely, though a borrowing of ideas inevitably occurred.

The trajectory of new-town interest on the Continent followed the British pattern. Interest was present after the war, but grew greatly in the period from 1960 to 1975 and since then has declined precipitously. From the first, though, it was generally recognized that the garden-city model of free-standing, low-density, and self-contained towns of fixed and small size was only one of several approaches. Although all developed nations shared a common concern with urban growth and how this should occur, there were important differences in what was regarded as appropriate or even ideal. Much of the postwar enthusiasm for new-town programs among planners tended to disregard rather than clarify differences.

Individual nations responded to postwar planning needs in ways that reflected their special circumstances and planning precedents. Once more, architects and planners battled over desirable density levels. Continental planning generally relied on multi-story housing, although green space was usually interspersed among the built-up areas. This, in part, reflected the pressing need for rapid construction of low-cost housing and the ease with which cost-saving industrial techniques could be employed in tower construction. It also often expressed a preference for high-density development as more appropriate for an urban society. For the most part, what was absent in postwar debate over community was the explicit ideological positions related to environment so strongly present in the 1930s. The tenor of discourse after 1945 was more flexible and pragmatic.[1]

Reorganized after the war, the Congrès International d'Architecture Moderne continued fitfully in existence until 1960, but no longer was it fired by the iconoclastic zeal of the avant-garde. By and large, the "International Style" prevailed in architectural circles but now represented more an aesthetic than social statement. Carnel Van Eesteren, supervising the postwar design and construction of Amsterdam's new suburbs according to his 1935 plan, often referred to them as garden cities, a term not only inaccurate but also which before the war he would have abjured as negative. Disagreements over high- versus low-density development tended to be couched in functional terms—such as more effective utilization of land and sites, or quality of life issues as related to whether a family environment should emphasize stimulation or tranquility.[2]

Though receiving much less international attention than Britain, the Scandinavian countries and The Netherlands also led the way in postwar new-town planning among advanced nations. By the late 1940s, schemes were in place for high-density suburban communities relying largely for employment and services on core cities. In promoting linkage between planned new suburbs and their central cities, north European practice remained consistent with the principles of the C.I.A.M. as expressed by Corbusier and Ernest May, both of whom remained active and influential as planners until the 1960s.

Continental planners did not seek to reduce the importance of large cities. Their thinking was in terms of structuring inevitable urban growth and often referred to as "centralized-decentralization." New communities were regarded as a form of urban extension, a means of siting necessary new housing to allow for lower densities in older inner-city neighborhoods. But the high density of the latter was unacceptable only in terms of crowded conditions in the existing aged housing stock rather than in absolute terms. For the most part, Continental planning rejected the strategy of urban decentralization that British planners attempted. Most of postwar planned development in metropolitan areas represented, in effect, a form of suburban extension in small communities with their own shopping centers. Only in the late 1950s did interest develop in including significant employment opportunites to accompany this housing.

Emphasis on linkage between central city and planned metropolitan extension encouraged planning in terms of rapid movement along axes. As early as 1947, Danish planners presented a "Fingerplan" for Copenhagen. This called for the city's future growth to occur in corridors extending from the core city as "fingers" stretching outward from the palm. Land lying between the fingers was reserved for agriculture or recreational open space. Running through the corridors were rapid-transit systems. Much admired, the Danish approach attracted considerable interest in the United States where cities confronted an explosion of suburban development.[3]

Stockholm's postwar planning relied largely on undeveloped municipally owned land. A general plan adopted in 1950 projected future growth channeled parallel to a subway system "radiating out like spokes" from the main railroad station. Concentrated tightly around carefully sited stations at regular intervals, new high-density suburbs for a population of about fifty thousand each were internally organized into neighborhood units. Initially the Swedes gave little thought to anything but commuter bedroom suburbs, but influenced by the British example and concerned with overburdening the metropolitan road systems, they showed interest by the mid-1950s in providing employment in new communities.[4]

Vallingsby, twenty minutes from central Stockholm, was built in the early 1960s as the prototype of the Swedish satellite community, or "ABC-city" (an acronym for work, housing, and center). Vallingsby borrowed from the British model. A well-designed town center was to meet the needs (cultural as well as commercial) of the resident population and of those people in the surrounding areas. Despite this, however, most of Vallingsby's working residents were employed in central Stockholm. In appearance, Vallingsby was very impressive; in planning terms, it did not really achieve the goal of a satellite community as a lever for redirecting metropolitan organization.[5]

By the early 1960s, planners throughout the world cited British and Scandinavian new towns as models of proper, planned urban expansion. Western nations had experienced a rapid and unexpected increase in population. Those continuing to drift to the cities encountered a deteriorating housing stock in short supply. New towns, regardless of their architecture, layout, or even rationale, appeared not only as an answer to these problems but also as the key to establishing "national growth policies" directing regional economic development. Differences among planners concerning strategy on such issues as housing type appeared secondary to achieving the acceptance of new towns as an instrument of national planning.[6]

There was reason for optimism. Media interest in planning in the 1960s was high, while many planners regarded new towns as their discipline's most important activity. The United Nations sponsored new-town conferences, including several devoted to new-town planning as a developmental tool in the Third World. By the mid-1960s, nations formerly aloof were climbing aboard what now seemed a new-town bandwagon. Such was the American experience.[7]

Washington's involvement in America's postwar building boom was profound, although indirect. In various ways it promoted the rapid build-up of suburbs by private developers. As a massive movement of the white middle and working classes occurred, their place was often taken in the older cities by migrating southern blacks and other minorities. This, in turn, speeded "white flight." In the 1950s, a federally subsidized urban renewal program directed at central-city blight engaged in selective rebuilding, only to incur criticism for placing commercial interests before the needs of displaced residents of razed neighborhoods. By the 1960s, urban decline and escalating racial tension as matters of national concern underscored the need for a new federal approach to the problems of the cities.[8]

Nor was all well on the "crabgrass frontier." Social critics decried that frontier as a spawning ground of a vacuous materialism and conformity, while public administrators bemoaned suburbia's political Balkanization and inefficient delivery of public services. Above all, the suburbs were perceived as promoting tendencies within American society to divide the races physically and socially, allowing the white majority to retreat into socially indifferent "privatism" and to disregard the plight of urban ghettos. American interest in new towns in the 1960s thus reflected a desire for federal support of a new radical approach to city and suburb which in one fell swoop attended to the needs and excesses of both.[9]

As early as 1947, the brothers Paul and Percival Goodman, one an architect and the other a social critic, in *Communitas: Means of Livelihood and Ways of Work* declared that the American city must be made over. In their design of a visionary community, they emphasized a fraternal associationism in both design and values to break with the values of consumer capitalism and its tendency to force life and its various roles into tightly sealed-off compartments. Ignored at publication, *Communitas* would be much acclaimed by the counterculture of the 1960s and Paul Goodman would be honored—one of the few from the older generation—by the "youth generation."[10]

A second to be so revered would be Lewis Mumford. In 1948, Mumford and Clarence Stein revived the Regional Planning Association of America, intending this time a lobbying organization modeled after the then highly successful British Town and Country Planning Association. To their older arguments they added a contemporary note. In the context of the high tension of the Cold War and concerns over the dawning of the nuclear age, they urged urban dispersal as a priority of national defense and survival. In the rush to suburbia and amidst the beginning of an era of unprecedented growth and affluence, their message fell on deaf ears, and within a few years organizational efforts were halted.[11]

A dozen years later, the pendulum swung dramatically. Mumford's *The City in History* (1961), adopted by a book club, sold several hundred thousand copies to achieve his first commercial success. Its condemnation of the contemporary city as "tyrannopolis" repeated old arguments, but the postwar suburbs came under scathing attack as a "low-grade environment from which escape is impossible." Never would Mumford's Jeremiahs sound more menacing and relevant. In the summer of 1964, black ghettos burst into flames amidst riotings and warnings of worse to come. Armageddon indeed appeared at hand.

The administration of John F. Kennedy struck a note of activism and social concern, and his assassination in late 1963 only enhanced a sense of urgency. To demonstrate commitment to meeting the problems of America's communities, the Department of Housing and Urban Development (H.U.D.) was established in 1965 with a black man, Robert Weaver, named secretary. Federal commissions proliferated to examine the problems and recommend solutions. Legislation proposing federal assistance for new-town development as a bold new approach was placed before Congress in 1966.[12]

American planners and their principal professional organizations rallied behind a new-town approach. Most planners, as liberals, were highly sensitive to a mounting criticism which held them accountable for the damage to neighborhoods and the urban fabric caused by large-scale expressway construction and urban renewal. A new-town program promised planners an answer to their critics, a truly radical reconstruction of the metropolitan region which could right many of the wrongs of the disadvantaged in housing, education, community, family life-style, and even jobs while environmentally contributing to the greening of America.

A few planners did express reservations. One who did was Lloyd Rodwin, author of a critical study of the British new towns, who publicly doubted on the basis of the English experience that an American counterpart could offer much help to the cities. The real opposition to a new-town program came not from intellectuals and academicians but from interest groups who believed they had something to lose. Mayors of large cities, anxious over their funding, joined in opposition with suburban officials concerned about forced racial integration and groups representing the

building industries who anticipated that a new-town program might lead to
a comprehensive national land-use policy. For two years they blocked congressional action.[13]

To win its passage in 1968, the program was tailored to reduce opposition, falling far short of what its advocates intended. Private developers
were to build the new towns with money provided at low interest by the
government. For the most part, it was assumed that developers would avoid
highly experimental-type communities or other controversial actions and
that the program would be modest.[14]

Supporters of the new towns envisioned them as the means to a major
restructuring of American society. The National Committee on Urban
Growth in 1969 projected a greatly increased population by the year 2000
and recommended that this be accommodated in planned communities. It
proposed building a hundred new towns of one hundred thousand each and
an additional ten new cities of a million each. This program would break
traditional patterns of residential segregation, avoid suburban sprawl, and,
of course, create communities vastly superior to the usual in attractiveness
and efficiency.[15]

The Housing and Urban Development Act of 1970 called for a national
policy on urban growth. Its recommendations were clearly reminiscent of
the philosophy of the Regional Planning Association of America. The drift
to older cities was to be reversed; city centers, revitalized. New towns would
be located to create balanced regional development and orderly metropolitan development. The legislation, however, created no agenda, established
no priorities, and only went so far as to establish a new-town agency within
H.U.D. as the mechanism for the implementation of its national urban-
growth policy.

Moreover, this agency, the New Community Development Agency, lacked
the power to select sites or designate new towns, as did the British Planning
Ministry. Its role was only to establish basic guidelines for new communities,
approve private developers for funding under these guidelines, and guarantee that these funds were used appropriately. The program's success
depended initially on whether enough developers would be attracted by
low-interest money to venture the risks and red tape involved. Even if
interest were found, the amount of money available made ludicrous any
hope that the federally sponsored new towns could really dent the nation's
urban problems. Furthermore, by relying on private developers who would
tend to be attracted to prime sites awaiting development, the program
could not really hope to achieve the regional balance and metropolitan
reordering that the 1970 legislation grandiosely envisioned.[16]

The orienting of the program to private developers in search of profit
was largely done for political reasons, but the way had been pioneered

earlier by two developers who greatly admired Ebenezer Howard. In the 1960s, the new communities of Reston, Virginia, and Columbia, Maryland, were started with the intention of being planned for living, work, and play. Columbia was by far the more daring and successful of the two. Its developer, James Rouse, intended an example to others in his industry that "good planning was good business measured by the bottom line." Moreover, Rouse intended Columbia to be racially and economically mixed. A team of sociologists worked with the planners to envision the details making for a "rewarding communal experience" as part of a better way of life. It was hoped that developers working with the New Community Development Agency would be similarly motivated.[17]

The New Town program, however, proved short-lived. In 1975, with fifteen new towns approved, the Republican administration, lukewarm from the first to a program thrust upon it by a Democratic Congress, decided to accept no further applications. A year later, H.U.D. announced that federal involvement was to be phased out entirely due to disappointing results. Little housing had been created, and most of the development companies were in serious financial trouble. There was no point in throwing good money after bad. Not even bothering to undertake a comprehensive evaluation of a program that had cost several hundred million dollars, H.U.D. walked away. Neither press nor public took much note. Riots were no longer occurring in the cities, and the national mood had by then moved to the right. Between 1977 and 1987, H.U.D.'s allotment fell from 7.4 percent of the national budget to less than 1 percent. The President's Commission on Housing, reasoning from "Reaganomics," concluded in 1982 that the nation's problems required the "genius of the market economy" unfettered by federal policies.[18]

As in Britain and elsewhere, collapse of the American New Town program happened during hard times that nurtured conservative thinking. Social experimentation was blamed for having exacerbated the situation by working up expectations that government could not meet, either because they were too radical or otherwise deemed unrealistic. A shift in thinking was also under way, and particularly notable was the weakening of the environmentalist approach to social behavior which had long undergirded the rise of modern city planning and the welfare state. Conservative thinkers increasingly shifted the debate on social issues away from a concern with housing, community, and the improvement of the environment to emphasize the importance of individual values and behavior.

Politicians of the Right assured receptive audiences that "you can take people out of the slums, but you can't take the slum out of the people." The Harvard social scientist Edward Banfield disconcerted many of his colleagues with a view that "the lower class individual in the slum sees little or no reason to complain. He does not care how dirty and dilapidated his housing is either inside or out, nor does he mind the inadequacy of such public facilities as schools, parks, libraries. Indeed, where such things exist he destroys them by acts of vandalism if he can. Features that make the slum repellent to others actually please him."[19]

Even earlier, however, in the early 1960s, many planners had lost interest in environmental issues. They moved away from being essentially concerned with issues of design and community as related to the preparation of comprehensive plans to a fascination with a "systems-analysis approach" that emphasized the process of problem solving almost regardless of the problem. City planning no longer was to be regarded as a process of decision making primarily concerned with the physical environment. It was increasingly thought of as the efficient delivery of public services. For many radicals attracted to the "systems-analysis" approach, this meant entirely novel services directed at redistributing wealth and power to the poor so as to fundamentally alter society.[20]

There was of course nothing inherently radical or conservative in a "systems-analysis" approach. It offered only a methodology for seeking control over any complex process of change. The systems analyst regarded planning as a continuous consideration of alternatives. Planners would quantify a mass of information in order to establish correlations between different factors. Relying on techniques from the field of econometrics, models would be created capable of "generating predictive ability," that altered as new data fed in, "allowing for rational choice under conditions of uncertainty." One enthusiast for the "systems-analyst" approach exclaimed that "model design is the most complex and fascinating chore facing the planner." Skeptics scoffed that planners preoccupied with refining mathematical models had lost track of the real world. Others warned that obsessions with model building represented a form of technocratic idol worship that encouraged planners to ignore the issue of human values in their pursuit of a scientific method.[21]

Interest in a "systems-analysis" approach was a natural consequence of a groping for a more sophisticated handle on the complex nature of modern change suggested by the advent of the computer. It also reflected a disillusionment in some circles with traditional professional concerns which were derided as "brick-and-mortar planning." The limitations of trying to shape desirable social values through architecture and design at a time of little consensus over what these were supposed to be was evident. Moreover, planners were being asked to think of social values in new ways. No longer were they to be simply tagged desirable and undesirable. Planners must recognize that all social values emanated from a class system. Accordingly, values conventionally regarded as desirable should be suspect when held up to the poor if they served the interests of the powerful who, after all, needed an industrious and submissive working class. Indeed, planners were told to question their own values and motives and to stop hiding self-seeking behind the pose of professional detachment.

In the 1970s, planners increasingly came from different fields, with fewer trained in architecture and landscape. Less and less did planners agree on the nature and purpose of their profession. The long-standing view of the profession as one entrusted with a special responsibility to safeguard the public interest in regards to housing, community, and the environment had to be reconsidered, as did indeed the view of planners as the spearhead of society's collective effort to shape a higher civilization.[22]

The visionary impulse of early-twentieth-century planning, of which the Garden City movement was representative, has not flourished in recent years. This is at least in part because we no longer share the communitarian conviction that the community must be at the center of change. Perhaps this expectation reflected an ideology which looked backward to a simpler setting and technology than our own. Modern trends and consumer capitalism do not appear conducive to a concept of community based on mutual cooperation and place. Our society places individual fulfillment above attachment to community, and we are increasingly involved in complex relationships extending well beyond personal and community ties to distant connections often of an abstract and obscure nature but, nonetheless, real and demanding.

The future is, of course, as much of a mystery to the historian as to the planner. Even so, it does not appear probable that new-town planning and the Garden City movement will soon, if ever, regain favor in the developed West. The propitious circumstances that fostered these in the postwar decades have altered dramatically.

Present low birthrates in the Western World with attendant implications for negligible population increase appear a durable consequence of structural changes in modern societies. Accordingly, the great growth of cities and suburbs may well be over in the West, although the relationship between the two remains in flux, and regional shiftings of population will continue. New polynucleated metropolitan areas acquired shape in the last two decades as traditional central-city economic functions increasingly dispersed.

The suburbs are now fully areas of employment as well as consumption. Two-thirds of all jobs created in the United States between 1960 and 1980 were located in the suburbs. An environmental order Howard could not have anticipated, spread cities of industrial parks, office campuses, shopping malls, and residential neighborhoods extend outward from older areas of concentration. Neither country nor city, this pattern of geographic sprawl might have dismayed the reformers of the turn of the century. They optimistically anticipated that a new technology and a reshaping of the city and country would combine the best of both these worlds, but "spread city" appears admirably suited to our prevailing values that emphasize mobility and pursuit of the material.

What, of course, could not have been foreseen was the private passenger automobile as a ubiquitous conveyance offering comfort and convenience of travel to the masses without parallel in history. The automobile and the culture it has generated are so deeply imbedded in Western society that alternatives now seem virtually inconceivable. Yet the automobile exacts a heavy toll. The once urban phenomenon of gridlock is now a commonplace of suburban intersections. On the vaunted freeways of Southern California, the average travel speed is expected to drop to fifteen m.p.h. by the year 2000, and newspapers already report impatient motorists expressing aggression by shooting at each other. Still our love affair with the automobile and the status it confers continues. We are instructed by commercials, "you are what you drive."[23]

Howard believed garden-city dwellers would perceive themselves as members of a cohesive community, bound together by shared moral and social values. Relying as it does on the concept of the "community of place," this ideal with its communitarian affinity appears strongly out of place in our nomadic modern world. Technology incessantly redefines our meaning of time and space and gives more meaning to nonspatial forms of community, while eroding those dependent upon geography. The quest for community will certainly continue, but it will increasingly be in terms of common interests and "affinity groups" rather than shared space.

Sociologists inform us, and personal experience confirms, that with affluence we substitute hired professional assistance for services previously provided by informal or even governmental support networks. The impersonality of a cash transaction is simpler and perhaps even more efficient than the human demands or bureaucratic complexity of the other two, while allowing great freedom of action. Indeed, such hallmarks of communitarian thinking as the common dining hall and collective recreational facilities are routinely supplied for a fee by condominium housing for the affluent. Planned unit development for retirement villages or colonies of second homes is a common occurrence nowadays. On a larger scale, even an occasional new town is created by developers whose motivation is profit, not social idealism.[24]

Rancho Santa Margarita presently under way in Southern California for an anticipated population of fifty thousand promises to provide job, shopping, recreational, and social opportunities in a "scenic setting within traffic-free proximity to a wide variety of affordable housing." This approach, the developers believe, will meet the needs of contemporary life, where most married women work and commuting is a hassle. Early sales and common sense suggest they are right. Eschewing social goals, Rancho Santa Margarita attracts residents and industry by promising an "upscale life-style" in a community sprinkled with golf courses, tennis courts, and gourmet restaurants. It may represent the new town of the future, where the market researcher and not the social visionary determines the ideal community. Of course this consumer utopia will not pretend to offer the solution to society's social problems, and the poor will have to go elsewhere. Indeed, this is a great part of its appeal.[25]

Columbia, Maryland, in 1989 had a population of about seventy thousand, or about thirty thousand shy of the one hundred thousand anticipated. Despite this shortfall, growth is still vigorous and homes and apartments are occupied almost as soon as they are finished. The cluster arrangement of apartments, town houses, and single-family detached homes organized into villages has made good real-estate sense, proving attractive to residents and the market. Its diversity of housing stock has encouraged an economic and social mix. But this has not generated the social experiment intended. Social divisions have not eroded, and community organizations are what might be expected in any American town. Nor do residents stay put any more than elsewhere. Columbia serves to demonstrate what good planning can do in the way of creating an attractive, diverse, and convenient community. And it also appears to demonstrate the limits of planning in shaping the social nature of the community.

Our sense of community as spatially defined and distinctive has eroded. Most new developments are much like the fast-food chains which service them, an interchangeable experience. They, and we, are largely indifferent to local roots. They reflect the values of a mobile society where individuals move every few years for a new job or to mark a "life-style change" or simply to change scenery and climate. In consequence, our communities are increasingly open-ended in terms of people and space. Location is now principally valued in terms of proximity to expressways and airports. We look to the mass media and consumer styles for the shared values formerly derived only over time by a population living together under stable conditions. If the "community of place" is no longer important to most of us, its decline began not with the postwar world but well over a century ago with the changes that concerned Howard.

Historically, modern planning emerged at the confluence of four very different streams of development. One was the complex and technical nature of the urban infrastructure at the end of the nineteenth century with the pressing need for coordinating diverse service activities and anticipating future requirements. Another was the environmental reform movement, which was itself an outgrowth of the earlier public-health and model-housing movements. The third was the growing conviction that society could be reconstructed through collective political action with government properly taking the lead in shaping the future. Finally, there was a humanitarian, perhaps utopian, theme, which represented a secularized version of the old aspiration for the New Jerusalem and an evolutionary statement of the communitarian dream of the Cooperative Commonwealth. This presumed a society of social harmony and efficient production in which all could attain a life of individual fulfillment and the nation a "higher civilization." It looked toward the design of communities which would further a genuinely ethical and civic life while providing the individual a sense of connection and order.

The fusion of these themes created a tension between utopian and pragmatic thinking. Among planners, a rhetoric of grandiose expectations had to be moderated to influence those with the power to act. Accordingly, the history of much of city planning, including the Garden City movement, has been one of accommodation.

Even in *To-morrow,* Howard's thinking was influenced by the need to make his scheme appealing to others. Letchworth altered his ideal to a model industrial village that fitted into a framework of philanthropy and self-help acceptable to "enlightened capitalists." Not until World War I did the New Townsmen regard government itself as the proper means of achieving garden cities. This, in turn, raised new issues that still perplex. Should government engage in expensive new-town developments which benefit their residents but whose costs are borne by the population as a whole? And if the answer is, "only under special circumstances," then specifically what are those circumstances? Certainly schemes that appeared plausible at one point in time, such as the turn-of-the-century ideas of labor colonies for the unemployed or model industrial towns built by employers, are now not acceptable.

We no longer believe in either the efficacy or desirability of social engineering as practiced by planners or others. A persistent interest of planners and architects devoted to the Garden City movement has been housing and its arrangement to promote a sense of community, or, as it is sometimes called, "social architecture." By the mid-1960s, many planners conceded the limitations of this approach. It is, of course, possible through design to increase greatly the encounters of people living in proximity. This does not, however, guarantee that these will be either significant or pleasant. Planners do not have the professional ability to engender, in Howard's words, "the soft notes of brotherhood and goodwill." They can design for efficiency, convenience, attractiveness, and even to discourage (or at least make more difficult) antisocial behavior, but the planned community alone cannot be expected to elevate morals or raise civic loyalty. More fundamental economic, political, and social factors determine these. Society is presently perceived largely in terms of individual and group interests offering little potential for a consensual community.[26]

The environmental reform movement of the early twentieth century was a response to the emergence of the industrial city with its myriad problems. In focusing on the problems of the city, reformers understandably sought in its new physical form explanations of social problems. Alienation and the indifference of those of means to the urban poor were perceived as inherent to living in large cities; the unhealthiness of urban life was accepted as scientific fact.

It is, of course, incontrovertible that the present conditions of most of our cities remain deplorable, the contrasts between rich and poor as extreme now as then, the need for reform as great. But what has indeed changed is our perspective of the city. Long since accepted as part of modern life, our cities are hardly regarded as spearheads of change or employed as a metaphor for social transformation. Great cities are now the norm. The formerly important cultural dichotomy between urban and rural life has very largely eroded. Cities may still at times be dangerous, but advances in medical science mean they are not necessarily any unhealthier in advanced nations than the country.

For the most part, the problems of the city are those of society at large. If they appear more prominent in urban settings, it is because of scale, visibility, and the undeniable fact that cities serve society as a repository of problem populations. Both the sociological and the environmental arguments against city living have very largely run their course, and with this development, so has much of the perceived need for garden cities.

If one projects the future from the present (what planners refer to as trend extrapolation), the Garden City movement in much of its philosophy and certainly in its cheerful expectations and confident hopes appears now something of a museum piece. This need not be the case. Reliance on trend extrapolation has its limitations. It leaves little room for the unexpected and ignores the possibility that the heterodox occasionally enters the mainstream. Indeed, Howard's view of the need for smaller experimental communities still retains much appeal for many of our own dissenters and "simple-lifers," who still aspire to an "organic community" in which individual wishes and community claims are reconciled and participatory democracy flourishes in a setting consistent with a natural order.[27]

Since the 1960s, a social-issue-oriented ecology movement has predicted that our consumer culture and its technology is threatened by contradictions. With warnings about the ozone layer, pollution, the greenhouse effect, and the depletion of natural resources, environmentalists call for limits on economic and population growth. They urge us to use our environment congruent with and not in violation of natural imperatives. Perhaps this message will be as ignored in the future as it has been in the past. Still the challenges to the environment could, in time, force a reconsideration of our present values and the cities and suburbs they have created. Certainly the summer of 1988 with its drought and heat spell frightened many and added a sense of urgency to ecological considerations of a growing greenhouse effect. Only time will tell whether the summer's discomfort was an ordinary occasional occurrence or a harbinger of troubles to come.

Our suburbs are particularly vulnerable to any future restraints on auto use required to curb pollution and climatic changes—or indeed in response to an oil shortage. Under such circumstances, suburban diffusion may be forced to become more cohesive and self-contained—to evolve into sub-centers that are more compact and urban than at present. Garden City themes might then return to fashion in planning and governmental circles as they reevaluate old solutions in the hope of finding answers to new problems. Oscar Wilde enjoined his readers that "A map of the world that does not contain Utopia is not worth looking at. For it is the one place that man is always landing."

Utopias, Lewis Mumford has reminded us, arise from the reality of the known environment—ours appears to be fraught with menace. Future efforts at depicting or even enacting a utopia will no doubt have as a principal concern the design of a satisfactory or even superior life-style which will pose less peril to the planet than our own. Thought will have to be given to how our desire for mobility and access to jobs, homes, and services can be reconciled with the need to conserve energy and protect our environment. Interest in alternative cultures is far from dead. Since the 1960s, there has been an increased tendency for individuals to declare for change by simply living in a different way. The search for utopia is often not only a rational exercise but perhaps on a deeper level also a quest for a collective consciousness based on the universal experiences of work, family, and community. It may represent our modern way of creating the myths about returning to or arriving at an age of innocence and goodness so commonly found among primitive people.[28]

The last two decades of the nineteenth century experienced a rush of speculation and high expectation about the future that is absent today. Perhaps in part this is because of twentieth-century experiences with totalitarianism, wars, holocausts, and the uncertainties of a nuclear age that have sobered our imaginations and curbed our optimisms. Probably more important is the absence of a satisfactory new model of change which together with a strong sense of moral imperatives fuels visionary thinking. The professionalization of planning and the rise of relativistic thinking may have promoted a tendency to search for neutral technical solutions.

Two very powerful models of change were developed in the course of the nineteenth century. The Marxist assumed that all history was the working out of internal contradictions present in societies because of their class nature and required intervals of abrupt revolutionary outbursts and sudden transformation. The evolutionary model of Darwin assumed slow change over time. Both were, however, optimistic in believing that change led to progress, even if the process was painful. They both assumed the reality of historical movement and invested change with some unified and ultimate meaning, in contrast to, for example, the fatalism of the ancient Greeks and Romans who regarded history as essentially a continuous recurrence, a series of endless repetitions or cycles signifying nothing. In a sense, Marxism and Darwinian evolution offered secular substitutions for Christian millenarianism and thus met the nineteenth-century need for a substitute faith as traditional religious beliefs waned. As early as 1861, Herbert Spencer in his *Social Statics* proclaimed that "progress is not an accident but a necessity. Instead of civilization being artificial it is part of nature; all of a piece with the development of the embryo and the unfolding of a flower."

Twentieth-century liberalism has envisioned national history as a process proceeding purposefully to a "higher civilization." The broad characteristic of this intended civilization is a society oriented to allowing the individual a full and dignified life in the expression of humane values. It also assumes an ordered, equitable, and rational social organization representing a collective effort to achieve the common good and to manage resources and shape the future accordingly. Society had to secure for individuals the rights and conditions necessary for their full development of moral capacity. This has been the vision behind the positive state in the West. It is teleological, but not necessarily deterministic, and it rests on faith in a discernible social ideal sufficiently powerful to unify conflicting interests. In the last several decades, this vision yielded to an indeterminacy which appears to deny that one can make valid public judgments about the relative legitimacy of different conceptions of progress.

Events in the twentieth century have warned us away from a facile enthusiasm for a positivistic approach to progress. We well know that change will bring advances and retreats, hopes and fears, and that the actual details of the future will always be different from what we envision. In William Morris's famous remark in the "Dream of John Ball": "Men fight and lose the battle, and the thing they fought for comes about in spite of their defeat, and when it comes turns out not to be what they meant and other men have to fight for what they meant under another name."

The visionary impulse in planning revealed by the history of the Garden City movement is one that has an increasing, not decreasing, relevance today. Planning must be about substance as well as process, and at the heart of the former are important questions about how human life should best be lived. Can means be intelligently chosen without an end in view? Utopian thinking is important in opening up a consideration of alternative possibilities. The history of the Garden City movement also indicates the constraints of vision and the importance of the process by which it is actualized. Neither planners nor other experts esteemed as trustees of the public good should be allowed to impose their own notions. The planning process is all important in terms of offering safeguards against arbitrariness, authoritarianism, and self-interest posing as the general good. But planners must do more than determine and efficiently deliver what people want. They must contribute to providing alternative visions of what is socially desirable.

The concept of planning as an important function of the positive state in shaping the future took root at the turn of the century. It was intended as a remedy in one way or another of a market system whose consequences were found socially wanting. We end our own century acutely aware of the shortcomings of the positive state and, for that matter, of society's inability to handle adequately apparently intractable social problems. Confidence in human rationality, altruism, and potential has greatly diminished in recent times.

Partly in response to this, there has been increasing regard for the efficiency of the market in allocating resources. Our neo-conservatives insist that market efficiency must be the single or at least most important determinant of social issues and questions. This is to ignore the historical experience of the nineteenth century that allowing market forces and an entrepreneurial ethos to exclusively determine the technology, values, and life-styles of the future invites social indifference and courts disaster. Long ago, John Maynard Keynes warned that businessmen disregard long-term goals when their "thoughts are excited by the possibility of a quick fortune and cleaning out."

Another related snare that has entrapped generations of reformers is the assumption that social progress is necessarily identical to economic efficiency, when indeed they may represent contrary impulses and needs. Planning must go beyond the merely technical concerns of infrastructure, land-use control, and even general interest in the delivery of public services to grapple with environmental issues and the management of resources for the public good which synthesize social requirements and personal pleasures. When it does this, however, it becomes too important to entrust exclusively to the professional. Visionary planning is most viable when it involves the collective imagination of the community and perhaps taps unconscious yearnings. As our sense of community based on spatial considerations and the intersecting demands of work, family, and neighborliness weakens, there is need to fashion new forms of social bonding—or perhaps reinforce old ones. A political scientist, George Kateb, has suggested that future utopias will "derive their form from the shifting and dissolving movement of society that is replacing the fixed locations of life." Certainly the idea that impelled reformers—increasing economic interdependence requires new ways of thinking about community—remains valid.

Those who pursued the will-o'-the-wisp of the Cooperative Commonwealth a century ago were eager for social experimentation to resolve society's contradictions. They envisioned an alternative culture set in a landscape that was neither city nor country as a middle way between individualism and collectivism. The questions they raised remain largely unanswered but are still important.

A major concern of this study has been to place the Garden City movement in its historical setting by demonstrating that Howard essentially worked within a paradigm established at the end of the nineteenth century by those attracted to the notion of a communitarian approach to reform— one which looked to the miniature rather than the large scale model for achieving a humanistic society and which accepted the notion of the community as a social invention. What is clear to me is that people drawn to this approach sought spiritual and ethical values to counter the enveloping materialism of skeptical rationalism and capitalistic development. To them, God was a force leading to a higher goal. For this reason, they were often attracted to heterodox faiths. The particular type of faiths they were drawn to tended to offer almost a Platonic sense of an immanent ideal—a natural, harmonious, and perfect design of which our world constitutes an imperfect version which must be made to correspond, or catastrophy would result. Such a vision can transform the very sense we have of reality and invite social action, but it does not easily accommodate itself to the conceptual tools we provide our professionals or to the political and financial constraints within which they must work. Above all, it does not accord with our view of change as open-ended and limitless.

The tension between idealist and realist may, however, prove a positive and energizing force keeping the professional from retreating into stultifying bureaucracy and the idealist from naive excess. Utopian thinking that seeks not only to arrest deterioration but also to explore a variety of possibilities may enrich mainstream thinking. Lack of it may be indicative of our tacit acceptance that the twenty-first century will only continue the present. The theologian Paul Tillich has written, "Where no anticipating utopia opens up possibilities, we find a stagnant sterile present—we find a situation in which not only individual but also cultural realization of human possibilities is inhibited and cannot win through to fulfillment. . . . This is the fruitfulness of utopia—its ability to open up possibilities."[29]

The richness of modern reform has long owed much to people representing dissenting traditions oriented toward moral and material progress for the individual and the commonwealth. It is from their ranks that from time to time individuals have stepped forward to call to us, as did Cotton Mather in *Theopolis Americana* (1710): "Come hither and I will show you an admirable Spectacle! Tis an Heavenly City . . . A CITY to be inhabited by an Innumerable Company of Angels and by the Spirits of Just Men. . . ."

Notes

CHAPTER 1

1. Alfred Marshall, "Three Lectures on Progress and Poverty," *Journal of Law and Economics*, XII (Apr. 1, 1969), 184.

2. For a brief account of experiences which contributed to his conceptualization of the garden city, see "Ebenezer Howard," *Garden Cities and Town Planning*, new series, XVI (July 1926), 132–34.

3. Alfred Baker, *The Life of Sir Isaac Pitman* (London, 1930). Howard's selection of stenographic work might have been significant. When he began his interest in stenography, it was still a controversial or at least innovative system that had not yet gained general acceptance. Pitman's first advocates in the United States were two inveterate communitarians, Stephen Pearl Andrews and Ulysses G. Marrow. Marrow headed a stenographic school in Chicago during the 1870s when Ebenezer Howard resided there and, like Howard, was interested in spiritualism and the mechanical improvement of the typewriter.

4. An autobiographical essay by Howard, marked number 6, in the Frederic J. Osborn Papers, Central Library, Welwyn Garden City. This collection is henceforth cited as W.G.C.

5. For an interesting contemporary depiction of Chicago in the early 1870s by a "booster," see Everett Chamberlain, *Chicago and Its Suburbs* (Chicago, 1874). Chamberlain predicted that within ten years the city would have a population of 800,000 and occupy an area of 125 square miles. On the Chicago park system, see John H. Rauch, *Public Parks: Their Effects Upon the Moral, Physical and Sanitary Condition of the Inhabitants of Large Cities* (Chicago, 1869), and Galen Cranz, "Models for Park Usage: Ideology and the Development of Chicago's Public Parks," (Ph.D. dissertation, Univ. of Chicago, 1971), 1–72. An important analysis of environmental factors as it influenced social and reform thought of the 1870s is provided by Marlene Stein Wortman in "Domesticating the Nineteenth-Century City,"

Prospects: An Annual of American Cultural Studies, III (1977), 531–41. Chicago's streets were arranged according to a rigid grid plan, a feature of almost all American cities that startled visiting Europeans.

6. Autobiographical essay by Ebenezer Howard, marked number 6, W.G.C.

7. On numerous occasions, Howard acknowledged Richmond's influence, as in the autobiographical article cited above (note 6). Shortly before his death, he repeatedly told close friends of the importance of her teachings to him, Dugald MacFadyen, *Sir Ebenezer Howard and the Town Planning Movement* (Manchester, 1933), 10. In conversation with this author, F.J. Osborn stated his belief that Howard had lost interest in spiritualism at the time Osborn met him shortly before World War I and that Howard's interest only revived in the 1920s when he was ill. In 1910, however, Howard wrote an essay, "Unity," in support of spiritualism. This is in the Ebenezer Howard Papers, Hertfordshire County Archives, henceforth cited as H.C.A. Ebenezer Howard in his autobiographical writings recalled meeting Richmond personally in 1876. For Richmond's life see H.D. Barrett, *Life Work of Cora L.V. Richmond* (Chicago, 1895), 725–59. She described her occult powers in "Psychic or Supermundane Experiences," *Arena,* XVIII (1897), 98–107.

8. Adin Ballou, *History of the Hopedale Community* (Loncel, Mass., 1897), reprinted in 1972 by Porcupine Press of Philadelphia. John L. Thomas, "Antislavery and Utopia," in Martin Duberman (ed.), *Antislavery Vanguard* (Princeton, 1965), 249–54. John S. Garner, *The Model Company Town* (Amherst, Mass., 1984), 117–235. Despite Ballou's unhappiness with this development, Garner believes the model factory town was exemplary, and its work force content at least until the twentieth century.

9. "Certain Dangerous Tendencies in American Life," *Atlantic Monthly,* XLII (Oct. 1878), 391–92. In this highly critical article, spiritualists are described as "especially hostile to belief in any authority except that of the individual soul . . ." and espousing the view that all existing organizations and institutions be replaced in order to "begin anew." Historians of "Modern Spiritualism" emphasize its attack on orthodoxy, the latter being regarded as an impediment to individual enlightenment and social progress.

10. Frank Podmore, *Modern Spiritualism,* vol. I (London, 1902), 134–37. Podmore was a member of the Society of Psychical Research, a biographer of Robert Owen, and a founder of the Fabian Society to which he contributed its name. In 1886, he presented a paper to the Fabians on the American socialist colonies.

11. Though finding Richmond the most impressive trance speaker he had encountered, Podmore still described her "utterings" as virtually incomprehensible, "the protoplasm of speech," *Modern Spiritualism,* vol. I, 137; the quote from Henry James is cited in Howard Kerr, *Mediums and Spirit Rappers, and Roaring Radicals* (Urbana, Ill., 1972), 197. Howard, however, wrote in 1926: "I say without hesitataion that she was the most eloquent extempore speaker I have ever heard." Ebenezer Howard, *Garden Cities and Town Planning,* new series, XVI (July 1926), 132–33.

12. Kerr, 190–222.

13. *Chicago Times,* Nov. 15, 1875; *Chicago Tribune,* Nov. 15, 1875. For the subject of the remainder of Richmond's appearance in Chicago on this occasion see her *Experience of Judge J.W. Edmonds in Spirit Life* (Chicago, 1876). Soon after this stay in Chicago, Cora Richmond was offered a position by the First Spiritual Society of Chicago. Richmond remained in Chicago until her death in 1923.

14. Cora L.V. Richmond, *The Soul, Its Nature, Relations and Expressions in Human Embodiments* (Chicago, 1888). This book was dedicated by Richmond "to my classes in England and America."

15. Ibid., 49–54. Of special interest is Richmond's novel *Zulicka* (Chicago, 1890). Written "under the control of Ovina," this novel has as its plot an English aristocrat's establishment of a model industrial village, which in time becomes a cooperative society.

16. Howard, "Unity," H.C.A.

17. Dugald Macfadyen, 13–14.

18. Ebenezer Howard to Elizabeth Howard, Nov. 3, 1879, W.G.C.

19. Ebenezer Howard, "Spiritualism: A Paper Presented to the Holborn Literary and Debating Society, Feb. 14, 1880," *The Medium and Daybreak*, XI (Apr. 16, 1880), 241–45. On the Zetetical Society, see Norman and Jeanne MacKenzie, *The Fabians* (New York, 1977), 35.

20. J.J. Morse, *Leaves From My Life* (London, 1877), 53. This work compares American and British spiritualists from the point of view of the latter; also Podmore, *Modern Spiritualism*, vol. I, 209–10, 216–17. The best recent work on 19th-century American spiritualism is Lawrence Moore's *In Search of White Crows* (New York, 1977). Its counterpart on English spiritualism is Janet Oppenheimer's *The Other World: Spiritualism and Psychical Research in England, 1850–1914* (Cambridge, 1985). Spiritualism among English working-class radicals is considered in Logie Barrow, *Independent Spirits: Spiritualism and English Plebians, 1850–1910* (London, 1986).

21. James Burns published Richmond's English lectures, and her foreword acknowledged his friendship and support—*Discourse Through the Mediumship of C.L.V. Tappan* (London, 1875). On Burns, see Barrow, 101–7, 256–62.

22. Letters from Howard and his wife to Cora Richmond are in Barrett, 693–94.

23. Moore, 168–69.

24. Laurence Veysey, *The Communal Experience: Anarchist and Mystical Communities in Twentieth-Century America* (Chicago, 1978), 47–49. After 1900, "Modern Spiritualism" tended to fuse with "New Thought," examples of which are Christian Science and Eastern occult religions. These latter stressed an inward quest for self-fulfillment rather than an outward effort at a social mission. The present religious phenomenon known as "New Age" can be traced to the counterculture of the 1960s which after a period of intensive communitarian experimentation, entered a stage where the emphasis is on inner quest. Veysey's study finds a general belief in a "New Age to arrive for all mankind brought about by a mixture of willful effort and inbuilt astrological determinism."

CHAPTER 2

1. Alfred Marshall, "The Housing of the London Poor: Where to House Them," *Contemporary Review*, XLIV (Feb. 1884), 224–31. For examples of early-nineteenth-century use of the term "home colonies" see P.C. Harrison, *Quest for the New Moral World: Robert Owen and the Owenites in Britain and America* (New York, 1969), 23. On the intellectual roots of nineteenth-century colonization enthusiasm, the most valuable study is Frank E. and Fritzie P. Manuel, *Utopian Thought in the Western World* (Cambridge, Mass., 1979), 413–580.

2. Max Beer, *A History of British Socialism*, vol. 2 (London, 1920), 246–53; Elwood P. Lawrence, *Henry George in the British Isles* (East Lansing, Mich., 1957). For George's influence on the Fabian Society, see A.M. McBriar, *Fabian Socialism and English Politics* (Cambridge, 1966), 29–36.

3. Beer, 250.

4. The standard biography of George is Charles Albro Barker's *Henry George* (New York, 1955). Useful in understanding George in the context of American radical culture is John L. Thomas, *Alternative America* (Cambridge, Mass., 1983). Thomas's study also treats two other American social critics of importance to Howard: Edward Bellamy and Henry Demarest Lloyd.

5. On the use of the term "single tax" see Barker, 291, 607. For Barker's comments on George's distinctive treatment of urban land values, 77; Henry George, *Progress and Poverty*, treats urban land value primarily in Chapter Six, "Effect of the Expectations Raised by Material Progress." Here is found George's famous statement: "When we reach the limits of the growing city—the actual margin of building, which corresponds to the margin of cultivation—we shall not find the land purchasable at its value for agricultural purposes . . . but we shall find that for a long distance beyond the city, *lands bears a speculative*

value, based upon the belief that it will be required in the future for urban purposes [emphasis mine]."

6. Writing in 1894, Sidney and Beatrice Webb confirmed the change: "Instead of the Chartist cry of 'Back to the Land' still adhered to by rural labourers and belated politicians, the town artisan is thinking of his claims to the unearned increment of urban land values, which he now watches falling into the coffers of great landlords," cited in Barker, 413. It should be recalled that the same small group of aristocratic families possessed vast urban holdings as well as extensive rural estates. David Cannadine, *Lords and Landlords* (Cambridge, 1980), and David Cannadine (ed.), *Politicians, Power and Politics in Nineteenth-Century Towns* (New York, 1983).

7. The two essays "Mr. George in California" and "Mr. George in England" appeared in the appendix of Arnold Toynbee, *Lectures on the Industrial Revolution* (London, 1896 edition), 264–319. The circumstances of the lectures are given in F.C. Montague, *Arnold Toynbee* (Baltimore, 1889), 51–52. Charles Booth also offered an interesting but brief criticism of *Progress and Poverty,* which has not been published, Booth MS 797: II 127/13, Library of the University of London.

8. Alfred Marshall's lectures appeared in the Bristol *Times and Mirror* 20, 27 Feb. and 3 Mar. 1883. Certified transcripts are in the Henry George Collection, New York Public Library, A slightly different version from these transcripts has been published by George Stigler as "Alfred Marshall's Three Lectures on Progress and Poverty," *Journal of Law and Economics,* XII (Apr. 1969), 184–212. An exchange of correspondence between Marshall and Alfred Russel Wallace concerning these lectures which appeared in the *Western Dial Press* is also included, *Journal of Law and Economics,* XII, 222–27, as well as a transcript of a rowdy meeting at Oxford University where George, after speaking and being questioned by Marshall, was heckled by students, *Journal of Law and Economics,* XII, 217–22.

9. Alfred Marshall, "The Housing of the London Poor: Where to House Them," *Contemporary Review,* XLV (Feb. 1884), 224–31. According to his student F.Y. Edgeworth, Marshall "valued improvement in physical surroundings chiefly as rendering it possible for the many to lead a noble life," cited in Martin J. Wiener, *English Culture and the Decline of the Industrial Spirit, 1850–1980* (Cambridge, 1981), 90.

10. Carl E. Schorske, "The Idea of the City in European Thought," in Oscar Handlin and John Burchard (eds.), *The Historian and the City* (Cambridge, Mass., 1963), 105–7. Raymond Williams, *The Country and the City* (Oxford, 1973), 302–6. In *The Housing Question,* originally written as a series of three articles in 1872, Engels asserted that only through socialism could the problem of great cities be resolved; although favoring "the abolition of the antithesis between town and country," he refused to state the way this would occur since "utopia begins . . . when one ventures from existing conditions to prescribe the form in which this or any other antithesis of present-day Society is to be resolved" (Moscow, 1970), 89.

11. Alfred Russel Wallace to Henry George, June 3, 1882, and June 7, 1882, in Henry George Collection, the New York Public Library. The correspondence between Wallace and Darwin are in James Marchant, *Alfred Russel Wallace: Letters and Reminiscensces,* vol. I (London, 1916), 316–17. Also see A.R. Wallace, *My Life,* vol. II (New York, 1905), Chapter XXXV, and Wallace's response to Henry Fawcett's cutting review of both Wallace's and George's books which appears in Wallace's *Studies Scientific and Social* (London, 1890), Chapter XVII.

12. Wallace's new enthusiasm for a collectivist economy was influenced by reading Edward Bellamy's *Looking Backward.* Wallace, *My Life,* vol. II, 266. The 1890 article appeared in the *Fortnightly Review,* XLVI (Sept. 1890), 272–82.

13. The term "utopian socialism" (or "utopianism") was used by Engels and others on the Left in two senses: meaning either the advocacy of the founding of socialist colonies or the drawing up of detailed blueprints of any future socialist society. Frederick Engels, *Socialism: Utopian and Scientific,* seventh revised edition (Moscow, 1970). For an example of Engels's use of the term, see above, note 10. E.P. Thompson has commented that in

orthodox Marxism: "Speculation as to the society of the future was repressed and displaced by attention to strategy. Beyond 'the Revolution' little more could be known than certain skeletal theoretical propositions, such as the 'two stages' forseen in *The Critique of the Gotha Programme*," E.P. Thompson, *William Morris: Romantic to Revolutionary* (New York, 1977), 788.

14. The quote from Owen is cited in Beatrice Potter (Webb), *The Co-operative Movement in Great Britain* (London, 1930), 18.

15. Sidney Pollard has asserted that a majority of early industrial "model towns" came about as the result of necessity rather than of social idealism on the part of their founders, "The Factory Village in the Industrial Revolution," *English History*, LXXIX (1964), 513–22; for a further discussion of this issue see, J.D. Marshall, "Colonization as a Factor in the Planting of Towns in North-West England," in H.J. Dyos (ed.), *The Study of Urban History* (London, 1968), 215–30, and Martin Gaskell, "Model Industrial Villages in S. Yorkshire/ N. Derbyshire and the Early Town Planning Movement," *Trends in History*, vol. II (1981), 437–57. For an important group of manufactures who were motivated by social interest, the Bradford-Halifax School, see Walter Creese, *The Search for Environment* (New Haven, 1966), 13–60. Some reformers did perceive or at least sense a relationship between communitarian interest and model factory town, see Gustav Stickley, *The Craftsman* (June 1913), 296; Stickley thought both represented branches from a common trunk, representing efforts at an ideal community based on avoidance of class antagonisms and the provision of a countrified urban setting. Also Henry Demarest Lloyd, "Pullman," an unpublished manuscript in the Lloyd Papers, Box 36, Wisconsin Historical Society.

16. For the Society for Promoting Industrial Villages, see William Ashworth, *The Genesis of Modern British Town Planning* (London, 1954), 133–38. The University of London Library in its Solly Collection has miscellaneous press clippings, pamphlets, and correspondence concerning the society. Solly was also the founder of the Workingmen's Club movement and this aspect of his career is considered in Peter Bailey, *Leisure and Class in Victorian England* (Toronto, 1978). British model villages are the subject of Walter Creese, *The Search for Environment*. Earlier efforts along similar lines are discussed in W.H.G. Armytage, *Heavens Below: Utopian Experiments in England, 1560–1960* (London, 1961).

17. H. Solly, *Industrial Villages: A Remedy for Crowded Towns and Deserted Fields* (London, 1884), 3.

18. Roy Douglas, *Land, People and Politics: A History of the Land Question in the U.K., 1878–1952* (New York, 1976); Avner Offner, *Poverty and Politics, 1870–1914: Landownership, Law, Ideology, and Urban Development in England* (Cambridge, 1981); H.J. Perkin, "Land Reform and Class Conflict in Victorian Britain," in J. Butt and I.F. Clarke (eds.), *The Victorians and Social Protest* (Newton Abbot, 1973), 177–217.

19. H.V. Emmy, *Radicals, Liberals and Social Reform* (London, 1973). Also of interest in understanding this important transition is Stefan Collini, *Liberalism and Sociology* (Cambridge, 1979).

20. Douglas, 111–14.

CHAPTER 3

1. Richard T. Ely, "Pullman: A Social Study," *Harper's Monthly* LXX (1885), 452–66. On the American model town, see Stanley Buder, *Pullman: An Experiment in Industrial Order and Community Planning* (New York, 1967). Certain features of Howard's garden city resemble Pullman—for example, a central arcade, a brickyard, and the use of treated human waste as a fertilizer in surrounding fields. But these were often proposed features of colonization schemes: see Howard Segal, *Technological Utopianism in American Culture* (Chicago, 1985).

2. Olmstead, Vaux, and Company, *Preliminary Report Upon the Proposed Suburban Village at Riverside Near Chicago* (New York, 1868). F.L. Olmstead, "Public Parks and the Enlarge-

ment of Cities," *Journal of Social Science,* III (1870). Albert Fein, *Frederick Law Olmsted and the American Environmental Tradition* (New York, 1972). On London suburbs, see Alan A. Jackson, *Semi-Detached London* (London, 1973), 21–30; F.M.L. Thompson, *Hampstead: Building a Borough, 1650–1964* (London, 1974), 296–334. Also of use is M.A. Simpson and T.H. Lloyd (eds.), *Middle-Class Housing in Britain* (Hamden, Conn., 1977), and the studies of H.J. Dyos, D.J. Olsen, and F.H.W. Sheppard on estate and suburban development.

3. On rent as a percentage of income, see "Statement of Men Living in Certain Districts of London," British Parliamentary Papers, 1887, LXXI, pp. XIV–XV. The problems of managing a London household on Howard's estimated income may be gleaned from Eliza Warren, *How I Managed My House on Two Hundred Pounds a Year* (London, 1865). In his *Prosperity and Parenthood* (London, 1954), J.A. Banks regarded 300 pounds per annum as the dividing line between the lower-middle and middle-middle classes in late-nineteenth-century Britain. On that income, he believed a family could keep the "maid-of-all-work," which the popular mind identified with middle-class status, 48. For a further discussion of who constituted the lower-middle class and comments on their life-style, see Geoffrey Crossick (ed.), *The Lower Middle Class in Britain, 1870–1914* (New York, 1977), especially S. Martin Gaskell's contribution, "Housing and the Lower Middle Class," 159–83.

4. Ebenezer Howard to Elizabeth Howard, Mar. 4, 1885, W.G.C. At about this time, a young man who later became Howard's principal interpreter and disciple, Raymond Unwin, wrote: To be a socialist nowadays a man must first have enough discontent with his surroundings to look for something better"—"Social Experiments," *Commonweal* (Mar. 5, 1887), 313.

5. John R. Kellett, *The Impact of Railways on Victorian Cities* (London, 1969), 244–314; Gareth Stedman Jones, *Outcast London* (Oxford, 1971), 159–78.

6. Gareth Stedman Jones, 281–314; Paul Thompson, *Socialists, Liberals and Labour: The Struggle for London, 1885–1914* (London, 1967), 5–16.

7. Charles Booth, *Life and Labour of the People in London,* vol. I (London, 1902), 115, 119, 151, 159.

8. M. Dorothy George, *London Life in the Eighteenth Century* (London, 1966), 103.

9. John Ruskin, *Sesame and Lillies* (New York, 1888). In the third and final essay of this book, Ruskin called for social action so that housing be provided "in groups of limited extent, kept in proportion . . . and walled around so that there may not be festering and wretched suburb anywhere but clean and busy street within and the open country without, with a belt of beautiful gardens and orchards around the walls, so that from any part of the city perfectly fresh air and grass and sight of far horizon might be reachable in a few minutes walk." On the Victorian cult of domesticity see Walter E. Houghton, *The Victorian Frame of Mind* (New Haven, 1957).

10. Patricia Branca, "Image and Reality: The Myth of the Idle Victorian Woman," in Mary S. Hartman and Lois Banner (eds.), *Clio's Consciousness Raised* (New York, 1977), 179–91. Michael Young and Peter Willmott, *The Symmetrical Family* (New York, 1973), 65–101. Geoffrey Crossick (ed.), *The Lower Middle Class in Britain, 1870–1914* (New York, 1977).

11. For birthrates, see J.A. Barks and Olive Banks, *Feminism and Female Planning in Victorian England* (New York, 1964).

12. Young and Willmott, 19, 27–33.

13. Although occasionally inaccurate on details, the works of George Jacob Holyoake are essential to an understanding of the 19th-century cooperative movement: *History of Co-operation in England,* 2 vols. (London, 1875), and *Bygones Worth Remembering,* 2 vols. (London, 1905). Still useful is Beatrice Potter (Webb), *The Co-operative Movement in Great Britain* (London, 1891). A recent study is Philip N. Backstrom, *Christian Socialism and Cooperation in Victorian England* (London, 1974). According to Paul Thompson, the cooperative movement was weak in London—a fact often explained as the result of a migratory life-style which mitigated against corporate organization. *Socialists, Liberals and Labour: The Struggle for London, 1885–1914,* 40–41. Stephen Mayor has pointed out that the cooperative move-

ment depended largely on the dissenting churches for its supporters, and these were underrepresented in London's population as compared with the north. *The Churches and the Labour Movement* (London, 1967), 152–53. On the relationship of cooperators and socialism, see, for example, *Twenty-second Annual Co-operative Congress, Manchester, 1890*, pp. 12–15. Many cooperators believed that they and the socialists shared common ends and only differed in means. For an account by the American social reformer Henry Demarest Lloyd of interest among British cooperators in home colonization, see his *Co-partnership* (New York, 1893), 97.

14. C.R. Fay, *Co-operation at Home and Abroad* (London, 1923), 222–37; "Labour Association for Promoting Co-operative Production Based on the Co-partnership of the Worker, First Report," (London, 1885), 1–6. The organization soon shortened its name to the Labour Co-partnership. As early as 1889, G.B. Shaw denounced labor co-partnership as "joint stock capitalism masquerading as cooperation" whose purpose was to allow a safety valve for mounting pressure for real social change. *Fabian Essays* (London, 1889), 83. The Fabians consistently opposed labor co-partnership: Edward R. Pease, *Profit Sharing and Co-partnership: A Fraud and a Failure*, Fabian Tract 170 (London, 1913).

15. The quote from Carpenter is from *My Days and Dreams* (London, 1916), 245. Also see E.P. Thompson, *William Morris* (New York, 1977), 427; Stanley Pierson, *Marxism and the Origins of British Socialism* (Ithaca, 1973), 217–43; R.C.K. Ensor, *Modern Socialism* (London, 1907), 427.

16. Peter Marshall, "A British Sensation," in Sylvia Bowman (ed.), *Edward Bellamy Abroad* (New York, 1962), 86–118.

17. Ebenezer Howard, "Spiritual Influences Towards Social Progress," *Light* (Apr. 30, 1910), 195. Howard in this article recalled the occasion of his reading *Looking Backward* as the moment when he started to give thought to a new colony. The evidence suggests that he did not start working out or writing down his ideas of a colony until 1891 at the earliest. In 1890, Howard did change the name of a jobbing press he was planning to start to the Bellamy Cooperative Press and decided to organize it along labor–co-partnership lines. I suspect Howard in later life confused this event as the start of his thinking about a colony.

18. Peter Marshall, 90–94.

19. Peter d'A Jones, *The Christian Socialist Revival, 1877–1914* (Princeton, 1968), 331–37. A description of the Rectory Road Congregational Church is in Booth, vol. I, 224–25. For Williams's view on London's housing problems, see *Morning Leader*, Sept. 19, 1899. A useful work on the much-studied theme of the nonconforming churches as a moral force in British reform is Clyde Binfield, *So Down to Prayer: Studies in English Nonconformity, 1780–1920* (Totowa, N.J., 1977).

20. H.G. Wells, "Faults of the Fabians," privately printed (London, 1906). Wells's paper to the Fabian Society on Feb. 9, 1906, appears in its entirety in Samuel Hynes, *The Edwardian Turn of Mind* (Princeton, 1968), Appendix C, 390–409.

CHAPTER 4

1. For early-19th-century community activity in America, the best book is Arthur Bestor, *Backwards Utopia: The Sectarian Origins and the Owenite Phase of Communitarian Socialism in America*, 2nd edition enlarged (Philadelphia, 1970). For the revival of communitarian efforts, see Alexander Kent, "Cooperative Communities in the U.S.," *Bulletin of the Department of Labor*, VI, no. 35 (July 1901), 604–12, 617–18. A sympathetic account of these efforts is in William Alfred Hinds, *American Communities and Cooperative Colonies*, 2nd edition revised (Chicago, 1908), and for criticism, see *People*, Aug. 6, 1893, and Jan. 6, 1895.

2. Crane Brinton, *The United States and Britain* (Cambridge, Mass., 1945); Richard Heinde, *The American Impact on Britain* (Philadelphia, 1940); Sylvia Straus, "The American Myth in Britain," *South Atlantic Quarterly*, LXXII (1973), 66–81. For contemporary views by radi-

cals on an Anglo-American mission to create a new social order, see the *New Nation* I (May 16, 1891), 245. On the difference between native-born, middle-class American radicals and their European immigrant counterparts, see Howard Quint, *The Forging of American Socialism* (Columbia, S.C., 1953), 86–87. Robert Wiebe, *The Search for Order, 1877–1920* (New York, 1967), provides useful insight into American social change. In Wiebe's analysis, the last quarter of the 19th century is a time of the breakdown of the relatively socially and economically self-sufficient American town and city, what he calls "the island community," before the rise of big business and a national economic network. There is little question that communitarian activity reflected at least some nostalgia for the disappearing worlds of the "island community" and rural life.

3. Lawrence Gronlund, *The Cooperative Commonwealth* (New York, 1884), 64. The first British edition published in London in 1885 contains an introduction by the then obscure G.B. Shaw. The best edition of Gronlund's book is by the Belknap Press of Harvard University Press with an excellent introductory essay by John L. Thomas (Cambridge, Mass., 1965).

4. Herman I. Stern, "Who Are the Utopians?" *The Nationalist* 3 (Oct. 1890), 167.

5. Bestor, 230–52.

6. Adin Ballou, *History of the Hopedale Community* (Loncel, Mass., 1897), 241–42.

7. Bestor has catalogued 106 American communities in the period from 1800 to 1860; Robert Fogerty has compiled a list of 150 communities for the period 1860 to 1918. For an assessment of these figures, see Dolores Hayden, *Seven American Utopias* (Cambridge, Mass., 1976), 365. For differences between early and late communitarian movements, see Charles Pierce LeWarne, *Utopias on Puget Sound, 1885–1915* (Seattle, Wash., 1975), 5–7. Biographic information on Albert K. Owen and an account of his community is provided by Ray Reynold in *Cat's Paw Utopia*, privately printed (1973). Also see Albert K. Owen, *Integral Cooperation: Its Practical Application*, a collection of writings by Owen published in 1885 and reprinted by the Porcupine Press of Philadelphia in 1975 as part of a series of reprints of primary material on American utopias under the editorship of Robert J. Fogerty. Sometime around World War I, survivors of the Topolobampo community settled in the mountains northeast of Fresno, Calif. The records of the colony consisting of nine uncatalogued file cabinets of material and including hundreds of photographs are now in the library of Fresno State University of California, henceforth referred to as Fresno Col.

8. John Reps, *The Making of Urban America* (Princeton, 1965), 403–4.

9. "Integral co-operation is a system in which a colony owns all forms of businesses, acting as sole employer of men. The men, however, are paid varying rates according to skill, need, and experience." Herbert B. Adams (ed.), *History of Co-operation in the United States* (Baltimore, 1888), 365. The first use of the term in the U.S. appears to have occurred in the 1880s and may have been introduced by an English immigrant, Henry G. Sharpe, active in the Knights of Labor, who tried to start a colony in Eglinton, Mo., in 1881.

10. Two plans of residential-block arrangement and street layout prepared by the Philadelphia architectural firm of Deery and Keerl are in Owen's *Integral Cooperation*, 106, 122; Albert K. Owen, *A Dream of an Ideal City* (London, 1897).

11. An account of John Lovell's life and the New York bohemian circle is in Madeline Sterns, *Imprints in History* (Bloomington, Ind., 1956), 259–79. Lovell formerly had been an important supporter of Henry George, but the latter disapproved of his interest in colonies— John Lovell to Henry George, Nov. 28, 1882, Henry George Collection, New York Public Library. Lovell was also a spiritualist and as publisher promoted the publication of cheap editions of books on the women's movement and the occult.

12. Sterns, 274.

13. Edward Aveling, *The Working-Class Movement in America* (London, 1891), 190–93. This is an enlarged and revised edition of the work originally published in 1889 by Lovell. There is an irony in the fact that Aveling provided the first English translation of Frederick Engels's important attack on communitarianism, *Socialism Utopian and Socialism Scientific* (London, 1891).

14. Among those Owen met in Britain were Annie Besant of the Fabian Society and Henry

Mayers Hyndman, the founder of the Social Democratic Federation: Annie Besant to Albert Owen, Mar. 13, 1889; Henry Mayers Hyndman to Albert Owen, Jan. 19, 1889, Fresno Col. *Pall Mall Gazette,* Sept. 30, 1889. At this time Besant was writing an attack on colonization schemes which appeared as "Industry Under Socialism" in George Bernard Shaw (ed.), *Fabian Essays on Socialism* (London, 1889). After breaking with the Fabians to become a leader of the Theosophy Society, Besant became interested in such efforts. Hyndman warned Owen, "you cannot create an oasis of cooperation and harmony amidst a wilderness of competition and war"; he advised the American to direct his energies toward "achieving" state socialism. Twenty-two letters from Evacustes Phipson, the earliest from 1884 and the latest from 1902, are in Fresno Col. According to Robert Beevers, *The Garden City Utopia: A Critical Biography of Ebenezer Howard* (New York, 1988), 38, and W.H.G. Armytage, *Heavens Below: Utopian Experiments in England, 1560–1960* (London, 1961), Phipson visited Owen's colony, but I found no evidence of this. Armytage also notes that Phipson had used a 16,000-pound legacy in 1881 to establish a colony in Australia in 1881. Phipson corresponded extensively with John Samuel, secretary of the National Cooperative Union of America, writing him in 1894 that "I am still anxious to see a . . . colony started by real solid and true Rochdale cooperators." Clifton Yearly, Jr., *Britains in American Labor* (Baltimore, 1958), 298.

15. Peter d'A Jones, *The Christian Socialist Revival, 1877–1914* (Princeton, 1968), 335–40; A.G. Higgins, *A History of the Brotherhood,* privately printed (1982), 2–8. This work (a copy of which is with the Osborn Archives at the Welwyn Garden City Central Library) is by a longtime member of the Brotherhood Church, which as of date of publication still existed at Stapleton near Pontefractin, Yorkshire. Higgins had access to an unfinished manuscript by a W.R. Hughes who had been authorized by J. Bruce Wallace's daughter to write his biography. It appears from Higgins's confused text that the Brotherhood group at Stapleton was a break-off from a group which in 1894 itself broke off from Wallace's followers to form the Brotherhood Church of Croyden under J.C. Kenworthy. For Kenworthy's efforts to start an intentional community along Tolstoyan lines, see Dennis Hardy, *Alternative Communities in Nineteenth Century England* (London, 1979). For J. Bruce Wallace's inclusive reform program, see *Brotherhood* (Apr. 27, 1888) and (Oct. 7, 1889).

16. J. Bruce Wallace to Albert K. Owen, Aug. 2, 1890, Fresno Col.

17. For Bliss's life, see entry in W.D. Bliss (ed.), *The New Encyclopedia of Social Reform* (New York, 1908); Quint, 109–25, 256–68. For Bliss's approach to reform, see *Dawn* VII (Jan. 1890), 1; for his view on colonies, see *Dawn* VIII (Nov. 1891), 7–8. For Edward Bellamy's views on colonies and Kaweah in particular, see the *New Nation* I (May 2, 1891). Many of Bellamy's supporters continued to remain interested in colonies—see Quint, Chapter III.

18. Accounts by Wallace of his American trip are in *Brotherhood* (Nov. 12, 1890), 98, (Feb. 16, 1891), 200, (Mar. 4, 1891), 228. Lawrence Gronlund, *The Cooperative Commonwealth* (London, 1885), 16; Lawrence Gronlund, *The New Economy* (New York, 1907), 192–95. An account of the Kaweah community is in Robert V. Hine, *California's Utopia Colonies* (New York, 1973), 78–100.

19. For Flürscheim's life, see Charles Albro Barker, *Henry George* (New York, 1955), 531–39. Letters from Flürscheim to George are in the Henry George Collection of the New York Public Library and his correspondence with Albert K. Owen is in Fresno Col. Flürscheim published a utopian fable, *The Real History of Money Island* (London, 1896), with J. Bruce Wallace's Brotherhood Press and dedicated it to Wallace. For the final years of the Topolobampo experiment, see *Cat's Paw Utopia,* and also Leopold Katschen, "Owen's Topolobampo Colony," *American Journal of Sociology,* XII (Sept. 1906), 145–75. Katschen was a professor at the University of Leipzig interested in home colonies in Germany who extensively corresponded with Owen in the years 1895 to 1906, which he refers to in his article. A letter from Marie Howland to J. Bruce Wallace on the end of the Mexican colony was published in *Brotherhood* (Nov. 23, 1902), 72. By this time the irrepressible Howland was a member of yet another colony, the Fairhope community, and was a Theosophist.

20. Carlos A. Schwantes, *Radical Heritage: Labor, Socialism and Reform in Washington and British*

Columbia, 1885–1917 (Seattle, 1979), 87–93; Charles Pierce LeWarne, *Utopias on Puget Sound, 1885–1915* (Seattle, 1975), 55–113; Quint, 283–317.

21. Debs's involvement in colonization schemes and the struggle over this issue is described in Nick Salvatore, *Eugene V. Debs* (Urbana, Ill., 1982), 152–69; Quint, 299–320. Also see H. Wayne Morgan, "The Utopia of Eugene V. Debs," *American* (Summer 1959), 120–35.

22. Hinds, 586.

23. A typewritten copy of this article dated Nov. 1983 is in the Henry Demarest Lloyd Collection, Box 38, Wisconsin Historical Society. A revised version was published in Henry Demarest Lloyd, *Mazzini and Other Essays* (New York, 1910), 201–33. On Lloyd, see John L. Thomas, "Utopia for an Urban Age: Henry George, Henry Demarest Lloyd, Edward Bellamy," *Perspectives in American History*, VI (1972), 135–63.

24. Gustav Stickley, *The Craftsman* (June 1913), 296.

CHAPTER 5

1. Robert Flint, *Socialism* (London, 1895), 3.

2. J. Bruce Wallace to Albert K. Owen, Oct. 24, 1891, Fresno Col.

3. J. Bruce Wallace to Albert K. Owen, Feb. 6, 1892, Feb. 13, 1892, Fresno Col.

4. *Labour Nationalisation News* (Feb. 1892); *Brotherhood* (Feb. 7, 1892). Also see Peter Marshall, "A British Sensation," in Sylvia Bownan (ed.), *Edward Bellamy Abroad* (New York, 1962), 97–102.

5. *Brotherhood* (Sept. 14, 1892), (Dec. 20, 1892), (Jan. 10, 1893).

6. A detailed account of circle cooperation as well as indications of Wallace's interest in starting a colony is in *Brotherhood* (Sept. 9, 1887). Also see J. Bruce Wallace, *Towards Fraternal Organization* (London, 1894). *Brotherhood* (Mar. 16, 1888). Members of the Fellowship of the New Life communicated with Albert Owen before starting their experiment— Dyke Smith to Albert K. Owen, May 2, 1888, Fresno Col. Sidney Webb described Wallace as "a comrade whom we all respect for sincerity and boundless energy" but then chided him as one who eschewed building up a Municipal Works Department under the London County Council "and preferred the glorious but impractical vision of a cooperative commonwealth which was to be created overnight." Sidney Webb, *Socialism True and False*, Fabian Tract 51 (London, 1894), 10–12.

7. Marie Howland, *The Kingdom Comes* (Topolobampo, Mexico, 1889). Theodore Herzka, *Freeland* (London, 1892). On Herzka's ideas and movement, see Richard Wheatley, "Ideal Communities," *Methodist Review*, LXXV (July 1893), 594–603, and more important, Frank and Fritzie Manuel, *Utopian Thought in the Western World* (Cambridge, Mass., 1979), 752–59.

8. Evacustes Phipson to Albert K. Owen, Jan. 4, 1892, and Mar. 7, 1892, Fresno Col. Owen, however, on his own had established contact with Herzka. Theodore Herzka to Albert K. Owen, Dec. 3, 1891. This letter and three others from Herzka were written in German and translated by a Topolobampo colonist into English. The German originals appear to be missing.

9. Albert K. Owen to J. Bruce Wallace, July 11, 1892. Published in Albert K. Owen, *Pacific City Studies* (New York, 1893), 19–27. Evacustes Phipson to Albert K. Owen, Oct. 20, 1892, Fresno Col. This letter discusses the rift which had developed in the London group.

10. Howard's involvement in Wallace's group has been pieced together from a variety of sources, including *Brotherhood* and the *Labour Nationalisation News* for 1892 and early 1893; newspaper clippings concerning the Feb. 11, 1893, meeting in "Ebenezer Howard Scrapbook," W.G.C.; Evacustes Phipson letters to A.K. Owen, Sept. 18, 1892, Oct. 20, 1892, Apr. 1, 1893, Fresno Col.; J. Bruce Wallace to A.K. Owen, June 15, 1892, Oct. 3, 1892, Feb. 4, 1893; the *New City*, Dec. 8, 1892, p. 4; the *New City*, Dec. 22, 1892, p. 3. The *New City* was a newspaper published sporadically by Marie Howland, and issues, though not the entire run, are in Fresno Col.

11. Royal Commission on Labour, *Report of the Royal Commission on Labour*, British Parliamentary Papers, 1894, XV.

12. "Common Sense Socialism," item 45, W.G.C. This also may be found in Howard Papers, folio 10, H.C.A.

13. For Howard's version of his abandonment of Bellamy's Nationalism, see Dugald Mac-fadyen, *Sir Ebenezer Howard and the Town Planning Movement* (Manchester, 1933), 20–21. As with most of his important ideas, Howard attributed this to a dramatic insight which suddenly came upon him. Evidence suggests a slower development. Note, for example, that in *To-morrow* Howard cited Owen's Topolobampo as an instance of a colony which floundered as a consequence of an overcentralized economy—*Garden Cities of To-morrow* (London, 1902), 98–99. Howard also referred to Owen's *Integral Cooperation* in his foot-notes and employed this term several times in his manuscript.

14. See "Summary of E. Howard's Proposal for a Home Colony," *Labour Nationalisation News* (Feb. 1893), 20–21.

15. Ibid.

16. *Brotherhood* (Dec. 14, 1896), 128. This letter was originally written in Jan. 1894 in response to an inquiry on how to go about beginning a colony. A collection of articles by Kropotkin which appeared in the journal *The Nineteenth Century* from 1888 to 1890 were collected and published in Peter Kropotkin, *Fields, Factories, and Workshops* (London, 1899). Here Kropotkin argued that the dawning age of electricity allowed for rapid urban decentraliza-tion and called for the creation of new small "industrial villages." For Kropotkin in Lon-don, see J.W. Hulse, *Revolutionists in London* (Oxford, 1970).

17. The meeting was reported in several small London radical and neighborhood newspapers—for example, *Weekly Times and Echo*, Feb. 12, 1893; and the *Morning Leader*, Feb. 13, 1893. Clippings concerning this meeting are to be found at the rear of a scrapbook, "Ebenezer Howard Scrapbook," 138–45, W.G.C., otherwise used for reviews of *To-morrow* and early accounts of the Garden City Association. For this reason, the clippings escaped the attention of researchers until I noticed them in the fall of 1967. Stanley Buder, "Ebenezer Howard: The Genesis of a Town Planning Movement," *Journal of the American Institute of Planners*, XXXV (Nov. 1969), 390–98.

18. The writers Howard acknowledged as foreshadowing his work were Edward Gibbon Wakefield, Alfred Marshall, Thomas Spence, and James Silk Buckingham, but he denied familiarity with their ideas until after he had thought through his scheme for the garden city. He claimed that the only relevant book he read before beginning work on the garden city was Dr. Benjamin Richardson's *Hygeia, A City of Health* (London, 1876). This he remembered reading in the United States before returning to Britain in 1876. E. Howard, "Spiritual Influences Towards Social Progress," *Light* (Apr. 30, 1910), 196. Richardson's book was originally presented in the form of a lecture, and the date and place of publica-tion suggest that Howard misremembered the time when he read it. Sometime during the 1890s, Howard wrote to Richardson describing his scheme for a new community but received no reply. Richardson also wrote a utopian work, *The Son of a Star: A Romance of the Second Century* (London, 1887).

19. Ebenezer Howard to Elizabeth Howard, July 13, 1893, W.G.C.

20. *Brotherhood* (Dec. 14, 1893). The meeting was "to clarify various schemes for a colony of which so many are being urged." The flurry of activity that followed this meeting is discussed in W.G.H. Armytage, *Heavens Below: Utopian Experiments in England, 1560–1960* (London, 1961), 342–46.

21. Dennis Hardy, *Alternative Communities in Nineteenth Century England* (London, 1979), 177–79, 194–95.

22. Ebenezer Howard to C.B. Purdom, Jan. 4, 1913. At this time, Howard expected Purdom to be his biographer. He warned Purdom that several people claimed to have worked with him in developing the Garden City concept before the publication of the book. Howard denied this was true. The letter is in W.G.C. Purdom later noted that Howard was very reticent about anything connected with the inception of his ideas. C.B. Purdom, *The Building of Satellite Towns* (London, 1949), 27–39. For Ebenezer Howard's comments on Topolobampo, see *Garden Cities of To-morrow* (London, 1902), 98–99.

CHAPTER 6

1. The earliest drafts of Howard's manuscript refer to the community as Unionville. In the years 1895 and 1896, Howard called it Rurisville, and then Garden City. Howard later regretted that he had not retained the name Rurisville as less open to misunderstanding. *The Garden City,* VIII (Feb. 1908), 17.

2. *Builders' Journal and Architectural Record,* Oct. 25, 1899, W.G.C.; *Brotherhood* (Feb. 11, 1901), 155. Lecture to the Fabian Society, Jan. 11, 1901, holograph in W.G.C.; Ebenezer Howard to F.J. Osborn, May 30, 1917, W.G.C.

3. On the Continent, especially in parts of Germany, factory workers still grew much of their food needs. The Krupp model factory towns in Essen, Germany, for example, contained allotment gardens. American and British model industrial villages tended not to provide these. After 1890, the "allotment movement" encouraged providing them as a means of adding to the real income of workers.

4. One of those active in the 1892–93 meeting, Evacustes A. Phipson, wrote in 1895: "The ideal system, is . . . modelled after a cobweb. The principal avenues radiating from a central space around which should be grouped the chief public buildings, while the subsidiary streets are arranged in concentric circles." Evacustes A. Phipson, *Art Under Socialism* (London, 1895), 11–12.

5. The idea of a world of federated colonies can be traced at least as far back in communitarian thought as Fourier. It is unclear whether he originated the concept. The idea that the world of the future should be composed of a federation of free communes was advanced actively in the 1880s by the Russian anarchist Peter Kropotkin. See, for example, *Freedom* (Jan.-Feb. 1894), 436–42.

6. Any consideration of anti-urbanism as a historical theme encounters formidable problems of language and methodology. Much of 19th-century "anti-urbanism," for example, was directed at the city as symbol of capitalism or modernism. Other aspects of "anti-urbanism" were directed at very specific and legitimate concerns of public health. In short, the subject must be handled with great care and sensitivity. Of the many books on this theme, the following are of value: Raymond Williams, *The Country and the City* (New York, 1973); Morton and Lucia White, *The Intellectual Versus the City: From Thomas Jefferson to Frank Lloyd Wright* (Cambridge, Mass., 1962); Andrew Lees, *Cities Perceived: Urban Society in European and American Thought, 1820–1940* (New York, 1985).

7. Adna F. Weber, *The Growth of Cities in the Nineteenth Century* (Ithaca, 1965), 1–2. This is a reprint of a work originally published in 1899 which remains the standard reference on 19th-century urban demographics.

8. William Ashworth, *The Genesis of Modern British Town Planning* (London, 1954), 47–117.

9. Gareth Stedman Jones, *Outcast London* (Oxford, 1971), 303–22; S. Martin Gaskell, "The Suburb Salubrious: Town Planning in Practice," in Anthony Sutcliffe (ed.), *British Town Planning: The Formative Years* (London, 1981), 16–56.

10. Robert Owen, *A New View of Society* (London, 1927), 72; Robert Owen, *The Revolution in the Mind and Practice of the Human Race* (London, 1849), 62–63. J.F.C. Harrison, *Quest for the New Moral Order: Robert Owen and the Owenites in Britain and America* (New York, 1969), 22–23; Frank E. and Fritzie P. Manuel, *Utopian Thought in the Western World* (Cambridge, Mass., 1979), 682–85. While Owen is best known as an atheist, he became involved with spiritualism in the 1850s and under its influence designed a community very different from his earlier efforts. For Owen's ideas on community as a spiritualist, see his *The Future of the Human Race* (London, 1853) and *The Millennium in Practice* (London, 1855).

11. William Hazlitt, *Table-Talk,* vol. I (Paris, 1823), 215–51. For a brief general discussion of late-19th-century environmentalism, see Roy Lubove, *The Progressives and the Slums* (Pittsburgh, 1962), 46–48. On the influence of Darwin on late-19th-century housing reformers' and environmentalists' thinking, see the article on "Housing" in the 11th edition of the *Encyclopaedia Britannica* (London, 1909). Related to environmentalism was the aesthetic principle of "associationism," according to which an individual reacted to the sight of a

natural or historical subject, or its reproduction by an artist, as an evocation of earlier memories. Although found in the late 18th century, "associationism" was given wide hearing by the writings of Pugin and Ruskin. James S. Buckingham, *National Evils and Practical Remedies with the Plan of a Model Town* (London, 1849); Buckingham deplored blind alleys which might lead to "the morose defiance of public decency which such secret haunts generate in the inhabitants." He also stipulated that all families with children were to have no less than three rooms. For temperance reformers and environmentalism, see Brian Harrison, *Drink and the Victorians: Temperance Question in England, 1815–1872* (Pittsburgh, 1972).

12. James Phillips Kay, *The Moral and Physical Condition of the Working Classes* (Manchester, 1832), 6; Southward Smith, *Results of Sanitary Improvements, Illustrated by the Operation of the Metropolitan Societies* (London, 1854), 21–23.

13. Benjamin Richardson, *Hygeia, A City of Health* (London, 1876); James H. Cassidy, "Hygeia: Mid-Victorian Dream of a City of Health," *Journal of the History of Medicine and Allied Sciences,* XVII (Apr. 1962), 217–27. John Stuart Mill in his *Autobiography* suggested that "nothing contributed more to nourish elevation of sentiment in a people than the large and free character of their habitations." Selwyn K. Troen, "The Evolution of a Transatlantic Literature of Urban Planning," unpublished paper delivered to the Organization of American Historians, Apr. 1984.

14. H.D. Trail, "In Praise of Country," *Contemporary Review,* LII (1887), 479–81; W.M. Frazer, *A History of English Public Health, 1834–1939* (London, 1950). In *The Housing Question* (Moscow, 1970), 38–41, which he wrote in 1872, Engels charged that the public-health movement arose out of middle-class fears of the spread of disease from working-class districts into their own. Earlier, in *The Conditions of the Working Class,* Engels had observed that "everyone in a position to do so prefers to live in the suburbs. . . ." He also commented "that great cities have grown up so spontaneously . . . that it is all extremely convenient for the ruling class to ascribe all evils to this apparently unavoidable source."

15. For criticism of model tenement housing in London by early supporters of the Garden City movement, see letters to the editors by C. Fleming Williams in *Morning Leader,* Sept. 19, 1899, and F.W. Steere in the *North Herald,* Oct. 21, 1899. Howard's views on the subject appeared in the *Stoke Newington and Islington Record,* Dec. 9, 1898, and the *Citizen,* Sept. 2, 1899. Also of interest is John Nelson Tarn's well-done architectural analysis, *Five Per Cent Philanthropy* (Cambridge, 1973), 150–81; Anthony Sutcliffe (ed.), *Multi-Storey Living* (London, 1974), 19–41, 88–121. London County Council, *Housing of the Working Classes in London, 1855–1912* (London, 1913).

16. Gareth Stedman Jones, *Outcast London* 330–31; C.F.G. Masterman (ed.), *The Heart of the Empire: Discussions of Problems of Modern City Life in England, with an Essay on Imperialism* (London, 1901). G.A. Lonstaff, "Rural Depopulation," *Journal of the Royal Statistical Society,* LVI (Feb. 1893).

17. Ashworth, 118–57; Tarn, 121–42; Derek Fraser, *The Evolution of the British Welfare State* (New York, 1973); Michael Freeden, *The New Liberalism: An Ideology of Social Reform* (Oxford, 1978).

18. Fabian Society, "Facts for Socialists," Fabian Tract 5; Smith R. Maudie, *The Religious Life of London* (London, 1904), 38–44; Liberal Land Enquiry, *Report of Liberal Land Enquiry* (London, 1913), 114–22. Willard Wolfe, *From Radicalism to Socialism* (Newttavon, 1975); Stefan Collini, *Liberalism and Sociology* (Cambridge, 1979).

19. Tarn, 143–57; Ashworth, 147–57; Anthony Sutcliffe, *Towards the Planned City: Germany, Britain, the United States and France, 1780–1914* (New York, 1981), 62–63.

20. Philip Abrams, *The Origins of British Sociology* (Chicago, 1968), 77–105; Patrick Geddes, *The Garden City,* new series, I (Aug. 1906), 151–52.

21. Dolores Hayden, *Seven American Utopias: The Architecture of Communitarian Socialism, 1790–1975* (Cambridge, Mass., 1976); Helen Rosenau, *The Ideal City in Its Architectural Evolution* (Boston, 1951); Thomas A. Reiners, *The Place of the Ideal Community in Urban Planning* (Philadelphia, 1963).

CHAPTER 7

1. *Fabian News*, Dec. 1898. Reviews of *To-morrow* are to be found in Howard's scrapbook, W.G.C.

2. The *Clarion*, Apr. 29, 1893. For Webb's remark, see his *Socialism in England* (London, 1890), 7. The quote from Shaw is to be found in Dan H. Lawrence (ed.), *George Bernard Shaw: Collected Letters, 1898–1910* (New York, 1972), 103. All the important Fabian leaders frequently spoke out against colonization. In June 1894, Sidney Webb debated J. Bruce Wallace and asserted: "I assume the continuance of large and populous communities . . ." *Brotherhood* (July 1894), 40. A few years later Webb wrote that "down to the present generation every aspirant after social reform . . . naturally embodied his ideas in a detailed plan. . . . But modern Socialists have learned the lesson of evolution . . . and it cannot be said too often that Socialism to Socialists is not a utopia which they have invented, but a principle of social organization," Sidney Webb, *The Difficulties of Individualism*, Fabian Tract 64 (London, 1896), 1. G.B. Shaw succinctly stated the Fabian attitude in Aug. 1896: "the Fabian Society desires to offer all projectors and founders of Utopian communities in South America, Africa and other remote localities, to apologize for its impatience with such adventures. To such projectors, and all patrons of schemes for starting similar settlements and workshops at home, the Society announces emphatically that it does not believe in the establishment of Socialism by private enterprise." *Report on Fabian Policy*, Fabian Tract 70 (London, 1896), 1.

3. Karl Marx and Frederick Engels, *The Communist Manifesto* (Moscow, 1955), 57.

4. Ebenezer Howard, *Garden Cities of To-morrow* (London, 1902), 28–30. For Howard's comments on how in *To-morrow* he handled the financing of the garden city, see *The Garden City*, VI (Feb. 1905), 2. Also informative is Howard's interview with *Daily News Weekly*, July 22, 1899.

5. The Manchester branch of the Garden City Association, for example, was "drifting aimlessly" until Adams took charge. "Minutes of the Manchester Branch," Garden City Association, 1–5, archives of the Town and Country Planning Association, London, henceforth cited as T.C.P.A. See also C.B. Purdum, *The Garden City* (London, 1913), 24; and letter to editor by S.H. Milford, *Co-operative News*, May 20, 1901. A description by Howard of the movement before Neville and Adams arrived is in the second printing of the 1902 *Garden Cities of To-morrow* (London, 1902), Postscript, 161–67. For the inability of J. Bruce Wallace to marshal support from the cooperative movement, see *Brotherhood* (Jan. 1901), 138. Robert Beevers, *The Garden City Utopia: A Critical Biography of Ebenezer Howard* (New York, 1988), 72.

6. Ebenezer Howard, "The Relation of the Ideal to the Practical," *The Garden City*, I (Feb. 1905), 15.

7. The title of the article written by Neville was "Co-operation and Garden Cities." This and other articles by Neville were published in Ralph Neville, *Papers and Addresses on Social Questions* (London, 1919).

8. On Thomas Adams, see Michael Simpson, *Thomas Adams and the Modern Planning Movement* (London, 1984). J.D. Hulchanski, *Thomas Adams: A Biographical and Bibliographic Guide* (Papers on Planning and Design, no. 15, Department of Urban and Regional Planning, University of Toronto, 1978).

9. Simpson, 6.

10. The Garden City Conference at Bournville, 1901, *Report of Proceedings;* The Garden City Conference at Port Sunlight, 1902, *Report of Proceedings.*

11. For Howard's talk to the Fabians on Jan. 11, 1901, see *Brotherhood* (Feb. 1901), 55–57. G.B. Shaw to Ralph Neville (undated holograph, but probably written at the end of 1901), British Library, Shaw Collection, Addn. MS, 50513, ff.247–67. I am indebted to Robert Beevers who kindly called this letter to my attention and allowed me to read his typed transcript of the holograph. See Beevers, 74–77.

12. Anonymous, "A Plan for Social Experiments," *The Race Builders* (May 1906), reprinted in

its entirety in *The Garden City,* new series, I (Aug. 1906), 159. F. Knee, letter in *Justice,* XXX (July 1906).

13. "Report Mr. Ralph Neville, K.C. on the Question of Land Tenure, June 20, 1903," in the Garden City Museum, Letchworth, henceforth cited as G.C.M.L.; Ralph Neville to Ebenezer Howard, June 28, 1903, H.C.A.; Beevers, 87–88.

14. The Garden City Conference at Bournville, 1901, *Report of Proceedings;* "Report Mr. Ralph Neville, K.C. on the Question of Land Tenure, June 20, 1903," G.C.M.L; Beevers, 94–95.

15. Evacustes Phipson to Albert K. Owen, Dec. 25, 1903, Fresno Col.

16. Ibid.; R. Morrell to Thomas Adams, Apr. 25, 1902, G.C.M.L.

17. The fullest account of the building of Letchworth is provided by C.B. Purdom, *The Garden City: A Study in the Development of a Modern Town* (London, 1913). But also useful is E. Bonham-Carter, "Planning and Development of Letchworth Garden City," *Town Planning Review,* XXI (1950), 362–76, and Beevers, 92–107.

18. The three main plans entered in the competition are in the Garden City Museum, Letchworth. The submission of W.R. Lethaby and Holsey Ricardo is only a layout of the town center and residential areas and appears in C.B. Purdom, *The Letchworth Achievement* (London, 1963), between pages 24 and 25.

19. Frank Johnson, *Sir Raymond Unwin: Architect, Planner and Visionary* (London, 1985); Walter L. Creese, *The Search for Environment: The Garden City Before and After* (New Haven, 1966); Walter L. Creese (ed.), *The Legacy of Raymond Unwin: A Human Pattern for Planning* (Cambridge, Mass., 1967); Michael Day, "The Contribution of Sir Raymond Unwin and Barry Parker to the Development of Site-Planning Theory and Practice, 1890–1918," in Anthony Sutcliffe (ed.), *British Town Planning: The Formative Years* (London, 1981), 156–65. Mervyn Miller, "Raymond Unwin," in Gordon E. Cherry (ed.), *Pioneers in British Planning* (London, 1981), 72–99.

20. Donald Drew Egbert, *Social Radicalism and the Arts* (New York, 1970), 399.

21. Raymond Unwin, "On the Building of Houses in the Garden City," in the Garden City Conference at Bournville, 1901, *Report of Proceedings,* 70–76. According to Barry Parker, Howard in early 1900 read something he and Unwin had written and corresponded with them to arrange a meeting. Barry Parker to F.J. Osborn, Feb. 6, 1944, W.G.C. Parker joined the Manchester branch of the Garden City Association on March 21, 1902. "Minutes of the Manchester Garden City Association," T.C.P.A.

22. In a letter to C.B. Purdom, Feb. 4, 1913, Howard wrote a lengthy critique of Letchworth, W.G.C. An edited excerpt of this letter was printed as Appendix H in Purdom, *The Garden City,* 289–94.

23. Barry Parker to F.J. Osborn, Feb. 6, 1944, W.G.C.

24. Purdom, *The Garden City,* 211–21.

25. C.B. Purdom, *Life Over Again* (London, 1951), 53.

26. Ibid.

27. Ibid. Also Purdom, *The Garden City,* 51–55. For excerpts of descriptions of the Letchworth community in newspapers see *The Garden City,* new series, II (Oct. 1907), 51 and (Jan. 1908), 492. For the reaction of transplanted Bermondsey workers to Letchworth, see the *Garden Cities and Town Planning,* new series, III (May-June, 1908), 79. It should be noted that the name of the association's journal was changed from *The Garden City* to the *Garden Cities and Town Planning* with the Mar. 1908 issue.

28. For quote from the *Daily Mail,* see *The Garden City,* new series, II (Jan. 1908), 491; also of interest is *The Garden City,* new series I (June 1906), 120.

29. George Hicks, "Garden Cities and the Workers," *Garden Cities and Town Planning,* new series, XVIII (Mar. 1928), 61.

30. F.N. Heazell, chairman of the Guild of Help, "Circular Letter," July 1910, G.C.M.L.

31. Letter to editor by A. Wright, *Letchworth Citizen,* Jan. 26, 1913; *Letchworth Citizen,* Jan. 24, 1913; Letter to editor by A.J. May, *Letchworth Citizen,* Jan. 13, 1913, and news story entitled "For What Does Garden City Stand?" in same issue; *Hertfordshire Express,* Jan. 31, 1913; *North Hertfordshire Mail,* Jan. 31, 1913.

32. Purdom, *Life Over Again,* 51.
33. For the harm done by the Cheap Cottage Exhibit, see *Town Planning Review,* IV (Apr. 1913), 62.
34. *The Garden City,* new series, I (Oct. 1906), 187.
35. A.T. Edwards, "A Criticism of the Garden City Movement," *Town Planning Review,* IV (Apr. 1913), 155. Also by Edwards, "A Further Criticism of the Garden City Movement," in *Town Planning Review,* IV (Apr. 1913), 316–17. Thomas Adams, letter to the editor, *The Garden City,* new series, II (Apr. 1907), 329.
36. Letter to the editor by H.A.G. [Henry A. Gill], *The Garden City,* new series, II (Nov. 1907), 468.

CHAPTER 8

1. "Relationship of Association and Company, Memorandum by Secretary, Thomas Adams, Jan. 8, 1904," G.C.M.L.
2. *Western Mail,* Sept. 17, 1903.
3. "Relationship of Association and Company, Memorandum by Secretary, Thomas Adams, Jan. 8, 1904," Appendix I, "Memorandum by Herbert Warren," 10–11, G.C.M.L.
4. *The Garden City,* I (Oct. 1904), 6.
5. Though earlier efforts along similar lines can be traced to 1888, tenant co-partnership effectively started with a scheme at Ealing near London in 1901. Until 1906, the Ealing, Ltd., erected conventional row housing, but later building was "along advanced garden suburb lines." In 1907, a central body, the Co-partnership Tenant, Ltd., was formed to coordinate the activities of the local societies. By 1914, there were fourteen of these with a total of 3,000 houses. Societies were active at Letchworth and Hampstead Garden Suburb. The advantages of tenant co-partnership were given as low interest capital, economies of scale in construction and management, and pride of ownership for tenants. The quote from the *Daily Mail* appeared in *Garden Cities and Town Planning,* new series, III (May-June 1908), 183; Henry Vivian, "Co-partnership in Cottage Building," *The Garden City,* I (July 1905), 65; Ralph Neville, "Garden Cities: As a Solution to the Housing Question and from an Industrial Point of View," *The Garden City,* new series, I (Apr. 1906), 63–65.
6. Anthony Sutcliffe, *Towards the Planned City: Germany, Britain, the United States and France, 1780–1914* (New York, 1981), 69–73.
7. C.B. Purdom, *The Garden City: A Study in the Development of a Modern Town* (London, 1913), 9.
8. Sutcliffe, *Towards the Planned City,* 72.
9. Martin Gaskell, "The Suburb Salubrious: Town Planning in Practice," in Anthony Sutcliffe (ed.), *British Town Planning: The Formative Years* (London, 1981), 10–13.
10. Purdom, *The Garden City,* 201–2.
11. Ewart G. Culpin, *Garden City Movement Up-to-date* (London, no date), pamphlet published by the Garden Cities and Town Planning Association in 1913—see especially pp. 12–13.
12. Fred Knee to Thomas Adams, Sept. 9, 1902, G.C.M.L.
13. "Minutes of the Executive, Garden Cities and Town Planning Association, 1912–1916," p. 221, T.C.P.A.
14. *The Garden City,* new series, II (Nov. 1907), 446.
15. *Garden Cities and Town Planning,* new series, IV (Aug. 1909), 215.
16. Ebenezer Howard, "Spread the People," *Garden Cities and Town Planning,* new series, I (Feb. 1911), 21–23.
17. *The Garden City,* new series, II (Sept. 1907), 415; *The Garden City,* new series, II (Nov. 1907), 464–66.
18. *The Garden City,* new series, I (Nov. 1906), 203; *The Garden City,* new series, II (Mar. 1907), 298–99.
19. Raymond Unwin, *Nothing Gained by Overcrowding! How the Garden City Type of Development*

May Benefit Both Owner and Occupier (London, 1912). This pamphlet was published by the Garden Cities and Town Planning Association.

20. Aston Webb (ed.), *London of the Future* (New York, 1921), 177–92.

21. Gaskell in Sutcliffe, *British Town Planning*, 19–20.

22. Gordon Cherry, *The Evolution of British Town Planning* (Leighton Buzzard, 1974).

23. Ibid.

24. Ewart Culpin, "Our Aims," *Garden Cities and Town Planning*, new series, I (Feb. 1911), 1–2.

25. *Transactions of the Royal Institute of British Architects: Town Planning Conference, London, October 10–15, 1910* (London, 1911).

26. Raymond Unwin, "American Town Planning," *Garden Cities and Town Planning*, new series, I (Aug. 1911), 162–73; Thomas Adams, "Garden Cities and Town Planning in America," *Garden Cities and Town Planning*, new series, I (Sept. 1911), 196–98.

27. G.L. Pepler, "A Belt of Green Round London," *Garden Cities and Town Planning*, new series, I (Mar. 1911), 41–43, 65–68; Thomas Manson, *Civic Art* (London, 1911), 13–19.

28. A.T. Edwards, "A Criticism of the Garden City Movement," *Town Planning Review*, IV (Apr. 1913), 155.

29. *Garden Cities and Town Planning*, new series, III (May-June 1908), 82. Culpin originally made this remark in the introduction to a pamphlet entitled *Town Planning in Theory and Practice* which was a collection of papers read at a 1908 Guildhall conference which I have not been able to locate.

30. For Purdom's life, see his autobiography, *Life Over Again* (London, 1951).

31. Ibid., 58–62.

32. *Minutes of the Executive, Garden Cities and Town Planning Association, 1916–1920*, pp. 109, 197, T.C.P.A.

33. C.B. Purdom, "A Criticism," *Garden Cities and Town Planning*, new series, IV (Mar. 7, 1914), 124–25.

34. *Minutes of the Executive, Garden Cities and Town Planning Association, 1912–1916*, p. 198, T.C.P.A.

35. *Minutes of the Executive, Garden Cities and Town Planning Association, 1916–1920*, pp. 128, 131, T.C.P.A.

36. Osborn claimed to be the sole author of this pamphlet, but Purdom asserted it was a collaborative effort, and Beevers accepts the latter's view, *The Garden City Utopia*, 155–56. In 1942, a second revised edition was published as a book by Dent, the original publisher, under Osborn's name.

37. *Minutes of the Executive, Garden Cities and Town Planning Association, 1916–1920*, pp. 183, 230, T.C.P.A.

38. For criticism of the housing bill by the Executive of the G.C.T.P., see ibid., p. 219. According to Purdom, the act was "popularly supposed to be a garden city measure. . . ." C.B. Purdom, *The Building of Satellite Towns* (London, 1949), 181. Mark Swenarton, *Homes Fit for Heroes: The Politics and Architecture of Early State Housing in Britain* (London, 1981), 93. William Ashworth, *The Genesis of Modern British Town Planning* (London, 1954), 193–95.

39. Swenarton, 93.

40. Frederic J. Osborn to Ebenezer Howard, May 5, 1919, W.G.C.

41. Letter to the editor by Ebenezer Howard, *Letchworth Citizen*, May 9, 1918.

42. Ashworth, 195.

CHAPTER 9

1. Howard's second wife was mentally unstable and on occasion institutionalized. On his death, she destroyed many of his papers. Barry Parker to F.J. Osborn, Feb. 16, 1944; also see Robert Beevers, *The Garden City Utopia: A Critical Biography of Ebenezer Howard* (New York, 1988), 124.

2. For Thomas Adams's condescending attitude toward Howard, see Barry Parker to F.J. Osborn, Feb. 16, 1944. W.G.C. Culpin described Howard as a "small man, almost insignifi-

cant. . . . He did not seem to be endowed with any extraordinary talent, and he had no knowledge of the big business world." E.G. Culpin to F.J. Osborn, Feb. 21, 1944, W.G.C. Osborn at this time was researching a biographical essay on Howard.

3. H.G. Wells, "Utopianism: I, The Garden Cities," *Daily Mail*, Mar. 18, 1905; "Utopianism: II, A Cottage in a Garden," *Daily Mail*, Mar. 30, 1905; "Utopianism: III, State Babies," *Daily Mail*, Apr. 20, 1905; "Utopianism: IV, Joint Housekeeping—Daring Socialist Suggestion," *Daily Mail*, May 25, 1905. With the exception of the material on joint housekeeping, there was little original in these articles. Almost all the ideas had appeared earlier in Wells, *Anticipations* (London, 1902).

4. Ebenezer Howard, "Garden Cities by Their Inventor," *Daily Mail*, Mar. 22, 1905. Also see Keeble Howard (no relation), "The Dream Cottage: A Reply to H.G. Wells," *Daily Mail*, Apr. 4, 1905; H.G. Wells to Ebenezer Howard, *Daily Mail*, Mar. 24, 1905. Wells in an undated postcard (in W.G.C.) to Howard indicated approval of an effort at joint housekeeping at Letchworth but noted that he was too busy to help. He asked Howard to join the Fabians. At this time, Wells was a vice president of the Garden City Association, which was of course a purely honorific title. This card is apparently referred to in *The Garden City*, I (July, 1905), 64. Northcliffe and the *Daily Mail* were strongly pro–garden city and his brother, Cecil Harmsworth, was active in the association.

5. Introduction to Harper and Row reprint edition, *Women and Economics* (New York, 1966), vii. *The Home: Its Work and Influence* was reprinted in 1972 by the Univ. of Illinois Press. Gilmore also wrote a popular novel, *What Diantha Did* (New York, 1911), which describes cooperative housekeeping.

6. H. Clapham Lander, "The Advantages of Cooperative Dwellings," The Garden City Conference at Bournville, 1901, *Report of Proceedings*.

7. Ebenezer Howard, "Cooperative Housekeeping," *The Garden City*, new series, I (Aug. 1906), 170. This is apparently a reprint of an article originally published in the *Daily Mail;* Ebenezer Howard, "A New Way of Housekeeping," *Daily Mail*, Mar. 27, 1913, p. 4.

8. H. Clapham Lander, "Associated Homes, A Solution of the Servant Problem," *Garden Cities and Town Planning*, new series, V (Apr. 1911), 71–72; Raymond Unwin, *Town Planning in Practice* (London, 1909), Chapter 11.

9. Beevers, *The Garden City Utopia*, 149–51.

10. C.B. Purdom, *The Building of Satellite Towns*, 2nd edition (London, 1949), 184–89.

11. "Preliminary Announcement of a Garden City in Hertfordshire for London Industries, 1919." In early 1922, large billboards were erected on both sides of the train tracks traversing the site announcing: "London's First Satellite Town."

12. F.J. Osborn to Norman Macfadyen, Mar. 22, 1955, W.G.C.

13. Purdom, *The Building of Satellite Towns*, 215.

14. On governmental loans under the 1921 act see ibid., 321–22. Other types of governmental loans were also received. On Purdom's departure from the company, see Beevers, 175.

15. Purdom, *The Building of Satellite Towns*, 331.

16. Ibid., 256–62, 266–67.

17. Ibid., 278.

18. Ibid., 315–16; W.H.G. Armytage, *Heavens Below: Utopian Experiments in England, 1560–1960* (London, 1961), 403–5.

19. Lynn F. Pearson, "Cooperative Housekeeping," *Planning History Bulletin*, VI, 2 (1984), 33–43. For American interest in cooperative housing, see Dolores Hayden, *The Grand Domestic Revolution: A History of Feminist Designs for American Homes, Neighborhoods, and Cities* (Cambridge, Mass., 1981), and David Handlin, *The American Home: Architecture and Society, 1815–1915* (Boston, 1979), especially pp. 391–405.

20. Catherine Bauer, *Modern Housing* (New York, 1932), 158.

21. Louis de Soissons and Arthur W. Kenyon, *Site Planning in Practice as Welwyn Garden City* (London, 1927).

22. For neo-Georgian architecture and its relationship to the Arts and Crafts movement, see

Roderick Gradidge, "Edwin Lutyens, the Last High Victorian," in Jane Fawcett (ed.), *Seven Victorian Architects* (University Park, Pa., 1977), 130–31.

23. F.J. Osborn, *Green-Belt Cities: The British Contribution* (London, 1946), 113–28.
24. Henry Wright, "The Autobiography of Another Idea," *The Western Architect*, XXX (Sept. 1930), 5.
25. *International Town Planning Conference, New York, 1925, Report* (London, no date), 7–10.
26. *Barlow Report* (report of the Royal Commission on the Distribution of Industrial Population), Cmd. 6153 (London, 1940); an excellent brief treatment of the problem is S.B. Dennison, *Location of Industries and Depressed Areas* (London, 1939).
27. Osborn believed that his lower-middle-class upbringing in London and his experience as an estate manager provided him with insight into popular preferences. F.J. Osborn, *Green-Belt Cities*, 117–18. For Osborn's view of how he differed from Howard, see Michael Hughes (ed.), *The Letters of Lewis Mumford and Frederic J. Osborn: A Transatlantic Dialogue, 1938–70* (New York, 1972), 9. On Osborn's life, see Michael Hebbert, "Frederic Osborn, 1885–1978," in Gordon Cherry (ed.), *Pioneers in British Planning* (London, 1981), 177–202.
28. Hughes (ed.), 69.
29. *Thirty-eighth Annual Report of the Garden Cities and Town Planning Association, 1936;* also see Hughes (ed.), 126, 137 for Osborn's view of these years.
30. Hebbert in Cherry (ed.), *Pioneers in British Planning*, 184–85.
31. Ibid. Hebbert is not convinced that the G.C.T.P. and Osborn influenced the commission as profoundly as the latter claimed, but he is prepared to accept Osborn's view that he greatly enhanced the importance of the document, in effect making it into a major statement of policy, while also exaggerating its agreement with the G.C.T.P. position. For the G.C.T.P. testimony to the Barlow commission, see F.J. Osborn, "The Problem of the Great City: A Royal Commission at Work," *Political Quarterly*, IX, 3 (1938), 408–20. For Osborn's estimation of the importance of the report, see F.J. Osborn and Arnold Whittick, *The New Towns: The Answer to Megalopolis* (London, 1969), 88.

CHAPTER 10

1. *Transactions of the Royal Institute of British Architects: Town Planning Conference, London, October 10–15, 1910* (London, 1911), 368.
2. For a penetrating analysis of the transatlantic discourse on philosophy and political theory, which illuminates national differences in outlook and ideology, see James T. Kloppenberg, *Uncertain Victory: Social Democracy and Progressivism in European and American Thought, 1870–1920* (New York, 1986). For comparisons of national town- and city-planning movements, see Anthony Sutcliffe, *Towards the Planned City: Germany, Britain, the United States and France, 1780–1914* (New York, 1981). Andrew Lees, *Cities Perceived: Urban Society in European and American Thought, 1820–1940* (New York, 1985), is useful for understanding attitudes toward urbanization.
3. For the German Garden City movement, see Kristina Hartmann, *Deutsche Gartenstadtbewegung; Kulturpolitic und Gesellschaft Reform* (Munich, 1976), and Franzika Bollery and Kristina Hartmann, "A Patriarchal Utopia: The Garden City and Housing Reform in Germany at the Turn of the Century," in Anthony Sutcliffe (ed.), *The Rise of Modern Urban Planning, 1800–1914* (New York, 1980), 135–64.
4. The similarities between Howard's and Fritsch's schemes have been exaggerated. Both did emphasize community land ownership, house and garden, planned concentric development, segregation of function, and the importance of green space. Fritsch, however, explicitly regarded his scheme as equally applicable to town extension planning as well as de novo town planning. Moreover, he offered no mechanism for limiting population size and appears to have thought in terms of a range of 100,000 to one million. Thomas Reimer, *The Place of the Ideal Community in Urban Planning* (Philadelphia, 1962), 36–39. Originally published in Leipzig in 1896, *Die Stadt der Zukunst* appeared in a second edition

in 1912 with the term "Gartenstadt" added to the title. According to *The Garden City*, new series, I (May 1906), 94, a Swede, Dr. G. Stjernstrom, had written a work in 1899 advocating a scheme close to Howard's.

5. Albert Weiss, *Can the Present-Day Evils of the Living Conditions Be Remedied* (Berlin, 1912). A seventeen-page precis in English of this German-language pamphlet was prepared by the author and sent to, among others, George Hooker, an American housing reformer associated with the Chicago City Club and Hull House, and is in the George Hooker Collection, Univ. of Chicago Library. Hooker had toured England and Germany in 1910 and was an ardent advocate of planned communities. All references to Weiss refer to the precis.

6. Ibid., 3–6; Professor Eberstadt, "The Problem of Town Development," *Garden Cities and Town Planning*, new series, III (Aug. 15, 1913), 200–205.

7. T.C. Horsfall, "The Real Enemy of Great Britain and of Germany," *Garden Cities and Town Planning*, new series, III (Feb. 1913), 33–36; Weiss, 7.

8. Weiss, 16; Hartmann, *Die Deutsche Gartenstadtbewegung* (Berlin, 1911), 7–9.

9. Bollery and Hartmann, 151. On the German civil service, Kloppenberg, 167–68, 176–79, 389–90. Useful on German planning developments is Sutcliffe, *Towards the Planned City*, 27–47.

10. "A German Bournville," *Garden Cities and Town Planning*, new series, I (June 1911), 129–30.

11. Jon Kleber, "The German City of Hellerau: A German Housing Development," *The Architectural Review*, XXXV (Feb. 1914), 151–61; Upton Sinclair, *The Autobiography of Upton Sinclair* (New York, 1963), 184–86, 193.

12. Bollery and Hartmann, 153–54.

13. Nicholas Pevsner, *Pioneers of Modern Design from William Morris to Walter Gropious* (London, 1936).

14. For Gide's social ideas, see *Consumers' Cooperative Societies* (London, 1921) and *Communist and Cooperative Colonies* (New York, 1930); for his life, see Karl Walters (ed.), *Cooperation and Charles Gide* (London, 1931).

15. Sutcliffe, *Towards the Planned City*, 149–50; interview with Benoît-Lévy, July 17, 1968. Two of several articles by J.W. Petavel are "A Scheme for Town Development," *The Garden City*, new series, II (Dec. 1907), 475–76, and "The Town Planning of the Future," *Westminister Review*, CLXXII (Oct. 1909), 398–408. Also of interest is Charles Gide, "The Town of the Future," *The Garden City*, new series, II (May 1907), 331–32. George Collins, "V Ciudad Lineal Madrid," *Journal of the Society of Architectural Historians*, XVIII (May 1959), 8–53, and "Linear Planning Throughout the World," *Journal of the Society of Architectural Historians*, XVIII (Oct. 1959), 74–93.

16. Georges Benoît-Lévy, *Cités-jardins de France*, 3 vols. (Paris, 1911). An excellent analysis of Benoît-Lévy's distortion of the garden-city idea is in Marcel Smets, *L'Avènement de la cité-jardin en Belgique* (Brussels, 1977), 78–81. According to Smets, Benoît-Lévy influenced the ideas of the first Belgian garden-city advocates who organized an association in 1904. On linear planning in the U.S.S.R. in the 1930s, see Hans Blumenfeld, "Regional and City Planning in the Soviet Union," *Task* (1942), 33–52, and N.A. Miliutin, *Sotsgorod: The Problem of Building Socialist Cities* (Cambridge, Mass., 1974).

17. Tony Garnier, *Une Cité industrielle: Etude pour la construction des villes*, 2 vols. (Paris, 1918); Dora Wiebenson, *Tony Garnier: The Cité Industrielle* (London, 1970).

18. For the Russian Garden City movement, see Maurice Parkins, *City Planning in Soviet Russia* (Chicago, 1953), especially the first two chapters; Etienne de Groer, "Town Planning in Russia," *Garden Cities and Town Planning*, new series, VI (July–Aug. 1922), 117–23; A. Bloch and V. Semionov, "The Housing Question and the Garden City Movement in Russia," *Garden Cities and Town Planning*, new series, XII (July 1914), 107–9. My discussion is indebted to S. Frederick Starr, "The Revival and Schism of Urban Planning in Twentieth-Century Russia," in Michael Hamm (ed.), *The City in Russian History* (Lexington, Ky., 1975); Catherine Cook, "Russian Response to the Garden City Movement," *The Architectural Review*, CLXIII (June, 1978), 354–63; Eric Richard, "The Garden City in Russian Urbanism, 1904–1933," unpublished senior thesis in history, Princeton Univ., 1972.

19. A. Bloch and V. Semionov, 108; Richard, 71–76.
20. Cook, 357; Alexander Block, "Land Problems and Town Planning in Soviet Russia," *Garden Cities and Town Planning,* new series, XVIII (Mar. 1927), 336–38. Block left Russia at the time of the Revolution and lived in Letchworth until his death.
21. Parkins, *City Planning in Soviet Russia,* 43–48.
22. "An International Association," *Garden Cities and Town Planning,* new series, III (May 1913), 140; "International Garden Cities and Town Planning Association," *Garden Cities and Town Planning,* new series, III (Aug. 15, 1913), 224–26.
23. "International Garden Cities and Town Planning Association," *Garden Cities and Town Planning,* new series, III (Aug. 15, 1913), 224–26.
24. The quote from Antonio Sant' Elia is from his "Manifesto of Futurist Architecture," July 1914. See *Futurismo i Futurismi,* catalogue for the exhibit at Palazzo Grassi Spa, fall 1987, Venice, Italy, 417; S. Giedion, *Space, Time and Architecture,* 3rd edition enlarged (Cambridge, Mass., 1959), 442–43; Leonardo Benevelo, *History of Modern Architecture,* vol. II (Cambridge, Mass., 1971), 396–406.
25. For the relationship between cooperators and socialists in various European countries, see Charles Gide, *Consumer Co-operative Societies* (London, 1921), especially Chapter 16, "Co-operation and Socialism," 222–42. An early proponent of the Garden City movement in the Netherlands was Frederick van Eeden, a leading cooperator and an advocate of the Arts and Crafts movement. His journal *De Pioneer* advocated community land ownership as well as the Garden City movement. Van Eeden also began the colony of Walden. S.J. Fokema Andrae, "The Garden City Ideal in the Netherlands Before 1930," *Stedebouw and Volkshuivesting* (May 1963), 95–97. A brief description of Dutch supporters appeared in *The Garden City,* new series, I (Sept. 1906), 178. For Belgian supporters, see *The Garden City,* new series, I (Feb. 1905), 12.
26. Gide, *Consumer Co-operative Societies,* 233–36; Kloppenberg, 217–20.
27. Ashok K. Dott and Frank J. Costa, *Public Planning in the Netherlands* (Oxford, 1985), 139–60; Bauer, 124–37; Benevelo, vol. II, 396–99.
28. Benevelo, vol. II, 398–423, 651–53; E.A. Gutkind, *Revolution of Environment* (London, 1946), 111–58; Gordon Cherry, *The Evolution of British Town Planning* (Leighton Buzzard, 1977). For more general treatments on the important topic of modern professionalization, see Eugene Haskell, *The Emergence of Professional Social Science* (New York, 1977), and Haskell (ed.), *The Authority of Experts* (New York, 1982); Edward Bledstein, *The Culture of Professionalism* (New York, 1982).
29. Benevelo, vol. II, 651–53.
30. Several hundred Belgian refugees lived in Letchworth during World War I. For the activities of the international association in 1918, see *Rebuilding Belgium: Conference of the International Garden Cities Federation, London, Sept. 7–9, 1920.*
31. Purdom described Chapman as an insular Englishman attached to "beer, roast beef and cricket." C.B. Purdom, *Life Over Again* (London, 1951), 63.
32. *Transactions of the International Garden Cities and Town Planning Federation Congress, Paris, Oct. 1922,* pp. 6–8.
33. Ibid., 9–16.
34. Lewis Mumford, *The City in History* (New York, 1961), 514–17.
35. Raymond Unwin, "Some Thoughts on the Development of London" in Aston Webb (ed.), *London of the Future* (New York, 1921), 177–92.
36. See the following articles by Raymond Unwin, "The Town and the Best Size for Good Social Life," in C.B. Purdom (ed.), *Town Planning Theory and Practice* (London, 1921), 80–102; "Need for a Regional Plan," *Transactions of the International Garden Cities and Town Planning Federation Congress, Amsterdam, 1924,* pp. 15–30; "Methods of Decentralization," *Transactions of the International Garden Cities and Town Planning Federation Congress, New York, 1925,* pp. 150–65; "Regional Panning," *Journal of the Royal Sanitary Institute* (Aug. 1929), 229–34; "Regional Planning, With Specific Reference to the Greater London Regional Plan," *Journal of the Royal Institute of British Architects,* XXXVII (Jan. 1930), 183–

93. Also see Frank Jackson, *Sir Raymond Unwin: Architect, Planner, Visionary* (London, 1985), 140–58.

37. Arthur Comey, "Response to Raymond Unwin," *Transactions of the International Garden Cities and Town Planning Federation Congress, Gothenberg, 1923*, pp. 66–71, 114–17; also see Arthur Comey, "Answer to the Garden City Challenge," *American City*, XIX (July 1923), 36–40.

38. Max Ermers, "Planned Housing in Vienna," in F.J. Osborn (ed.), *Planning and Reconstruction Yearbook, 1942* (London, 1942), 26–39; Bauer, 132–36; Benevelo, vol. II, 509–10.

39. Walter Gropious, *The New Architecture and the Bauhaus* (Cambridge, Mass., 1965).

40. Benevelo, vol. II, 495–506; Sigfried Giedion, "On C.I.A.M.'s Unwritten Catalogue," *Journal of the Society of Architectural Historians*, III (Jan.-Apr. 1943), 43–46; Catherine Bauer Wurster, "The Social Front of Modern Architecture in the 1930s," *Journal of the Society of Architectural Historians*, XXIV (Mar. 1965), 48–52.

41. For a critical view of the C.I.A.M., see Michael Hughes (ed.), *The Letters of Lewis Mumford and Frederic J. Osborn: A Transatlantic Dialogue, 1938–70* (New York, 1972), 83. An interesting analysis of technocratic currents present in the C.I.A.M. is in Charles S. Maier, "Between Taylorism and Technocracy: European Ideologies and the Vision of Industrial Productivity in the 1920s," *Journal of Contemporary History*, V (1970), 27–61.

42. Giedion, 688.

43. For bibliographies of housing studies in the period, see Bauer, 312–25, and International Federation of Housing and Town Planning, *Horizontal or Vertical Buildings?* (Paris, 1937), 117–36.

44. Bauer, 215–24; International Housing Association, *Slum Clearance* (Frankfort, 1935); James Ford, *Slums and Housing* (Cambridge, Mass., 1937).

45. Hans Kampffmeyer to Edith Elmer Wood, Jan. 14, 1927; Mar. 1, 1927; Nov. 6, 1928, Edith Elmer Wood Collection, Avery Library, Columbia Univ., Folder H, Box 65.

46. Ibid.

47. Catherine Bauer Wurster, "The Social Front of Modern Architecture in the 1930s," 48–49.

48. W. Dougill, "Amsterdam: Its Town Planning Development," *Town Planning Review*, XIV (June 1936), 123–40; *Transactions of the International Federation of Housing and Town Planning Congress, London, 1935*, pp. 148–52. Also of interest is Karin Gaillard, "The Amsterdam School and Public Housing," in Wim de Wit (ed.), *The Amsterdam School and Public Housing* (Cambridge, Mass., 1983), 145–62. For Belgium, see Emil Cammaerts, "The Reconstruction of Belgian Towns," *Journal of the Royal Society of Arts*, LXIII (Apr. 1925), 538–48; Smets, 78–81.

49. Harry Barnes, *The Slum: Its Story and Solution* (London, 1931), 323–32; Bauer, 168–69.

50. Hughes (ed.), 12–13, 46.

51. Maxwell Fry, *Fine Building* (London, 1954), 86–114; Anthony Jackson, "Politics of Architecture: English Architecture, 1929–51," *Journal of the Society of Architectural Historians*, XXIV (Mar. 1965), 314–406; Arthur Korn and Felix Samuely, "A Master Plan for London," *The Architectural Review*, XCI (June 1942), 143–50. An excellent critique of this plan is offered by the Bauhaus planner Ludwig Hilberseimer in *The New City* (Chicago, 1944), 151–54.

52. Bauer, 103; Maxwell Fry, *Autobiographical Sketches* (London, 1975), 122, 126, 138–42, 160–61.

53. Fry, 138–42, 160–61.

54. "Report to the Executive Committee, 1932, International Housing Association"; John Ilder to Edith Elmer Wood, June 30, 1937. Both documents are in the Edith Elmer Wood Collection, Avery Library, Columbia Univ., Folder H, Box 65.

55. *Transactions of the International Federation of Housing and Town Planning, Congress, Mexico City, 1938*, p. 7.

56. Raymond Unwin, "Housing and Town Planning Lectures, 1936–37." These lectures, delivered at Columbia Univ. while Unwin was a visiting professor, were apparently mimeographed by the Subcommittee on Research and Statistics, Central Housing Committee,

Washington, D.C. They are reprinted in part in Walter Creese (ed.), *The Legacy of Raymond Unwin* (Cambridge, Mass., 1967), 167–213.

57. *Transactions of the International Federation of Housing and Town Planning, Congress, Mexico City, 1938*, p. 44.

CHAPTER 11

1. *Municipal Affairs*, VI (June 1902), 287–90.
2. Unwin quote cited in Jon A. Peterson's MS, "A Comprehensive Vision: The Birth of Modern American City Planning, 1840–1917," Chapter 9. My analysis of American city planning in the period 1900 to 1918 relies heavily on Peterson's important work.
3. Peter Marcuse, "Housing Policy and City Planning: The Puzzling Split in the United States, 1893–1931," in Gordon Cherry (ed.), *Shaping an Urban World* (New York, 1980), 23–58. For the 19th-century American urban environmental tradition and the importance of F.L. Olmsted to this, see David Schuyler, *The New Urban Landscape: The Redefinition of City Form in the Nineteenth Century* (New York, 1987).
4. The significance of the Progressive Era is a matter of controversy among American historians. Recent works of value are Daniel T. Rogers, "In Search of Progressivism," *Reviews in American History*, X (1982), 113–32; David P. Thelen, *The New Citizenship: Origins of Progressivism in Wisconsin, 1885–1900* (Columbia, Mo., 1972); Richard L. McCormick, *From Realignment to Reform: Political Change in New York State, 1893–1910* (Ithaca, 1981). The controversy centers on whether Progressivism constituted a reform movement, and, if so, was it essentially of a conservative nature—preoccupied with social control and efficiency—or an authentic effort at social justice. In large part, the problem of analysis is due to the blurring of significantly different visions of the good society by all sorts of reformers who tended to employ (in their efforts at discourse and consensus) a common utilitarian rhetoric of efficiency.
5. *The Garden City*, I (Oct. 1904), 24.
6. *The Garden City*, new series, II (Jan. 1907), 257; *The Garden City*, new series, II (Feb. 1907), 268–69; The program of the American Garden City Association and a list of its officers appears in full in "The Garden City Association; What the Garden City Ass'n Is," *The Village* (July 1907), 295–98.
7. On the National Civic Association, see James Weinstein, *The Corporate Ideal in the Liberal State, 1900–1918* (Boston, 1968), 3–39; Gordon M. Jensen, "The National Civic Federation: American Business in an Age of Social Change and Social Reform, 1900–1910" (unpublished Ph.D. dissertation, Princeton Univ., 1956). For Ralph Peters and the Long Island Rail Road, see "The Garden City Association of America: Workingmen's Model Homes and Villages in America," *The Village* (Oct. 1907), 417–19.
8. Letter to editor, *Garden Cities and Town Planning*, new series, II (July 1907), 380–81.
9. On Stickley, see T.J. Jackson Lears, *No Place of Grace: Antimodernism and the Transformation of American Culture, 1880–1920* (New York, 1981), 68–71, 85–95. For the Arts and Crafts movement in America, see Eileen Boris, *Ruskin, Morris, and the Craftsman Ideal in America* (Philadelphia, 1986). Stickley had visited England in 1898 and had met Parker and Unwin at the Manchester Art Worker's Guild. Frank Jackson, *Sir Raymond Unwin* (London, 1984), 34–37. An interesting statement by Stickley on community is "Rapid Growth of the Garden City Movement Which Promises to Reorganize Social Conditions All Over the World," *The Craftsman* (Dec. 1909), 296–310.
10. See Alfred B. Yeomans (ed.), *City Residential Land Development: Studies in Planning* (Chicago, 1916). This book contains the major entries for the 1913 competition, including an entry by Frank Lloyd Wright. Walter Burley Griffin offered part of his prize money to the British Garden Cities and Town Planning Association to finance a lecture series by W.R. Davidge in Australia that does not appear to have occurred. *Minutes of the Executive, Garden Cities and Town Planning Association, 1913*, p. 6, T.C.P.A. Gwendolyn Wright,

Moralism and the Model Home; Domestic Architecture and Cultural Conflict in Chicago (Chicago, 1980), 280–91.

11. Roy Lubove, *The Urban Community: Housing and Planning in the Progressive Era* (Englewood Cliffs, N.J., 1967), 11–13; Graham Romeyn Taylor, *Satellite Cities: A Study of Industrial Suburbs* (New York, 1915), 263–301. Taylor's use of the term "satellite cities" for industrial suburbs is the earliest instance of this employment that I am familiar with.

12. Harvey A. Kantor, "Benjamin C. Marsh and the Fight Over Congestion," in Donald A. Krueckenberg (ed.), *The American Planner: Biographies and Recollections* (New York, 1983), 58–74. For Marsh's program in his own words, see "City Planning in Justice to the Working Population," *Charities and Commons,* XIX (Feb. 1908), 1514–18, and an *Introduction to City Planning* (New York, 1909). After 1912, Marsh abandoned his interest in city planning. Invaluable in its treatment of the dispute between Olmsted and Marsh is Jon Peterson's MS, Chapter 9.

13. Cited in Peterson MS, Chapter 9; Frederick Law Olmsted, Jr., "Introductory Address on City Planning," *Second National Conference on City Planning and the Problems of Congestion* (Boston, 1910), 15–30.

14. Olmsted was a colleague of Henry James who until his death in 1910 influenced a generation of Harvard students, including Walter Lipmann, to adopt a pragmatic view toward social values and change—see Kloppenberg, 392–93.

15. The best account of Veiller's philosophy of regulatory reform and his leadership in the area of housing is offered in Roy Lubove, *The Progressives and the Slums* (Pittsburgh, 1962).

16. Cited in Ralph Henry Gabriel, *The Course of American Democratic Thought* (New York, 1956), 253.

17. The quote from Unwin is cited in Jackson, *Sir Raymond Unwin,* 113. For the quote from Veiller, see "Housing Reform Through Legislation," in American Academy of Political and Social Science, *Housing and Town Planning* (Philadelphia, 1914), 74.

18. Lawrence Veiller to Ebenezer Howard, June 15, 1918, W.G.C.; Lawrence Veiller, "Are Great Cities A Menace?: The Garden City As a Way Out," *Architectural Record,* LI (Feb. 1922), 175–84. In this article, Veiller mentions meeting with Howard shortly before writing this article. Of interest is a pamphlet by Veiller critical of British postwar planning policies as overly ambitious and too costly: *How England Is Meeting the Housing Shortage* (New York, 1920).

19. Robert L. Fishman, "American Suburbs/English Suburbs: A Transatlantic Comparison," *Journal of Urban History,* XIII (May 1987), 237–51, and Kenneth T. Jackson, "Suburbanization in England and North America: A Response to a 'Transatlantic Comparison,' " *Journal of Urban History,* XIII, 302–6.

20. The most effective study of the R.P.A.A. is Roy Lubove's insightful *Community Planning in the 1920s: The Contributions of the Regional Planning Association of America* (Pittsburgh, 1963). Also of interest is Daniel Schaffer, *Garden Cities for America: The Radburn Experience* (Philadelphia, 1982). Both writers have relied heavily, perhaps too much so, on Mumford's various accounts of the R.P.A.A., which are usefully summarized in Lewis Mumford, *Sketches from Life* (New York, 1982), 333–51.

21. Lubove, *Community Planning in the 1920s,* 38–40. Whittaker was an ardent opponent of Veiller's approach to housing, see Eugenie Ladiner Birch, "Edith Elmer Wood and the Genesis of Liberal Housing Thought," unpublished Ph.D. dissertation, Columbia Univ., 1975, pp. 58–59. For Whittaker's ideas, see his "Foreword" to *The Housing Problem in War and in Peace* (Washington, D.C., 1918), and *The Joke About Housing* (Boston, 1920), and "An American View of Letchworth," *Garden Cities and Town Planning,* new series, XIII (June 1923), 113–23.

22. Lubove, *Community Planning in the 1920s,* 31–32.

23. Roy Lubove, *The Progressives and the Slums* (Pittsburgh, 1962), 228. See, for example, Carol Aronovici, *Housing and the Housing Problem* (Chicago, 1920), and John Murphy, Edith Elmer Wood, and Frederick Ackerman, *The Housing Famine* (New York, 1920).

24. Cited in Schaffer, *Garden Cities for America*, 83. The most complete presentation of Mac-Kaye's ideas is in his *The New Exploration* (New York, 1928)—see especially Chapters 11 and 12. (See note 37 of this chapter.)

25. For Mumford, see Lubove, *Community Planning in the 1920s,* and Park Dixon Goist, "The City as Organism: Two Recent American Theories of the City," unpublished Ph.D. dissertation, Univ. of Rochester, 1967.

26. Mumford, *Sketches from Life,* 340.

27. Birch, "Edith Elmer Wood and the Genesis of Liberal Housing Thought," 126–31.

28. The fullest history of Radburn is Schaffer's *Garden Cities for America: The Radburn Experience.* For Radburn's influence, see Eugenie L. Birch, "Radburn and the American Planning Movement; The Persistence of an Idea," *Journal of the American Planning Association,* XLVI (Oct. 1980), 424–39.

29. The *Citizen* (Letchworth), Mar. 5, 1943, contains an interview with Stanley Parker in which he describes English influence on Radburn. For Stein's view of various English sources of the plan, see Clarence Stein, "Acceptance Speech, Ebenezer Howard Medal," Mar. 17, 1960, Clarence Stein Collection, Cornell Univ. Library. Also of interest is Regional Planning Association of America, "Summary of Discussion of Problems Connected With a Garden City, Oct. 8–9, 1927," Clarence Stein Collection, Cornell Univ. Library.

30. Birch, "Radburn and the American Planning Movement: The Persistence of an Idea," 424–39.

31. Michael Hughes (ed.), *The Letters of Lewis Mumford and Frederic J. Osborn: A Transatlantic Dialogue, 1938–70* (New York, 1972), 223–24; here Mumford criticized Osborn for identifying the Garden City movement with one type of town and one type of planning: "It seems vital to me to conceive of maintaining garden city principles in towns that represent wide variations in design and considerable differences both in residential density and in the manner of layout."

32. Mel Scott, *American City Planning Since 1890* (Berkley, 1969), 250–51. According to Scott, planners, while sympathetic, believed the Garden City movement was of very limited relevance. John Nolen, the nation's most prestigious planner, was strongly for planned new towns and had joined the British association in 1909, but he also recognized that most housing could not be in planned communities. John Nolen, *New Towns for Old* (Boston, 1927).

33. Lewis Mumford, "Regionalism and Irregionalism," *Sociological Review,* XIX (Oct. 1927), 277–78; "The Theory and Practice of Regionalism," *Sociological Review,* XX (Jan. 1928), 18–33, 131–41.

34. Lewis Mumford, "The Fate of Garden Cities," *Journal of the American Institute of Architects,* XV (Feb. 1927), 37–38.

35. Lubove, *Community Planning in the 1920s,* 83.

36. Ibid.

37. MacKaye's background and ideas are discussed in Mumford's introduction to MacKaye's *The New Exploration* (Urbana, Ill., 1962). This is a reprint of a work originally published in 1928.

38. Ebenezer Howard to Patrick Geddes, Nov. 3, 1904, in Geddes Papers, MS10612, National Library of Scotland. In 1914, the association provided substitute material for an exhibit Geddes intended to present in India which was destroyed in transit. Geddes's relationship with the association was cordial but not close, and his ideas were not actively promoted by the association; Helen Meller, "Cities and Evolution: Patrick Geddes as an International Prophet of Town Planning Before 1914," in Anthony Sutcliffe, *The Rise of Modern Urban Planning, 1800–1914* (New York, 1980), 199–223.

39. Patrick Geddes, *Cities in Evolution: An Introduction to the Town Planning Movement and to the Study of Civics* (London, 1915).

40. Lubove, *Community Planning in the 1920s,* 89.

41. *Survey Graphic,* LIV (May 1, 1925). A selection of articles from this issue has been repub-

lished: Carl Sussman (ed.), *Planning for the Fourth Migration: The Neglected Vision of the Regional Planning Association of America* (Cambridge, Mass., 1976). Sussman notes in the introduction that the journal articles "convey the essential thought of the R.P.A.A."

42. On Adams's career in Canada, see Olive Saarinen, "The Influence of Thomas Adams and the British New Towns Movement in the Planning of Canadian Cities," in Alan F.J. Artibise and Gilbert A. Stelter (eds.), *The Usable Past: Planning and Politics in the Modern Canadian City* (Toronto, 1979).

43. Lewis Mumford, "The Plan of New York: I," *The New Republic*, LXXI (June 15, 1932), 121–26; "The Plan of New York: II," *The New Republic*, LXXI (June 22, 1932), 146–53. Mumford's major criticism was of the final volume, *Building the City*, by Thomas Adams which had just been published. The fullest statement of the R.P.A.A.'s preferred approach to planning for the New York region is the *Report of the New York Commission of Regional Planning* (New York, 1926). Although Stein was the commission's chairman, the report was mainly written by Henry Wright.

44. Thomas Adams, "A Communication in Defense of the Regional Plan," *The New Republic*, LXXI (July 6, 1932), 207. On Adams and the New York regional plan, see Michael Simpson, *Thomas Adams and the Modern Planning Movement* (London, 1985), 143–68, and David Johnson, "Regional Planning for the Great American Metropolis: New York Between the World Wars," in Daniel Schaffer (ed.), *Two Centuries of American Planning* (Baltimore, 1988), 167–96.

45. Clarence A. Perry, "The Neighborhood Unit, a Scheme of Arrangement for the Family Life Community," monograph one in *Neighborhood and Community Planning*, vol. VII of *The Regional Survey of New York and Its Environs* (New York, 1929). Useful for an understanding of Perry's ideas is James Dahir, *The Neighborhood Unit Plan: Its Spread and Acceptance* (New York, 1947).

46. Perry occasionally attended meetings of the R.P.A.A. and was well regarded by the group. Lubove, *Community Planning in the 1920s*, 40.

47. Lewis Mumford, *The Culture of Cities* (New York, 1938), 471–79. On the influence of Perry's ideas in Britain, see E.C. Kaufman, "Neighborhood Units as New Elements of Town Planning," *Journal of the Royal Institute of British Architects*, XLIV (Dec. 19, 1936), 165–75; P. Collison, "British Town Planning and the Neighborhood Idea," *Housing Centre Review*, V (Dec. 1956), 190–92. For Osborn's reservation concerning the neighborhood unit, see Hughes (ed.), 203–4, 244–45.

48. In May 1933, several members of the R.P.A.A. prepared "A Housing Policy for the United States Government," which they distributed to the press. Edith Elmer Wood Collection, Avery Library, Columbia Univ., Box 6-B. According to Birch, a split between "housers," such as Edith Elmer Wood, and planners, such as Stein and Mumford, always just beneath the surface, now erupted as the prospect of public action became imminent and contributed greatly to the end of the R.P.A.A. Birch, 180–83. In addition, an estrangement had occurred between Stein and Wright. Hughes (ed.), 410.

49. On F.D.R. and New Deal planning, see Scott, *American City Planning Since 1890*, 299–303; Paul Conkin, *Tomorrow a New World* (Ithaca, 1959).

50. The best single-volume study of the politics of the New Deal is William Leuchtenberg, *Franklin D. Roosevelt and the New Deal* (New York, 1963).

51. The standard work on the greenbelt communities is Joseph L. Arnold, *The New Deal in the Suburbs: A History of the Greenbelt Town Program, 1935–54* (Columbus, 1971), which should be supplemented with Paul Conkin's *Tomorrow a New World*.

52. Scott, 300–301.

53. Cited in Conkin, 34.

54. Mark Gelfand, *A Nation of Cities: The Federal Government and Urban America, 1933–1965* (New York, 1975), 112–40; Mabel L. Walker, *Urban Blight and Slums* (Cambridge, Mass., 1938), 8–35, 68–73.

55. Gelfand, 150–70.

56. Ibid., 144–49.

57. The Delano quote is cited in Gelfand, 134; for views of urban decline and return to the countryside, see Conkin, 93–108; Frank Lloyd Wright, "Broadacre City: A New Community Plan," *Architectural Record*, LXXVII (Apr. 1935), 243–54.

58. Alvin Hansen and Guy Greer, *Urban Redevelopment and Housing: A Plan for Post-War America* (Cambridge, Mass., 1942). For postwar planning in wartime, see Otis L. Graham, Jr., *Toward a Planned Society: From Roosevelt to Nixon* (New York, 1976); Phillip J. Funigiello, *The Challenge to Liberalism: Federal City Relations During World War II* (Knoxville, 1978); Marion Clawson, *New Deal Planning: The National Resources Planning Board* (Baltimore, 1981).

59. Scott, 367.

CHAPTER 12

1. Patrick Abercrombie, *Greater London Plan, 1944* (London, 1945). This plan was preceded by J.H. Forshaw and Patrick Abercrombie, *County of London Plan* (London, 1943)—in important ways a harbinger of the 1944 work.

2. The official history of British governmental new-town planning is J.B. Cullingworth, *Environmental Planning, 1939–1969*, vol. III, *New Town Planning* (London, 1979). For Osborn's reaction to Silkin's appointment, see Frederic Osborn and Arnold Whittick, *The New Towns: The Answer to Megalopolis* (New York, 1963), 83–85. His account of wartime and postwar planning is in *The New Towns*, 65–89. My account of the politics of planning has benefited from a year spent working on a daily basis with Sir Frederic Osborn, who arranged interviews for me with Lords Reith and Silkin as well as Sir Graham Vincent. Osborn was determined that he and the T.C.P.A. be credited with passage of the New Town Act of 1946 and with shaping its initial implementation. I have tried to offer a balanced view, while acknowledging that I have not regarded this subject as warranting for my needs the thorough investigation required to assess Osborn's claims.

3. Interview with Lord Silkin, June 25, 1968; Cullingworth, 13–16.

4. On Osborn as a lobbyist, see Donald L. Foley, "Ideas and Influence: The Town and Country Planning Association," *Journal of the American Institute of Planners*, XXVIII (Feb. 1962), 10–17; Michael Hebbert, "Frederic Osborn: 1885–1978," in Gordon Cherry (ed.), *Pioneers in British Planning* (London, 1981), 182–88. Also of interest is Donald Foley's *Controlling London's Growth: Planning the Great Wen, 1940–1960* (Berkeley, 1963). An American planner, Foley accepted Osborn's view of developments and the association's role in them. Ministry of Town and Country Planning, *Final Report of the New Towns Committee*, Cmd. 6876 (London, 1946). Also see *Interim Report of the New Towns Committee*, Cmd. 6759 (London, 1946), and *Second Interim Report of the New Towns Committee*, Cmd. 6794 (London, 1946). For Osborn's views at this time, see his *Green-Belt Cities: The British Contribution* (London, 1946), 131–65. A revised edition with an introduction by Lewis Mumford was published in 1961.

5. Osborn, *Green-Belt Cities*, 42; *Final Report of the New Towns Committee*, 9–16.

6. Meryle Aldridge, *The British New Towns: A Program Without a Policy* (London, 1979), 32–34.

7. Michael Hughes (ed.), *The Letters of Lewis Mumford and Frederic J. Osborn: A Transatlantic Dialogue, 1938–70* (New York, 1972), 203–4; Osborn's critical comments on the neighborhood unit did not influence Mumford as demonstrated by the latter's "The Neighborhood and the Neighborhood Unit," *Town Planning Review*, XXIV (Jan. 1954), 256–70.

8. Aldridge, 33; Osborn told me in conversation that the two theaters were Reith's idea.

9. Aldridge, 33.

10. F.J. Osborn and Arnold Whittick, *The New Towns: The Answer to Megalopolis* (New York, 1963), 87–88. The quote of Silkin is in the *House of Commons Debates* CCCCXXIII (Hansard), col. 1091.

11. Aldridge, 69–75, 86–91; Lloyd Rodwin, *The British New Town Policy* (Cambridge, Mass., 1956), 72–86; P.H. Levin, *Government and the Planning Process* (London, 1976); Gordon Cherry, *The Politics of Planning* (London, 1982).

12. Cullingworth, *New Town Planning*, 362–66; Peter Willmott, "Social Research and the New

Community," *Journal of the American Institute of Planners*, XXXIII (Nov. 1967), 387–97; Aldridge, 89–91. Ironically the Reith committee had recommended a central advisory agency to coordinate research and experience.

13. Cullingworth, *New Town Planning*, 362–66.

14. Rodwin, 57. For an excellent brief analysis of Mark I towns, see Rodwin, 51–53.

15. See, for example, Harold Orlans, *Utopia Ltd.* (New Haven, 1953). This was published in the United Kingdom under the title *Stevenage: A Sociological Study of a New Town* (London, 1952). It offers a critical appraisal of the concept of "balance" by a social anthropologist. Even Osborn, however, admitted that Stevenage was the weak sister of the new communities. Hughes (ed.), 214. An examination of the class structure of new towns is in B.J. Heraud, "Social Class and the New Towns," *Urban Studies*, V (Feb. 1968), 33–58.

16. Aldridge offers a balanced view of a controversial topic, 43–47. For a very critical approach, see Bob Mullan, *Stevenage Ltd.* (London, 1980).

17. Rodwin, 85–89; J.M. Richards, "Failure of the New Towns," *The Architectural Review*, CXIV (July 1953), 31–32; G. Cullen, "Prairie Planning in the New Towns," *The Architectural Review*, CXIV, 34–35; L. Brett, "Failure of the New Towns," *The Architectural Review*, CXIV, (Aug. 1953), 119. Despite some searching questions on social and economic policies and achievements, the thrust of *The Architectural Review* attack was essentially on aesthetic issues.

18. Wyndham Thomas, *New Town Blues* (Chicago, 1964); Peter Willmott, "East Kilbride and Stevenage," *Town Planning Review*, XXXIV (Jan. 1964), 307–16; Peter Willmott, "Social Research and New Communities," *Journal of the American Institute of Planners*, XXXIII (Nov. 1967), 387–98; Gillian Pitt, "A Consumer's View," in Hazel Evans (ed.), *New Towns: The British Experience* (New York, 1972), 140–41. The term "new-town blues" came into use in the late 1950s, popularized by the well-known study of Michael Young and Peter Willmott, *Family and Kinship in East London* (London, 1957).

19. Cumbernauld Development Corporation, *Cumbernauld New Town Preliminary Planning Proposals* (Apr. 1958), *First Addendum Report* (May 1959), *Second Addendum Report* (Jan. 1962); *Cumbernauld Extension Area Outline Plan* (Feb. 1974). Peter Willmott, "Housing in Cumbernauld," *Journal of the Town Planning Institute*, L (May 1964), 195–200; Mayer Hillman and Stephan Potter, "Movement Systems for New Towns," in Gideon Golany (ed.), *International Urban Growth Policies: New Town Contributions* (New York, 1978), 38–40; C. Carter, *Innovations in Planning Thought and Practice at Cumbernauld New Town, 1956–62* (Milton Keynes, 1983). A criticism by the architect Arnold Whittick, a staunch supporter of Osborn, is in "Cumbernauld—Outstanding Success or Failure," *Town and Country Planning*, XXXVIIII (May 1970), 236–40.

20. Peter Self, *Cities in Flood* (London, 1957). Self, a professor of public administration at the London School of Economics, became editor of *Town and Country Planning* in 1966 and the director of the association in 1969. T.C.P.A. Executive, "Planning Problems of the Large Towns," *Town and Country Planning*, XXXVIII (June 1968), 200–205.

21. David Eversley, *The Planner in Society: The Changing Role of a Profession* (London, 1973); Robert Cowan and Kelvin MacDonald, "Changing Views on Town Planning in Great Britain," *Annals of the American Academy of Political and Social Science*, CCCCLI (Sept. 1980), 130–42. Peter Hall, *Urban and Regional Planning* (New York, 1982), 197–98. Hall makes the important point that suspicion of planners and their own professional confusion was not of course unique at a time when authority and professionalism in general was under attack.

22. Derek Diamond, "New Towns in Their Regional Context," in Evans (ed.), *New Towns: The British Experience*, 54–65; Thomas Ray, *Aycliffe to Cumbernauld: A Study of Seven New Towns in Their Regions* (London, 1969), especially the conclusion which treats the changing perception of the role of new towns in economic regional planning; Frederic J. Osborn and Arnold Whittick, *The New Towns: The Answer to Megalopolis* (London, 1977). This work originally appeared in 1963, in a revised edition in 1968, and was again revised for the 1977 edition. For this reason, the three editions provide a plumb line to the diverse and

changing roles the new towns were intended to fulfill, and how these changing roles influenced their design and planning.

23. Aldridge, 135; "T.C.P.A. Evidence to Hunt Committee," *Town and Country Planning,* XXXVI (May 1968), 237–55.

24. Aldridge, 143–47; P.H. Levin, *Government and the Planning Process* (London, 1976); S. Holland, *The Regional Problem* (London, 1976).

25. C. Buchanan et al., *Traffic in Towns* (London, 1963); Peter Hall, *London 2000,* revised and expanded edition (London, 1969), 217–18; John Tetlow and Anthony Goss, *Homes, Towns and Traffic* (London, 1965).

26. Frederick Gibberd, "The Master Design; Landscape; Housing; The Town Centres," in Evans (ed.), 93–95; *Runcorn New Town: Master Plan, 1967;* R. Berthoud, *Runcorn Travel Survey* (London, 1973). Hillman and Potter in Golany (ed.), 40–43.

27. Frank Schaffer, "The New Town Movement in Britain," in Gideon Golany (ed.), 16–22.

28. Peter Self, "A New Vision for New Towns," *Town and Country Planning,* XL (Jan. 1972), 4–9. Frederic Osborn concurred with this new view; see his *Green-Belt Cities* (New York, 1969), note 145(1) on p. 192.

29. Hillman and Potter in Golany (ed.), 43–46; Richard Llewelyn-Davies, "Changing Goals in Design: The Milton Keynes Example," in Evans (ed.), 102–16. This article, by a leading planner of international stature, is important in indicating changes in planning theory that had taken hold in the 1960s; see also *The Plan for Milton Keynes* (Mar. 1970) prepared by the Milton Keynes Development Corporation for the Minister of Housing and Local Development.

30. Llewelyn-Davies, 105; Christopher Alexander, "The City Is Not a Tree," *Architectural Forum* (Apr. 1965), 58–62, and (May 1965), 58–61. Another planner whose ideas are said to have influenced the planning of Milton Keynes was Melvin Webber, who attacked the neighborhood-unit approach, arguing that voluntary association not residential propinquity was the key to social associations and community.

31. Llewelyn-Davies, 107; "Milton Keynes: A Progress Report," *Architectural Design* (June 1973), 117–23; also see *City Structure,* a confidential report of the Milton Keynes Development Corporation intended for limited distribution. Undated, but prepared in 1980, this report admits the lack of "overall structure at any finer grain than the grid roadwork system."

32. Hillman and Potter in Golany (ed.), 37.

33. Ibid., 46.

34. Ibid., 45.

35. Frank Schaffer, *The New Town Story* (London, 1970), 244.

36. Bernard Crick, *Essays in Reform* (London, 1968); A. Wildavsky, "If Planning Is Everything, Maybe Its Nothing," *Policy Science,* IV, 2 (1973), 127–53.

37. Anthony Sampson, *The Changing Anatomy of Britain* (New York, 1982), 190–94; Patsy Healy et al. (eds.), *Planning Theory: Prospects for the 1980s* (Oxford, 1980).

38. Patsy Healy et al. (eds.), 224–36.

39. Aldridge, 147–51.

40. Sampson, 210; "Save Our Cities: A Strategy to Fight Urban Decay," (London) *Sunday Times Magazine,* Nov. 23, 1976, pp. 56, 61. Peter Hall (ed.), *The Inner City in Context* (London, 1981). Also useful is David H. McKay and Andrew M. Cox, *The Politics of Urban Change* (London, 1979), Chapter 7, and Paul Lawless, *Britain's Inner Cities: Problems and Policies* (New York, 1981).

41. Douglas E. Ashford (ed.), *Financing Urban Government in the Welfare State* (London, 1980).

42. Aldridge, 150–51; *Policy for the Inner Cities,* Cmd. 6845 (London, 1977).

43. *The Economist* (5–11 Dec. 1987), 61–62.

CHAPTER 13

1. Lloyd Rodwin, *Nations and Cities* (Boston, 1970); papers presented at United Nations symposia held in Stockholm in 1961 and Moscow in 1964 appear in the United Nations,

Planning of Metropolitan Areas and New Towns (1967), ST/ SOA/ 65; Gideon Golany (ed.), *International Urban Growth Policies: New Town Contributions* (New York, 1978); Peter Hall, *The World Cities* (London, 1966); Brian J.L. Berry, *Comparative Urbanization: Divergent Paths in the Urban Experience of the Twentieth Century* (New York, 1981), 114–81.

2. J.L. Sert, "What Became of C.I.A.M.," *The Architectural Review* (Mar. 1961), 14; "Reorganization of C.I.A.M.," *Journal of the Royal Institute of British Architects*, CXIV (Oct. 1957), 505. The most important postwar C.I.A.M. statement is Jacqueline Tyrwhitt et al., *Heart of the City* (London, 1952).

3. Hans Blumenfeld, "A Hundred Year Plan: The Example of Copenhagen," in Hans Blumenfeld, *The Modern Metropolis* (Cambridge, Mass., 1967), 93–112. One American plan based on the Danish example was *A Policy Plan for the Year 2000* issued by the National Capital Regional Planning Council in 1961. Ironically, the Danes were by then accepting the limitations of "finger planning" and modifying the original approach. Blumenfeld, 93. An interesting theoretical consideration of linear planning is L. Hilberseimer, *The New City: Principles of Planning* (Chicago, 1944).

4. David Pass, "Swedish Urbanization Policy: Contributions of New City Districts," in Golany (ed.), 115–20; Yngve Larson et al., *Stockholm Regional and City Planning* (Stockholm, 1964); Kell Astrom, *City Planning in Sweden* (Stockholm, 1967).

5. David Popenoe in *The Suburban Environment: Sweden and the United States* (Chicago, 1977) compares Vallingby with the American suburb of Levittown near Philadelphia. See also, David Goldfield, "Suburban Development in Stockholm and the United States: A Comparison of Form and Function," in Ingrid Hammerstrom and Thomas Hall (eds.), *Growth and Transformation of the Modern City* (Stockholm, 1979), 139–56. The most acclaimed Scandinavian new town was Tapiola built by a nonprofit housing corporation as a commuter suburb of Helsinki. Often called the "Finnish garden city," Tapiola has become in recent years an upper-class suburb noted for its attractive appearance—Berry, 148.

6. For example, see Niles M. Handon, "Criteria for a Growth Centre Policy," in Antoni Kuklinski (ed.), *Growth Centres in Regional Planning* (The Hague, 1972), 103–24; Pierre Merlin, "The New Town Movement in Europe," *The Annals of the American Academy of Political Science*, CCCCLI (Sept. 1980), 76–85.

7. United Nations, *Planning of Metropolitan Areas and New Towns* (1967), ST/ SOA/ 65.

8. Kenneth T. Jackson, *Crabgrass Frontier: The Suburbanization of the United States* (New York, 1985), 225–48, is excellent on describing the transformation of American society and life by the new importance of the suburb after 1945. Sam Kaplan's *The Dream Deferred* (New York, 1979) conveys with wry humor the political chaos that often characterizes suburban government. Two very good accounts of the urban crisis of the late 1950s and 1960s are Jeanne R. Lowe, *Cities in a Race With Time* (New York, 1967), and Charles Abrams, *The City Is the Frontier* (New York, 1965). Both of these deal with the highly controversial urban renewal program but may be usefully supplemented by Scott Greer, *Urban Renewal and American Cities* (Indianapolis, 1965). Invaluable for understanding the confusion among American city planners is Jane Jacobs's powerful *The Death and Life of Great American Cities* (New York, 1961), though she is often wrong on historical details and seriously misrepresents the Garden City movement and Howard's ideas.

9. A particularly incisive contemporary critique of the mushrooming postwar American suburb was David Riesman's "The Suburban Sadness," in William Dobriner (ed.), *The Suburban Community* (New York, 1958), 375–408.

10. Paul and Percival Goodman, *Communitas: Means of Livelihood and Ways of Life* (Chicago, 1947); a second revised edition was published in New York in 1960. While sympathetic to the integrative aims of a garden city, the Goodmans did not approve of their low density and their emphasis on single-family housing and explicitly regarded Unwin as the principal theoretician of the garden city. Paul Goodman's *Growing Up Absurd* (New York, 1960) became an important manifesto of the counterculture of the 1960s, and Paul Goodman and a few others, such as Mumford and the economist Kenneth Boulding, represent

linkages between an older and newer radical tradition that historians are presently exploring. Percival Goodman taught at the School of Architecture, Columbia Univ.

11. A letter from Lewis Mumford to F.J. Osborn, Sept. 27, 1948, announced the formation of the Regional Planning Association of America, W.G.C. It soon merged with the Regional Development Corp. headed by Albert Mayer. Michael Hughes (ed.), *The Letters of Lewis Mumford to Frederic J. Osborn: A Transatlantic Dialogue, 1938–70* (New York, 1972), 410–11.

12. As of yet, scholars have given little attention to the short-lived American federal new-town program. The most comprehensive account is Carol Corden, *Planned Cities: New Towns in Britain and America* (Beverly Hills, 1977). For a general treatment of federal policies toward cities and suburbs leading up to the new-town program, see Mark Gelfand, 345–79, which concludes at the very point that new-town interest becomes significant. The first several years of H.U.D. are described in Harold L. Wolman, *The Politics of Federal Housing* (New York, 1971). For the activity of planning organizations in the 1960s, see the concluding chapter, "The Search for a New Comprehensiveness," in Mel Scott, 554–652, especially pages 647–48 which deal briefly with the "New Communities Act of 1968." The entire issue of the *Journal of the American Institute of Planners*, XXXIII (Nov. 1967) was devoted to the theme of new communities, while *Architectural Record*, CLVIII, 7 (Dec. 1973), was given over to the federally financed new towns.

13. Alonso Hamby, "The Mirage of New Towns," *The Public Image* (Spring 1970), 3–17. Suzanne Farkas, *Urban Lobbying: Mayors in the Federal Arena* (New York, 1971), 211–13.

14. Farkas, 211–13; Scott, 647–48.

15. Donald Canty (ed.), *The New City* (New York, 1969), 172–74. The National Committee on Urban Growth Policy was not an official governmental committee but was sponsored by such prestigious groups as the National League of Cities, the National Association of Counties, the U.S. Conference of Mayors, etc. A foreword for the book was provided by Vice President Spiro Agnew, and it was funded by the Ford Foundation. Rich in pictures, short on text, and with much of its research hurried and slipshod, *The New City* was intended essentially to promote a planning and new-town approach to urban problems and not to be a thoughtful consideration of the subject. More useful is James Bailey (ed.), *New Towns in America: The Design and Development Process* (New York, 1973), 155–65, which contains an extensive bibliography of articles, books, and reports on new-town activity.

16. Eleanore Carruth, "Private Developers Are Making the Big Move to New Towns," *Fortune*, LXXXIV (Sept. 1971), 95–97; John E. Kegan and William Rutzick, "Private Developers and the New Communities Act of 1968," *Georgetown Law Journal*, LVII (June 1969), 1119–58; Myron Lieberman, "New Communities; Business on the Urban Frontier," *Saturday Review*, LIV (May 15, 1971), 20–24.

17. James Rouse, "Statement Before Subcommittee on Housing of the Home Banking and Currency Committee on H.R. 12946, Title II, 89th Congress, 2nd session, March 25, 1966"; Richard Brooks, "Social Planning in Columbia," *Journal of the American Institute of Planners*, XXXVII (Nov. 1971), 373–79; Morton Hoppenfeld, "A Sketch of the Planning Process for Columbia, Maryland," *Journal of the American Institute of Planners*, XXXIII (Nov. 1967), 398–409.

18. Condon, 124; Alan Oser, "U.S. Re-evaluating 'New Towns' Program," *New York Times*, July 23, 1976; New Communities Administration, *New Communities: Problems and Potentials*, a report published in Dec. 1976. To the best of my knowledge this is the last published report of the New Communities Administration. In 1981, officials of H.U.D. informed me that the records of the New Communities Administration were not yet available for scholarly research.

19. Edward C. Banfield, *The Unheavenly City: The Nature and the Future of Our Urban Crisis* (Boston, 1970), 62.

20. J.W. Forrester in *Urban Dynamics* (Cambridge, Mass., 1969) treated the city as an interacting set of systems represented by a computer model; Archibald C. Rogers, "Systems Design: An Overview," in Bailey (ed.), 45–48; Robert W. Morans and Willard Rogers,

"Evaluating Resident Satisfaction in Established and New Communities," in Robert W. Burchell (ed.), *Frontiers of Planned Unit Development: A Synthesis of Expert Opinion* (New Brunswick, 1973), 197–227; Ernest Erber, (ed.), *Urban Planning in Transition* (New York, 1970), passim, but especially part two, "The State of the Art," and part three, "The Professional Planner's Role." This book was a publication of the American Institute of Planners and is invaluable in offering insight into the heated debate over the nature of planning and the planner's role which occurred at the end of the 1960s and still continues. For developments in Britain at this time, see David Eversley, *The Planner in Society: The Changing Role of a Profession* (London, 1973).

21. On the origins and development of the systems-analysis approach, see Erber (ed.), 138–39. J.W. Forrester has described his approach in *Urban Dynamics* as "based on methods for studying complex systems that form a bridge between engineering and the social sciences."

22. Erber (ed.), 142–92; Scott, 640–53; Michael Lee Vasu, *Politics and Planning: A National Study of American Planners* (Chapel Hill, 1979); Howell S. Baum, *Planners and Public Expectations* (Cambridge, Mass., 1983); and by the same author, "The Planning Profession in the 1980s," in Daniel Schaffer (ed.), *Two Centuries of American Planning* (Baltimore, 1988), 231–64.

23. David Boyle, "Cities of the Future Look Set to Spread," (London) *Sunday Times*, May 17, 1987, p. 34; President's Commission for a National Agenda for the Eighties, *Urban America in the Eighties Perspectives and Prospects* (Washington, D.C., 1980); Gary Gappert and Richard V. Knight (eds.), *Cities in the 21st Century* (Beverly Hills, 1982); *Changing Cities: A Challenge to Planning*, special, September 1980 issue of *The Annals of the American Academy of Political Science*.

24. A useful analysis of community theory is provided by Thomas Bender, who also offers a historical context of the role of community in the United States in his *Community and Social Change in America* (New Brunswick, 1978); an analysis of the relationship of modernization and urbanization is in Gerald D. Suttles, *The Social Construction of Communities* (Chicago, 1972), 258–60; Suzanne Keller's *The Urban Neighborhood: A Sociological Perspective* (New York, 1968) vividly describes the erosion of community involvement and networks by market forces.

25. On Rancho Santa Margarita, see Bernie Bookbinder, "Searching for the New Levittown," *Newsday Magazine*, Oct. 11, 1987, pp. 8–15ff.

26. Robert Sommer, *Personal Space: The Behavioral Basis of Design* (Englewood Cliffs, 1969), 153. Two important articles by Herbert J. Gans are "Planning and Social Life: Friendship and Neighbor Relations in Suburban Communities," *Journal of the American Institute of Planners*, XXVII (May 1961), 134–40, and "The Balanced Community," *Journal of the American Institute of Planners*, XXVII (Aug. 1961), 176–84.

27. See, for example, Murray Bookchin, *The Limits of the City* (New York, 1973), and his *The Rise of Urbanization and the Decline of Citizenship* (San Francisco, 1987). Bookchin, a libertarian anarchist and ecological activist, calls for small communities based on participatory and cooperative democracy as a way of achieving democratic socialism. He offers a superficial analysis of urbanization but a disturbing indictment of our society.

28. Laurence Veysey, *The Communal Experience: Anarchists and Mystical Communities in Twentieth-Century America* (Chicago, 1978).

29. Paul Tillich, "Critique and Justification of Utopia," in Frank E. Manuel (ed.), *Utopias and Utopian Thought* (Boston, 1967), 296–309.

Bibliographical Essay

After Ebenezer Howard's death in 1928, his second wife, believing his friends held her responsible, destroyed in anger most of his papers. What remains is to be found in three collections, each of which often contains duplicates of the others' holdings. The most important repository is "The Ebenezer Howard Papers," Hertfordshire County Archives, Hertford, England. The Garden City Museum, Letchworth, in addition to material on Howard, also holds the records of the First Garden City, Ltd., and much material on the first garden city. "The Frederic J. Osborn Archives" at the Welwyn Garden City Central Library includes material collected by Osborn for a biography of Howard that he never completed, as well as material spanning his long involvement in the movement; this material is presently being catalogued by Michael Hughes of the library staff. The basic biography of Howard is Robert Beevers's *The Garden City Utopia; A Critical Biography of Ebenezer Howard* (New York, 1988), which supersedes Dugald Macfadyen's pietistic *Sir Ebenezer Howard and the Town Planning Movement* (Manchester, 1933). A superb comparative study of the ideas of Howard, Frank Lloyd Wright, and Le Corbusier is Robert Fishman, *Urban Utopias in the Twentieth Century* (Cambridge, Mass., 1982).

The second edition of *To-morrow: A Peaceful Path to Real Reform*, published in 1902, had a different title—*Garden Cities of To-morrow*. It differed from the original in deleting the final chapter and several quotes cited by Howard in other chapters and in omitting some of the original illustrations, probably because they contained material that might appear radical. In addition, the illustrations, unlike those in the first edition, are marked "A Diagram Only, Plan Must Depend Upon Site Selected" on the advice of Raymond Unwin. The 1946 edition of the book prepared by Sir Frederic Osborn restored a portion of the 1898 text and contains important essays by Osborn and Lewis Mumford. In 1985, Attic Books of the United Kingdom published an edition of *Garden Cities of To-morrow* using the 1902 text but adding several of the 1898 illustrations that had been omitted. It also includes a most useful annotated bibliography prepared by Ray Thomas and Stephen Potter of the Open University.

The London office of the Town and Country Planning Association has the association's minutes and miscellaneous pamphlets and reports. Dennis Hardy of Middlesex Polytechnic is presently preparing an authorized history of the Town and Country Planning Association. The International Federation of Housing and Town Planning, headquartered in Amsterdam, lost most of its early records during World War II but does have a complete set of its annual meetings and some miscellaneous pamphlets. I found the "Edith Elmer Wood Papers" at the Avery Library, Columbia University, contained much useful material, especially correspondence, on the activities of the international association in the interwar years. The "Clarence Stein Papers" at Cornell University on the Regional Planning Association of America, however, proved disappointing. Mary Ellen Huls has prepared the incomplete but still useful *The History of the Garden City Idea: A Bibliography* (1986) as part of the *Architecture Series: Bibliography* published by Vance Bibliographies of Monticello, Illinois.

The Topolobampo material in the library of the California State University at Fresno fills seven filing cabinets and fifteen shelves. For the most part, it has not been catalogued. In addition to much varied material on the Topolobampo colony—including several hundred photos—it holds Marie Howland's scrapbooks of press clippings on late-nineteenth-century social experiments related to colonization schemes compiled when she was the community's librarian.

Index

251

68; and integral cooperation, 39–40, 42–
43, 44, 54, 55, 56–57, 60, 61; and the international movement, 134, 136, 138, 141;
and land reform, 55–56; and the Left,
141; and Letchworth, 94–95; and Marxism, 141; and the middle class, 141; and
religion, 54–55, 62; and socialism, 34, 38–
39, 45–46, 52, 55–56; in the United States,
38–39, 42–43, 44, 160; and urbanization,
52; and utopianism, 10; and Welwyn Garden City, 124; and the working class, 66,
141. *See also* Associated housing
Cottage housing, 86, 97–98, 102, 150, 153,
154, 189
Council housing, 102
Credit Foncier, 42, 43, 44, 47
Crickmer, C. M., 121, 126
Crow, Arthur, 108
Cullingworth, J. B., 184, 187
Culpin, Ewart, 102, 103, 106, 109, 153
Cult of domesticity, 32
Cumbernauld (British new town), 188, 189

Darwin, Charles, 8, 9, 96
Davidge, W. R., 106
Davidoff, Paul, 192
Davis, William Morris, 171
Debs, Eugene, 48
Degler, Carl, 118
Delano, Frederic, 175
Denmark, 201
Denny, E. M., 90
Density, 71, 75, 81–82, 86, 87, 97–98, 100,
184–85, 200
Downing, Andrew Jackson, 164
Draper, W. H., 8
Dyckman, George, 62

Ecology, 211–12
Edwards, A. T., 94
Edwards, Trystan, 108
Efficiency, 27–28, 36, 66–67, 118–19
Egbert, Donald Drew, 85
Ely, Richard, 28
Emerson, Ralph Waldo, 52
End-state planning, 192
Engels, Friedrich, 19, 21, 79
England. *See name of specific community or per-
son*
Entrepreneurial ethos, 214
Environmentalism: and Adams, 82–83, 98;
in Britain, 70–76, 101–2, 103; and cities,
64, 71–76; and collectivism, 72; and
communitarianism, 65, 74–75; and the
definition of a good environment, 74; and
density, 75; and ecology, 211–12; and the
Garden Cities and Town Planning Association, 103; and the Garden City Association,
81–83, 99; and government, 72, 142; and
Howard, 64–76, 103; and individualism,
73; and the international movement, 156;
and land reform, 72; and Letchworth, 109;
and materialism, 73; meaning of, 69–70;
and the middle class, 71, 73, 76; and model
housing/villages, 71, 73; and the New
Town program (Britain), 185; and planning, 206, 209–10; and population redistribution, 73, 75; and post-WW II housing,

200; and professionals, 143; and the public
health movement, 101–2; purpose of, 211;
roots of, 70; and services, 74; and Social
Darwinism, 71–72; and social issues, 66,
72–73; and social reform, 72, 74–75; 76;
and street design, 101; and suburbs, 71,
100; in the United States, 158, 163, 164,
167, 170, 206; and urban-rural synthesis,
73, 75; and utopianism, 76; and the working class, 70, 71, 73, 76, 81
Erickson, Kai, 147
Esperanto, 90, 120, 140

Fabian Society, 9, 15, 37, 40, 50, 54, 77–78,
82, 86
Factory towns, 23, 27–28, 159
Fairhope, Alabama, 47
Familistère (France), 44
Family, 29–30, 32, 52, 86, 117, 161, 174, 185
Farringdon Hall scheme, 3–4, 26, 40, 54,
57–63
Federated town development (Unwin), 145
Fellowship of the New Life, 77
First Garden City, Ltd., 84, 88, 89, 90, 92,
93, 94, 98, 117
Flürscheim, Michael, 47, 57, 59
Forest Hills Gardens (New York, NY), 161
Fourier, François-Marie-Charles, 21, 79, 138
France, 138–39, 142
French Garden and Linear Cities Associa-
tion, 138
Fritsch, Theodor, 135
Fry, Maxwell, 154

Garden cities. *See name of specific city*
Garden Cities and Town Planning Associa-
tion, 103, 106–7, 108, 130, 131, 181
Garden Cities and Town Planning (journal),
103, 108
The Garden City (journal), 99
Garden city, definition of, 103
Garden City, selection of the name of, 62, 65
Garden City Association, 78–83, 86–87, 97–
103, 117. *See also* Letchworth; *name of spe-
cific person*
Garden City Association of America, 40
Garden City Tenants Association, 93
Garden village, 103
Garnier, Tony, 139
Gavin, J. C., 17
Geddes, Patrick, 73, 165, 171–72
Geographic sprawl, 207–8
George, Dorothy, 31
George, Henry: and Bliss, 40; and colonization schemes, 46, 47; critiques of, 15, 16,
17–18; impact in Britain of, 15–16, 17;
importance of, 16; as an influence on Howard, 15, 17, 25, 33, 37; in Ireland, 15–16;
and the Labour party, 184; and landlordism, 16, 17; and land reform, 15–17,
18, 20, 21, 23, 25; and a market economy,
20; and Marshall, 17–18; movement away
from thinking of, 51; and population redistribution, 18; and progress, 14; and rent
theory, 16–17; and the rise of cities, 18;
and Shaw, 16; and socialism, 21; and
speculation, 16–17, 18; and Toynbee, 17;
and Wallace (Alfred Russel), 16, 20, 46